BLACKSTONE'S GUIDE TO THE

Sexual Offences Act 2003

GW00726058

BLACKSTONE'S GUIDE TO THE

Sexual Offences Act 2003

Kim Stevenson, Anne Davies, and Michael Gunn

OXFORD
UNIVERSITY PRESS

OXFORD

UNIVERSITY PRESS

Great Clarendon Street, Oxford OX2 6DP

Oxford University Press is a department of the University of Oxford.
It furthers the University's objective of excellence in research, scholarship,
and education by publishing worldwide in

Oxford New York

Auckland Bangkok Buenos Aires Cape Town Chennai
Dar es Salaam Delhi Hong Kong Istanbul Karachi Kolkata
Kuala Lumpur Madrid Melbourne Mexico City Mumbai Nairobi
São Paulo Shanghai Taipei Tokyo Toronto

Oxford is a registered trade mark of Oxford University Press
in the UK and in certain other countries

Published in the United States
by Oxford University Press Inc., New York

© Kim Stevenson, Anne Davies and Michael Gunn 2004

The moral rights of the authors have been asserted

Crown copyright material is reproduced under Class Licence Number CO1P0000148
with the permission of HMSO and the Queen's Printer for Scotland

Database right Oxford University Press (maker)

First published 2004

British Library Cataloguing in Publication Data

Data available

Library of Congress Cataloging in Publication Data

Data available

ISBN 0–19–927000–7

5 7 9 10 8 6

Typeset in Times
by Cambrian Typesetters, Frimley, Surrey
Printed in Great Britain
on acid-free paper by
Ashford Colour Press Limited, Gosport, Hampshire

Acknowledgements

The authors wish to acknowledge the suggestions and guidance offered by colleagues Russell Heaton and Liz Rodgers. In particular they also express their gratitude to the final year LLB students at Nottingham Law School who opted to study our Sexuality and the Law module 2002–3 and 2003–4. Their questions and contributions concerning the various draft Bills helped us to formulate our own ideas and to interpret the provisions.

Kim Stevenson, Anne Davies, and Michael Gunn, December 2003

Contents—Summary

Contents

Contents

Table of Cases

Tables of Legislation

PRIMARY LEGISLATION

SECONDARY LEGISLATION

CONVENTIONS

List of Abbreviations

ASBO	Anti-Social Behaviour Order
CA 1989	Children Act 1989
CACAD	Court of Appeal Criminal Division
CDA 1998	Crime and Disorder Act 1998
CJA 1988	Criminal Justice Act 1988
CJCSA 2000	Criminal Justice and Courts Services Act 2000
CJPOA 1994	Criminal Justice and Public Order Act 1994
CPS	Crown Prosecution Service
HO	Home Office
NHSA 1997	National Health Service Act 1977
NSPCC	National Society for the Prevention of Cruelty to Children
OAPA 1861	Offences Against the Person Act 1861
OPA 1959	Obscene Publications Act 1959
PACE 1984	Police and Criminal Evidence Act 1984
PCA 1978	Protection of Children Act 1978
RSHO	Risk of Sexual Harm Order
SMD	Special Measures Direction
SOA 1956	Sexual Offences Act 1956
SO(A)A 1976	Sexual Offences (Amendment) Act 1976
SOA 1993	Sexual Offences Act 1993
SOA 1997	Sexual Offenders Act 1997
SOA 2003	Sexual Offences Act 2003
SOO	Sex Offenders Order
SOPO	Sex Offences Prevention Order
SOR	Sex Offenders Register
The Review	*Setting the Boundaries*
USI	Unlawful Sexual Intercourse
YJCEA 1999	Youth Justice and Criminal Evidence Act 1999

Note: shortened references to official publications and responses are cited in the chapters. Full references appear in the summary of Official Publications and Responses (Appendix 3).

1

INTRODUCTION

1.1 OVERVIEW

On 25 January 1999 the Government announced that it was commissioning a review of the law relating to sexual offences, the aims of which were to modernize and strengthen the existing legal provisions, make them clearer and more coherent and thereby to increase the protection of children and vulnerable persons (Jack Straw, then Home Secretary, Foreword, *Setting the Boundaries: Reforming the Law on Sex Offences*, HO 2000). Introducing the subsequent White Paper, the Home Secretary, David Blunkett, described the existing framework as 'archaic, incoherent and discriminatory' (Foreword, *Protecting the Public,* HO 2002). The resulting Sexual Offences Act 2003 (SOA 2003) is a landmark statute that repeals almost all of the Sexual Offences Act 1956 (SOA 1956) and many other statutory provisions enacted since, delivering, in effect, a new criminal code of sexual offences. The Act has considerable implications for all those working in this field, whether with victims or offenders, adults or children, directly engaged within the legal process or closely associated with pre-trial or post-trial work. Perhaps more than any other type of crime it is within the context of dealing with sexual offences that so many different agencies are drawn together, whether they be professionals; such as legal practitioners, the police, probation service, health and social services, educational or penal services, or voluntary and charitable organizations such as Victim Support, the NSPCC, and the Rape Crisis Federation. This Guide is intended to be of practical benefit to all such practitioners, whether legally qualified or not and aims to set out and explain the provisions of this major enactment in an understandable and accessible fashion.

The SOA 2003 not only introduces a considerable number of new offences and criminalizes certain types of conduct not previously subjected to the written law but also substantially redefines many sex crimes incorporating new terms and language deemed more appropriate to contemporary society. The Act is therefore the culmination of a major review and public consultation exercise conducted by the Home Office. It is not simply a consolidating or codifying measure but a considered and detailed revision of the existing legislation relating to virtually all sexual activities.

1.2 FACTORS PRECIPITATING REVIEW

The Sexual Offences Act 1956 (SOA 1956) was drafted nearly half a century ago and many of its provisions date back even further to the Offences Against the Person Act 1861 and the Criminal Law Amendment Act 1885. Predominantly a consolidating statute, the SOA 1956 received minimal debate and its main provisions regarding sexual violations, particularly rape, indecent assault, defilement, and procuration, were simply reproductions of existing nineteenth-century provisions. The 1956 Act contained some 50 clauses that potentially created over 200 offences taking into account all the possible permutations but a number of these were rarely used underlining their outdated nature. Certain offences, such as incest and unlawful sexual intercourse, were by way of definition, gender- and age-specific, reflecting historical perspectives and patriarchal attitudes about the nature of sex and female and male sexuality. Such provisions reinforced stereotypical views about masculine sexuality as dominant and aggressive, and feminine sexuality as submissive and incapable of initiating sexual aggression or abuse. Many aspects of the statute were discriminatory and could no longer be justified, particularly the criminalization of homosexuality; and a number of anomalies existed relating to criminal responsibility and sentencing. In the light of public acknowledgement about the existence and extent of child sexual abuse over the last two decades, the omission of any specific offences to deal with this phenomenon also proved problematic. A review of the substantive law of rape was undertaken in 1984 by the Criminal Law Revision Committee, which concluded that no major revision was necessary though it was intimated that the criminal law might not always be appropriate in all cases of incest. The Committee made a number of recommendations but these were largely ignored. Otherwise no major review of the law in this area has been undertaken since the enactment of the Criminal Law Amendment Act 1885 which itself attracted considerable controversy. Interestingly, it was the issue of the trafficking of children which precipitated the passage of that Act, and today the globalization of trafficking and child prostitution has again focused minds on reform as the need for new powers and offences to deal with this problem has become self-evident. Also since 1956 a more liberal and enlightened understanding within society towards both sexual activity and sexual identity has led to greater awareness and more tolerant attitudes. The enactment of the Human Rights Act 1998 and incorporation of the European

Convention on Human Rights further reinforced the realization that a more gender-neutral approach acknowledging personal sexual autonomy was long overdue. It is now universally accepted that many of the provisions of the SOA 1956 are inappropriate to contemporary sexual behaviour and orientation. The new Act aims to address these limitations and therefore not only seeks to protect and empower but also to liberate as well as criminalize.

1.3 WHO CONDUCTED THE REVIEW?

Two bodies were commissioned to undertake the Review—a Steering Group comprised of representatives of the Home Office, Department of Health, lawyers, and charitable organizations directly involved in working with victims such as the NSPCC and Victim Support; and the External Reference group comprising of representatives from other organizations and pressure groups with relevant experience to advise the Steering Group. Interest groups represented included those concerned with women's issues, children's charities, gay and lesbian rights, and medical, ethical, legal, and religious interests. Their remit was to review the existing sex offences in the common and statute law of England and Wales and make recommendations that would:

(i)   Provide coherent and clear sex offences that would protect individuals from sexual violation, especially children and the more vulnerable

(ii)   enable offenders to be appropriately punished

(iii)   be fair and non-discriminatory.

Underpinning these aims a utilitarian principle was adopted as the benchmark. The intervention of the criminal law into people's private sexual lives would only be justified where harm to an individual could be shown and generally any sexual activity should only be subject to legal control where it is non-consensual. The recommendations made by the two review teams were subsequently published in *Setting the Boundaries: Reforming the Law on Sexual Offences* and *Review of Part 1 of the Sex Offenders Act 1997* (HO 2000).

1.4 *SETTING THE BOUNDARIES*

In July 2000 the Home Office published the first stage of this review as *Setting the Boundaries* (the Review), which included 62 recommendations. Most of these were subsequently formulated into specific proposals sponsored by the Home Secretary, David Blunkett, and published in the 2002 White Paper, *Protecting the Public*. This was generally well received though it did attract some criticism concerning the shift in responsibility onto the defendant in terms of establishing consent in cases of rape, the over-criminalization of sexual activity between young teens, and the replacement of the old offences of indecent exposure with a new clause criminalizing sexual activity in the open air. Soon after, on 28 January 2003, a draft Sexual Offences Bill 2003 was introduced into the Lords. When presented to the Commons on 18 June 2003 almost all the House was united in its concern about the 'champagne challenge', how to address the issue of under-age sex and balance the extent to which sexual experimentation should be condoned with the need to protect immature teens from themselves. A major amendment was also inserted which would have extended the protection of the anonymity of rape victims to those charged with or suspected of rape but this was rejected by the Commons and led to some last minute negotiations between the two Houses. This was particularly prescient in the light of the allegations of group rape made against certain premiership footballers in October 2003 and the suppression of their identities by the press and prosecuting agencies. Arguments over whether such anonymity should apply at pre-arrest, pre-trial and/or pre-conviction stage proved problematic and the amendment was lost. Royal Assent was granted on 20 November 2003 and it is intended that the Act become fully operative by Commencement Order in May 2004.

Perhaps one of the most important distinctions between the Review and subsequent enactment of this legislation and all that has gone before it is, for the first time ever, the significant involvement and input of a feminine perspective. While feminist campaigns in the past may have secured the promise of legislative reform, few female participants were able to engage in the actual legislative process. The involvement of leading female academics such as Professors Jennifer Temkin and Liz Kelly, comment from those with direct experience of working with victims such as Helen Jones and Cathy Halloran (Rape Crisis Federation), and the legal and political expertise provided in the Lords by Baronesses Kennedy, Mallalieu, Scotland and Walmesley, etc., together with, post 1997, a considerably more feminized Parliament, has meant that women, just as much as men, have been able to have a say in the making of legislation that affects them in the most personal and intimate way.

1.5 IMPACT AND EFFECT

The Act repeals almost all the previous existing provisions relating to sexual offences and abolishes the time limits within which certain prosecutions must be brought (see Table of Changes (Appendix 2)). The statute also introduces some brand new provisions such as the sexual penetration of a corpse, exposure, and voyeurism, which has led to comment from some quarters of over-criminalization and unnecessary interference with an individual's sexual autonomy. Part One of the Act details the substantive provisions consequent to the *Setting the Boundaries* recommendations and Part Two focuses on the management of sex offenders in response to the second review of the Sex Offenders Act 1997. Some of the major changes include:

4

1.5.1 Rape and other non-consensual sexual offences

Over the last two decades it has become apparent that not only were there limitations and difficulties with the content of the substantive law of rape but also with its practical application. To some extent this has been ameliorated by recent changes to the law of evidence which can facilitate the delivery of testimonies in court and preserve the freshness of evidence through the use of video recording and video links (a brief summary of these evidential provisions can be found in Chapter 10). Equally there has been some restriction on cross-examination in relation to the previous sexual history of the complainant but recent public concern regarding conviction rates for rape—only one out of every thirteen reported rapes led to a conviction in 1999 down from one in three in 1977—demanded a more robust response (*Report on the Joint Investigation into the Investigation and Prosecution of Cases Involving Allegations of Rape*, HMCPSI April 2002). As a result the crime of rape is redefined and extended to cover non-consensual oral sex as well as penile penetration of the vagina or anus, and the controversial defence of genuine or mistaken belief in consent, however unreasonable, removed. The Act introduces a new statutory definition of consent based on capacity and reinforced by two sets of presumptions, an evidential set, which may be rebutted by the defendant, and a set of conclusive presumptions that are irrebuttable. New offences to cover those who actively encourage or incite sexual violations are included and a newly worded offence of sexual assault replaces indecent assault. The issue of what constitutes consent is detailed in Chapter 2 followed by an examination of the substantive offences in Chapter 3.

1.5.2 Child sexual abuse

Continuing challenges from those convicted of offences involving the sexual abuse of children led many to question the efficacy of the law's protection. The percentage of child sex abusers acquitted is much higher than for other offenders and the number of children known to be at risk is significant. The Government has responded positively creating four new offences specifically directed at those who target children under 13 years including the revision of sexual intercourse with a child under 13 as statutory rape. These are examined in Chapter 4 together with a number of offences prohibiting a wide range of sexual activity conducted with children under 16 and, controversially, any sexual activity between under 16 year-olds. The existing offence of abuse of position of trust is strengthened to cover those professionals who look after young persons under 18 years and who not only engage directly in sexual activities but cause or incite others to do so; these offences are addressed in Chapter 5. The increasing recognition of the abuse of people with a mental disorder including those with special needs or learning difficulties prompted the need to remove the inappropriate and outdated concept of unlawful sexual intercourse with a mental defective. The Act therefore creates a number of separate provisions which specifically protect such vulnerable persons, whether children or adults, and incorporates special offences for care workers who sexually abuse or violate such individuals as identified in Chapter 6.

1.5.3 Familial sex offences

For the first time since 1956 the law relating to incestuous relationships has been comprehensively reformed. Perhaps the most important issue in this context is the separation of offences relating to children in a family and offences between adults. The list of persons who can be guilty of a sexual offence committed against children in a family is extended greatly to reflect the looser structure of modern families. In fact, the offences that can be perpetrated against a child can even be committed by those who are not related to the child at all, provided that they are involved in the care of the child. For these offences, a child is regarded as someone under the age of 18 years, reflecting the intention to strengthen protection for the vulnerable. The Act creates new offences concerning sexual activity between related adults and again widens the range of relatives who could be guilty of an offence. This new approach to incestuous relationships is examined in Chapter 7.

1.5.4 Child pornography and prostitution

Public concern about child pornography made it inevitable that the law relating to indecent photographs of children would be strengthened. The law relating to prostitution has also been given a thorough overhaul. Existing child pornography offences have been amended, principally by raising the age of a child for the purposes of the offences to someone under the age of 18 years. It could be argued that this is too high, when the Act regards 16 years as the appropriate age for a child to consent to sexual intercourse as discussed in Chapter 8. The chapter also deals with a number of new offences, which prohibit involvement in child prostitution and child pornography. The Act has also amended and replaced existing offences relating to adult prostitution, making them gender-neutral and removing any distinctions between homosexual or heterosexual prostitution. There are also a number of new offences which deal with the problem of trafficking.

1.5.5 Preparatory offences

Chapter 9 examines preparatory offences and a number of other new provisions, such as voyeurism, which is criminalized for the first time. Some of these offences are controversial, such as the new offence of 'committing an offence with intent to commit a sexual offence', which is so widely drafted that Liberty has criticized it as being unfair to defendants. Specific offences relating to homosexual behaviour, such as soliciting for an immoral purpose, have been repealed and in their place the Act has introduced the new gender-neutral offence of 'sexual activity in a public lavatory'. Originally, the intention was to create an offence of 'sexual activity in a public place' but this did not survive the Bill's scrutiny by Parliament.

1.5.6 Sex offenders

In the last few years public attitudes towards sex offenders, particularly paedophiles, have hardened culminating in demands for a more punitive approach and stringent monitoring. Part Two of the Act strengthens the existing provisions in relation to those obliged to notify and register their details on the Sex Offenders Register requiring more details and more frequent registration. The Act also consolidates the various Sex Offender Orders that may be applied for by the police or imposed at the discretion of the court in order to maximize such preventative measures. These changes are detailed in two related chapters, Chapters 11 and 12.

2

THE ISSUE OF CONSENT

2.1 INTRODUCTION

Consent, or rather its absence, is a vital factor in some of the offences created by the Sexual Offences Act 2003 (SOA 2003). Consent is not relevant to some offences, such as sexual intercourse and other assaults against children under 13 (ss 5–8), where there is harm sufficient to warrant criminalization regardless of consent or its absence. If the offences rely upon the absence of consent, such as rape, it is that absence of consent that enables a differentiation to be made between lawful and criminal activity. This chapter addresses the general principles in relation to consent under the Act. In relation to those sexual offences where consent is a defence, the activity is lawful unless consent is absent. So, absence of consent is an essential definitional element of those offences. Consent is absent where the person does not want to have sexual intercourse. This is most obvious when she says no, or refuses, or where she is not capable of providing consent.

The Act introduces a new statutory definition of consent based on a person's capacity to make that choice (s 74). There are two sets of presumptions about consent. The first set consists of evidential presumptions that may be challenged by the defendant (s 75); the second set consists of conclusive presumptions that are not subject to challenge (s 76). With respect to a belief that a person consented, such a claim must meet a clearly objective standard.

2.2 THE LAW PRIOR TO THE ACT

Before the Act, there was no definition of consent. Prior to the decision of the Court of Appeal in *R v Olugboja* [1982] QB 320, there was, though, a set of circumstances in which consent would be regarded as being absent (see J. Temkin, 'Literature Review of Research into Rape and Sexual Assault' (1999) in *Setting the Boundaries*, p 85, J. Temkin, *Rape and the Legal Process* (2002, 2nd ed.), pp 91–2). The full list was (*Setting the Boundaries*, para 2.2.2):

[C]onsent is not present if

- It was achieved by the use of force or fear of force (which *may* extend to threats to a third party);
- The complainant was incapable of consenting because they were unconscious. This includes sleep (*Larter and Castleton* (1995) [[1995] Crim LR 75]; *Howard* (1965)[[1966] 1 WLR 13]);
- There is fraudulent misrepresentation as to the nature of the act—for example a deception that the act was not a sexual act (*Flattery* (1877) [(1877) 2 QBD 410] and *Williams* (1923) [[1923] 1 KB 340]);
- Impersonation of another—s 142(3) of the Criminal Justice and Public Order Act 1994 re-enacted the previous statute that 'a man . . . commits rape if he induces a married woman to have intercourse with him by impersonating her husband'; *Elbekkay* (1995) [[1995] Crim LR 163] extended that impersonation to a partner;
- The complainant is fundamentally mistaken as to the nature of the act (*Clarence* (1889) [(1888) 22 QBD 23]);
- The complainant did not have the understanding and knowledge to decide whether to consent or resist (whether by age, disability, or illness) (*Howard* (1986) [(1985)) 82 Cr App R 262]; *Lang* (1975) [(1975) 62 Cr App R 50]);
- The complainant was so drunk or drugged they could not consent (*Camplin* (1845) [(1845) 1 Car & Kir 746]).

The Court of Appeal in *Olugboja* did not provide a definition of consent, but also appeared not to accept that there was a set of cases in which consent would be absent if the facts were established (Temkin (1999), p 86). The Court stated (pp 331–2) that the SOA 1956, as amended by the SO(A)A 1976, simply defined rape 'as being unlawful sexual intercourse with a woman who at the time of the intercourse does not consent to it'. There was no need to establish 'force, fear, or fraud' affecting the woman's consent. A judge's direction would include telling the jury that

consent, or the absence of it, is to be given its ordinary meaning and if need be, by way of example, that there is a difference between consent and submission; every consent involves a submission, but it by no means follows that a mere submission involves consent.

While in many cases, little more would need to be said,

in the less common type of case where intercourse takes place after threats not involving violence or the fear of it . . . [the jury] should be directed to concentrate on the state of mind of the victim immediately before the act of sexual intercourse, having regard to all the relevant circumstances . . . Where [the dividing line between real consent and mere submission] is to be drawn in a given case is for the jury to decide, applying their combined good sense, experience and knowledge of human nature and modern behaviour to all the relevant facts of the case.

This decision was viewed by some as emphasizing the importance of sexual autonomy as it focused upon determining what the woman was deciding (see S. Gardiner, 'Appreciating *Olugboja*' (1996) 16 *Legal Studies* 275). *Olugboja* emphasizes that simply submitting to another's wishes does not necessarily mean that a woman is consenting. Were this to have been taken up properly, the argument that a woman must have been consenting to sex when she decided to have sex rather than to risk violence would have had less credibility even than it currently has. In stressing that all that must be established is that the woman did not consent, not whether the absence of consent was a product of fear or force, it underpins respect for sexual autonomy. A proper understanding of that decision would have produced the same conclusion as is now laid down in legislation: that it is for the complainant to decide whether they wish to have sexual intercourse with the alleged offender. Consent is not present unless someone agrees to the activity.

On the other hand, others thought *Olugboja* gave the jury too much leeway and failed to ensure that similar cases were to be decided consistently and according to an appropriate standard of what is consent. As it happens the old cases had not completely disappeared, e.g., on the question of induced mistake, the courts subsequently, in *R v Elbekkay* [1995] Crim LR 163, extended the impersonation of a husband to include the impersonation of a partner and, in *R v Linekar* [1995] QB 250, decided that a deception not going to the quality of the act but to the question of a woman being paid for sex was not a deception that could vitiate consent.

Whatever view may be taken of the decision of the Court of Appeal in *Olugboja*, there is no doubt that the law could be improved and so lead to more consistent decision-making. In addition, there was a deep fear that the law was failing to protect women by not recognizing when women were not consenting to sexual intercourse (*Setting the Boundaries*, section 2.10). In order to address these issues, the Act introduces a statutory definition, supported by presumptions that provide a clearer legal position for the set of circumstances that, at least at one time, had been recognized as determining that there was no consent.

2.3 THE DEFINITION OF CONSENT

Section 74 provides:

For the purposes of this Part, a person consents if he agrees by choice, and has the freedom and capacity to make that choice.

2.3.1 Agreement by choice

Parliament elected to define consent as being an agreement by choice. Originally, the intention had been to require that the agreement be 'free', but this word was not used because it might have suggested that monetary or other payment in kind were part of the definition. In fact, had that word been used, it should have meant that the decision made by the complainant was one that was freely arrived at, that is without undue influence. The same end is achieved by requiring the complainant to have the freedom to make the decision (see below). Rumsey, discussing the original concept of free agreement, states that the definition should mean that 'sexual encounters should involve the communication of desires, likes and dislikes in the absence of force, coercion, or fraud'. So what the law may encourage is the increasing influence of what he calls 'communicative sexuality within rape law' (P.N.S. Rumsey, 'The Review of Sex Offences and Rape Law Reform: Another False Dawn?' (2001) 64 *Modern Law Review* 890, p 898). It is possible that what the definition will, therefore, require is that men will have responsibility to ensure that consent is present and that women will have the responsibility to communicate clearly (Rumsey (2001) p 901).

What the first part of the definition requires is that the complainant agrees or chooses to have sexual intercourse with the alleged offender. If she does, then it is not rape (or any other sexual offence requiring the absence of consent). If she does not agree to the sexual intercourse, then it occurs without consent and so constitutes the actus reus of the offence of rape.

If agreement by choice must be present, it might be anticipated that some decisions under the old law could go a different way. In *Linekar* a prostitute only agreed to have sexual intercourse with a man on the basis that he would pay for it. He never intended so to do. Was her agreement by choice? Would it not be possible to argue that there was no real agreement as, had the woman known the truth, she would not have agreed to have sex with the man? What if a man does not reveal, when asked, that he is HIV positive? The woman, on finding out that he is HIV positive, states that she would not have had sex with him had she known, though at the time, in ignorance of this issue, she was very happy having sex with him. It seems unlikely that the courts will accept an argument that the act that takes place is different in nature from that agreed to (D.C. Ormerod and M.J. Gunn, 'Criminal Liability for the Transmission of HIV' (1996) 1 *Web Journal of Current Legal Issues*), but could it be argued that she did not agree by choice because, had she known the truth, she would not have agreed to sex? It is entirely possible that arguments like this might be run (and are not dissimilar, e.g., to the matters raised by E. Finch and V. E. Munro, 'Intoxicated Consent and the Boundaries of Drug-assisted Rape' [2003] *Criminal Law Review* 773 in relation to drug- and alcohol-assisted rape). What is their chance of success? First, they will need to be assessed on the new law. Under the old law there was no definition of consent and so the courts should now consider the implications of the new definition. However, reference to the presumptions reveals that much of the old case law will continue to have relevance. All the presumptions provide is that, if they are satisfied, a particular conclusion must be reached. This does not, necessarily, limit the scope of the definition itself. While, therefore, the courts could revisit the effect of deception and reach a different conclusion, it is thought that the old distinctions will continue to be of determinative relevance.

2.3.2 Freedom to make the choice

The woman must have the *freedom* to make the choice. In cases where violence is threatened, for example, such freedom will not be present. By analogy with the civil law, what will take away the woman's freedom will be something that so affects her will that she is not truly making a choice. Whilst not necessarily directly applicable, the concept of undue influence might be of value as an analogy. For example, in a healthcare treatment case, *Re T* [1992] 4 All ER 649, the majority of the Court of Appeal, that authorized a blood transfusion, decided it on the basis that there was no evidence that Miss T was a Jehovah's Witness and yet, after meeting with her mother in hospital, she espoused that she was and so appeared to be refusing the transfusion. Another case that might be valuable as an analogy is *Freeman v Home Office* [1984] QB 524 where it was determined that, just because someone was in prison, it did not automatically follow that they were not capable of making a voluntary decision or a decision without undue influence. The law relating to undue influence in the civil law has recently been reviewed by the House of Lords in *Royal Bank of Scotland plc v Etridge (No.2)* [2001] UKHL 44 in which Lord Nicholls (at paras 8 and 9) reiterated the general position as follows.

Equity identified broadly two forms of unacceptable conduct. The first comprises overt acts of improper pressure or coercion such as unlawful threats. Today there is much overlap with the principle of duress as this principle has subsequently developed. The second form arises out of a relationship between two persons where one has acquired over another a measure of influence, or ascendancy, of which the ascendant person then takes unfair advantage . . . In cases of this latter nature the influence one person has over another provides scope for misuse without any specific overt acts of persuasion. The relationship between the two individuals may be such that, without more, one of them is disposed to agree a course of action proposed by the other. Typically this occurs when one person places trust in another to look after his affairs and interests, and the latter betrays this trust by preferring his own interests. He abuses the influence he has acquired.

The presumptions are also relevant, e.g., if an issue similar to that in *Freeman* arose, reference would be made to one of the rebuttable presumptions, s 75(2)(c), which deals with the effect of unlawful, rather than lawful, detention (see below). Since violence or the fear of violence may be involved in limiting freedom of choice, the relevant presumptions will also be considered (see s 75(2)(a) and (b), below).

2.3.3 Capacity to make the choice

The woman must have the *capacity* to make a choice. Capacity is not defined, although consideration was given to introducing a definition. What there is, though, is a phrase that appears in the offences related to sexual offences and persons with a mental disorder. The phrase 'unable to refuse' is used. There is the prospect for some confusion here, as it may occur in practice that there is a debate as to the distinction between capacity to choose and inability to refuse. Concern was expressed in Parliament about this possibility. However, the way in which the phrase 'unable to refuse' is defined demonstrates that the two concepts are closely related and that, indeed, a person who is unable to refuse (s 30(2)) is a person who does not have the capacity to make the choice (s 74).

'Unable to refuse' is defined in the same manner in each of the relevant offences (for further discussion of these offences, see ch 6). As an example, s 30(2) states:

B is unable to refuse if—

(a) he lacks the capacity to choose whether to agree to the touching (whether because he lacks sufficient understanding of the nature or possible consequences of what is being done, or for any other reason), or

(b) he is unable to communicate such a choice to A.

The interrelationship between capacity to make a choice and inability to refuse is made clear by s 30(2)(a). A first question is whether someone who is unable to communicate a choice that they have made is not only unable to refuse but also is not capable of making the relevant decision. The person to consider is someone whose communication skills are so limited that they cannot make the other person understand what they have decided. Clearly, this person is unable to refuse. By analogy with the draft Mental Incapacity Bill 2003, they would also be incapable of choosing. This is because, ever since the Law Commission's report on Mental Incapacity (1995) Law Com No 231, it has been accepted that a person who is not able to communicate a choice, even one that has been made, is incapable. Since the origins of the phrase 'unable to refuse' lie within the Law Commission's work on mental incapacity and its subsequent development, it is reasonable to posit the view that a person not able to communicate a choice is not only unable to refuse but is also not capable of choosing. Thus, the man who has sexual intercourse with a woman who cannot communicate her choice commits the actus reus of rape, as the sexual intercourse is non-consensual. He also commits the offence of having sexual activity with a person with a mental disorder impeding choice, contrary to s 30, on the basis that she is unable to refuse. In the old law, it was stated that the consent of the woman did not need to be communicated (see *R v Lang* (1975) 62 Cr App R 50).

Section 30(2)(a) adopts the functional approach to capacity which means that the question of capacity is related to the individual's abilities at the time that the decision is made. It means that their status (e.g., having a profound learning disability) does not determine capacity, but its presence is relevant to assessing whether capacity exists. It also means that the outcome of a decision does not determine capacity. The fact that a decision is irrational or unreasonable from an objective standpoint does not make the person incapable, although the more irrational or the more frequently unreasonable decisions are made the more relevant that information is in the assessment of capacity. So, in deciding whether a person is incapable, the need is to examine whether they had the abilities to agree to sexual intercourse. The legislation focuses this question on whether she lacks sufficient understanding of the nature or possible consequences of what is being done. Two matters need to be teased out here.

2.3.3.1 *What needs to be understood?*

This presents a considerable range of potential issues. The guidance in the legislation is that it is the nature of the act and its possible consequences that are to be considered. The nature of the act would refer to whether the individual understands the mechanics of sexual intercourse. It is predicted that, if a person does not understand that sexual intercourse involves the insertion of the (erect) penis into the vagina or that there must be movement by the man and/or woman and that it terminates by withdrawal or ejaculation of spcrm and withdrawal, that person does not understand the nature of the act. For example, the young girl in *R v Williams* [1922] All ER 322 did not understand what constituted sexual intercourse to the extent that she thought what was being done to her was an operation to improve her singing voice. The late Ann Craft often used an example of sex education for adults with a learning disability where the educators had discussed sexual intercourse by using the phrase 'going to bed'. When asked what they had learned, one person made clear, through a drawing of two people in bed, that they had taken the phrase literally and understood that sexual intercourse involved two people lying down in bed and that was it. In both cases, there would be an inability to understand the nature of the act. What also is illustrated is that, with appropriate sex education, the people in question might have learned what is involved in having sexual intercourse and that would have provided an ability to exercise autonomy. Decisions as to whether to agree to sex and knowledge that sex need not be agreed to are vital in enabling people to make decisions meaningfully and to understand when what is being proposed is abuse.

In addition to understanding the nature of the act, the legislation requires an understanding of its possible consequences. This must mean that there has to be an understanding of the possibility of contracting a sexually transmitted disease and the possibility of the woman (where one is involved) becoming pregnant. No doubt there will be argument about what both these elements mean, particularly in terms of the level of detail and specificity of the consequence, and the likely impact upon the individual.

This approach will provide considerable assistance to the determination of capacity, since determining what must be understood makes clearer what must be looked for in capacity assessments and so understanding may be judged by hearing what the person in question can tell the assessor what they know of sexual intercourse. This is verifiable, as others can assess whether an initial decision was within an acceptable spectrum of assessments. Of course, what matters is that the standard that the assessors of capacity set is proper, but this can be achieved by careful research, education, and learning to underpin the practical application of an assessment procedure and process.

2.3.3.2 *How well must something be understood to be sufficiently understood?*

This is always a difficult factor in capacity assessments in the civil law (M.J. Gunn, J.G. Wong, I.C.H. Clare and A.J. Holland, 'Decision-Making Capacity' (1999) 7 *Medical Law Review* 269; M. Gunn, J. Bellhouse, I. Clare, T. Holland and P. Watson, 'Families and new medical dilemmas—capacity to make decisions' (2001) 13 *Child and Family Law Quarterly* 383). What is clear, in civil law, is that the level of understanding is not high. This is because there is a theme of requiring understanding in broad terms and simple language and because there is a presumption that all people are capable of making relevant decisions, unless the contrary is established. There is an assumption that the vast majority of people are capable of making such a decision, so that the individuals who are not capable form a relatively small group of people. Setting the level of understanding too high would exclude too many people from the group of those assumed to be capable. G.H. Murphy and A. O'Callaghan ('Capacity to Consent to Sexual Relationships in Adults with Intellectual Disabilities' (2003, unpublished)) have considered this issue, amongst others, in relation to capacity to consent to sex, and have drawn attention to one route to assist. This is that, since most 16 year-olds are assumed to be capable of consenting, then the normal level of understanding of a 16 year-old must be assumed to be the sort of level of understanding that is required. Therefore, in determining whether the individual's understanding is sufficient, too high a level must not be required and attention must always be paid to whether what is being expected of the individual would not be achieved by other people assumed to be capable of consenting.

How will these matters be resolved? In Parliamentary debate, it was suggested that this is not a difficult issue for, e.g., magistrates to determine. It is submitted that rather more assistance may need to be provided, especially as there cannot be confidence that, without assistance, the issues as highlighted above are being properly taken into account. Thus, when capacity is in issue, it is likely that expert witnesses will be sought to endeavour to determine, or rather to assist the court in determining, whether she was capable of providing consent.

Assuming that this approach is adopted to the meaning of capacity to consent, it will prevent a bad decision being reached such as that in *R v Jenkins* (unreported). This trial decision was explained by Lord Adebowale in the Committee stage of the House of Lords as follows:

. . . Jenkins was a support worker in a residential unit. He admitted having sexual intercourse with a woman resident. When it was discovered that she was pregnant DNA tests confirmed he was the father, At the trial experts agreed that the woman could name only some body parts, could not distinguish acts of sexual intercourse from other pictures shown to her and had no understanding of pregnancy or contraception. Plainly, she lacked the capacity to consent, as we would understand the term. However, the judge ruled that she had given consent through her 'animal instincts'. (HL Deb 10 April 2003, col 395.)

One matter in the new definition leads to some uncertainty. It will be seen, in s 30(2)(a), that the lack of capacity may be 'for any other reason'. It is frankly hard, if not impossible, to see to what this phrase might refer. No examples were given in Parliament, but the Government wanted it in to avoid any possible inappropriate acquittals. However, not only were no examples given in Parliament, but also none of the bodies with a deep interest in these matters were able to identify to what this phrase might refer (as indicated by Lord Adebowale, Chief Executive of Turning Point, the charity that coordinated the group).

2.4 CONSENT AND THE PRESUMPTIONS

Some assistance on deciding whether a woman has consented is provided by the presumptions introduced by ss 75 and 76. In Parliament, there was considerable debate about these presumptions in part because they often seemed to confuse rather than clarify the issues and also because of a fear that they involved a breach of Article 6(2) of the ECHR (see also H. Power, 'Towards a Redefinition of the Mens Rea of Rape' (2003) 23 *Oxford Journal of Legal Studies* 379). The rationale for the presumptions is that, after the examination of the current position and proposals for reform in *Setting the Boundaries*, the view was taken that the courts needed assistance in determining consent and, in consequence, raising the likelihood of convictions in appropriate cases. Therefore, what the Act does is to introduce two sets of presumptions. One is a set of evidential presumptions that are rebuttable by the defence and one is a set of presumptions that are conclusive.

2.4.1 Evidential presumptions

The evidential presumptions are to be found in s 75. Such presumptions only arise (s 75(1)(a)) where it has been established in the normal manner by the prosecution that the defendant did the 'relevant act' (defined in s 77). If it is then proved by the prosecution, beyond a reasonable doubt, that any of a set of circumstances existed and that the defendant knew that they existed (s 75(1) (b) and (c)),

the complainant is to be taken not to have consented to the relevant act unless sufficient evidence is adduced to raise an issue as to whether he consented, and the defendant is to be taken not to have reasonably believed that the complainant consented unless sufficient evidence is adduced to raise an issue as to whether he reasonably believed it (s 75(1)).

The burden to adduce 'sufficient evidence' is on the defendant. The set of circumstances is listed in s 75(2):

(a) any person was, at the time of the relevant act or immediately before it began, using violence against the complainant or causing the complainant to fear that immediate violence would be used against him;

(b) any person was, at the time of the relevant act or immediately before it began, causing the complainant to fear that violence was being used, or that immediate violence would be used, against another person;

(c) the complainant was, and the defendant was not, unlawfully detained at the time of the relevant act;

(d) the complainant was asleep or otherwise unconscious at the time of the relevant act;

(e) because of the complainant's physical disability, the complainant would not have been able at the time of the relevant act to communicate to the defendant whether the complainant consented;

(f) any person had administered to or caused to be taken by the complainant, without the complainant's consent, a substance which, having regard to when it was administered or taken, was capable of causing or enabling the complainant to be stupefied or overpowered at the time of the relevant act.

In relation to each of these evidential presumptions, the Government in debate explained that it was introducing an evidential rather than persuasive burden. Taking words from Baroness Scotland, Minister of State in the Home Office, the Explanatory Notes on the legislation advise that,

in order for those assumptions not to apply, the defendant will need to satisfy the judge from the evidence that there is a real issue about consent that is worth putting to the jury. The evidence relied on may be, for example, evidence that the defendant himself gives in the witness box, or evidence given on his behalf by a defence witness, or evidence given by the complainant during cross-examination. If the judge is satisfied that there is sufficient evidence to justify putting the issue of consent to the jury, then the issues will have to be proved by the prosecution in the normal way. If the judge does not think the evidence relied on by the defendant meets this threshold, he will direct the jury to find the defendant guilty, assuming the jury is sure that the defendant did the relevant act, that the circumstances in subsection (2) applied and that the defendant knew that.

2.4.1.1 *Use of violence and fear of violence*

The use of violence and the fear of violence each clearly affect the ability and freedom of a woman to agree by choice. Normally people do not consent when threatened with violence, so it is proper to have a presumption to that effect. However, it is still possible that the woman did consent (e.g., because she enjoys sado-masochistic sex), and so it is a presumption that can be rebutted.

Section 75(2)(a) applies where violence is used or it is feared that immediate violence will be used against the complainant. Section 75(2)(b) is concerned with its use or anticipated use against another person. As regards the latter, there is no requirement of any particular connection between the complainant and the third person, but it can be anticipated that the presumption will be much harder effectively to rebut where the violence is threatened against a woman's young and dependant child than against an adult man. The Explanatory Notes advise that the violence or threat must occur either at the time of the relevant act or immediately before it began.

The word 'violence' is used. This is not defined in the Act. In normal usage, this word would refer to a level of harm that is greater than would satisfy the meaning of the word 'force'. In Parliament, it was indicated that it would relate only to harm to the person and not to harm to property.

2.4.1.2 *Unlawful detention*
A person who is unlawfully detained has their ability freely to make decisions reduced, but it is not necessarily removed. Whilst most people kidnapped do not form real affection for their kidnappers, it is not unknown. Being an evidential presumption, allowance is made for this, admittedly rare, possibility. Detention of itself does not necessarily deprive a person of their capacity to make decisions.

2.4.1.3 *Unconsciousness*
A person who is asleep cannot give agreement to an act. They are factually incapable of doing so. In the old law, a woman who was asleep was said not to be able to provide consent (*R v Larter and Castleton* [1995] Crim LR 75). It is proper, there-fore, to presume the absence of consent unless the defendant can raise some factor to the contrary, which is most likely to be about the defendant's belief that the woman was not asleep (see below), assuming the evidence establishes that she was indeed asleep (similarly also for any other cause of unconsciousness). If drunkenness produces unconsciousness (as was the case in *R v Camplin* (1845) 1 Car & Kir 746), it falls within s 75(2)(d). If it does not produce that state of unconsciousness, the presumption in s 75(2)(f) may be relevant (see below).

2.4.1.4 *Inability to communicate from physical disability*
A person who cannot communicate may be incapable as a result of a physical or a mental disability. Where it is as a consequence of a physical disability, the presump-tion in s 75(2)(e) will arise. Since such a disability is likely to be relatively obvious, it makes sense to raise a presumption, that the defendant can rebut, both about the state of facts and the defendant's belief about them. It is perhaps surprising that this presumption only applies where the inability to communicate is a product of a physi-cal disability. Although that may be more obvious on the basis of observable facts about the woman, nevertheless it is hard to fathom its limited application. If, as suggested above, there is a link between a person's inability to refuse and capacity to choose, this presumption may be unnecessary, as a person not able to communicate is not able to refuse and therefore cannot choose. On the other hand, the concept of inability to refuse only appears in the offences concerned with the protection of people with a mental disorder, whereas this presumption applies to people with a physical disability in the whole range of general offences. A better option would have been a definition of capacity to consent that included the inability to communi-cate, howsoever produced. The presumption would not have been necessary in rela-tion to whether the complainant could consent, but might have been necessary in relation to the defendant's belief about the ability of the complainant to consent.

2.4.1.5 *Substances non-consensually administered capable of stupefying or overpowering*

This evidential presumption was introduced late in the Parliamentary life of the Bill and even though the Home Secretary had been reluctant to do so having indicated a concern about 'mischievous accusations' (*Protecting the Public* (2002)). The objective of this presumption is to be a response to concerns about drug-assisted rape. It will also have a role to play in relation to the offence of administering a substance with intent contrary to s 61 (see ch 9). The presumption does not just apply to such drugs as Rohypnol or GHB, but to any substance capable of causing or enabling stupefaction or overpowering of the woman. The substance to which this is most likely to apply is alcohol. It may well assist in some cases where the woman is stupefied or overpowered and so the man can have sexual intercourse with her. In some cases, the consequence of the administration is to make the woman more likely to 'be a willing participant in sexual activity that she would usually refuse or find repugnant' (Finch and Munro (2003), p 776). This type of case will present an interesting matter for the court, since the evidence is that she was consenting at the time of the sexual intercourse, but that this was a product of the administration of a substance which was capable of producing a different consequence, but had not done so at that time (the drugs and alcohol eventually induce unconsciousness but do not do so immediately). Even so, the presumption is to apply, evidentially, and indicates that she was not consenting. The counter-evidence will be that she was consenting! As the presumption requires that the person doing the administering knows (s 75(1)(c)) that the circumstances existed, i.e., that the substance is capable of causing or enabling her to be stupefied or overpowered, it is entirely understandable that he should be convicted of rape (see Finch and Munro).

2.4.2 Conclusive presumptions

The conclusive presumptions are to be found in s 76. Such presumptions only arise where it has been established in the normal manner by the prosecution that the defendant did the 'relevant act' (defined in s 77) (s 76(1)). If it is then proved by the prosecution, beyond a reasonable doubt, that any of a set of circumstances existed (s 76(1)),

it is to be conclusively presumed

    (a) that the complainant did not consent to the relevant act, and

    (b) that the defendant did not believe that the complainant consented to the relevant act.

Whilst the prosecution does not have to prove anything with regard to the defendant's belief under s 76(1), this is not a strict liability provision, as the set of circumstances that have to be proved rests on the defendant intentionally doing something. The set of circumstances is listed in s 76(2).

    (a) the defendant intentionally deceived the complainant as to the nature or purpose of the relevant act;

(b) the defendant intentionally induced the complainant to consent to the relevant act by impersonating a person known personally to the complainant.

These two presumptions are a product of what the defendant does. He, therefore, has relevant knowledge about the circumstances. He knows that he has deceived the woman as to whether it is sex that is occurring or who he is. In both cases, the pre-existing law made clear that an apparent consent was not valid. It is unarguable that, where these circumstances exist, the woman did not consent. Further, there can be no mistake being made by the defendant, as it must be proved that he induced it intentionally. Therefore, the creation of a presumption is valid. And there is nothing wrong with it being conclusive, since there is no possible argument that can be made against its application and consequences. The presumption only deals with mistakes created by the defendant. If a similar mistake occurs as a result of some other cause and the defendant takes advantage of it, that would not appear to give rise to a presumption, but would have to be handled in determining whether there was an agreement by choice by the woman to having sexual intercourse.

2.4.3 Presumptions: compatibility with the European Convention on Human Rights

One matter that will no doubt arise is whether either set of presumptions or a particular presumption survives challenge under Article 6(2) ECHR. Article 6(2) sets its face against reverse burdens of proof. Both types of presumption could be argued to fall foul of this provision. In *Salabiaku v France* (1988) 13 EHRR 379, the European Court of Human Rights made clear that, even where it was a true reversal of the burden, there was not necessarily a breach of the Convention. The factors that the English courts are taking into account in determining whether such a provision is in breach are: the seriousness of the offence, the public interest to be served by the provision, and the ease with which the defendant could discharge the burden upon him. Even where an offence carries a high maximum penalty, the provision may not breach Article 6 provided the public interest is sufficient to warrant it (see, e.g., *R v Lambert* [2001] 3 WLR 206; *AG's Reference (No 4 of 2002)* [2003] HRLR 15; *Blackstone's Criminal Practice 2004*).

In sex offences, the public interest to be served by the presumptions would be the need to protect women and vulnerable people from a serious infringement of their freedom of the person that is not adequately provided by the current law. There is a public interest in securing more rape convictions. It would seem that there is a strong argument that the presumptions in the Act will survive challenge. In discussion of each of the presumptions a rationale has been provided that would satisfy the policy element requirement. In short, the policy is that the rate of convictions is so low and dealing with protecting women from rape is so poor that action has to be taken, but that it is a balanced approach. In the case of the evidential presumptions, there is no doubt that, if the necessary facts are proved, there is no consent, unless something unusual is raised which challenges that presumption. Such an issue is likely to be within the peculiar knowledge of the defendant, and so imposing upon him a burden of raising the matter is appropriate. It is then for the prosecution to disprove it. Thus, the evidential presumptions can be argued as being proportionate. In the case of the conclusive presumptions, they are established on the basis of something that the defendant has done with intention, they only arise where the prosecution has proved the facts and, if that is achieved, there is no possible argument that the defendant could raise that could challenge the conclusion reached by application of the presumption and therefore the approach is proportionate.

If absence of consent is established (and the other elements of the relevant offence are also established), the question then is the relevance of the defendant's belief that, contrary to the facts of the matter, he believed that the woman was consenting.

2.5 BELIEF IN CONSENT

2.5.1 The law prior to the Act

If the defendant committed the actus reus of a sexual offence, what is left to be considered is his mens rea. In the offence of rape, the mens rea for this offence has traditionally focused on the belief in consent of the defendant.

The House of Lords in *DPP v Morgan* [1976] AC 182 decided that a defendant is not guilty of rape where he has an honest belief that the woman consented to sexual intercourse, even if he was mistaken and she did not, in fact, consent. This was put into statutory form by amendment to the SOA 1956:

. . . at the time he knows that the person does not consent to the intercourse or is reckless as to whether that person consents to it (s 1 SO(A)A 1976).

According to case law interpreting the statutory provision (*R v Kimber* [1983] 1 WLR 1118 and *R v Satnam and Kewal* (1984) 78 Cr App R 149), a defendant is reckless where he knows there is a risk that she does not consent or his attitude is one of indifference whether she consents or not, which is alternatively put as being that he could not care less whether she consented (for a valuable recent summary of positions, see Power (2003)).

In the end, what this all means is that, if a defendant honestly believes that the woman does not consent, he is not guilty. This issue, of course, does not arise until it has already been established that she did not, in fact, consent to what the defendant did. The belief held by the man need not be reasonable, but the more unreasonable it is the more likely it is that his belief will not be accepted by the jury as its reasonableness is relevant to their decision.

The decision in *Morgan* and its continued application in English law has been a matter of considerable controversy. Described as a 'rapist's charter', it was thought to allow defendants to get off rape when they should not, and to limit the likelihood of a woman being prepared to allow an allegation of rape to get to court (Temkin (1999) and Power (2003)). Therefore, it was said to reduce the likelihood of convictions when such convictions should be reached. Whilst there was a need for improvements in procedure, there was also a contribution that the substantive law could make. A decision has to be made as to whether it is acceptable to use a negligence standard in determining guilt in relation to belief about consent. The Law Commission usefully summarized the arguments in support of what might be termed the objective and subjective approaches in its 2000 Policy Paper entitled, 'Consent in Sex Offences' (*Setting the Boundaries*, vol. 2) as follows:

Arguments in support of an objective element

(1) Belief in consent is an easy defence to raise but hard to disprove.

(2) It encourages defences to be run which pander to outmoded and offensive assumptions about the nature of sexual relationships. The more stupid and sexist the man and his attitudes, the better chance he has of being acquitted on this basis.

(3) The damage is done to the woman by the act of rape. She is entitled to expect the protection of the criminal law where, on any view, the man has acted on an unreasonably held assumption about her consent.

(4) The mistaken belief arises in a situation where the price of the man's (gross) neglect is very high, and paid by the woman, whereas the cost to him in time and effort of informing himself of the true position is minimal by comparison.

(5) Under new provisions in section 41 of the Youth Justice and Criminal Evidence Act 1999, a complainant will be substantially better protected from intrusive cross-examination where the issue is actual consent (that is, whether she is lying when she says she did not consent) than where the issue is *belief* in consent (where it may be conceded that her evidence is truthful). The complainant ought not to have less protection from such cross-examination merely because the defendant runs a defence of honest but unreasonable mistake in tandem with a defence of actual consent. Therefore the retention of the defence of honest but unreasonable mistake would serve to undermine this enhanced protection for the witness.

Arguments in favour of retention of the subjective test

(1) A person should not be guilty of a serious criminal offence on the basis of strict liability or on the basis of negligence. Liability at this level of seriousness should be based only on intent or recklessness.

(2) The burden is on those who argue for a change to an objective basis to demonstrate that persons are being inappropriately acquitted by running a bogus 'unreasonable belief' defence. No such evidence has been produced. It appears that *Morgan* is not, in practice, a problem.

(3) If the availability of the defence is based in law on 'reasonableness', then whose reasonableness is being applied? Is it that of the defendant, the members of the jury, the person on the Clapham omnibus? The concept of 'reasonableness' has been the source of endless, and continuing, difficulty in relation to provocation in homicide. Many cases in which provocation is raised occupy the same type of contested space as is occupied by rape,

namely intimate relationships between the genders in extremis. There is no reason, therefore, to suppose that the same difficulties would not be encountered if the same concept were introduced in this context. Any proposal to reform the law should not lightly be made which carries the risk of making it more complex and unpredictable.

(4) This difficulty would be even more pronounced if, instead of a test of reasonableness, the test were to be one akin to 'gross negligence', as a further level of complexity would be involved.

(5) A modern jury, properly directed on the question whether the person did or did not have such a belief, will be well able to root out the true from the bogus defence of belief in consent. Anyway it is seldom, if ever, that a defendant would put forward a defence that he had such a belief for which he acknowledged there were no reasonable grounds.

(6) The rate of conviction for rape is already alarmingly low. Juries appear already to be uncomfortable in convicting men of a very serious offence in circumstances that appear to them to be ambiguous. If there were a rule of law that, however honest a belief, the jury had no option but to convict in the absence of reasonable grounds for it, a perception of unfairness might arise, which might result in fewer convictions than were the jury left themselves to judge whether an assertion of belief is genuine or just a fanciful story unworthy of belief.

A choice has to be made as to which of the above arguments seem to be the more compelling. In Parliament, the majority of the lawyers who spoke were in favour of retaining *Morgan*. However, the Government was convinced that a change was necessary and chose to go down the route of introducing an objective element. In the Committee stage in the House of Lords, Lord Falconer (then Minister of State in the Home Office) explained that,

there is no justice in a situation where a person who has been raped, or subjected to other forced sexual activity, sees an assailant go free because of a belief that society as a whole would have found unreasonable or completely unreasonable or totally unreasonable. In considering where justice lies, it is important to consider not only the interests of the defendant but also the interests of the victim. In circumstances where the defendant has behaved wholly unreasonably in believing that there is consent and could have taken steps to put the position beyond doubt, where should the risk lie? Should it lie with the victim who has, through her own experience, been raped in the sense that she has sexual intercourse forced upon her without her consent; or should it lie with the defendant who, although extraordinarily unreasonably, honestly believed that she consented? The defendant would be acquitted, rightly, under the current law—but, we would say, wrongly as a matter of justice—whereas the victim will suffer from the humiliation of being raped and not receiving justice. It is a difficult balance. It should not be determined by political correctness but by something that reflects people's understanding of what is or is not just. (HL Debs 31 March 2003, Col 1089, see also HL Debs 2 June 2003, Col 1060.)

Initially, the Government proposed that the introduction of an objective element should be achieved by asking whether the reasonable person would have doubted whether the woman consented to the act. So, clause 1(3) of the Bill as originally introduced into the House of Lords adopted the Canadian approach and stated:

This subsection applies if—

(a) a reasonable person would in all the circumstances doubt whether B consented, and

(b) A does not act in a way that a reasonable person would consider sufficient in all the circumstances to resolve such doubt.

As a minimum, this would have obliged the man to have asked the woman if she did really consent. However, in Parliament concerns were raised about this formulation, because it was felt that it would catch those who could not perceive things that would be perceived by a reasonable man (e.g., some people with a learning disability would not be able to perceive that which would be perceived by a reasonable person and judging them by that standard would lead to their conviction when there was nothing they could have done to have avoided that conviction). This was accepted by the Government as a problem and thus, broadly speaking, the New Zealand example was adopted and introduced as what is now s 1(1)(c) and (2):

(1) ...

(c) A does not reasonably believe that B consents.

(2) Whether a belief is reasonable is to be determined having regard to all the circumstances, including any steps A has taken to ascertain whether B consents.

Thus, what is to be focused upon is the reasonableness of the belief held by A, the defendant. The question is whether that belief is a reasonable one. In determining whether it is reasonable, account, it is expected, will be taken of the characteristics of the defendant (e.g., any learning disability, mental disorder, or exceptional inexperience of sex). However, the statute uses the word, 'circumstances', rather than something such as 'characteristics of the defendant'. Whilst lessons from the law of provocation give some indication of the potential problems in identifying the relevant characteristics of the defendant (see *Blackstone's Criminal Practice 2004*), it is entirely possible, though hopefully not likely, that the courts will take the view that the personal characteristics of the defendant, such as his learning disability, are not 'circumstances' and so are not to be taken into account (for the possibility of this approach, see *R v P* (1993) 10 CRNZ 250). Will the 'circumstances' include the nature of the relationship between the two? A full answer to this question will depend upon the extent to which the evidence will be admissible as it will examine sexual history (see ch 10) and the relevance of the presumptions about violence (below), but the reasonableness of a belief might well be related to the past experience of a particular sexual relationship, e.g., where violence has been consensually used in the past, might that not be relevant to determining whether his belief that she was consenting (when she was not) was a reasonable one (see, e.g., *R v McFall* [1994] Crim LR 226). Further, whilst the test is left open for consideration by the jury or magistrates, it is emphasized that they must take into account, in particular, any steps that the defendant has taken to ascertain whether the woman does indeed consent. This will best be satisfied where the two negotiate and overtly agree exactly what they are going to do and so comply with the concept of communicative sexuality (see Rumsey (2001), pp 898–904), but it is unrealistic to anticipate that this would be a requirement for compliance. Sexual encounters do not always involve overt, verbal interactions, and yet may be fully consensual. Unless there were to be a major change in societal attitudes, the law must accommodate the range of approaches adopted that in normal behaviour secure clarity about consent prior to a sexual engagement.

There are four examples of cases in which a man can be acquitted under the *Morgan* rule that may be taken as measures of whether the new law has made an improvement (Temkin (1999)). Professor Temkin states these to be:

1. D has sexual intercourse with V at the invitation of another man, X. V struggles and protests but X explains that this is mere play-acting and D believes him;

2. V explicitly states that she does not consent and attempts to resist. D, because of his superior strength, is able without much force to overcome her. He, believing that women always behave in this way, interprets her no as yes and her resistance as token;

3. D has so terrified V by his conduct that V dare not register her non-consent. He may, for example, have broken into her home or violently assaulted her before attempting to have sexual intercourse. He interprets her lack of protest as consent;

4. V is a child or mentally disabled.

In determining how these examples might work out under the SOA 2003, account must also be taken of the presumptions to the extent that they apply to the reasonableness of the defendant's belief. In example 1, D's belief would have to be reasonable. There is no third party presumption, though one was in the original Bill, and it was lost because

it would be unfair to impose a conclusive presumption in relation to the reasonableness test where the defendant was a person with a mental disorder or learning disability, who could not be expected to understand that a third party was deceiving him as to the truth (Baroness Scotland, HL Debates, 17 June 2003, cols 671–2).

It is for the jury to determine whether it thought that D's belief was reasonable or not (see also Baroness Scotland, col 672). This case could go either way, and it will depend upon the strength of the case as presented in court. It should be borne in mind that V's sexual history may be introduced into a court if the trial judge gives permission under the Youth Justice and Criminal Evidence Act 1999, s 41 (see *Blackstone's Criminal Practice 2004*). As the belief must be reasonable, there is less likelihood of acquittal than under the existing law. As Temkin points out,

it is not clear that V's non-consent should necessarily be obvious to D. Sado-masochism is practised by some and D may believe what he has been told . . . [T]he law should require that D should make it his business to find out whether or not she is truly consenting by asking her . . .

If he does so ask her, it is less likely that his belief will be regarded as unreasonable and the fact that the jury is required to take into account any steps that he has taken to ascertain whether she consents confirms the importance, though not determinative, nature of this simple task by D. It may also be relevant that, in sado-masochism, 'yes' and 'no' are not normally used to indicate when violence should cease, but that keywords are used to achieve that end (N. Bamforth, 'Sado-Masochism and Consent' [1994] *Criminal Law Review* 661).

In example 2, it seems likely that D will be convicted because it seems unlikely that a jury would regard his belief as being reasonably held, especially as she states explicitly that she does not consent. It is, though, relevant that he believes that women always behave in that way and interprets her 'no' as 'yes'. The viability of this argument is now more difficult to sustain because it would seem, prima facie, to be an unreasonable belief. If he comes from a society or culture in which these are generally held beliefs that might make it more possible for him to be acquitted, but even in those cases, it would be a difficult task.

In example 3, there is a presumption that will help in some aspects. In s 75, there is an evidential presumption that the defendant's belief that the woman consented is not reasonable where someone uses violence against her or someone causes her to fear violence. Violence is not further defined in the Act, but in Parliamentary debate any presumption on the basis of harm to property was rejected so it is to be presumed (as would also be suggested by the ordinary meaning of the word) that it is violence to the person that is required. Thus, to the extent that the example focuses upon harm to property, no presumption applies in relation to it, but the presumption does apply to the violent assault upon V. What will be necessary in the case of D breaking into V's home will be to focus upon any harm to the person and whether that amounts to violence. Clearly if V fears violence that is sufficient as that would satisfy s 75(2)(a). If, however, she is scared of what might happen then such apprehension may not amount to violence or the fear of violence.

In example 4, it is to be recalled that, although there are special offences that may deal with these instances (i.e., sex with a girl under the age of 13 (s 5) or sexual activity with a person with a mental disorder (s 30)), the question here is whether there was a rape. The sex may be non-consensual either because the woman was not capable of consenting as a result of age or mental disability or, though capable, did not consent. Thus, D's belief may be either that he thought that the person was not a child or had a mental disability or that the person did consent, despite being a child or having a mental disability. It will not be sufficient for D simply to assert his belief. It is for the prosecution to establish that the belief was unreasonable. The most straightforward cases will be where the person is obviously either a young child or someone with a severe mental disability. In these cases, it will be extremely difficult if not impossible for any defendant successfully to assert that their belief was reasonable. The older the child or the less apparent the person's mental disability, the more likely that a belief may be held to be reasonable. However, even here it is less likely than before that the defendant will be acquitted.

In summary, the likelihood of conviction is raised by the introduction of the requirement that the belief held by the defendant must be reasonable, and in some cases this is assisted by the application of one or more of the presumptions about consent in ss 75 and 76 (a similar outcome would be reached were the case categories identified by Power (2003) at p 384 to be analysed in similar fashion). The conviction rate for rape is very low, and this change in the law should make a difference. Many barristers, speaking in Parliament, were of the view that the change would have very limited impact because they were, anecdotally, not aware of many, if any, cases where honest belief was run in court. In these debates, it was frequently erroneously suggested that the only case that could be recalled was *Morgan* itself, but here, though the judge directed the jury incorrectly, the House of Lords applied the then proviso and upheld the conviction, basically on the ground that no jury properly directed could have accepted the defendant's story as it was so unreasonable.

2.6 PROCEDURAL CHANGE AS A RESULT OF THE SUBSTANTIVE LAW CHANGE

It is clear that the issue in relation to belief in consent is not just one that had an effect at trial. The anticipation of what would happen at trial appears to have reduced the confidence that women had about reporting to the police or, if reported, pursuing the matter further. In a Memorandum submitted to the Home Affairs Select Committee by the Metropolitan Police Service, an insight is provided into the difficulties presented to one police force by the decision in *Morgan*. As it happens, the difficulties highlighted are, it is submitted, a product of a misunderstanding of the law prior to the 2003 Act since unreasonableness is relevant to determining whether the belief was honestly held by the defendant and that seems not to be taken into account. But whether the cause was an inaccurate or accurate understanding of the law, it is the effect that matters. The Metropolitan Police Service stated that:

It is virtually impossible to prove 'reckless' intent when all the suspect has to say is that 'he believed she/he consented'. We contest that suspects are hiding behind the *Morgan* ruling despite behaviour that was totally unreasonable in the circumstances (e.g. a minicab driver raping a woman passenger). The *Morgan* ruling means that legitimate questions about the behaviour of a suspect cannot be put in interview to test '*mens rea*' further. Once a suspect has stated that 'he honestly believed she consented' that is normally the end of an interview. Furthermore, in these cases, the onus then frequently focuses on the victim to subsequently prove that she did not consent rather than on the suspect, by both police and courts, to prove that she did. This leads to victims being questioned vigorously on their behaviour with no similar questioning permitted of the suspect. We contend that this is an imbalance that needs addressing. (House of Commons, Home Affairs Committee HC 639 (2003), Written Evidence Appendix 22 at para 4; and as to the effect of existing law on police practice, see Temkin (1999), pp 94–5).

The change in the substantive law should be relatively easy to understand, so that it should be clear that the belief of the defendant would have to be a reasonable one.

Thus, feeling impotent when the alleged offender states that he thought she was consenting need not arise. So, questioning tactics will have to change so as to enable evidence to be raised that can allow the reasonableness of a belief to be tested by the police and in court. This assumes that the defendant raises the belief. Of course, if he does not, his failure to do so before trial is something that the jury can take into account in deciding whether to believe him under the Criminal Justice and Public Order Act 1994, ss 34 and 35 (see ch 10 and *Blackstone's Criminal Practice 2004*).

3

SEXUAL VIOLATION:
RAPE AND SEXUAL ASSAULT

3.1 INTRODUCTION

One of the main factors driving the reform of rape law was public concern over the increasingly high attrition rates for rape convictions, which, according to Home Office figures fell from 25% in 1985 to 7% in 2000. It was estimated that in the preceding year (1999) only 1 in 7 of the 61,000 rapes estimated to have occurred was reported to the police. Of these 9,008 reported rapes, only 1 in 13 resulted in conviction (*Rape and Sexual Assault of Women: Findings from the British Crime Survey*, HO 2002). Such figures underline the inherent difficulties in prosecuting rape and securing convictions, particularly in cases of 'date' or acquaintance rape. It is now acknowledged that rape is a diverse crime embracing a range of circumstances, relationships, and sexual violations including serial rape, marital rape, stranger rape, male rape, gang rape, date rape, acquaintance rape, and child rape. Equally, it is recognized that apparent consent can be induced by threats, violence (to victim or third party), drugs, alcohol, sexual innocence, and fraud. As consciousness of the vagaries of rape heightened it became apparent that the 'one size fits all' approach of the existing legislation was no longer sustainable.

Rape was first enacted as a statutory crime in 1861. The Offences Against the Person Act simply stated 'it is a felony for a man to rape a woman'. It was therefore left to the judiciary to establish the constituent elements and develop the factors that might vitiate an apparent consent: threats, fear, and fraud. Section 1 of the consolidating SOA 1956 failed to provide any further guidance or substantive definition. It was only after the controversy surrounding the decision of *DPP v Morgan* in 1975 and the uncertainty of whether a jury would be convinced by the defence of an honest but unreasonable belief that the victim consented (as highlighted in the previous chapter), that Parliament responded with a limited definition of mens rea based on knowledge and recklessness as to consent (s 1 Sexual Offences (Amendment) Act 1976 (SO(A)A 1976)). Similarly Parliament belatedly abolished the marital rape exemption *only after* the House of Lords declared it to be a common law fiction in *R v R* [1993] 1 All ER 747. The CJPOA 1994 extended the definition of s 1 to cover male victims and to include any penile rape by anus whether male or female (s 142). But apart from some reflections on the law by the Heilbron Committee in 1975 and the Criminal Law Revision Committee in 1984, the Review and subsequent enactment of the SOA 2003 is the first serious attempt at fundamental evaluation and systematic definition of rape's constituent elements. The Review did consider whether a gradation scheme should be introduced establishing different categories of rape as in some other common law jurisdictions. This was discounted on the grounds it might trivialize the seriousness and sexual emphasis of the crime and that current judicial guidelines on sentencing, recently updated in *R v Millberry* (2003), in practice achieve the same result (see table below). The Government was also unwilling to introduce a specific offence of date rape for similar reasons.

Not surprisingly it was concluded that the existing law failed to offer appropriate protection for victims or to acknowledge the true impact of rape and other sexual assaults perpetrated on them. To redress the balance new classifications of non-consensual penetrative and non-penetrative forms of sexual assault are introduced together with guidelines for establishing non-consent and determining what constitutes a sexual activity.

The first four offences in Part One of the Act deal with the most serious non-consensual sexual acts: the crime of rape and other associated offences reflecting the gravest sexual violations. When initially drafted, the Bill offered four paired offences, the basis of each being identical. The first offence e.g., rape, applied universally; the second applied specifically to child victims aged under 13, e.g., rape of a child under 13. However, this arrangement proved somewhat confusing as the main provisions dealing with child sex offences are grouped together in the next section of the Act. After its Reading in the Lords these paired offences were reorganized and those relating to children under 13 years collated into their own discrete section.

The Act clearly establishes that rape can only be committed by *penile* penetration and therefore, subject to a possible exception noted below, remains a gender-specific offence. Non-penile penetration (the insertion of objects or other parts of the body) is termed *assault by penetration*. New offences of *sexual assault* and *causing a person to engage in sexual activity* replace the former offence of *indecent assault* and emphasize the *sexualized* aspect of such assaults. A controversial amendment supported by the House of Lords was inserted to allow a defendant or man charged with rape the protection of anonymity but this was rejected by the Commons. Media coverage of allegations of sexual assault made against celebrities such as John Leslie and Matthew Kelly and certain Premier League footballers propelled the issue into the public spotlight. Instead the Attorney General, Lord Goldsmith QC, has issued stringent guidance to stop any pre-judicial coverage in an attempt to curb such 'trial by media' (Speech delivered to Law for Journalists Conference, RSA, London 28 November 2003).

3.2 RAPE

Section 1(1) provides that rape is now committed where:

A intentionally penetrates the vagina, anus, or mouth of another person B with his penis,

B does not consent, and

A does not reasonably believe that B consents

Section 1(2) provides that:

Whether a belief is reasonable is to be determined having regard to all the circumstances, including any steps A has taken to ascertain whether B consents

A person found guilty is liable to life imprisonment.

Section 1(1) is the general rape provision that replaces and extends s 1 SOA 1956. Because of the requirement of penile penetration the offence is gender-specific as far as the offender is concerned and can only be legally performed by male perpetrators aged 10 years or over (the presumption of sexual incapacity was abolished by s 1 SOA 1993). Note that the provision not only includes penetration of the vagina or anus but also encompasses non-consensual oral sex as this was agreed to be just 'as abhorrent, demeaning and traumatizing' a violation and 'equally, if not more, psychologically harmful than vaginal and anal rape' (Government Reply to Fifth Report Home Affairs Committee 2003). Females cannot be charged as principals under this section but if they act as accomplices of a male rapist can be convicted of a new offence of causing a person to engage in sexual activity (see below). The Review recommended (para 2.8.4) that surgically reconstructed male or female genitalia should be expressly included in the legal definition of rape. This recommendation is not directly expressed in s 1 but is implied by virtue of s 79(3), the general interpretation provision, which confirms that references to a part of the body e.g., penis, include references to 'a part surgically constructed, in particular through gender reassignment therapy'. Female to male transsexuals who have undergone reconstructive penile surgery may therefore commit rape as the wording 'any person' would apply to those who have undergone physical gender change but are unable or not permitted to change their legal gender identity. In the case of any doubt the offence of assault by penetration should be charged (see below). The sole issue

33

seems to be whether there was penile penetration of the prohibited orifice, if gender becomes an extra issue it would be up to the court to determine this based on medical evidence, or amended birth certificate where appropriate. It is immaterial whether the person raped is male or female. Although the section is again silent as to reconstructive surgery, s 79(3) ensures that artificially constructed vaginas are included. This was held to be the position under the previous law in *R v Matthews* (unreported) Reading Crown Court, 24 October 1996 where penile penetration of a male-to-female transsexual's artificially constructed vagina amounted to rape.

3.2.1 Rape—elements to be proved

Essentially there are four elements which must be proved:

3.2.1.1 *that D* intentionally *penetrated the vagina, anus, or mouth of another person male or female*

The concept of intent has generally produced little difficulty in terms of interpretation and application as there are arguably few circumstances where D could claim any penetration was accidental. If D aims to have sexual intercourse without consent, he intends it. Once any degree of penetration is established, an intent to penetrate must be taken as read. Only if the penetration is minimal, or if D claims that he 'meant to stay on the outside', could there be any issue but given the wide view of penetration this is unlikely. D does not need to know that he is legally penetrating his victim, he need only intend to do an act that the law says constitutes penetration. Where he forces his victim to the ground, roughly removes their underclothes and attempts penetration, even if ultimately he is physically unable to complete the act, intent is present. Similarly, a simple admission from D that he intended to have sexual intercourse or bragged of his intent to his peers, made suggestive advances to the victim, or evidence that his penis was erect, could be sufficient to prove this element. As rape remains a crime of basic intent, self-induced intoxication cannot be relied on as a defence (see *R v Woods* (1981) 74 Cr App R 312 following *DPP v Majewski* [1976] 2 All ER 142).

Initially reference was made to recklessness in the draft Bill re-opening the whole debate about recklessness as to consent. The concept of recklessness as an element of the mens rea attracted considerable judicial discourse as this had never been defined in statute. This resulted in the confused position post *R v Caldwell* [1982] AC 341 and *R v Pigg* (1982) Cr App R 352 as to whether a subjective or objective standard should be applied. *R v Satnam and Kewal Singh* (1984) 78 Cr App R 149 apparently settled the issue in favour of subjective recklessness. More recently the House of Lords effectively overruled any remaining vestiges of *Caldwell* type objective recklessness and affirmed the primacy of subjective recklessness in cases of serious crime: *R v G and another* [2003] UKHL 50. Irrespective of such clarification the removal of all references to recklessness and limitation of the mens rea to intent should substantially simplify the position.

3.2.1.2 *that the vagina, anus, or mouth was* physically penetrated *by the defendant's penis*

The actus reus element relating to the physical act of intercourse is now penetration which replaces the former requirement of (*unlawful*) sexual intercourse (unlawful, meaning outside the bonds of marriage was dispensed with as surplusage in *R v R* [1991] 4 All ER 481) thereby removing any arguments as to when intercourse commences, how long it needs to last, and whether it is a continuing act (*R v Kaitamaki* [1985] AC 147). D must penetrate a woman's vagina or anus, a man's anus or the mouth of either with his penis. Penetration is defined in s 79(2), which formalizes the decision in *Cooper v Schaub* [1994] Crim LR 531 that penetration is a continuous act from entry to withdrawal. The slightest degree of penetration is sufficient. Vagina includes vulva (s 79(9)) confirming that full entry is not necessary. Thus the act of sexual intercourse may incorporate a 'number' of penetrations for each of which (theoretically) consent is required if culpability is to be avoided. Consent may be withdrawn at any time during this process at which point withdrawal should occur *R v Tarmohammed* [1997] Crim LR 458. Judicial guidance is silent as to whether this should be immediate or within a reasonable time but s 1(2) now provides a reasonableness test as to consent to be applied in such circumstances (see previous chapter). Thus where the penetration is initially consensual but B then withdraws her consent, perhaps because A is being aggressive and causing pain and discomfort, provided A is aware of this but carries on regardless he cannot claim that as the penetration was consensual so too was the sexual intercourse. The provision in s 44 SOA 1956 that it is not necessary to prove emission of seed has been retained raising the question as to why this was not incorporated into the new Act for ease of reference.

Evidence that the penis entered the prohibited orifice can be shown by witness testimony and/or supported by medical evidence where available; see *AG's Reference (No 25 of 1990) (Doheny)* (1992) 13 Cr App R(S) 220 for a detailed description of the range of physical injuries sustained where the female victim was raped both vaginally and anally.

3.2.1.3 *that the victim did* not consent

The issue of the actus reus element of consent has been dealt with in full in the preceding chapter. Consent is defined as a person freely agreeing by choice and who has the freedom and capacity to make that choice (s 74). Generally this will not be considered to be the case where a person is unconscious, drugged, abducted, subjected to threats of violence, or in fear of serious harm. Consent will inevitably be a matter of fact for the jury to determine based on all the available evidence and circumstances and using their own experience and sense: *R v McAllister* [1997] Crim LR 233.

3.2.1.4 *that the offender* did not reasonably believe *that B consents*

The issue of whether D should be able to avail himself of the defence of honest or mistaken belief in consent exercised the minds of the Review team and caused some disagreement between the External Group and the Steering Group. The case of *DPP v Morgan* [1975] Crim LR 717 was thought by some (e.g., Metropolitan Police Service) to have unjustifiably attracted the status of a precedent whereby defendants could hide behind the ruling claiming honest belief and making it harder for the police to prove intent, despite the rulings in cases such as *Pigg*. The External Group recommended that the pre-*Morgan* position be restored in that any such defence must be subjected to a test of reasonableness. The Steering Group preferred to fetter the use of such a defence by tying it into the definition of consent and requiring that D prove he had taken all reasonable steps that a reasonable person might expect in order to verify belief.

The compromise was a recommendation that a defence as to consent of honest but mistaken belief in free agreement should not be available where it was due to self-induced intoxication, there was recklessness as to consent, or where D failed to take all reasonable steps that might be expected in the circumstances (*Setting the Boundaries*, para 2.13.14). In the first draft Bill where D did not believe that B was consenting two alternatives were stipulated in clauses 1(2) and 1(3): a subjective test requiring the jury to be satisfied that D did not believe that B was consenting whether because D knew that B did not consent or gave no thought to the matter or otherwise. If D did believe B was consenting, the jury had to be satisfied that a reasonable person would have doubted that B was consenting taking into account all the circumstances, and that the *behaviour* of the defendant in the eyes of a reasonable person was sufficient to resolve any such doubt. The final revised s 1(2), which applies to all four non-consensual offences and appears as the second clause in each, is more simply and tightly drafted. It addresses the concerns raised about the potential injustice of the objective *reasonable person* test by substituting a more subjective approach requiring the jury to consider 'all the circumstances' including the individual characteristics of the defendant. The first key point is that the prosecution must adduce evidence to 'prove' that D did not reasonably believe that B consented—primarily the allegation of rape itself. The second key point is that in order to discharge this burden the Act provides the prosecutor with two means of assistance to determine what 'reasonable' means.

Section 1(2) provides that whether a belief in consent is reasonable may be determined having regard to all the circumstances and what D did, or did not, do. He might 'care' and make a genuine mistake but it could still be an 'unreasonable' one. Thus the prosecution must show that the circumstances were such that D could not have genuinely believed that B was consenting. If he then claims that he reasonably believed B did in fact consent the test for the jury would be whether a reasonable person would agree that his behaviour and actions (or lack of them) were conducive to such belief. Any ambiguity concerning what *he thought* was genuine consent might rely on any attempts made to resolve such doubts. The Government did not want to make date rape a specific offence but in practice this provision should tighten up the position as there is now a greater onus on the man to ensure that his sex partner was genuinely consenting. The thorny question of whether 'No' can in fact mean 'Yes' uttered in a sexual game or fantasy might now require D to be absolutely certain that there was no ambiguity as to its actual meaning. Any doubt, e.g., change in voice tone or physical expression, potentially demands that he re-establishes consent, otherwise he might have to explain to a jury why he failed to make any attempt so to do. He now bears more of a burden to show that he acted responsibly in ensuring that consent was freely and continuously given with full agreement and capacity.

The prosecution may also seek to rely on one or more of the rebuttable or conclusive presumptions listed in ss 75 and 76 as already discussed in Chapter 2. Consent may be presumed to be vitiated, for example, if induced by threats, force, or unlawful detention unless D can adduce evidence to the contrary in respect of s 75. In relation to s 76, where D intentionally deceives the complainant as to the nature of the act or induces consent by impersonation, the presumption cannot be rebutted at all.

3.2.2 Statutory rape of a child under 13

Where the victim is under 13 the Act creates a specific provision in s 5 of statutory rape of a child under 13. This is virtually a strict liability offence as there is no requirement whatsoever to prove non-consent and while intent must be proved it is nearly impossible to think of any situation where such an act would be accidental or justified. This provision is discussed in full in Chapter 4.

3.2.3 Recent guidelines on rape sentencing

In the light of recent criticism of some rape sentences the Court of Appeal took the opportunity in *Millberry* [2002] EWCA Crim 2891 to update the *Billam* (1986) 82 Cr App R 347 guidelines on rape sentencing. The court stressed that these should apply equally to stranger/relationship/acquaintanceship rape, male rape, and anal rape. The starting points are tabulated overleaf. These tariffs should be increased where any of the aggravating features listed in the end column apply. The sentencing tribunal must consider three dimensions when calculating the final tariff:

(i)   degree of harm to the victim

(ii) level of culpability of the offender

(iii) level of risk posed by the offender to society.

While the above guidelines were designed to ensure that appropriate penalties are meted out in practice this has not always been the case. In October 2003 the Solicitor General, Harriet Harman, succeeded in convincing the Court of Appeal to double a 5 year sentence imposed by the trial judge on a man who conducted a campaign of rape against his sister-in-law where at least three of the aggravating features identified in *Millberry* were present thus forcing the attention of the judiciary onto these guidelines, *AG's Reference (No 26 of 2003) sub nom R v M* [2003] EWCA Crim 2736.

Recent guidelines on rape sentencing

Contested trial:	Starting point	Aggravating Factors
Single offence on adult victim (where timely guilty plea)	5 years	Excessive violence
Contested trial: 2 or more offenders	8 years	Use of weapon
Offender in position of responsibility		
Victim abducted/held captive		Offence was planned
Victim child/vulnerable person		
Racially aggravated or homophobic		Serious physical or
Repeated rape in one attack, vaginal and anus		mental effect
Offender has life-threatening sexually transmitted disease		(pregnancy)
Repeated rape of same victim over course of time	15 years	Further degradation
Multiple victims		of victim
		Forced entry into place victim living
		Presence of children
		Covert use of drug to overcome resistance
Offender has perverted or psychopathic tendencies	Life	History of sexual
Offender has personality disorder		assaults
Danger to women		
Previous conviction rape/serious offence (s 109 Powers of Criminal Courts (Sentencing) Act 2000)	Automatic life sentence	

Young offenders: custodial sentence as above but significantly shorter
Defendant's good character: to be taken into account but does not justify substantial reduction

3.2.3.1 *Automatic life sentences*

In addition note should be made of s 109 Powers of Criminal Courts (Sentencing) Act 2000 (replacing s 2(1) Crime Sentences Act 1997) which requires the court to impose a mandatory life sentence on any person aged 18 or over convicted of a serious offence committed after 30 September 1997 and who, at the time the offence was committed, had been convicted in any part of the United Kingdom of another serious offence. Where the person is aged 21 years or over this will be a sentence of life imprisonment, but if aged under 21 but over 18, a sentence of custody for life is imposed. Aside from serious violent offences such as murder, manslaughter and ss 18 and 20 OAPA 1861, the specific sexual offences classified as 'serious offences' are now rape, assault by penetration, causing a person to engage in sexual activity without consent (must involve penetration), these same three offences committed against a child under 13, and sexual activity (i.e., penetration), or causing, or inciting the same with a person with a mental disorder (Sch 6 SOA 2003). Thus where D has a previous conviction for rape and is convicted on a second occasion of rape the sentence is automatically life unless there are exceptional circumstances relating to either of the offences. The court must be satisfied that the individual presents a considerable risk to the public and so factors such as the time that has elapsed between the offences may be relevant in deciding the degree of risk, see *R v Stark* [2002] EWCA Crim 542. The age of a defendant and the potentially different nature of the offences may also, in some circumstances, give rise to the conclusion that the case is exceptional, see *R v Offen* [2001] 1 Cr App R 24. Interestingly the Court of Appeal held in *R v Stephen Robert Wood* [2001] 1 Cr App R(S) 8 that a previous conviction for non-consensual buggery committed against his female partner in 1990 was not a 'serious offence' for the purposes of this section. The judicial rationale was that the old law did not require the prosecution to prove absence of consent in relation to buggery as there was no crime then of anal rape. This demonstrates a somewhat strict judicial interpretation and so until the implementation of the SOA 2003, s 109 will only catch those convicted of buggery as separate offences after the CJPO 1994 amended the crime of rape to include anal rape.

3.3 ASSAULT BY PENETRATION

The Review concluded that the offence of indecent assault did not sufficiently reflect the gravity of serious sexual assaults perpetrated by the penetration of the anus or female genitalia by the insertion of an object, or other part of the body e.g., digital penetration. The forced entry of physical objects such as bottlenecks (broken or otherwise), gun shafts, vibrators, and screwdrivers can often cause as much or more fear and distress, and potentially worse internal injuries, than penile rape. A new offence of assault by penetration reflects this and not only carries the same penalty, life imprisonment, as for penile penetration (rape) but is also made a serious arrestable offence for the purposes of PACE. Section 6 provides an identical offence in relation to children under 13 (see ch 4). The offence is committed contrary to s 2(1) where:

A intentionally penetrates the vagina or anus of another person B with a part of his body or anything else,

> the penetration is sexual,
>
> B does not consent to the penetration and
>
> A does not reasonably believe that B consents.

As with rape, whether a belief is reasonable is to be determined having regard to all the circumstances, including any steps A has taken to ascertain whether B consents (s 2(2)). The offence is gender-neutral. It can be committed against both males and females and equally both sexes can commit it and be convicted as principals.

3.3.1 Assault by penetration—elements to be proved

Apart from the aspect of non-penile penetration this offence is identical to rape and so the mens rea aspect of '*intentionally* penetrated the vagina or anus of another person male or female' and the actus reus that *penetration occurred* are the same as discussed above.

3.3.1.1 *that the vagina or anus is penetrated by a* part of the body *or* anything else

In addition to the digital penetration of the vagina or anus, a 'part of the body' would also include penetration by fist (fisting), tongue (rimming), and toes. Thus where D inserted his hand into the complainant's vagina and twisted it causing injuries as in *R v Boyea* [1992] Crim LR 574, and where such activity is non-consensual, assault by penetration would be the appropriate charge. As discussed above in relation to rape, a part of the body includes a part that has been surgically constructed, in particular through gender reassignment therapy such as a neo-phallus constructed as part of sex reassignment surgery or reconstruction of the penis by phalloplasty. While s 79(3), the interpretative section, emphasizes the context of gender reassignment therapy, the provision must be intended to include other non-sexual surgical constructions such as an artificial hand, finger, or toe. Equally it is presumed that it is intended to apply to all forms of reconstruction, not just those utilizing human tissue.

'Anything else' is not defined but is sufficiently all-embracing to limit any judicial pontification over what it may or may not cover. Obviously physical items such as vibrators and other inanimate objects would suffice but what of animate objects as in the somewhat bizarre practice of 'felching'? In the absence of any definition it would seem that small animals such as hamsters could constitute 'anything else'. Other issues for interpretation might include the forced entry of liquid douches or pessaries except where justified as healthcare treatment or anal irrigation. For example, in *R v Brian P* [2003] EWCA Crim 453 where D was convicted of indecent assault for forcing a showerhead up his female partner's anus who suffered from multiple sclerosis, he would now be convicted of assault by penetration. Unlike penile penetration the provision does not extend to penetration of the mouth so it would not be an offence under this section if A forced a vibrator or mock phallus into the mouth of B as s 2 (unlike s 1 rape) is confined to penetration of the anus or female genitalia. In this case an alternative charge would be s 3 sexual assault (see below).

The Review also recommended that where the means of penetration is not clear, perhaps where a number of different objects were inserted, or where the victim was blindfolded or suffered from memory loss, this offence should apply. The wording of the offence confirms this as it does not require that the precise object be identified as where this is unknown it must be caught by 'anything else'.

3.3.1.2 *the penetration is sexual*

The requirement that the penetration be sexual is perhaps somewhat superfluous and difficult to reconcile in light of the aim to address violent assaults where the intent is not predominantly 'sexual'. The rationale appears to be the justification of 'non-sexual' penetration in the context of medical treatment or therapy, something that might have been easier to facilitate by way of an exception or defence. In establishing whether any activity is sexual s 78 provides an objective test based on the reasoning in *R v Court* [1988] 2 All ER 2 (see below) whereby context and secret intent are relevant in assessing the sexual nature of an act. An activity is sexual where a reasonable person would consider that:

a) whatever its circumstances or any person's purpose in relation to it, it is because of its nature sexual *or*

b) because of its nature it may be sexual and because of its circumstances or the purpose of any person in relation to it, (or both) it is sexual.

Virtually any penetrative act would satisfy this test unless conducted in the course of bona fide medical examinations, treatment, or intimate searches by the police and other enforcement agencies. An issue here could be where a defendant claims that any forced insertion of an object such as a gun-barrel or spanner was intended only to cause *internal physical* injuries and that there was no associated sexual pleasure intended or experienced by him. Aside from the possibility of charges being brought for, say, grievous bodily harm, could a case under s 2 succeed? Whether the penetration is sexual is a question for the jury to decide applying this objective test. There are two potential aspects to consider.

Firstly, whether a reasonable person would consider that the nature of the penetration, irrespective of the circumstances or D's purpose, is sexual (s 78(a)). This demands some correlation between the nature of the activity and an associated sexual connotation. In terms of non-penile penetration, which is in essence simulating a sexual act, this is easily satisfied. It makes no difference whether items specifically manufactured as sex objects such as vibrators, dildos, or other sex toys are utilized, or those manufactured for non-sexual purposes such as gun barrels and rods. In each case the activity is 'because of its nature sexual'. However, it cannot be assumed that just because a sexual organ is penetrated by an object that this makes it sexual, as this would catch bona fide internal medical examinations that are invasive but have no sexual connotation. Similarly while not all may consider the penetration of the anus to be sexual as it is not a sexual i.e., reproductive, organ, most would undoubtedly consider that because of the nature of the penetration *it may be* sexual, especially when the purpose of the individual and the circumstances are taken into account. For example, where non-penile anal penetration is forced as a means of exerting power and humiliating the victim, the primary motivation may not be sexual but the purpose, and subsidiary aim, is to use sexual means to achieve this.

Thus the first para of s 78(a) of the reasonable person test applies where the nature of the sexual activity is unambiguous and does not require any further kind of contextual explanation such as that advanced by the House of Lords in *Court*. The second para of s 78(b) in effect puts the guidance given by their Lordships onto a statutory footing and deals with those activities where the sexual aspect is ambiguous but which may be regarded as being at least potentially sexual. Once D's purpose or intent is made clear, and/or the circumstances are fully understood, the ambiguity diminishes and it becomes self-evident that because of the nature of the activity *as a whole* it is in fact sexual. In *AG's Reference (No 3 of 2002)* [2003] EWCA Crim 2452, D, a psychiatrist specializing in psychotherapy, was convicted of two offences of rape and three of indecent assault committed upon vulnerable female patients who were referred to his surgery for counselling and therapy for depression and eating disorders. He suggested that sexual relations would assist in such counselling and be therapeutic. Applying s 78(a), a reasonable person must consider such activity to be sexual irrespective of any 'professional' purpose intended by D so if D penetrates B either digitally or with a mock-phallus his conduct could be sexual because of its nature. If, however, he used some type of medical instrument in the guise of therapy or treatment then the sexual nature of the activity, irrespective of the circumstances or D's purpose, may be less apparent. Applying s 78(b) no other conclusion could be drawn than that the nature of his activities *may be* sexual, and in the context of the circumstances and D's fraudulent purpose there is no question that they could be anything other.

3.3.1.3 *B does not* in fact consent *and D did not reasonably believe that B consented* As with rape the fact of non-consent must be proved and once this is established it is up to the prosecution to prove that any belief in consent was not reasonable (s 2(2)), shifting the burden to D to prove that he did act reasonably. The ss 75 and 76 presumptions also apply (s 2(3)).

3.4 SEXUAL ASSAULT

The offence of indecent assault (ss 14 and 15 SOA 1956) covered everything from groping and illicit touching to the sort of forced penetration with objects now controlled by s 2. Successful convictions necessitated proof of an assault or battery but did not require direct physical touching provided it was executed in circumstances that were deemed to be indecent. This was something that, given the particular circumstances, was not always clear; see *R v George* [1956] Crim LR 52, *Thomas* (1985) 81 Cr App R 331 and the leading case of *R v Court*. Where charges were brought for indecent assaults committed upon children there was the added complication of establishing the requirement of hostility, though this was somewhat mitigated with the enactment of the Indecency with Children Act 1960 (see ch 4).

The Review considered whether it would be more appropriate to adopt the term 'sexual touching' as used in some other jurisdictions, but decided to recommend the retention of an associated assault to clarify the context of the offence as not limited to just non-consensual touching. Despite the section's heading of 'sexual assault' surprisingly there is no reference to assault in the definition and in fact what the section delivers is an offence of sexual touching rather than a broader offence encompassing sexual assaults of the type where threats to commit a sexual violation are made. Thus 'assault' in the heading actually means 'battery'. The substitution of *sexual* for indecent recognizes the past difficulties associated with proving both the actions are indecent and that D had an indecent intent. While touching of the genitals is unquestionably indecent the position was always less clear-cut as regards the touching of buttocks (and possibly even breasts), kissing, or deliberately brushing up against a person (frottage). Where such touching is non-consensual but has associated sexual connotations it is now more likely to be caught as a sexual assault. Sexual assaults committed on a child under 13 are dealt with by s 7 (see ch 4); otherwise the offence is complete under s 3(1) where:

A intentionally touches another person B,

the touching is sexual,

B does not consent to the touching and

A does not reasonably believe that B consents

As with rape and assault by penetration, s 3(2) again repeats the reasonableness test as to consent. The maximum penalty is 10 years imprisonment if tried on indictment (the same as for the former offence of indecent assault), or 6 months/fine if tried summarily.

3.4.1 Sexual assault—elements to be proved

3.4.1.1 *that D* intended *to touch another person*
The general concept of intent applies as already discussed. In limiting the mens rea to intent and precluding any reference to recklessness s 3 formalizes Lord Ackner's view in *Court* that limited the mens rea of indecent assault to intent only. As Simester and Sullivan point out, from a practical perspective this does not unduly limit the offence's range of application as typically most sexual assaults are intentional; but an issue may arise in relation to self-induced intoxication. It is conceivable that where D is inebriated and wrongly believes B consented he may lack the necessary mens rea as he is incapable of forming any specific intent and subjective recklessness will not suffice (see A. Simester and G. Sullivan, *Criminal Law: Theory and Doctrine*, Hart, 2003, p 417).

In the context of non-penetrative offences there is another factor to be taken into account: whether it needs to be proved that there was the *intent* to touch a person *sexually*. Does the mens rea require a sexualized intent to touch the genitals as sexual parts of the body? Or simply to touch a part of the body that may not in itself be regarded as sexual but from which D enjoys some form of sexual gratification? Or would it be sufficient to prove that D intended to touch a non-sexual part, such as the face or arm, but in fact touched a sexual part? The section seems to make two requirements in subsections 1(a) and 1(b), that A intentionally touches another person, B, and that the touching is sexual. It does not seem to require any mens rea in relation to the intended touching being sexual. In *George* the removal of a shoe for sexual pleasure where D had a foot fetish was held not to be an indecent assault because there was no obvious sexual intent as any indecent motive was 'secret'. The House of Lords clarified the position regarding secret sexual intent in *Court* where D, who was a shop assistant, pulled a 12 year-old girl across his knees and spanked her on the buttocks over her shorts. When asked why he did it, he admitted he had a buttock fetish raising the question of whether this was sufficient to make it an indecent assault as on its own such desire would not necessarily constitute an indecent intent. The House of Lords identified three criteria in order to determine whether the circumstances of an assault are indecent where this is not obviously apparent from D's actions; these guidelines provided the basis for the s 78 definition of sexual and also have relevance in assessing whether any intention is 'sexual':

(i)   would the reasonable observer think the assault was inherently *decent*?

If an act is inherently decent then it cannot constitute an indecent, i.e., *sexual*, assault, thus combing a person's hair or touching a person's foot would not be inherently sexual so no sexual assault can be committed.

(ii)   are the circumstances surrounding the assault sufficiently unambiguous as to make it clear that the assault was in fact inherently *indecent*?

This classification is encapsulated in the s 78(a) definition of 'sexual' and would apply to those batteries that are inherently sexual and where there can be no doubt or ambiguity as to the sexual nature of the battery and therefore D's intent. Acts that are inherently sexual and would therefore constitute an obvious sexual assault would include groping a woman's sexual parts or man's penis.

(iii)   if the circumstances are not sufficiently unambiguous (as in *Court*) does the position become clear once D's proper intent is known?

D's motive is therefore a key factor and on this basis it was held that D did have an indecent intent when spanking the buttocks because of his secret sexual motive. This reasoning, drawing on contextual factors, has also been adopted in s 78(b) and in relation to proving intent any secret sexual intent must therefore be relevant. Presumably any 'inherently decent' touching cannot now become sexual unless a sexual motive can be shown such as in the case of a shoe fetishist who intends sexual gratification.

In most circumstances the sexual nature of the touching will be self-evident or the contemporaneous existence of any 'secret sexual motive' is likely to resolve any ambiguity as in the third classification. But the fact that there is no requirement to prove any *sexual* intent to touch obfuscates the position. It would appear that on the face of it a case could be made out that only an intent to touch the body, as opposed to an intent to *sexually* touch the body, is required. Perhaps an intent to caress the hair that spontaneously prompts the touching of a breast? Alternatively it could be argued that the touching intended: hair, must be 'sexual' and that it is not enough that there is an associated incidental, unintended touching which is in fact sexual. Clarification may be found in *R v Naveed Tabassum* [2000] 2 Cr App R 328. The

44

appellant appealed against his conviction for indecent assault on the grounds that no sexual motive could be proved. He had asked several women to take part in a breast cancer survey in order to create a database and they had consented in the mistaken belief that he was medically qualified. In order to undertake the agreed breast self-examination they removed their clothes in his presence and allowed him to feel their breasts. There was no evidence of any sexual motive but the Court of Appeal held that as the touching was prima facie indecent there was no requirement to prove any sexual motive. Interpreting s 3 in this light means that provided the touching is sexual it is not necessary to prove any sexual intent, only an intent to touch, therefore it is presumed that a sexual assault could now be committed in these same circumstances.

3.4.1.2 *that D in fact* touched *another person and the touching is sexual*

The actus reus appears to require that D physically touch his victim, and that the touching is sexual. Notwithstanding any complications about proving the sexual nature of any touching there is another potential difficulty here. The offence is termed a sexual *assault*, which like indecent assault beforehand, presupposes that it would encompass all forms of assault and battery as agreed by their Lordships in *Court* i.e., both physical and psychic indecent assaults. An indecent physical assault includes a battery or touching, whether the victim is aware of it and the surrounding circumstances or not. This is not a problem as all batteries necessitate an unlawful touching (*DPP v Taylor, DPP v Little* [1992] 1 All ER 299). An indecent psychic assault occurs where the victim apprehends or fears an immediate and unlawful indecent touching being perpetrated against him through words or gestures: it does not involve touching (*R v Ireland* [1997] 3 WLR 534). Section 3(1) specifically requires that the defendant actually *touched* the other person thereby limiting it to a battery. Any commonsense interpretation of touch must mean some form of physical contact however minor, so that a glancing touch would suffice. But it would appear that where there is no actual physical contact between D and the other person the offence is not made out. This would seem to be a retrograde step from the position in *R v Sargeant* [1997] Crim LR 50 where D forced a 16 year-old boy to masturbate into a condom after threatening him with a stick. There was no battery as such but the Court of Appeal held that the wielding of the stick constituted an indecent assault because the circumstances were indecent and a threat sufficient. It was not necessary to establish a battery. The court confirmed that if a man, without touching his victim, required her to remove her clothes at knife-point for the purpose of his own sexual gratification there could be no doubt that this was an indecent assault.

It would appear that these non-contact sexual assaults are intended to be caught by the new s 4 offence of causing another to engage in sexual activity without their consent but whereas *activity* needs further judicial interpretation to clarify its meaning, the meaning of *assault* has already been clarified as encompassing both assaults and battery. A verbal threat, providing there is an immediacy of violence, can constitute an assault but not a sexual assault, nor would it constitute sexual activity. A person who points a gun at someone and orders them to undress, or threatens to attack a child to make the mother undress, would have committed an indecent assault but does not commit a sexual assault. In respect of a conviction for s 4 it is the victim who has to be caused to engage in the sexual activity so only if the woman does undress could it now fall under causing or inciting sexual activity without consent. Other possible offences that might be considered include committing an offence with intent to commit a sexual offence (see ch 9) or possibly an attempted sexual assault. Finally some forms of sexual behaviour or 'activity' still fall outside the scope of the Act despite its comprehensive reach as illustrated in *R v Tinley* [2003] EWCA Crim 3032. The appellant suffered from a psychological condition known as 'paraphilia' where an individual derives sexual pleasure from visual sources. He suffered a particularly chronic form that involved him attempting to look up women's skirts in public places causing distress. As no threat was actually articulated it was not an indecent assault and no other suitable provision existed under the SOA 1956 so he was convicted of outraging public decency. Equally such conduct would not constitute a sexual assault nor it would seem any other statutory sexual offence.

3.4.1.3 *that the touching is* sexual

The requirement that the touching is sexual mirrors the offence of assault by penetration where it must be shown that any penetration is sexual. However, whereas the requirement that penetration be sexual is relatively easy to establish because it is restricted to penetration of the vagina or anus, the nature of what may or may not amount to sexual touching is less assured. Any doubt as to the sexual nature of the touching should be resolved by applying the objective test provided in s 78 i.e., whether a reasonable person would consider that whatever the purpose or circumstances the nature of the touching is sexual; or secondly, because of its nature the touching may be sexual and is in fact so because of its circumstances or the purpose of any person in relation to it. The Explanatory Notes cast doubt on whether 'obscure fetishes' such as in *George* might constitute sexual touching. In seeking to address the first stage, under s 78(a), the jury must consider whether a reasonable person would regard the nature of the activity as sexual, irrespective of purpose or circumstances. Touching a person's foot would not satisfy the requirement that 'because of its nature it is sexual'. However, applying the second stage s 78(b) a reasonable person may consider the nature of such touching to be sexual and may be satisfied that it is sexual once the defendant's purpose and circumstances are known. The wording of the section, however, presents the possibility of challenge. The phrasing of 'because of its nature it may be sexual' allows some room for manoeuvre as this needs to be established first before any contextual explanation as to purpose or circumstances is taken into account. Would a reasonable person think that the nature of combing a person's hair might be sexual? Knowing the secret motive of the comber could put an altogether different complexion on the touching particularly depending on the respective ages of the parties, but if this is conditional upon a positive acknowledgement that the touching may be sexual in the first place, the outcome is less assured. In *Court*, prima facie such inherently decent touching could be construed as indecent once D's purpose became clear; but it is difficult to see how this analogy could apply to parts of the body that are inherently non-sexual such as the foot or hair which may not be perceived by all as a form of sexual touching.

3.4.1.4 *that B does* not in fact consent *to the touching and D* did not reasonably believe *that B consented*

Both these elements apply as discussed above as do the ss 75 and 76 presumptions (ss 3(2) and 3(3)). In *Tabassum* D claimed that the complainants had given true consent as not only did he have experience in the field of breast cancer and two science degrees establishing his credentials (albeit he had never received any medical training) but he did no more than that to which each of them had consented. The Court of Appeal held even if they mistakenly believed that D was medically qualified they may have consented to touching for a medical purpose but not to any indecent behaviour so that there may be consent as to the nature of the act but not to its *quality*. Applying the two conclusive presumptions in s 76 would it now be presumed that the women did not give true consent? According to the Court of Appeal D did not intentionally deceive them as to the nature or purpose of the relevant act (s 76(1)(a)) only as to its quality. Provided this decision is followed such consent is vitiated. As regards the second presumption, the Law Commission suggested that a deception as to identity should include a deception as to any claimed professional qualifications but s 76(1)(b) is limited to where D impersonates a person known personally to the complainant (see J. Temkin, *Rape and the Legal Process*, Oxford University Press, 2002, p 104). Therefore it will not apply in respect of the deception practised by the defendant in *Tabassum*.

Groups representing those who practise sado-masochistic activities (e.g., Spanner Trust) expressed disappointment that the Government had failed to legalize such conduct and it has been suggested that s 3 criminalizes such encounters because of the presumption that violence negates consent. There is virtually no mention of sado-masochistic activities in *Setting the Boundaries* and it is doubtful whether this was the Government's intent, at least in respect of more minor injuries where consent could be implied because of the rebuttable presumption (see ch 2). Where injury is caused the position is less clear as only injuries equivalent to actual bodily harm (ABH), whether intended or caused, are needed to nullify consent. The question is whether this rule still applies to sexual offences or whether it is now impliedly abrogated by the presumptions in s 75(2)(a) and that consent is only vitiated where violence is used against the complainant or the complainant is fearful that immediate violence will be used against them. The claims by the appellants in *R v Brown* [1993] 2 All ER 75 that their 'injuries' resulting from sado-masochistic activities including whipping, caning, branding, the application of stinging nettles to the genital area and insertion of map pins and fish hooks into the penis, caused no permanent injuries, did not require medical treatment, and were no more than transient and trifling, failed to convince the majority in the House of Lords. Lord Jauncey considered that it was good luck rather than good judgment that prevented any serious injury occurring. Although the decision in *Brown* has not yet been overruled in the context of consensual same-sex masochistic activity, this 3:2 majority 10 year-old decision has been criticized as being anachronistic but has been confirmed by the Court of Appeal in *R v Emmet* [1999] Times LR 15 October 1, which effectively applied *Brown* to sado-masochistic practices in heterosexual relationships.

3.5 CAUSING SEXUAL ACTIVITY WITHOUT CONSENT

Previously where a person compelled another against their will to commit a sexual act either upon themselves, e.g., masturbation, or with the compeller, such as a woman demanding a man has sex with her, or with a third person, it was not clear with what offence, if any, they could be charged. Persons in positions of authority could thereby abuse their power over others and individuals forced to engage in such sexual violations might not only lose control of their personal sexual autonomy but possibly commit a sexual offence as well. The culpability of a woman in such forced acts was particularly vague, as she was unable to physically commit the actus reus of rape she could not be charged as principal. If a woman forced a man to have sexual intercourse with her without his consent she could not be charged with rape, only indecent assault. If she encouraged or incited other men to rape another woman then again she could not be charged with rape as a principal offender, only as an accessory by aiding and abetting, but could be punished as a principal. The increasing incidence of gang or group rapes, often at knife-point, involving numbers of complicit onlookers, committed by young persons and female participants (between 1997–2001, 14 women were charged as accessories to rape within the London area, BBC News website, 16 March 2001), further prompted the need for an appropriate provision. In 2001 Justice Pontius described 18 year-old Claire Marsh's role in the fourteen strong attack on a 37 year-old woman by the Regent's Canal in London as 'vicious and utterly merciless' (The Times, 9 May 2001). Though sentenced to 7 years imprisonment her conviction demonstrated the need to send a clear signal that such individuals should be charged as principals, not just secondary parties. Section 4(1) therefore creates a new offence of causing sexual activity without consent where:

A intentionally causes another person B to engage in an activity,

> the activity is sexual,
>
> B does not consent and
>
> A does not reasonably believe that B consents

As with all these four offences reasonable belief in consent is encapsulated in s 4(2) and the presumptions as to consent apply. The maximum sentence is life imprisonment where penetration occurs and in which case it would be classified as a serious arrestable offence; for non-penetration the sentence is 10 years on indictment or 6 months/fine if tried summarily. Section 8 creates an identical provision to protect children under 13 (see ch 4).

3.5.1 Causing sexual activity—elements to be proved

3.5.1.1 *that A* intentionally *causes another person to engage in a sexual activity*
The general concept of intent applies but it is not necessary to prove that A intended the sexual activity to take place, only that he or she intended to cause another, X, to engage in it. It is enough, that as in the case of Claire Marsh, she realized that the consequences of her actions in encouraging her male accomplices would result in the sexual violation of the complainant. Marsh punched her victim in the face and ripped off her top, she then held her down while a 15 year-old boy tore off the victim's trousers and committed rape followed in turn by an 18 year-old who also raped her. When the victim tried to escape after being pushed into the canal, Marsh dragged her naked along the towpath. It does not matter whether she intended that her accomplices rape, penetrate, or sexually assault their victim; only that she intended to cause or enable her associates to engage in such activities.

Section 4 should finally sound the death knell of *DPP v Morgan* both in respect of the husband who encouraged the rape of his wife and of his accomplices who claimed genuine belief. Any ambiguity as to an honest but unreasonable belief that the victim is consenting will no longer be sufficient to discharge culpability.

3.5.1.2 *that A* in fact causes *another to engage in a sexual activity*
The victim has to be caused to engage in the activity by A. Evidence must be adduced demonstrating a direct causal link between A's actions and the subsequent sexual conduct of the others involved, in other words that the outcome would not have occurred 'but for' A's actions. Thus, as in the Marsh case, where A plans, manages, and instigates a group rape or facilitates such by holding down or restraining the victim while others then sexually assault her, the offence is committed. A's acts need not be the sole cause of the ultimate assault but must be more than a minimal contribution; they must be a substantial operating cause: *R v Roberts* (1971) 56 Cr App R 96. Thus where a woman accepted a lift in a van from two men and then found another two men in the back of the van, all four of whom then participated in gang-raping her in a five hour ordeal (BBC News website, 29 August 2002), those who forcibly penetrated her commit rape contrary to s 1, and those who assisted in holding her down to allow the others to violate her would now commit the s 4 offence. The offence is gender-neutral and would apply to the case of a 14 year-old boy grabbed in an alleyway in Gillingham and seriously sexually assaulted by one youth while two others held him down (BBC News website, 22 August 2002).

It is not necessarily enough that A simply encouraged the others to engage in sexual activity, A's actions or omissions must be directly responsible for securing that end result. Some activities might therefore fall short of the line of causation in which case an alternative charge of aiding or abetting might have to be considered (s 8 Accessories and Abettors Act 1861, as amended by the Criminal Law Act 1977). Nor does the section directly address the culpability of bystanders or passive observers as in *R v Clarkson* [1971] 3 All ER 344 where no liability accrued to those who passively watched three soldiers rape their victim. Just because a person fails to act to stop a crime does not make him an accomplice and in not actively encouraging the principals those watching were acquitted of aiding and abetting. In such situations it may be difficult enough to establish any actus reus let alone any intent to assist or encourage the principal offenders, but should such individuals escape all culpability?

3.5.1.3 *the activity is* sexual

According to s 4(4) which lists the activities attracting a maximum sentence of life imprisonment, sexual activity automatically includes the penetration of B's anus or vagina with a person's penis, part of the body or anything else, and also the penetration of B's mouth with a person's penis. Thus in a group rape where some of the group are encouraged by others to rape the victim, anally or vaginally, or perform forced oral sex on him or her, those carrying out the violation would be charged as principals under s 1 and those inciting and compelling such acts under s 4. Sexual activity also includes any activity where B is forced by his protagonists to penetrate another person's anus or vagina with a part of his or her body, or by being forced to use anything else to so penetrate, or to penetrate another person's mouth with his penis. Such forced violations are unlawful irrespective of whether the other person consents or acquiesces. Thus the offence may be committed in a number of different ways. It may be the protagonists themselves who are the recipients of the forced penetration by B and as such receive direct sexual gratification. Where a man and a woman acting in concert threaten B and coerce him to have sexual intercourse with the woman while the man watches, she is a consensual recipient but also instigator so is equally culpable. The offence is also committed where a woman acting on her own forces a man to have sexual intercourse with her either vaginally or anally for her sexual gratification. Similarly where B is forced by his protagonists to put his penis into the mouth of a third person, male or female, who does not consent and from which his protagonists receive indirect sexual gratification, they commit the offence. In all these circumstances B of course will not be culpable as he is acting under duress and without consent. Notwithstanding any possible offences of causing prostitution (see ch 8), Simester and Sullivan suggest a potential limitation when s 4 is considered in conjunction with s 74 whereby consent is defined as an agreement by choice and the person has the freedom and capacity to make that choice. Where D offers an illegal immigrant work in his brothel as a prostitute knowing that she is forced to undertake it because of economic circumstances and therefore she 'agrees' but without full freedom and capacity, does he commit the offence of causing her to engage in sexual activity without consent? If he coerced her using threats or force then any 'consent' would be vitiated (s 75(a)) but it is less likely that a case could be made out for s 4 in such circumstances (see Simester and Sullivan p 421).

3.5.1.4 *that B does* not in fact consent *to the touching and D* did not reasonably
    believe *that B consented*

Both these elements apply as discussed above as do the ss 75 and 76 presumptions (ss 4(2) and 4(3)).

3.5.2 Young persons and teenage group rape

Identical provisions to deal with individuals who cause or incite children to engage in non-consensual sexual activities with other children or with adults appear in the next part of the Act. Where the offence is committed against children under 13, s 8 is the relevant provision, and in respect of children aged 13 but under 16, s 10 will be the appropriate charge; however, whereas the former carries the same sentence of life imprisonment for penetration as s 4, the latter only carries a maximum of 14 years. Also where a s 10 offence is committed by a person aged under 18 years the maximum sentence drops to 5 years by virtue of s 13. Thus taking the example of the 14 year-old girl raped by eight youths aged between 16–19 years in Moss Side, Manchester, in April 2002 (The Mirror, 28 September 2002) the 19 year-old would now face a maximum of life imprisonment, whereas the maximum sentence for those involved aged under 18 would be 5 years. However, the Act does permit the equivalent maximum adult sentence (where a person is aged 21 years or over) to be imposed in exceptional circumstances where the court is of the opinion that normal provisions are not suitable (Sch 6 amends s 91 Powers of Criminal Courts (Sentencing) Act 2000, see ch 4). Similarly in a case in Roehampton where three 15 year-old girls were indecently assaulted by ten 12–18 year-old males the adults would face a much stiffer sentence than their accomplices who might only be a few weeks younger (Bristol Evening Post, 7 August 2002). Of course the under 18 year-olds could be charged with s 4, or if they forcibly penetrated the victim with s 1 rape, but it does leave the possibility open towards what some may view as potentially too lenient an option.

3.6 ALTERNATIVE VERDICTS

There is an amount of overlap not just within the first four sections of the Act but potentially with subsequent sections such as administering a substance with intent to facilitate sexual activity (s 61), committing an offence with intent to commit a sexual offence (s 62), and trespass with intent to commit a sexual offence (s 63). In many cases it will therefore be prudent to charge in the alternative. Section 6(3) Criminal Law Amendment Act 1967 provides that an alternative verdict may be imposed where a guilty plea is entered though given the range of new offences it is likely that the Government did not intend this to be the norm. Thus in some circumstances the court might be prepared to accept a guilty plea to sexual assault as part of a plea-bargain in relation to say assault by penetration, but the acceptance of any such alternative verdicts would need to be justified in order to head off any adverse criticism (see also *Blackstone's Criminal Practice 2004*, para D17.30).

3.7 CONCLUSION

The Review team's term of reference was primarily to evaluate the legal definition of rape, not how it might operate in practice, thus it remains to be seen whether these new provisions will have any real impact in minimizing the incidence of rape and increasing the current low level of conviction rates. Ultimately the success of these reforms may depend less on their effective enforcement and subsequent interpretation by the judiciary; but largely on the willingness of victims to continue to come forward and give evidence in what is still seen by many as a largely unforgiving legal environment.

The Act fails to incorporate the Review's recommendation to include an offence of assault to commit rape or sexual assault by penetration on the basis that the law of attempts requires that for attempted rape the action must be 'more than merely preparatory' i.e., virtually tantamount to forced entry. The Review team concluded that where D is interrupted and dragged off his potential victim by rescuers the effects of such an assault with intent to commit rape could be traumatic and as such the offence should be distinguished from that of ordinary sexual assault. Section 62 creates a new crime of committing an offence with intent to commit a sexual offence and s 63 replaces the Theft Act provision of burglary with intent to rape (s 9(1)(a) Theft Act 1968) with a new offence of trespass with intent to commit a sexual offence. These additions do offer further options but they are more general provisions and not specifically targeted at potential rapists so it remains to be seen whether they are wide enough to cover all the likely scenarios as the Review team were hoping.

4

CHILD SEX OFFENCES

4.1 INTRODUCTION

From the 1980s onwards the phenomenon of child sexual abuse became embedded in the public consciousness. Awareness of its incidence expanded rapidly to the extent that the revelation of many abuses previously not thought possible are now acknowledged. One of the main criticisms levelled at the law was the lack of any specifically defined offence of sexually abusing children. Instances of child sexual abuse were largely regulated through the application of general sexual offences relating to the gender and age of the child rather than focusing on the relationship between offender and victim. The Review noted that this approach seemed to provide comprehensive protection (a somewhat questionable assertion given the number of new offences enacted) but as well as gender and age differentials there was no common rationale as regards defences and some offences were rarely utilized. Complexities in legal definition, the shortcomings of multi-agency responses and evidential difficulties combined with the notoriety of many child sex abusers in failing to admit their crimes or presenting ingenious defences meant that too often they escaped conviction. Such factors featured in a number of high profile scandals involving disputed diagnostic and interrogatory techniques, as yet unfounded allegations of satanic abuse, and persistent abuse of children in residential accommodation. A plethora of official inquiries, revelations of abuse perpetrated by the clergy, by extended family members and as a result of liaisons formed over the Internet, reinforced the need for substantive reform. Notwithstanding the difficulty in collating accurate statistics official police figures suggest that the incidence of child sexual abuse could be as high as 72,000 cases a year. And in respect of gross indecency the number of reports have more than doubled between 1985 and 1995 from 623 to 1,287 but at the same time the conviction rate has declined (see Grubin, *Sex Offending Against Children*, HO 1998).

The Government has responded positively by creating five new categories of offences in addition to the general non-consensual sexual offences in ss 1 to 4 of the Act. The age of consent remains at 16 years and any sexual activity with a child under that age is unlawful. Children under 13 years are deemed incapable of giving any legally significant consent and any act of sexual intercourse with a child under 13 is automatically statutory rape. Children aged 13 to 15 may 'voluntarily agree' to sexual activities but where the other person is aged *18 or over* such factual consent will not vitiate their legal culpability; where the other person is aged *under 18* a lesser offence is committed but the activity is still prima facie unlawful. Thus the intention is that however a child under 16 is sexually abused there will be a specific offence covering the violation. All time limits within which any prosecution must be instigated have been removed. The five categories are:

(i)   Statutory rape and other offences against children under 13 (ss 5–8)

(ii)   Child sex offences (ss 9–15)

(iii) Abuse of position of trust (ss 16–24 see ch 5)

(iv)   Familial child sex offences (ss 25–29 see ch 7)

(v)   Offences against persons with a mental disorder (ss 30–44 see ch 6).

4.2 STATUTORY RAPE AND OTHER OFFENCES AGAINST CHILDREN UNDER 13

The Government took the view that there should be an age below which the 'consent' of a child should not be legally significant, therefore a child under 13 cannot now consent in law to any sexual activity. Liberty expressed concern that this approach was too absolutist and that any distinction between consent in law and consent in fact is inherently problematic; not least because the Criminal Injuries Compensation Authority is precluded from awarding compensation for psychiatric injury where consent is given even though it is not recognized in law, and some young children may be *Gillick* competent as regards sexual behaviour and therefore competent to give factual consent (see *R v CICAP ex parte A* [2001] 2 WLR 1452, *R v CICAP ex parte J E* [2002] EWHC 1050, *Liberty's Second Reading Briefing*, July 2003).

Despite such concerns ss 5 to 8 create four separate offences that may be committed against children under 13 mirroring the non-consensual offences of rape, assault by penetration, sexual assault, and causing sexual activity. Consent is irrelevant in respect of all four. Where penetration occurs i.e., ss 5, 6, and 8, rape, assault by penetration and causing sexual activity respectively, the offence is now a serious arrestable offence for the purposes of PACE. Initially these four offences appeared as paired offences with the main substantive offence e.g., rape, paired with a second identical offence making it directly applicable to children under 13. This produced a rather messy layout and instead the final version collates them into a dedicated section. However, as the terminology used and its interpretation is the same as for the general non-consensual offences these need to be read in conjunction with their sister offences as detailed in Chapter 3.

4.2.1 Rape of a child under 13

Section 5 creates a new statutory rape provision, which in effect replaces the former s 5 SOA 1956 offence of unlawful sexual intercourse (USI) with a girl under 13. The offence is committed where

A intentionally penetrates the vagina, anus or mouth of another person, B, with his penis, and B is under 13.

Any penile penetration of the vagina, anus, or mouth of a child under 13 years is automatically statutory rape irrespective of 'agreement' or 'consent' and carries a maximum sentence of life imprisonment. Because of the requirement of penile penetration the offence is gender-specific and can only be physically performed by male perpetrators aged 10 years or over, the age of criminal capacity (the presumption of sexual capacity was abolished by the SOA 1993). As far as the child victim is concerned it is gender-neutral in that it recognizes, for the first time, the rape of boys under 13 as well as girls. For example, in February 2003 the 13 year-old teenager sentenced to 2 years for the 'wicked and shameful' rape of an 8 year-old boy would now be charged under this section rather than for the substantive s 1 offence of rape (BBC News website, 10 February 2003).

4.2.1.1 *Elements to be proved*
The prosecution must prove that D *intentionally* penetrated the vagina, anus, or mouth of a person under 13, male or female, and that *penetration occurred*. This is not a strict liability offence as intention must be proved but provided penetration by penis has in fact occurred it would be very difficult to argue that this was other than intentional. Penetration is a continuing act from entry to withdrawal (s 79(2)) and only the slightest degree of penetration is sufficient. It is not necessary to prove that the hymen was broken. There is no requirement whatsoever to prove non-consent. As consent is not at issue it may not even be necessary to call the child as a witness where medical evidence can confirm penetration occurred.

The prosecution must also prove that the child is in fact *under 13*. Proof of age would normally be sought by reference to a child's birth certificate together with evidence that identifies the person as the one named on the certificate. If unavailable other documentary evidence may be adduced to assist the court such as entries in foreign registers (see *Blackstone's Criminal Practice 2004*, para F8.15).

There is no recourse to any defence under this section. D cannot claim that he reasonably believed the child to be over 13, the onus is on him to have established beforehand that the child was older if he wishes to avoid culpability under this provision.

4.2.1.2 *No alternative charge*

Where sexual intercourse has taken place with a child under 13, even where s/he is compliant and 'agrees', rape must be charged. There is no alternative option of USI as s 5 SOA 1956 is repealed. The redefinition of USI with a girl under 13 as statutory rape is designed to ensure that offenders are given an appropriate sentence. In *AG's Reference (No 4 of 1991) (David Christopher Noble)* (1992) 13 Cr App R(S) 182 a stepfather was sentenced to 2½ years for USI with his 8 year-old stepdaughter whom he had indecently assaulted since she was 5 years old. The sentence was increased to 4 years acknowledging his guilty plea as a mitigating factor but some may still consider this somewhat lenient. Where the sexual intercourse occurs in the context of familial sexual abuse there is the alternative option of a charge under s 25, sexual activity with a child family member (see ch 7), but the presumption that under 13 year-olds cannot consent means that statutory rape should be the preferred charge and s 25 charged in the alternative. Similarly the maximum sentence under s 25 is 14 years compared to life imprisonment for s 5 implying that there must be good reasons not to charge statutory rape, for example, where the perpetrator is also a child.

The lack of an available alternative charge applies equally to persons aged 10 years or over so where two 12 year-olds engage in sexual intercourse, the boy will commit statutory rape. The girl cannot commit rape but either commits sexual assault with a child under 13 (s 7), or sexual activity with a child under 16 (s 9), both of which carry 14 years imprisonment. By virtue of s 13, child sex offences committed by young persons, the maximum sentence for the latter is reduced to 5 years but no reduction accrues in relation to s 7 (see below). No such leniency applies to the boy who faces a charge under s 5 and maximum life imprisonment. So much for the Act not discriminating according to gender. Further, the 14 year-old boy arrested in Sheffield in 1999 for USI with his 12 year-old girlfriend who became pregnant and whom he said he would look after now commits the same offence as the 23 year-old man in the same news report who also had sexual intercourse with a 12 year-old resulting in her pregnancy (BBC News website, 9 September 1999). The Home Office have advised that where the partners are close in age and both have 'agreed', it may be more appropriate to deal with the matter through child protection procedures by applying the welfare principle than engaging the criminal justice process, especially where aged between 13 and 16 years (see below). Ultimately in cases such as the one involving the 14 year-old boy it will be up to the CPS to exercise their discretion and determine whether any prosecution is in the public interest.

4.2.2 Assault of a child under 13 by penetration

This is essentially the same offence as s 2; it is non-gender-specific so can be committed by males and females, and is intended to reflect the gravity of sexual violation falling short of penile rape. The offence is committed where:

A intentionally penetrates the vagina or anus of another person B with a part of his body or anything else, the penetration is sexual and B is under 13.

Where such penetration or intercourse occurs this should be the preferred charge as the fact of such violation proves the case. As with statutory rape the penalty is life imprisonment.

4.2.2.1 *Elements to be proved*

Intention and penetration must be proved. Penetration may be by a part of the body, e.g., finger; or by an object such as a child's toy, bottle, or vibrator. The penetration must be sexual as defined in s 78 and discussed in Chapter 3: i.e., whether a reasonable person would consider it is because of its nature sexual irrespective of the circumstances or any person's purpose; or that because of its nature it may be sexual, and because of its circumstances or the purpose of any person in relation to it, it is sexual.

A good example of the sort of interference that might now constitute assault by penetration on a young child is *R v Gascoyne* [1996] 2 Cr App R(S) 133, where in the process of changing a 15 month-old baby's nappy D inserted his finger into the child's vagina. Applying the reasonable person test it would be virtually impossible to come to any other conclusion than that the nature of the penetration was sexual (s 78(a)). The purpose and circumstances are irrelevant. D seized an opportunity for sexual gratification which could not possibly be regarded as an accidental or mistaken action ancillary to the changing of a nappy; see also *DPP v H* [1992] COD 266 where D inserted his thumb into a baby's anus.

4.2.3 Sexual assault of a child under 13

One of the problems associated with the former law in relation to indecent assaults committed on children was the requirement that proof of assault necessitated some form of hostile act towards the child. The acquiescence of young children when 'invited' to participate in sexual acts was used by defendants to avoid culpability and was accepted by the courts despite the legislature's clear intent that children under 16 were not deemed capable of giving consent. This was mitigated somewhat with the Indecency with Children Act 1960 but some ambiguity remained. In addition, females who invited young boys to have sexual intercourse with them could not be convicted of USI, only indecent assault necessitating proof of non-consent. As with s 3 in relation to the general non-consensual offences, s 7 replaces the concept of indecent assault with *sexual* assault prohibiting the direct touching of a child's sexual parts, or of other parts of the body where it is can be shown that the purpose of the perpetrator and/or circumstances of the assault are sexual. The offence attracts a maximum penalty of 14 years imprisonment or 6 months/fine and is committed where:

A intentionally touches another person B, the touching is sexual and B is under 13.

4.2.3.1 *Elements to be proved*

As with sexual assault the mens rea element of intent does not appear to require the prosecution to prove that D intended to *sexually* assault the child, only that he intended to actually *touch* her. This will not be a problem where the touching is 'inherently sexual' as discussed in the context of *Court* in relation to s 3 sexual assault, but, as with the combing hair example (see 3.4.1.1) the same issue is raised as to whether any 'secret' sexual intent must be contemporaneously present at the time A touches B. Where A merely intends to touch the child's face there may be no sexual intent but the mens rea aspect would be satisfied if on meeting no resistance he then decided to kiss her full on the lips and put his tongue in her mouth. The only possible contention D might have where there was no initial sexual intention is that he accidentally brushed past, touched, or bumped into the child, but this is hardly likely to explain or justify why he then touched or fondled her in a sexual manner.

Both *sexual* and *touching* are defined. As above any touching is *sexual* where because of its nature a reasonable person would consider that it is sexual irrespective of purpose or circumstances; or that because of its nature it may be sexual and taking into consideration the associated circumstances and/or purpose, it is sexual (s 78). This means that fathers (and mothers) should now feel more at ease when bathing their children as any wholly innocent touching in the process of washing should not be construed as either sexual or an intentional assault. 'Touching' is defined as 'touching with any part of the body, with anything else, through anything and in particular includes touching amounting to penetration' (s 79(8)). Thus directly touching a child's sexual parts with finger, mouth, or penis or with any sexual object such as a vibrator or dildo, or non-sexual object such as a doll or teddy bear, would suffice. In *AG's Reference (134 of 2002)* [2003] EWCA Crim 1211, D claimed that his partner, the mother of a 10 year-old girl, had asked him to rub some antiseptic cream on her daughter. While she was out he entered the daughter's bedroom and told her to lie down so he could rub some cream on her. She said she could do it for herself but he went ahead and rubbed cream between her buttocks and on her vagina. Applying the reasonable person test this would probably constitute sexual touching as although the touching may not be considered sexual, given the circumstances and D's refusal to allow the child to put the cream on herself, a jury might consider that the reasonable person would regard this as sexual (s 78(b)). On another occasion D instructed the girl to remove her clothes and took off his dressing gown. He said he was going to 'put some stuff on her' then masturbated himself and ejaculated onto her vaginal area. Here there is no direct physical contact, albeit the sexual aspect is clearly satisfied irrespective of circumstances or purpose. It is therefore presumed that 'touching by any other thing' will be construed to include such emissions as semen, urine, and saliva. Any other interpretation would deny Parliament's intent. 'Touching through' would cover touching and petting through the child's clothing, underwear, or bed-clothing where no direct physical contact is made with the skin. Teenage (and under 13s) sexual experimentation and exploration involving the usual 'groping' and petting 'behind the bike sheds' would also constitute such touching.

Where non-sexual parts of the body are touched then the actus reus may still be satisfied applying the reasonable person test to the circumstances in which it takes place. An example is *R v Sutton* [1977] Crim LR 569 where a sports coach, in the process of taking a team photograph, touched the arms, legs, and torsos of a group of 11 and 12 year-old boys in order to arrange their poses. He was fully dressed at the time; the boys partially undressed. No indecent assault occurred as the boys had 'consented', there was no direct sexual assault and no hostile intent on the part of the defendant. Applying s 78, a reasonable person might well consider such touching to be sexual taking into consideration the associated circumstances; that the boys were not fully dressed, team photos are taken wearing full kit and the defendant acted for his own purpose and did not intend to distribute the photograph for team promotion.

4.2.4 Causing or inciting a child under 13 to engage in sexual activity

Section 8 provides that D commits an offence

if he intentionally causes or incites another person, B, to engage in a sexual activity where B is under 13.

This offence is intended to cover the same type of situations as envisaged in s 4 but in relation to under 13 year-olds. Consent is irrelevant. The maximum sentence is life imprisonment where the objective is to facilitate either penile or non-penile penetration of the child; penetration of another person with any part of the child's body or by the child with anything else; or penetration of a person's mouth with the child's penis. In all other cases it is 14 years imprisonment or 6 months/fine if tried summarily (ss 8(2), 8(3)).

4.2.4.1 *Elements to be proved*
The offence has two limbs and may be committed either by causing or inciting.

4.2.4.2 *Causing*
In order to prove that D caused another to engage in a sexual activity with a child under 13 there must be some evidence that his involvement was substantive enough to secure that end result. In other words, there must be a direct causal link between D's actions or omission and the consequences, which would not have occurred, *but*

for his intervention or conduct. Causing could therefore include the use of threats, force, intimidation, application of improper pressure or use of authority. Any acquiescence on the part of the child will not break the chain of causation (*R v Tyrell* [1894] 1 QB 710). The Explanatory Notes suggest that this provision is intended to cover situations where A causes a child to strip for his, or another person's, sexual gratification. Cases that would now be caught under this provision include *R v Pratt* [1984] Crim LR 41 where two boys were forced to undress almost completely revealing their private parts. Pratt won his appeal on the grounds that his sole motive was to search for cannabis, which he thought the boys had taken from him, i.e., he had no indecent intent. Similarly an example was cited in the Commons debates of a case in 2002 where an estate agent had managed to convince two young children to undress in front of him. No offence could be found with which to charge him (Hansard 15 July 2003 col 245). These cases were defeated because there was no proof of any direct indecent or sexual intent. Section 8 simply requires proof of *intent to cause* a child to engage in sexual activity. Notwithstanding other possible offences such as s 61, administering a substance with intent, another scenario is *R v Liles* [2003] 1 Cr App R(S) 31 where the defendant allowed two small boys to inhale a solution of isobutyle nitrate causing dizziness and sickness. In this case the offence had no sexual connotation, but if young children are given such solvents as a precursor to sexual activity then the case could be made out. Any question as to whether D's actions *in fact* caused a child to engage in sexual activity is ultimately one for the jury appropriately guided by the judge.

4.2.4.3 *Inciting*
This limb of the offence is committed where the child is incited to penetrate or touch the defendant, himself or another person and updates s 1 Indecency with Children Act 1960 which made it an offence to incite a child under 16 to commit an act of gross indecency. Provided the incitement has taken place it is not necessary to prove that any sexual activity actually occurred. 'Incitement' was construed quite generously under the old s 1 as compared to its more general interpretation. For example, that incitement is only complete when it comes to the attention of the other person, as rarely would a child know or understand that they were actually being incited. It was also possible to attempt to incite an act of gross indecency: *R v Rowley* (1992) 94 Cr App R 95. The offence would apply where D invited a 9 year-old girl to touch his penis while urinating as in the earlier case of *Fairclough v Whipp* [1951] 2 All ER 83 or as in *R v Clayton* [1990] Crim LR 447 where D masturbated in front of his 12 year-old daughter, tried to get her to help him and subjected her to looking at pornographic magazines. The provision is also intended to close a loophole identified by a case in 2002. A 39 year-old sports coach induced two 12 year-old girls to undress, taking off their trousers and pants, by telling them they were being entered into a competition for a £50 prize but that they had to prove they were actually older than 15 years. Taking their clothes off, he said, would prove this (BBC News website, 24 January 2002). No indecent assault had occurred as there was no threat

or battery. Gross indecency could not be charged as there was no conduct directed at or towards the girls. No appropriate public order offence existed and in fact there was no other offence that could be utilized in these circumstances; s 8 however would now apply.

4.3 CHILD SEX OFFENCES

This group of offences, to be found in ss 9 to 15, address inappropriate sexual conduct with a child and generally replace the offences of USI with a girl under 16 (s 6 SOA 1956) and gross indecency with a child under 16 (s 1 Indecency with Children Act 1960 as amended by s 39 CJCSA 2000). The intention is to send a strong message that any adult who sexually abuses a child under 16, or encourages others to do so, commits a serious offence. Consideration was given to an over-arching single offence but the Review recommended that a series of offences clearly defining the conduct deemed unacceptable would be simpler and easier to enforce. A marriage defence was originally included on the basis of respecting international obligations as regards valid marriages in other jurisdictions where the age of consent is lower than in the UK. The defence was intended to apply to all the child sex offences in ss 9 to 12 where the child was aged 13 years but under 16 years. The provision was criticized as, notwithstanding any cultural norms, to condone such sexual intercourse with young teens under the guise of 'lawful' marriage would be contradictory to the Act's stated intent in terms of protection. In light of the growing problem of paedophiles making contact with children over the Internet a new offence of meeting a child following sexual grooming is included. The most controversial of this clutch of offences is s 13, which in effect criminalizes all sexual activity between youngsters under 16 years. Diverse views were submitted about this including a response from The Christian Institute that the age of consent be raised to 18 years to correspond with adulthood.

There is an apparent overlap with both the specific offences that may be committed against a child under 13 discussed above, and with the general non-consensual offences outlined in Chapter 3, i.e., sexual assault (s 3) and sexual assault on a child under 13 (s 7), causing a person to engage in sexual activity (s 4) and causing a child under 13 to engage in sexual activity (s 8). There are three distinctions:

(i) these child sex offences (except where s 13 applies) may only be committed by a person aged 18 or over whereas the offences in ss 7 and 8 may be committed by anyone aged 10 or more;

(ii) unlike ss 3 and 4 there is no requirement to prove non-consent as children under 16 are deemed incapable of giving consent;

(iii) there is a potential defence where D can prove he reasonably believed the child to be over 16.

4.3.1 Table summarizing child sex offences

Common elements	Provision	Specific element	Defence of reasonable belief over 16?	Maximum penalty
A 18 or over commits offence against B under 16	s 9 sexual activity with a child	*intentional sexual touching*	yes	14 years
A does not reasonably believe B is 16 or over	s 10 causing or inciting a child to engage in sexual activity	intentionally *causes* or *incites* B to engage in sexual activity	yes	14 years
	s 11 engaging in sexual activity in presence of child	intentionally *engages* in sexual activity for sexual gratification *in the presence* of child	yes	10 years or 6 months/ fine
	s 12 causing child to watch sexual act	intentionally causes B to *watch, or look* at image of, or third person engaging in, sexual activity	yes	10 years or 6 months/ fine
	s 14 arranging/ facilitating commission of child sex offence	intentionally arranges or facilitates commission of ss 9–13 offence	Defence of lack of intent? Defence of child's protection	14 years or 6 months/ fine
	s 15 meeting a child following sexual grooming	intentionally meets or travels with intention of meeting	yes	7 years or 6 months/ fine
Where offender is under 18	s 13 child sex offences committed by children or young persons	commits any ss 9–12 offence		5 years or 6 months/ fine

4.3.2 Sexual activity with a child

Section 9 sexual activity with a child and its subsequent permutations replace USI with a girl under 16 and committing an act of gross indecency with or towards a child under 16. There is some overlap here with s 3 sexual assault but that requires proof of non-consent, and s 7, sexual assault of a child under 13, to which consent is irrelevant. The substantive elements of s 9 are virtually identical:

A person aged 18 or over, commits an offence if

  he intentionally touches another person, B,

  the touching is sexual, and either

B is under 16 and A does not reasonably believe that B is 16 or over, or

B is under 13.

Where penile penetration or non-penile penetration occur the offence is indictable only and the penalty is 14 years imprisonment; in all other cases the maximum sentence is still 14 years but the offence may be tried summarily in which case the penalty is 6 months/fine.

4.3.2.1 *Elements to be proved*

The mens rea aspect is the same as for s 7 above in that an intention to touch must be proved. 'Sexual' and 'touching' have the same meaning and would now cover, for example, the case of 33 year-old mother Tracey Whalin who had an affair with a 13 year-old school boy where both ran away to Florida. On her return she was convicted of gross indecency and child abduction but could now be convicted of sexual activity with a child under 16 (The Independent, 5 December 1997). Similarly Joanna James, also 33 years, convicted of two offences of indecent assault for having sex with a 13 year-old boy and sentenced to 12 months imprisonment (BBC News website, 24 November 2003). The section is subtitled 'sexual activity with a child' implying a broader ambit than sexual assault and comparable to an act of gross indecency as in the former provision; but the wording in s 9 *specifically limits* the actus reus to sexual touching thus narrowing its remit. The Home Office state that this is not an oversight as other forms of sexual activity that fall short of touching will be caught by ss 10 to 12. But given that the objective of these offences is to 'catch-all' and plug any potential and unforeseen loopholes it is surprising that the provision does not extend to sexual activity as well as sexual assault. The illustration cited above where D masturbated over a child and emitted semen without any direct physical contact of skin on skin more easily satisfies the concept of sexual activity than a rather strained interpretation of touching. Similarly in *R v Speck* [1977] Crim LR 689, an 8 year-old girl approached D and placed her hand on his trousers touching his penis, D made no attempt to remove her hand and left it there for five minutes resulting in his erection. The Court of Appeal held that D's inactivity was sufficient to justify an offence of gross indecency but the wording of s 9 specifically requires that D actually *touches* the child.

4.3.2.2 *Defence of reasonable belief v aged 16 or over*

It must be proved that B was in fact under 16, proof of age would normally be confirmed by birth certificate or other testamentary evidence. A defence of reasonable belief that B was over 16 years is available where the child is aged 13 to 15 years. This is partly to mitigate the withdrawal of the 'young man's' defence to USI with a girl under 16; where D was under 24 years and had not been charged with a like offence (s 6(3) SOA 1956) and see *R v Kirk Russell* [2002] EWCA Crim 1580) and partly to address the confusion caused by the judiciary in declaring an implied mens rea requirement as to age into statutory provisions previously thought to be strict liability offences. In *B v DPP* [2000] 2 WLR 452 in relation to gross indecency with a child under 14 (s 1 Indecency with Children Act 1960, later amended to 16 years, s 39 CJCSA 2000) the House of Lords imported an obligation upon the prosecution to prove that D either knew the child was under 14 or gave no thought to the issue, despite the fact that the section was silent as to such stipulation. If D, as in *B v DPP* itself, proves he genuinely believed the child to be over 16 then the mens rea is negated. The court's justification was that unless Parliament clearly expresses otherwise, an appropriate mental element is to be imported as a necessary ingredient for all statutory offences, even ones of strict liability. Their Lordships followed this reasoning in *R v K* [2001] UKHL 41 confirming that mens rea must be imported into s 14 SOA 1956, indecent assault, requiring the prosecution to prove absence of honest belief. A schoolgirl, aged 14, told D that she was over 16 and he had no reason to disbelieve her. But as the Court of Appeal had indicated to Parliament (*R v K* (2000) Times LR 7 November), where the question is a mistake of fact the belief need only be genuine, it need not be reasonable. Thus the combined effect of these decisions was that, except for USI with a girl under 16, the age-based offences formulated in the SOA 1956, and those that failed to stipulate any mens rea fault requirements, were no longer sustainable as wholly strict liability offences, albeit their whole purpose was to protect children under 16. The apparent restriction of the young man's defence was challenged in *Kirk Russell* on the grounds it was incompatible with Articles 6 and 14 of the ECHR as it discriminated on age and gender, but the Court of Appeal responded that it was neither discriminatory nor disproportionate as a woman charged with aiding and abetting USI could claim the same defence.

4.3.2.2.1 *How the defence operates*   Parliament responded by expressly requiring the prosecution to prove that D, at the time of the incident, did not reasonably believe B to be over 16. Therefore where B falsely tells D that she is 16 the prosecution would need to proffer evidence countering D's claim of genuine belief and showing that such belief was unreasonably held. They would need to establish that D in fact knew, or should have reasonably known, that she was under 16, for example, that he knew she still attended school or associated with other under 16 year-olds, or that he made no attempt to discover her true age to resolve any doubt. This could then be rebutted if D can prove on a balance of probabilities that he reasonably believed B was in fact 16 or over. The requirement that such belief be reasonable avoids any potential difficulties associated with a genuinely, but unreasonably, held belief. Ashfaq Altaf, a 33 year-old solicitor, was charged with USI and indecently assaulting a 14 year-old girl whom he met through an Internet chatroom. She told him she was 19, he insisted that when they actually met he still believed her to be an adult as there was nothing about her demeanour that indicated she was only 14. Thus unless the prosecution can show that there was something in their conversations implying the contrary Altaf would now be able to claim that he reasonably believed her to be over 16 (BBC News website, 7 October 2003).

Where there is evidence that D has had previous relationships with under 16 year-olds more might be reasonably expected of him to discharge this burden. The irony is that, as with the former young man's defence, teenagers a year or two older than B who perhaps met her at school might find it harder to rebut a charge as they are more likely to know B's true age, or would be reasonably expected so to know, than adults who are considerably older.

4.3.3 Causing or inciting a child to engage in sexual activity

Section 10 extends the provisions in s 9 to cover anyone who

intentionally causes or incites another person, B, to engage in a sexual activity, B is under 16 and A does not reasonably believe that B is 16 or over, or, B is under 13.

Sexual activity has the same meaning as s 9. The sentencing threshold is identical in that penile penetration or non-penile penetration are indictable only and punishable with 14 years imprisonment whereas all other cases carry the same maximum sentence but may be tried summarily and attract 6 months/fine.

4.3.3.1 *Causing*

As with s 8 this provision covers the use of threats or force to cause a child under 16 years to engage in any form of sexual activity such as in *R v Sargeant* [1997] Crim LR 50 where D used threats to force a teenage boy to masturbate into a condom in front of him. The case of *DPP v K and C* [1997] Crim LR 121 would now be caught by s 10. A 14 year-old girl was threatened and falsely imprisoned by two other girls aged 11 and 14 who forced her to have sexual intercourse with a boy who was also under 14. The boy was never apprehended and so the magistrates dismissed the case on the grounds that the presumption of incapacity could not be rebutted. The Divisional Court ordered a retrial stating that the girls possessed the necessary mens rea for procuring the rape. Section 10 would now apply but being aged under 16 years a lesser penalty would be imposed by virtue of s 13.

4.3.3.2 *Inciting*

In the case of *R v Mason* [1968] 53 Cr App R 12 a 39 year-old woman encouraged a number of 14 and 15 year-old boys to engage in sexual intercourse with her. There being no offence of USI with a boy and no evidence of hostile intent she escaped liability. Now she could be convicted of inciting the boys to have sexual intercourse with her. Similarly if the situation involving the two 12 year-old girls induced to undress was practised against two 14 year-olds it would be caught by this clause. In *B v DPP* a 15 year-old boy was charged with inciting a 13 year-old girl to commit an act of gross indecency by asking her to give him a 'shiner', meaning to perform oral sex. Such an invitation would clearly constitute inciting.

4.3.4 Engaging in sexual activity in the presence of a child

This provision is intended to protect children from seeing and watching inappropriate sexual behaviour practised by adults, or involving other children directed by adults, who derive sexual gratification from such practices. Section 11 creates an offence where

A intentionally engages in a sexual activity for the purpose of obtaining sexual gratification, he engages in it

(i) when another person B is present or is in a place from which A can be observed, and

(ii) knowing or believing that B is aware or intending that B should be aware, that he is engaging in it, and either

B is under 16 and A does not reasonably believe that B is 16 or over, or

B is under 13.

Maximum imprisonment on indictment is 10 years or if tried summarily 6 months/fine.

4.3.4.1 *Elements to be proved*

As with all child sex offences intent must be proved implying that those involved in the sexual activity must deliberately intend the child to see what they are doing or at least suspect or believe that the child may be able to observe them from another room or location. Thus if a child unexpectedly enters their parent's bedroom in the middle of coition or other sexual play intent is not present. If, however, the adults once aware of the child's presence carry on regardless and do nothing to prevent the child watching their activities then intent may be shown either on the basis that they *know* the child is still physically there, or if they ignore their possible presence a jury might be convinced that they *believed* the child was aware. The stereotypical scenario is the paedophile who gains sexual pleasure knowing there is a young child in the room watching him masturbate or fornicate with another adult or child. Liability may also arise where children residing in premises used as brothels or where prostitution is rife are not screened or protected. Thus there is an implied expectation that adult individuals engaging in sexual activity must do so in private so they cannot be observed by any under 16 year-olds. Observation in this context means to directly observe (s 79(7)).

One potential difficulty is the circumstances of *R v Francis* (1989) 88 Cr App R 127 where D masturbated in front of 13 year-old boys in a swimming pool changing-room. Under the old law (s 1 Indecency with Children Act 1960) the issue was whether his conduct was directed at or towards the children. The Court of Appeal held he would be guilty if he knew that the children were watching him and gained sexual satisfaction from that but not if he believed they were not watching him. Here there would be no problem proving that he intentionally engaged in a sexual activity, i.e., masturbation; or even that it was for the purpose of sexual gratification but it must also be proved that he knew or believed that he was being observed or intended that he would be. Thus the prosecution must be able to refute any claims that D genuinely believed the children were not watching him, and did not intend that they would, however unreasonable that honest or genuine belief might be.

4.3.5 Causing a child to watch a sexual act

Section 12 provides that A commits an offence where

for the purpose of obtaining sexual gratification,

he intentionally causes B to watch a third person engaging in a sexual activity, or to look at an image of any person engaging in a sexual activity, and either

B is under 16 and A does not reasonably believe that B is 16 or over, or

B is under 13.

The penalty is 10 years imprisonment on indictment or 6 months imprisonment/fine if tried summarily. There is some overlap here with s 11 but the element of causation is the distinguishing factor requiring that D uses force, threats, or inappropriate pressure to make B watch a sexual activity or visual image. Also that the activity does not involve D, but a third person. The offence is aimed at those who force children to watch pornographic films or their equivalent in other visual mediums. 'Image' includes a moving or still image produced by any means such as film, photograph, and pseudo-photographs, and also 3-dimensional images such as computer generated graphics and visuals (s 79(4)). Critics have suggested that if this section is read in conjunction with s 13, 'under the bedclothes' experiences where young teens agree to look at pornographic images together may make them both liable for up to 5 years imprisonment. While technically such conclusions might be drawn they are reliant on a presumed broad interpretation by the courts of 'cause', which would be counter to Parliament's intent.

4.3.6 Child sex offences committed by children or young persons

This provision in s 13 has provoked considerable criticism in that it is unnecessary and over-criminalizes sexual activity between young teens turning them into criminals. In seeking to ensure that all potential paedophiliac activity is caught it appears that the Government initially accepted this as an inevitable side-effect. An offence is committed where:

A person under 18 does anything which would be an offence under any of ss 9 to 12 if he were aged 18.

The offence is punishable with a maximum term of 5 years imprisonment or 6 months if tried summarily.

The purpose of this offence is twofold: to ensure that where young teenagers exploit or abuse others, such as in *DPP v K and C*, there is an appropriate provision to deal with such behaviour, and secondly to permit a lower penalty in recognition that the offender is under 18. Concern was expressed in the Commons that even teenage kissing would be criminalized as a result, the so-called 'champagne challenge' (termed by Paul Hoggins MP whereby a bottle of champagne was offered to anyone who could resolve the conundrum). The House was assured that no such prosecutions had ever been instigated nor would be in the future (Hansard 15 July 2003 col 248). As with statutory rape the decision to prosecute falls solely within the discretion of the CPS. The *Code for Crown Prosecutors* specifically refers to the youth of the offender as a factor against the public interest (ss 6.5 and 6.9). Clearly there is a difference between sexual experimentation among prepubescent teenagers and young males with a history of sexually abusive behaviour, but reliance on agency discretion has not appeased all critics. Professor John Spencer acknowledges that there has been no oppressive prosecution of young teens but asserts that 'Banning swathes of human behaviour that is blameless or harmless, and leaving it to the authorities to decide which acts to prosecute . . . is flatly contrary to the rule of the law.' (The Times, 7 October 2003). Liberty suggest that either the *Code for Crown Prosecutors* should give clearer guidance, or that the consent of the DPP should be required, or that a separate offence should be created to cover situations where there is factual but not legal consent. At the very least Liberty argue, in cases of teen offenders, consent should be a heavily mitigating factor (see Liberty March 2001; Liberty July 2003). Home Secretary, David Blunkett, forced to respond to these concerns has publicly stated that 'there will be no prosecutions for sexual activity between children under the age of 16 where the activity is genuinely consensual, but the criminal law must cover under-age sexual activity in order to protect those who are victims of abuse' and has advised that new guidance to the CPS will be published to this effect (Sexual Offences Bill Receives Royal Assent, Home Office Press Release, 24 November 2003).

In practical terms it is unlikely that any more criminal prosecutions will result than those for USI, which have dropped significantly from 2,552 in 1988 to 1,133 in 1998 but the point is well made (*Setting the Boundaries*, para 3.2.9). Though given the advice that many teen magazines offer regarding sexual behaviour, there is an element of hypocrisy. Section 13 does remove the discriminatory aspects of USI criminalizing for the first time lesbian sexual activity between under 16s as well as homosexual acts by young males. The section also appears to override the long-established principle that where the purpose of a statutory provision is to protect a certain class of person, i.e., girls under 16 in the case of the former offences of USI or incest; such willing 'victims' who assisted in, or encouraged, the commission of those offences could not be charged as a secondary party. Thus formerly a girl under 16 could not be convicted for aiding, abetting, counselling, or procuring a man to have sexual intercourse with her (*R v Tyrrell* [1894] 1 QB 710; *R v Whitehouse* [1977] QB 868), nor could she be charged as principal. Now where a 16 year-old boy engages in sexual activity with a 14 year-old girl who 'consents' both are equally culpable and commit an offence under s 9.

However, if the primary objective of s 13 is to minimize the penalty for young offenders why not provide an alternative sentence of 5 years for s 9 sexual activity? Mixed messages are evident as Sch 6 now enables s 91 Powers of Criminal Courts (Sentencing) Act 2000, the power to detain offenders under 18 convicted of certain serious offences for specified periods, to be applied to this section. This provides that if the court is of the opinion that none of the other methods in which the case may legally be dealt with is suitable it may sentence the offender to be detained for such period, not exceeding the maximum term of imprisonment with which the offence is punishable in the case of a person aged 21 or over, as may be specified in the sentence. In other words this seems to imply that the adult tariff assigned to ss 9 to 12 could be imposed instead of the 5 year maximum if good cause could be shown; perhaps, for example, where a 17 year-old forces teenage girls or boys to watch sexual acts under threat of violence and is found to have a number of previous convictions for sexual assault.

4.3.7 Arranging or facilitating commission of child sex offence

The final offence in this series relating to sexual activity with children under 16 covers situations where a person intentionally arranges or facilitates any action which involves the commission of any offence under ss 9 to 13, or would do so but for the existence of any facts which would make such commission impossible. This offence, under section 14, is punishable with 14 years imprisonment or 6 months/fine if tried summarily and is committed where:

A intentionally arranges or facilitates something that he intends to do, intends another person to do, or believes that another person will do, in any part of the world, and doing it will involve the commission of an offence under ss 9–13.

Section 14 is potentially far-reaching as it extends to the intentional arranging or facilitating of something either D himself intends to do, or intends another to undertake anywhere in the world. D must either intentionally embark upon a course of action which he knows or intends will involve the commission of an offence under ss 9 to 13 above; or he must intend or believe that another person will engage in such action as a result of his organizational abilities.

4.3.7.1 *Arranging commission of child sex offence*

According to the Explanatory Notes this limb is intended to apply to scenarios where D approaches an agency requesting they procure a child for sex either for himself or another. It is targeted at those who seek out underground child sex agencies or who pay subscriptions to Internet procurers to provide children such as those investigated under Operation Ore where the FBI provided NCIS (National Criminal Intelligence Service) with a list of over 7,000 men suspected of using their credit cards to access websites containing child pornography. A number of these individuals are also believed to have been actively abusing children. The information only came to light when Texas computer consultant Thomas Reedy was jailed in August 2001 for 1,335 years for running an Internet child porn ring. The section's apparent remit might appear to be quite narrow (and criticism has been made in this regard) in that it focuses on those who contact or enter into agreements with a third party agency; but in terms of those individuals worldwide who might seek to make or offer such arrangements to procure children it is an important provision.

4.3.7.2 *Facilitating commission of child sex offence*

The second limb of s 14 is aimed at situations where D, through his actions, facilitates the commission of a sexual offence and this too potentially covers a wider range of possibilities; for example, a friend who allows his bedroom to be used by another person for illicit sex with a child under 16 intending or believing that this will occur, knowingly driving a person to the premises where an illicit encounter has already been arranged, or purchasing a camera or audio/visual equipment intending or believing it will be used by another to film sexually abusive activities involving children, or selling or supplying condoms or other sex aids knowing or believing that they will be used by the purchaser or another adult to engage in sexual activities with children.

4.3.7.3 *Defences*

An exception lies where a person is acting in order to protect the child such as an undercover police officer, healthcare worker or other concerned adult. Rarely would such individuals be charged but in exceptional circumstances D may rebut the mens rea requirement of intent if he can prove, on a balance of probabilities, that whatever arrangements were made he was acting in the best interests of the child by doing or facilitating something which would protect rather than harm her (s 14(2)). Section 14(3) defines four circumstances where a person would be regarded as acting to protect the child provided they act solely in the child's interests and, self-evidently, not for any sexually gratuitive purpose or to cause or encourage the child to participate in any type of sexual activity. Professionals and laypersons alike may claim the defence and there is also an apparent overlap with the general defence to child sex offences provided by s 73 (see 4.5) in relation to any ancillary offences of aiding and abetting. The specific circumstances covered in s 14 are:

(i) protecting the child from sexually transmitted infection

(ii) preventing the child from becoming pregnant

Thus where a healthcare worker, or organization such as Brooks Advisory Service, proffers advice about sexual health or supplies contraceptives to prevent disease or pregnancy no offence is committed by the professional or, say, the 14 year-old girl seeking contraception. From the Explanatory Notes it seems implicit that such professionals would be expected to warn the child that she and her partner will commit an offence if they go ahead and engage in any (protected) sexual intercourse. As The Christian Institute commented, the fact that such an exemption is included virtually implies that people engaged in such work might actually be committing criminal offences and questioned whether this is a message that Parliament intended. Criminalizing teen sex will not stop it but arguably stigmatizing those who promote and encourage sexual responsibility seems somewhat heavy-handed, especially given the measures now available to prevent individuals predisposed to abusing children from working in such environments.

(iii) protecting the physical safety of the child

In certain exceptional circumstances such as 'police stings' and undercover activity, the operation might require an accompanied child to identify a paedophile's address or location of sexual activity. Social workers too might need to undertake clandestine arrangements in order to protect or rescue a child. Such agencies would only wish to resort to such measures in extreme and urgent situations and as it is part of their professional duty this does raise a question about the need to flag it up as an exemption.

(iv) promoting the child's emotional well-being by the giving of advice

This exception would cover those professionals and others counselling teens on their sexual habits such as in association with sex education in schools and Government initiatives to promote and develop sexual awareness and responsibility.

4.3.8 Meeting a child following sexual grooming

The case of Michael Wheeler in October 2003 highlights the problem of paedophiles who 'groom' children through Internet chatrooms with the intention of gaining their trust prior to trying to meet them, and often deceiving the children into believing they are conversing with someone of a similar age and interest. Wheeler admitted having sex with two girls he had met through Internet chatrooms, he had lied about his age (he was 34 or 35 years old) and deliberately waited until they were 13 to avoid the higher sentence (maximum of life imprisonment) that could be imposed if convicted of USI with a girl under 13. He was convicted of five offences of USI with a girl under 16 (maximum 2 years imprisonment) and six of indecent assault (maximum 10 years) and sentenced by the Crown Court to an extended sentence of 5 years; 3 years imprisonment comprising two periods of 18 months in respect of each of the two girls, and a further 2 years under licence. Each 18 month period consisted of 15 months for USI and 3 months for the indecent assaults. The Attorney General appealed on the grounds that this was too lenient. The Court of Appeal made it clear that where an older man made contact with young girls through Internet chatrooms leading to the commission of sexual offences he should expect a sentence at the higher end of the scale. Equally that the sentence for indecent assault is not restricted to the maximum for USI where both are charged (see *R v Figg* (2003) EWCA Crim 2751. The proper sentence should be 18 months for the offences of USI and 12 months for the indecent assaults making a total of 5½ years imprisonment and an extension of the licence to 2½ years; the period of imprisonment was discounted to 4½ years to reflect the fact that Wheeler had had to go through the sentencing process twice making the final sentence 7 years: *AG's Reference (No 39 of 2003) R v Wheeler* [2003] EWCA Crim 3068. Section 15 now provides a new offence to deal with such practices and more straightforward sentencing provisions where:

A, having met or communicated with B on at least two earlier occasions, intentionally meets B, or

travels with the intention of meeting B in any part of the world, and,

at the time, he intends to do anything to or in respect of B, during or after the meeting and in any part of the world, which if done will involve the commission by A of a relevant offence, and

B is under 16, and

A does not reasonably believe that B is 16 or over.

The penalty on conviction is 10 years imprisonment on indictment or 6 months/fine. A relevant offence means any sexual offence in Part One of the Act so would include rape and non-consensual offences as well as child sex offences, sexual activity with persons suffering from a mental disorder and familial child sex offences (s 15(2)(b)). Offences committed outside England, Wales, and Northern Ireland that would be an offence if committed here are also included. This is largely a preventative offence and will require a high standard of proof. Wheeler, by arranging to meet the two girls would have committed this offence once he actually met them, or if the police could catch him en route, as he was making his way to the appointed time and place. Similarly, Douglas Lindsell, 64 years, described as Britain's most dangerous Internet 'groomer' and sentenced to 5 years in October 2003 would now be caught by this provision (The Times, 10 October 2003). Lindsell used a photograph of his teenage son to access Internet chatrooms and made contact with scores of young girls around the world. He sent sexually explicit emails including full frontal photographs of himself and telephoned some girls fraudulently claiming his voice did not sound like a normal teenager because of the drugs he was taking for cancer. This too was a lie. He most definitely 'communicated with other persons on at least two occasions by any means from, to or in any part of the world' (s 15(2)(a)). The requirement of two occasions is to demonstrate a persistent and continued course of conduct. Lindsell then tried to abduct at least two 13 and 14 year-old girls but both ran away when they realized how old he was. In orchestrating a meeting with them and physically attending he would now commit this new offence of grooming.

It is probable that the prosecution will need to show that the preliminary conversations contained some sexual content in order to prove D's intent and purpose in respect of meeting the child and what he intends to do. Such sexual content may be explicit or implicit using double entendres and other such ambiguous language. The Explanatory Notes suggest that this may not always be necessary citing an example where A gives B swimming lessons or meets her incidentally through a friend and then travels to a pre-arranged meeting with the intent to commit a relevant offence. Here it would be necessary to prove that D travelled to the meeting with items for the purpose of committing a sexual offence such as condoms, lubricants, or other sex aids. The planned offence does not need to take place but the travel to the meeting itself must at least partly take place in England, Wales, or Northern Ireland. The Metropolitan Police caution that they would never allow a child to physically meet an adult believed to be a danger to them and cited evidence where one individual sexually abused three children within 15 minutes of meeting them (Metropolitan Police Service, Response to Sexual Offences Bill). Liberty have criticized this provision arguing that it criminalizes an act which is not in itself criminal; i.e., the concept of a 'thought crime' but cases such as Wheeler clearly demonstrate the need for such an offence.

4.4 OFFENCES OUTSIDE THE UNITED KINGDOM

Section 72 replaces s 7 Sex Offenders Act 1997 and deals with sexual offences committed outside the UK by British citizens or residents, and is intended to discourage paedophiles who travel abroad to commit offences against children. The section does not change the law but updates it to include the new offences contained in the SOA 2003. The section provides that any act done outside the UK, which is an offence in that country and is also an offence in the UK constitutes an offence in the UK. The acts to which this section applies are listed in Sch 2. These include any of the offences in ss 5 to 15 and also the offences of rape or causing a person to engage in sexual activity, where the victim was under 16 years at the time of the offence. A wide range of other offences are also listed in the schedule, including abuse of a position of trust, offences against persons with a mental disorder, prostitution offences and administering a substance with intent. In all cases, the victim must have been under 16 years at the time of the offence for s 72 to apply. Offences relating to child pornography under s 1 PCA 1978 and s 160 CJA 1988 are also included but again the child must be under the age of 16 for s 72 to apply. The objective of this section, and of its predecessor is admirable but in practice the problems of obtaining evidence of actions carried out abroad mean that it is unlikely that there will be any more convictions under s 72 than there were under the old law.

4.5 EXCEPTIONS TO AIDING AND ABETTING

All of the offences in this Chapter are subject to s 8 Aidors and Abettors Act 1861 in that anyone who aids, abet, counsels, or procures their commission can be convicted as an accessory. However, where a professional or layperson offers justifiable advice about sexual relations and intercourse that is in the interests and best welfare of the child they will not be acting illicitly. This exception, to be found in the 'supplementary and general' section of the Act in s 73, adopts identical criteria to that specifically provided in s 14(2) and (3) relating to the offence of arranging and facilitating a child sex offence. It applies to offences committed against a child under 13 i.e., statutory rape, penetration by assault, and sexual assault of children under 13 (ss 5–7); sexual activity with a child under 16 (s 9) and where s 9 is committed by a person under 18 by virtue of s 13; abuse of position of trust (s 16), sexual activity with a child family member (s 25) and sexual activity with a child under 16 suffering a mental disorder (ss 30, 34, 38). The four circumstances where the exception applies are the same as already discussed in relation to s 14:

(i)   protecting the child from sexually transmitted infection

(ii)   protecting the physical safety of the child

(iii) preventing the child from becoming pregnant

(iv) promoting the child's emotional well-being by the giving of advice.

There must be no suspicion of any desire or purpose to obtain sexual gratification or any suggestion of encouraging or causing the child to participate or engage in any sexual activity. The provision addresses any concerns about *Gillick* competency for example where a child under 16 seeks advice on sexual matters and though under age is sufficiently informed to do so, and protects medical, healthcare, educational, and sexual welfare professionals as well as those acting in a voluntary capacity. Apart from the fact that this section extends the exclusion to a number of other offences in the Act it also acknowledges that not just under 16s, but under 13s, will engage in sexual activities and experimentation and at least tries to ensure that wherever possible this should occur in a safe, protected, and informed way.

4.6 SENTENCING TRENDS

Recently, as with rape, there have been clear signs that the Attorney General is pushing the judiciary to justify their sentencing practices and the appellate courts have started to respond to the Government's objective of tougher sentencing in relation to sexual offences as in the case of *Wheeler* where the Court of Appeal stated that there were no policy reasons preventing them dealing more severely with the indecent assault charge than the USI charge. However, there are numerous examples of questionable sentencing practices over the last few years in cases involving children both at the Crown Court and appellate level. In particular it will be interesting to see how the designation of sexual intercourse with under 13s as statutory rape rather than USI may impact upon judicial sentencing and to what extent previous convictions may be a factor. For example, in *R v Michael John L* [2000] 2 Cr App R(S) 177 the Court of Appeal reduced sentences totalling 9 years imposed on a 53 year-old man with 14 previous convictions between 1967 and 1997, including three for indecent assault and attempted rape, to 7 years for raping his 12 year-old stepson. The previous convictions dated back to 1970, 1982, and 1984 but the court said the trial judge was wrong to have taken them into account when determining sentence because of the long interval of time. D raped the boy twice and subjected him to oral sex, the boy's mother walked in on one of the rapes but failed to report what she saw. In an earlier case, *R v Steven Stepton* [1998] 2 Cr App R(S) 319, the sentence was also reduced from 9 to 7 years acknowledging the defendant's early admission and guilty plea. Six sample counts of rape and indecent assault on the same 9 year-old boy were charged. The 44 year-old defendant had given him lottery tickets in return for being allowed to bugger him, the boy suffered serious emotional damage as a result. Of course if a defendant is convicted on a second occasion and has a previous conviction for rape or other serious sexual offence then an automatic life sentence should be imposed (s 109 Powers of Criminal Courts (Sentencing) Act 2000) but cases like these where there may be an interval of time between convictions raise the possibility that perhaps the defendant was never caught in between. In another case of child grooming in June 2003, Stephen Jones, 27 years, was jailed for 12 months for USI with a 13 year-old girl suffering from emotional problems whom he had befriended over the Internet. The judge ordered a not guilty verdict on an alternative charge of rape (BBC News website, 23 June 2003).

In 2003 the Court of Appeal was invited to consider three references from the Attorney General all involving cases of indecent assault and gross indecency on young girls where the sentences were considered to be unduly lenient. Each case comprised different features such as the length of time the child took to disclose, that the abuse occurred some time ago, or that the trial judge applied the sentence he thought commensurate to the penalty that would have been imposed had the case been heard at the time the offence was committed. In all three cases the Court of Appeal confirmed that the original sentences were unduly lenient, see *AG v CCE, NJK, TAG* [2003] EWCA Crim 5.

4.7 CONCLUSION

The Government's avowed intent was to ensure that those who sexually abused children would be properly punished and certainly the new sentencing requirements reflect this. Clear distinctions are drawn between offences committed against children under 13 and those over that age. It appears that all potential loopholes have been plugged and that whatever sexual activity is perpetrated, and irrespective of the gender-relationship, there is an appropriate offence to charge. Further, an individual who commits any child sex offence abroad may be brought to trial in the UK for the equivalent sexual offence as expressed in the SOA 2003. However, despite assurances from the Home Office, there is still an issue about the desirability of criminalizing all teen sex under 16 years even though in real terms the position is not that different from before. Also, although the Review pressed hard for a new offence of persistent sexual abuse their recommendation was not taken up thereby entrusting the courts to punish such behaviour through a more general sentencing approach.

5

ABUSE OF POSITION OF TRUST

5.1 INTRODUCTION

During the 1990s, as revelations about the sexual abuse perpetrated by those entrusted with the care of vulnerable or disadvantaged children appeared in the public domain, a number of initiatives were introduced to address such betrayals of trust and prevent inappropriate persons from working with children. In June 1998 an Interdepartmental Working Group was set up to investigate the need for a legislative response, particularly in respect of protecting 16 and 17 year-olds, in light of the debates about lowering the age of homosexual consent (*Interdepartmental Working Group on Preventing Unsuitable People from Working with Children and Abuse of Trust,* HO December 1998). The Protection of Children Act 1999 imposed a statutory requirement on the Department of Health to maintain a list of individuals deemed unsuitable to work with children (see *SS Health v C* [2003] FCR 274). Similarly the Department for Education and Skills was also required to maintain a separate list (List 99) under the Restriction of Employment Regulations 2000. The combined effect of these lists was to control the employment of unsuitable persons in teaching establishments and organizations responsible for childcare. Simultaneously in 1998 the Criminal Records Bureau (established by the Police Act 1997), was set up as a single directory and central access point to incorporate all information on potential employees including these lists and other police information, such as that held on the Sex Offenders Register, to enable employers and voluntary organizations to check their existing staff and potential recruits. Different levels of checks can be applied for; Enhanced Disclosure where an individual works substantially with children or vulnerable persons; Standard Disclosure where he has regular contact; and Basic Disclosure in respect of all other circumstances (see www.crb.gov.uk/).

Formerly there was no specific offence of abuse of position of trust. Offenders could only be charged with general sex offences that addressed the sexual activity, e.g., indecent assault or gross indecency, but failed to reflect the aggravated nature of the offence resulting from the (usually) professional relationship between abuser and victim. The difficulties associated with prosecuting and convicting such individuals, especially for offences committed some years ago, were illustrated in the acquittals of Basil Williams-Rigby, 57 years, and Michael Lawson, 62 years, who were originally sentenced to 12 years imprisonment by Liverpool Crown Court in 1999 as part of the Merseyside police investigation Operation Care. This was one of the largest inquiries into systematic child abuse in children's homes in the 1970s and 1980s but the Court of Appeal ruled the convictions unsafe because of the lack of corroborating evidence and allegations that some complainants were motivated by possible compensation claims (*R v (1)X, (2)Y* [2003] EWCA Crim 693).

The Sexual Offences (Amendment) Act 2000 created a new offence of abuse of position of trust in response to these concerns (see *The Sexual Offences (Amendment) Bill: Age of Consent and Abuse of Position of Trust*, HC Research Paper 94/4). As a further preventative measure the Criminal Justice and Courts Services Act 2000 empowered the courts to disqualify individuals convicted of child sex offences from working with children in both a professional and voluntary capacity. The SOA 2003, in ss 16 to 19, repeals and re-enacts the former offence of abuse of position of trust replacing it with four offences utilizing the terms and language found elsewhere in the statute. Sexual contact between adults and children or young persons under 18 years in schools, colleges, and residential care is effectively prohibited in a bid to protect such potentially vulnerable individuals. But in raising the age threshold from 16 to 18 years the provisions may operate stringently in some cases involving 16 and 17 year-olds who consent in fact but cannot give valid legal consent, thus they do not sit easily with the general age of consent being set at 16. Provisions in the Act determine when a position of trust exists and whether a person is in fact in a position of trust, though these are somewhat convoluted in terms of expression.

Where an individual in a position of trust has sexual intercourse with a child under 13 this will automatically constitute statutory rape under s 5, similarly any other form of penetration falling short of penile penetration must be charged under s 6. Where the child is at least 13 but under 16 the offences overlap with the child sex offences provided in ss 9 to 12. Therefore these provisions do appear to be targeted more at protecting the 16 to 18 year-old group, especially as the maximum penalty for abuse of position of trust is 5 years compared to 14 years for the child sex offences. It would be nonsensical for the Government to have intended that a lesser penalty apply to any sexual abuse committed against a child under 16 by a person in a position of trust as the relationship itself and subsequent breach of trust makes the violation more serious. However, it may be considered appropriate in some cases to charge abuse of position of trust either as the principal charge or alternative charge where the sexual activity is perhaps relatively minor (e.g., kissing) but to emphasize the seriousness of the breach of trust in the context of the relationship.

5.2 DEFINITION OF POSITION OF TRUST

Section 21 lists a number of circumstances in which a person is deemed to be in a position of trust. The Secretary of State may, at a later date, specify further conditions constituting a position of trust. Generally a person will be in a position of trust where they *look after* or care for young persons aged under 18 years. 'Looks after' is defined as where a person is 'regularly involved in caring for, training, supervising or being in sole charge of such persons' (s 22(2)). The section does not mention that such individuals must be looking after the person solely on a professional basis (paid or otherwise) but this is the implication by virtue of the specified situations in which a position of trust exists (s 21) as these do not include relatives or other familial carers—specific offences to deal with familial relationships are considered in Chapter 7. Whether or not a person 'looks after' the child or young person will usually be self-evident such as where A looks after B on a day-to-day basis directly caring for him in residential accommodation, but there may be some occupations where the position is less clear-cut. In *R v Hassana Francis* (2000) WL 1720300 CA Crim Div the appellant was a domestic employee at the Royal London Hospital whose duties included filling patients' water jugs. She was convicted of indecently assaulting a 16 year-old boy who was a long-term patient suffering from cerebral palsy and a blood disorder necessitating him being in a spinal torso cast at the time of the offence. As an auxiliary it is unlikely that she would be regarded as being regularly involved in caring for children but at the time she was the only person present on the boy's ward highlighting the issue of who was actually looking after him. In some situations the position of trust will arise where a person 'looks after B on an individual basis', this too requires A to be regularly involved in the caring, training and supervision of B but A need not necessarily be in sole charge. Provided A has regular unsupervised contact with B, whether face-to-face or by any other means such as corresponding electronically or otherwise, then he is looking after B on an individual basis (s 22(3)). This covers childcare professionals working with children on a more intermittent basis perhaps as advisers, counsellors, or representatives etc. Teachers and instructors will be regarded as in a position of trust in respect of children and young persons enrolled as pupils or students at the institution where they teach (s 22(4)).

According to subsections 21(2)–(13) a position of trust will be deemed to exist in the following situations where A is in a position of trust in relation to another person B who is a young person aged under 18 years:

(i) Where A looks after persons detained in an institution by virtue of a court order or statutory provision and B is detained in that institution. For example, where B is convicted of a criminal offence and detained in a young offender institution, secure training centre, or probation hostel.

(ii) Where A looks after persons resident in a home or other place where accommodation and maintenance are provided by the local authority (s 23(2) CA 1989); or provided by voluntary organizations such as Dr Barnardo's and National Children's Homes. This category is quite broad but specifically covers accommodation in residential institutions so would include all residential care whether private or voluntary, secure accommodation, and semi-independent accommodation.

(iii) Where A looks after persons accommodated or cared for in a medical, therapeutic, or supportive context including a:

> hospital
>
> independent clinic
>
> care home, residential care home, or private hospital
>
> community home, voluntary home, or children's home
>
> home or other accommodation which provides facilities for children with special needs (s 82(5) CA 1989)
>
> residential family centre.

This category would include institutions where children receive medical or psychiatric treatment or other forms of therapy or support in respect of medical conditions and ill-health, physical or learning disabilities, mental illness and behavioural problems. It applies to both NHS and private institutions and in respect of under 18 year-olds who are either permanently or temporarily resident for the duration of treatment etc.

(iv) Where A looks after pupils and students receiving education at an educational establishment whether private or public, as boarders or day-attendees including primary schools, secondary schools, and colleges of further education. The subsection (s 21(5)) specifically requires that B receives such education at that institution and A does not, i.e., A is a teacher. This would include student exchanges and other programmes where students are enrolled at one institution but are studying at the institution where A works.

(v) Where A is engaged in the provision of special learning services and tuition and looks after B on an individual basis such as in the case of a Connexions personal adviser (pursuant to ss 8–10 Employment and Training Act 1973 and s 114 Learning and Skills Act 2000).

(vi) Where A regularly has unsupervised contact with B, whether face-to-face or by any other means, in relation to the provision of accommodation for children in police protection or on detention or remand; or as a result of being abandoned, having lost their parents, or where those with parental responsibility are unable to look after them (ss 20 and 21 CA 1989).

(vii) Where A is appointed as a reporter to the court in legal proceedings involving a child to report on the welfare of B (s 7 CA 1989) and has regular unsupervised contact whether face-to-face or by any other means such as telephone or electronic communications. This would include probation officers, local authority officers, other persons that the local authority considers appropriate and independent Children and Family Reporters appointed by CAFCASS (Children and Family Court Advisory and Support Service, see www.cafcass.gov.uk).

(viii) Where A is appointed by a local authority to act as a personal adviser in respect of children, normally 16 to 17 year-olds, in care or who have left care and looks after B on an individual basis. Primarily this covers social workers engaged as mentors to ensure that such children continue a 'family type' relationship (s 23B(2) CA 1989).

(ix) Where B is subject to a Care Order, Supervision Order, or Education Supervision Order under the CA 1989 and A looks after B or befriends on an individual basis under the authorization of that order.

(x) Where A is appointed as a guardian ad litem or children's guardian i.e., is an officer of CAFCASS in relation to adoption proceedings (s 41(1) CA 1989; Adoption Rules 1984 Rule 6 or Rule 18 and now see The Adoption (Amendment) Rules 2003; Family Proceedings Rules 1991 Rule 9.5) and has regular unsupervised contact whether face-to-face or by any other means.

(xi) Where A looks after B on an individual basis pursuant to any requirements imposed by a court order or on release from detention in respect of a criminal offence. For example, supervision of community sentences including probation order, combination order, community sentence order, supervision order, attendance centre order; bail supervision and where subject to conditions in association with release from detention. This category would also include members of Youth Offending Teams where they have sufficient contact and connection with the child, and court-approved counsellors in respect of drug rehabilitation services.

Though this is a fairly exhaustive list (and includes equivalent references to Northern Ireland) it is categorical and does not appear to cover 'non-professional' scenarios such as the case of Sarah Hubert, a 25 year-old scout mistress convicted of indecent assault for seducing a 14 year-old boy scout at scout camp whose parents had entrusted him into her care for the weekend (The Times, 23 October 1998). Similarly members of the clergy are not caught by this provision nor school caretakers, bus drivers and cooks etc.

5.3 KNOWLEDGE OF POSITION OF TRUST

Where A looks after B on an individual basis it will be presumed that he knew, or could have been reasonably expected to know, that he was engaged in a position of trust in relation to B and the circumstances of that position. It would therefore be up to A to discharge this burden by presenting evidence to the contrary. This is basically the combined effect of subsections 16(1)(d), 17(1)(d), 18(1)(e), and 19(1)(d) read in conjunction with subsection (4) of each of the four offences. For example, the Explanatory Notes suggest that in large institutions such as hospitals and schools it is reasonable to suppose that D may not be aware that the child is actually at that institution and so the defence could be claimed but it is expected that any such claims will be fairly limited.

An interesting and related legal development is the acknowledgment by the House of Lords that the employer of the person in a position of trust may be vicariously liable in the law of tort for the actions of his employee. In a ground-breaking decision Lord Steyn was satisfied that where the employee's torts were so closely connected with his employment it is fair and just to hold his employers liable, albeit this would be a matter of degree. In *Lister and others(AP) v Hesley Hall* [2001] UKHL 22, Hesley Hall Ltd., a commercial enterprise, entrusted the care of 12 to 15 year-old boys to a warden responsible for the day-to-day running of a boarding house annexed to a school. Their Lordships held that acts of sexual abuse perpetrated by the warden including mutual masturbation, oral sex, and buggery, were so inextricably interwoven with the carrying out of his duties that the employer was therefore potentially liable.

5.3.1 Relationships that pre-date position of trust

A further defence is provided in s 24 regarding relationships that *pre-date* the position of trust. Conduct between A and B that would otherwise have been an offence under ss 16 to 19, will not be an offence if *immediately before* the position of trust arose a sexual relationship existed. This defence is only intended to cover previous *lawful* sexual relationships. So, for example, where B, a 17 year-old girl, engages in a sexual relationship with a trainee teacher A who subsequently secures a teaching post at the school she attends, he would have a defence to any charge of abuse of position of trust as the relationship started before he undertook that position. However, if B was 15 when they first met the previous sexual relationship would not have been lawful and the defence will not lie (s 24(2)). A bears the responsibility of proving the existence of any previously lawful relationship (s 24(3)).

5.4 SUBSTANTIVE OFFENCES

The Act creates four new offences which replace the former offence of abuse of position of trust under s 3 SO(A)A 2000. All must be committed by a person aged *18 or over*, male or female, but may be committed against anyone *under* the age of 18. These offences have a broader ambit than the specific child sex offences dealt with in Chapter 4 in that, as with s 3 SO(A)A 2000, the complainant may be aged 16 or 17 years-old and so potentially capable of giving informed consent. The previous offence prohibited both sexual intercourse and sexual activity; sexual intercourse has now been removed and is covered by the broader concept of sexual activity as proscribed in the child sex offences in ss 9–12.

All four offences are rather lengthy and repetitive in that the subsections regarding proof and evidential burdens apply equally but are reproduced in full in respect of each offence. They also carry the same sentence of a maximum of 5 years imprisonment on indictment or 6 months/fine if tried summarily.

5.4.1 Abuse of position of trust

Section 16(1) creates the main offence of sexually abusing a child where the abuser is in a position of trust. This offence is committed where

A, aged 18 or over intentionally touches another person B,

the touching is sexual and,

A is in a position of trust in relation to B and

either B is under 18 and A does not reasonably believe him to be 18 or over,

or B is under 13.

The prosecution must prove that the offender intended to touch B anywhere on his body, that he in fact touched B and that the touching was sexual as defined in s 78 (see ch 4 for discussion of these points). The prosecution must also prove that the offender was *in fact* in a position of trust with B and that the relationship between A and B falls into one of the categories listed in s 21 above.

Examples of cases that could now be prosecuted under this provision include that of Mark Unsworth, 40 years, a PE teacher, sentenced to 12 months for USI with a 14 year-old girl whom he coached in the school football team (BBC News website, 17 March 2000). Similarly Amy Gehring, a supply teacher, cleared of indecently assaulting 14 and 15 year-old boys with whom she had engaged in sexual intercourse (BBC News website, 5 February 2002).

Of course if B does not consent to the sexual touching, rape, or another non-consensual offence should be charged, as in the case of the 17 year-old student raped after she refused to perform a sex act during an A-level practical examination in drama (BBC News website, 25 September 2002). If she had consented to sexual intercourse the offence of abuse of trust would have been applicable.

5.4.2 Variations

There are three alternatives to the substantive offence that may be charged. In each the main provisions are identical to s 16 and the actus reus elements such as causing, inciting etc., have the same meaning as for the child sex offences discussed in Chapter 4. Section 17 prohibits a person in a position of trust from causing or inciting a child to engage in sexual activity. Section 18 is similar to s 11 prohibiting sexual activity in the presence of a child where A, for the purposes of sexual gratification, engages in such activity when B is present or is in a place from which A can be observed. A must know or believe that B is aware of the child's presence or intends that B should be aware. Section 19 replicates s 12 and addresses the offence of causing a child to watch a sexual act, or image of a sexual act, for sexual gratification. The Hesley Hall case demonstrates all these variations as in systematically abusing the boys in his care, the warden committed all four offences in ss 16 to 19. The sexual abuse perpetrated took the form of mutual masturbation, oral sex, and buggery, which would not only constitute rape, assault by penile penetration, and sexual assault but also s 16 sexual activity, and s 18 sexual activity in the presence of another child. These actions were preceded by 'grooming' whereby the warden established control over the boys by offering unwarranted gifts, undeserved leniency, and trips alone, thus causing and inciting sexual activity and satisfying s 17. In allowing the boys to watch violent and x-rated videos in return for their sexual services such conduct could now be prosecuted under s 19.

5.5 DEFENCES

In addition to the defences relating to actual knowledge of position of trust whereby D may not be aware that he is responsible for a particular child in a large institution or where he has been involved in a previous lawful sexual relationship with B, two other defences are potentially available.

5.5.1 Defence of reasonable belief that B is aged over 18

The abuse of trust offences may be committed against anyone aged under 18. Except where B is under 13 the prosecution must prove that the offender did not reasonably believe that B was 18 or over. Assistance can be found in the presumption in subsection (2) of each of the four offences that once it is proved B is under 18 years it will be assumed that D had no reasonable grounds to believe that B was over 18. The evidential burden then shifts to D who must adduce evidence to show that there is an arguable case that he reasonably believed B to be over 18 years. This defence cannot be used where the child is under 13 as any age-based defence is irrelevant. In relation to most institutional and residential accommodation specifically provided for under 18s and in respect of certain positions such as a youth worker or professional working on programmes specifically targeted at young persons, this will be a very difficult burden to discharge.

5.5.2 Defence of marriage

A person, albeit in a position of trust, will not commit any offence under ss 16–19 if he can prove that at the time of the sexual activity he was lawfully married to B (s 23). Thus where a 17 year-old girl with parental permission marries her teacher or probation officer no offence is committed. The provision of this defence is questionable as on the one hand it seems to imply that it is acceptable for parents to condone such relationships, yet on the other denies the possibility that young adults could be pressurized or induced into marriage either by their parents or the adult in the position of trust. The onus is on D to prove that a valid marriage exists.

5.6 SENTENCING

The maximum sentence of 5 years may seem rather low, presumably this is to minimize the severity of the sentence where B is over 16 years, reflecting the possibility of, at least, factual consent, and implying that in respect of under 16s other non-consensual or child sex offences should be charged as appropriate. In *R v Bromiley* (2000) Times LR 4 July the Court of Appeal held that those in positions of trust and responsibility towards the young could expect to go to prison for a substantial period if they breached that trust and preyed sexually on those in their care. Caroline Bromiley, a 37 year-old care assistant, was sentenced to 5 years concurrently for 10 offences of indecent assault committed against five boys aged 12–14 years-old whom she had approached in the school dormitory and invited back to her flat on school premises. The court declared that if a man had been convicted of a similar offence he would have faced a long sentence and that sentencing for sexual abuse should therefore not be gender-specific.

An indication of the impact such offences have can be seen in *S (CICB: Quantum: 1999) (Sexual Abuse)* [2000] CLY 1528 where a 12 year-old boy was sexually abused by a 27 year-old male carer in a local authority residential home who touched his penis on two occasions. As an adult S suffered long-term psychological symptoms and found sexual intercourse distressing, his condition had failed to respond to therapy and the prognosis was poor. An award of £7,300 was made in his favour.

5.7 DISQUALIFICATION ORDERS

The Interdepartmental Working Group recommended that those whose previous conduct demonstrated their unsuitability to work with children should be banned from working with children. A new criminal offence to support this objective was introduced in the Criminal Justice and Courts Services Act 2000 (CJCSA). Section 28 provides courts with the power to impose a Disqualification Order where an individual is charged or convicted of a sexual or violent offence committed against a child and a qualifying sentence of 12 months or more is imposed. Section 35 makes it an offence for a person who is disqualified under s 28 to knowingly apply for or undertake any work in a regulated position as defined in s 36. This includes both paid and voluntary work with children and would extend to baby-sitting and sitting on a school's governing body. An employer who knowingly offers such work in a regulated position, or knowingly fails to remove someone with a Disqualification Order, also commits an offence. These offences are also punishable with 5 years imprisonment on indictment or 6 months summarily. The aim of the CJCSA 2000 is to ensure that courts impose Disqualification Orders where appropriate and that the police enforce any breaches. The order is of indefinite duration but a review process is incorporated whereby an individual may apply to the Child Protection Act Tribunal for a review 10 years after any disqualification order was imposed (see *Criminal Justice and Court Services Act 2000: Protection of Children Guidance*, HO December 2002).

Disqualification Orders should be used primarily where an individual presents a serious and ongoing risk of danger to a child or children: *R v MG* [2002] 2 Cr App R(S) 1. There has been some confusion, even amongst the judiciary, between Disqualification Orders issued under the CJCSA 2000 and Restraining Orders issued under s 5A SOA 1997 now s 104 SOA 2003 as discussed in Chapter 12. For example, in *R v David Christopher Yates* [2003] EWCA Crim 1917 it was not made clear by the trial judge whether the imposition of a Notice of Disqualification from Working with Children was a Disqualification Order or a Restraining Order. The order, which prohibited the appellant from working with, or in the vicinity of, children for a period of 20 years, was quashed by the Court of Appeal. Yates was convicted of indecent assault on a woman and indecent exposure and admitted eight other offences of indecent exposure that were taken into consideration. The court held that just because a person is deemed generally unsuitable to work with children is not a sufficient reason in itself to justify a ban, he must also present a potential risk to children. In *R v Field, R v Young* [2003] 2 Cr App R 3, s 28 was held to apply to all relevant convictions thereby including any offending behaviour which pre-dates the enactment of the CJCSA.

5.8 CONCLUSION

Few would dispute the fact that where an adult occupies a professional position in relation to a child any associated breach of trust must be perceived as an aggravating factor. But a virtually blanket prohibition of all such sexual relations involving 16 and 17 year-olds is at odds with the age of consent and fails to take into account their capacity to consent. Such an approach appears even more indefensible when provision for a defence of marriage is taken into account, especially in the context of 'forced' or arranged marriages where a 17 year-old may be allowed less of an opportunity to make an informed contribution about the relationship than in a voluntary and consensual love affair with their supervisor.

6

PEOPLE WITH A MENTAL DISORDER

6.1 INTRODUCTION

The Act creates three sets of offences where the victim is a person with a mental disorder. The first set consists of those general offences concerned with sexual activity involving a person with a mental disorder and apply where the person cannot consent to the sexual activity; the second set consists of those offences where the person's agreement to engage in sexual activity is secured through an inducement, threat, or deception; and the third set comprises those offences where the defendant is in some form of care relationship with the victim and they may be committed regardless of consent. In establishing these offences, a driving concern has been to ensure that vulnerable adults have protection from sexual abuse and exploitation, but without imposing improper and unnecessary barriers on their ability to develop, explore, and enjoy their sexuality (*Setting the Boundaries*, para 4.1.3). Of necessity, sexual offences will both impose limits upon the expression of and learning about sexuality and also provide protection against abuse. The danger is that, if the focus on protection from abuse is too great, laws are produced that improperly inhibit the right and need for sexual expression. This is a difficult balance to achieve, as has been the experience of those working with people with mental disorder under the SOA 1956 (M.J. Gunn, *Sex and the law: a brief guide for staff working with people with learning difficulties* (1996) Family Planning Association: London).

Over the past 20 years there has been serious debate about sexuality issues and people with learning disabilities, who form one group of people covered by the phrase 'person with a mental disorder' that is used in the new Act, but for whom this debate has particular resonance. On the one hand, there is the right of the person with a learning disability to their sexuality. There is no necessary reason, in most cases, why the fact of learning disability should prevent ordinary sexual development. With sexual development comes the need to understand and handle it and the opportunity to express it in a variety of ways. However, the learning disability may produce serious obstacles to learning and understanding that necessitate much assistance for the learning process to operate. On the other hand, it is the right of a vulnerable person not to be abused. Research into the prevalence of sexual abuse of people with a learning disability reveals a distressing history (*Setting the Boundaries*, para 4.2.5 and C. Keenan and L. Maitland, 'Literature Review of Research into the Law on Sexual Offences Against Children and Vulnerable People' in *Setting the Boundaries* (vol. 2)). People with a learning disability or a mental disorder have been the victims of a range of abuses. Their learning disability or mental disorder does not prevent them from being victims nor provide them with any protection. In the past, such abuse has often not been reported or, when reported, not dealt with well. A desire to improve the current position is revealed not only by the review of the substantive law achieved through the new Act, but also through the changes to the law of evidence in providing vulnerable witnesses with improved chances of presenting reliable evidence through the introduction of special measures by the Youth Justice and Criminal Evidence Act 1999 (see ch 10 and D. Birch and R. Leng, *Blackstone's Guide to the Youth Justice and Criminal Evidence Act 1999* (2000)).

The right to a private life, including a sexual life (*Dudgeon v UK* (1981) 4 EHRR 149), is provided for all citizens under Article 8 of the ECHR. The State has positive obligations under the Article which 'may involve the adoption of measures designed to secure respect for private life even in the sphere of the relations of individuals between themselves', *X and Y v Netherlands* (1985) 8 EHRR 235 at para 23. In that case, the European Court recognized the need to balance the right to sexuality with the right to protection from sexual abuse (*X and Y v Netherlands* (1985), at para 25 in the submission by the Dutch Government). The Court decided that there was a breach when a young adult with a learning disability was sexually abused by a care worker but he was not prosecuted. Dutch law required the victim to make a complaint. She was not capable of doing so, nor was her father entitled to make a complaint on her behalf. The positive obligation demanded that the State provide protection, through effective deterrence, by the criminal law. That standard was not met.

6.1.1 Sexual knowledge and understanding

The right to sexuality and the right to be provided with protection from abuse by the law are interlinked, especially when it is understood that an ability a person must have in order to help them in self action to prevent abuse is to have knowledge and understanding of their own sexuality. It is necessary for a person to know that she can set limits upon sexual behaviour and that the law also sets limits as to what is permissible. Sexuality is normally understood by someone recognizing and learning about their own sexuality and choosing to express it in the manner of their choice. Nowadays sex education can reduce the risks associated with purely experiential learning. For a person with learning disability, in particular, and also people with a mental disorder, this method of learning may simply not be possible. A person with a learning disability may well have difficulties of learning in the abstract (so the use of materials may not provide the necessary education); difficulties in learning from trial and experiment (so may not, e.g., improve sexual technique by trying an activity, such as masturbation, on repeated occasions, indeed staff have reported to one of the authors that some men with a learning disability are not able successfully to masturbate and continually try to do it thus causing themselves physical harm); and difficulties of meeting other potential partners (and so, even if sexual technique and desire are present, normal relationships may not easily be developed, if at all, thereby potentially causing deep frustration which can be difficult to handle especially for someone whose understanding of what is happening is relatively limited). While in most cases, normal approaches to sex education may be successful in achieving their aims, a much more direct and hands-on method, such as someone physically having to instruct by a hands-on teaching method how to masturbate, may be necessary to achieve the same level of success.

Under the SOA 1956, sex education of such a nature was extremely problematic. If the client were a person with a severe learning disability and so satisfied the definition of being a 'defective' (i.e., that he or she had 'a state of arrested or incomplete development of mind that included severe impairment of intelligence and social functioning', s 46), he or she could not provide consent to what might appear to be an indecent assault (ss 14(4) and 15(3)). The only means for arguing that such activity might be lawful, would be that it was not indecent on the basis that either a right-minded person would not regard the act as indecent and/or the purpose or intention with which someone acted was not indecent: *R v Court* [1989] AC 28. In cases where the genitalia were being touched, the essential argument would be that the touching was not indecent. If teaching a woman with severe learning disability about menstruation or a man or woman with severe learning disability about toileting are not indecent, then neither is teaching masturbation. It would have to be established that the activity cannot be explained to some people with a learning disability without using a hands-on method, that that method is identified, by a multi-disciplinary care group, as the right step to take at that particular time and that the group identifies the person to do it and in what circumstances and how it is to be done. The potential complexity and difficulty of this argument is necessary in order to establish that the activity was proper as opposed to being improper and therefore sexual abuse and deserving of punishment with the full vigour of the law.

6.1.2 The previous law

Until recently there was little effective response to sexual abuse, especially where the victim was a person with a learning disability. While there were difficulties with the substantive offences, the real problem was more a procedural issue associated with the gathering of information during an investigation and the giving of evidence in court. Of course, if the offence to be charged was that contrary to s 7(1) SOA 1956, this was relatively straightforward as all that would have to be proved is that the man had sexual intercourse with the woman who had a severe learning disability (that is, she was a 'defective'), that they were not married (that is, that the sex was 'unlawful') and that, if the matter was raised by the defendant, he could not avail himself of the defence that he did not know and had no cause to suspect that she was a defective, s 7(2). But, before DNA testing could establish that sex had taken place or where consent is in issue, there were real problems associated with the investigating and prosecuting agencies accepting that a person with a learning disability could be a reliable witness and the courts accepting that she could give evidence. Establishing that the woman was a 'defective', albeit expert evidence could be made available, 'effectively [put] that person on trial' (*Setting the Boundaries*, para 4.2.2). While significant progress has been made procedurally and culturally, such issues cannot be ignored as examining the substantive law on its own can too easily provide a false picture.

The SOA 1956 failed to achieve an appropriate balance in its offences dealing with persons with a mental disorder for a variety of reasons including the following:

(i) Some apparently protective sexual offences were over-inclusive as they relied upon status (i.e., whether she was a 'defective') and not functional ability (i.e., was she capable of deciding whether to have sexual intercourse);

(ii) The specialist offences only protected a person who had a severe learning disability (i.e., was a 'defective') and not any person with a different form of mental disorder;

(iii) The reference to a 'defective,' has been criticized as being 'demeaning and derogatory';

(iv) A capable person, though diagnosed as a 'defective', could not provide consent to sex or sexual activity, even if they desired the activity to take place if they carried a particular diagnosis;

(v) The only protection from abuse was provided by the ordinary offences and the specialist offences, but they failed to deal with sexual activity taking place in breach of trust or misuse of position.

6.2 OFFENCES AGAINST PEOPLE WITH A MENTAL DISORDER IMPEDING CHOICE

The first set of sexual offences in ss 30–33 establish four offences which deal with aspects of improper sexual activity with people with a mental disorder and mirror the child sex offences in ss 9–12 (see ch 4):

Sexual activity with a person with a mental disorder impeding choice (s 30);

Causing or inciting a person, with a mental disorder impeding choice, to engage in sexual activity (s 31);

Engaging in sexual activity in the presence of a person with a mental disorder impeding choice (s 32);

Causing a person, with a mental disorder impeding choice, to watch a sexual act (s 33).

6.2.1 Sexual activity with a person with a mental disorder impeding choice

The basic offence is in s 30. The essential elements to be proved are as follows.

6.2.1.1 *Intentional touching*

The offence consists of an activity by A, in this case the intentional touching of another, B (s 30(1)(a)). Activity short of touching would not, therefore, be covered. This marks a change as, under the old law of indecent assault, not only touching someone else would be covered, as a battery, but also causing the other to apprehend contact, as an assault, would have been covered. 'Touching' is defined in s 79(8) as including touching with any part of the body, with anything else, or through anything and in particular it includes penetration. So this offence covers both sexual intercourse and other sexual activity involving some form of touching. The touching must be intentional, so no accidental contact is affected.

6.2.1.2 *Sexual touching*

The touching must be sexual (s 30(1)(b)) as considered in Chapters 3 and 4. This will, therefore, capture many instances of abuse, whether it involves sexual intercourse or other sexual contact. Whilst there is no grooming offence, where that grooming leads to contact that is sexual, it will fall within this offence. One particularly contentious problem, which also illustrates some of the more general issues raised by this element of the offence, is to consider whether teaching masturbation by a hands-on method is sexual, when that is the only teaching method available? It does not fall within s 78(b) because of the non-sexual purpose, provided that is indeed established by the nature of the education programme and the way in which the multi-disciplinary care group identify the need for the teaching and the means of undertaking it. However, it might fall within s 78(a) as it involves touching the genitalia. But is it really sexual? What is actually being undertaken is teaching a necessary physical technique that cannot be taught by any other means and must be taught to prevent harm to the individual.

6.2.1.3 *Unable to refuse because of mental disorder*

B must be 'unable to refuse because of or for a reason related to a mental disorder' (s 30(1)(c)). The offence does not apply only to those with a severe learning disability as was the case under SOA 1956. By virtue of s 79(6), 'mental disorder' has the same meaning as s 1 Mental Health Act 1983. It means 'mental illness, a state of arrested or incomplete development of mind, psychopathic disorder and any other disorder or disability of mind'. 'Mental illness' is not defined in the Mental Health Act. There is broad professional agreement as to its parameters but there is the potential for serious disagreement in some situations (see P. Bartlett and R. Sandland, *Mental Health Law: Policy and Practice* (2003, 2nd ed.)). A 'state of arrested or incomplete development of mind' includes any learning disability regardless of its severity and regardless of any impact upon social functioning. 'Psychopathic disorder' is defined by the Mental Health Act as being 'a persistent disorder or disability of mind (whether or not including significant impairment of intelligence) which results in abnormally aggressive or seriously irresponsible conduct on the part of the person concerned'. Further 'mental disorder' includes 'any other disorder or disability of mind'. One condition that this might include is brain injury caused later in life (e.g., any time from a person's early 20s onwards). The development of mind has not been arrested or made incomplete, but there is a *'disability'* of mind. So, this sort of offence applies to a much larger range of people than the equivalent offences in the SOA 1956. However, a simplistic status approach is not being taken, since the presence of the mental disorder is not all that matters. Additionally, it must be established that the person must not, as a consequence of or for a reason related to the mental disorder, have the capacity to decide whether to engage in the sexual activity. This is, by s 30(2), one form of being 'unable to refuse'. The matter of capacity, whether through inability to choose or inability to communicate, is considered in more detail at Chapter 2 above.

6.2.1.4 *Knowledge of mental disorder*
A must know or could reasonably be expected to know that B has a mental disorder and that because of it or for a reason related to it B is likely to be unable to refuse (s 30(1)(d)). The burden of proving this, as with all other elements of the offence, lies upon the prosecution. A will not be able to claim simply that he honestly believed that B did not have a mental disorder, because of the reasonableness requirement. This element will be much more readily established where A is a carer of B or has professional expertise and/or experience of working with people with mental disorder. In other cases, it may prove to be difficult to establish that A could reasonably be expected to have the relevant knowledge, especially in cases where there are no external distinguishing features that might indicate mental disorder and A has no pre-existing knowledge of B. Not only must A have the necessary awareness of B's mental disorder, but also A must know or reasonably be expected to know that B is thereby likely to be unable to refuse. The combination will mean that the offence may well be prosecuted more regularly where B has a learning disability than any other form of mental disorder because the effect on capacity is more likely to be apparent to anyone where B has this type of mental disorder.

6.2.2 Causing or inciting a person, with a mental disorder impeding choice, to engage in sexual activity

The offence in s 31 follows the same pattern as that in s 30, though the activity is the causing or inciting of B to engage in a sexual activity (s 31(1)(a) and (b)). 'Causing' and 'inciting' are words regularly used in the criminal law and the same approach as in other offences will be taken (see, chs 3 and 4, and *Blackstones Criminal Practice 2004*).

6.2.3 Engaging in sexual activity in the presence of a person with mental disorder impeding choice

The offence in s 32 also follows the same pattern as the offence in s 30, though the required activity is engaging in a sexual activity (s 32(1)(a), (b)), when B is present or in a place from where A may be observed and A knows or believes that B is aware or intends that B be aware that A is engaging in it (s 32(1)(c)). There is, however, an additional requirement, which is that A must act with 'the purpose of obtaining sexual gratification' (s 32(1)(c)). If, therefore, the act is not done for that purpose, there is no offence. The presence of this element in s 32 might be thought to weaken the argument above that teaching masturbation can be lawful under s 30 on the basis that it is not sexual, but there is no explicit exception in the section for where A does not seek sexual gratification. Whilst this comparison between the two offences might present a problem, it is submitted that the logic and propriety of the argument in connection with s 30 is sufficient for it to stand nevertheless (see also Lord Falconer, HL Debs 28 April 2003, col 540–1).

6.2.4 Causing a person, with a mental disorder impeding choice, to watch a sexual act

The offence in s 33 also follows the same pattern as that in s 30, though here the activity is causing B to watch a third person engaging in a sexual activity or looking at an image of any person engaging in such activity (s 33(1)(a)). This offence also requires that A acts for the purpose of obtaining sexual gratification (s 33(1)(a)). The showing of a film for the purposes of sex education can, therefore, be lawful since A would not be showing the film for his sexual gratification nor indeed for that of B. A film would be an 'image', which is defined in s 79(4) as meaning a 'moving or still image and includes an image produced by any means and, where the context permits, a three-dimensional image'.

6.2.5 Sentencing provisions

The sentences available fall into two groups. In each group, higher maximum sentences have been created. This was a deliberate policy as the Government wishes to make clear the seriousness of such offences and this was best achieved by having high maxima. However, none of these offences have to be tried on indictment, so there is the possibility that they may be tried summarily.

6.2.5.1 *Sentence for ss 30 and 31*
Where A is convicted of an offence involving penetration contrary to s 30 or s 31, a substantial maximum sentence is available. It is imprisonment for life (s 30(3) and s 31(3)). In other cases, the offence is triable either way and, on conviction on indictment, the maximum sentence is imprisonment for 14 years and, on summary conviction, the maximum sentence is imprisonment for 6 months or a fine not exceeding the statutory maximum or both (s 30(4) and s 31(4)).

6.2.5.2 *Sentence for ss 32 and 33*
Where A is convicted of an offence contrary to s 32 or s 33, a substantial maximum sentence is still available, but these offences are less serious and so there is no possibility of a life sentence, and the maximum on indictment is lower. In all cases, the offence is triable either way and, on conviction on indictment, the maximum sentence is imprisonment for 10 years and, on summary conviction, the maximum sentence is imprisonment for 6 months or a fine not exceeding the statutory maximum or both (s 32(3) and s 34(3)).

6.3 SECURING AGREEMENT BY A PERSON WITH A MENTAL DISORDER TO SEXUAL ACTIVITY BY INDUCEMENT, DECEPTION, OR THREAT

6.3.1 The offences

The second set of offences are found in ss 34–37.

Inducement, threat, or deception to procure sexual activity with a person with a mental disorder (s 34);

Causing a person with a mental disorder to engage in or agree to engage in sexual activity by inducement, threat, or deception (s 35);

Engaging in sexual activity in the presence, procured by inducement, threat, or deception, of a person with a mental disorder (s 36);

Causing a person with a mental disorder to watch a sexual act by inducement, threat, or deception (s 37).

These offences are distinguished from the first set in that they only apply to people who are capable of deciding whether to engage in sexual activity, but their agreement in the particular case is improperly obtained. If B does not have the capacity to agree, these offences are not committed. Whilst the common elements of this set of offences are covered by discussion of the first set, attention must be paid to the inducement, threat, or deceptions necessary for commission of this offence. No definition of these terms is provided. It is not relevant to consider whether the validity of the agreement was affected, e.g., by considering whether B was deceived as to the nature and quality of the act, since the validity of the agreement is not in issue. So, not only would A's deception of B that the act was an operation to improve a singing voice be covered, but so also a promise to pay for sex or a promise to marry her. The only limitation appears to be that the inducement, threat, or deception must be used by A 'for the purpose of obtaining that agreement' or similar words (s 34(1)(c), s 35(1)(a), s 36(1)(d), s 37(1)(c)).

6.3.2 Sentence

As regards sentence for these offences, they fall into two groups.

6.3.2.1 *Sentence for ss 34 and 35*
Where A is convicted of an offence involving penetration contrary to s 34 or s 35, a substantial maximum sentence is available. It is imprisonment for life (s 34(3) and s 35(2)). In other cases, the offence is triable either way and, on conviction on indictment, the maximum sentence is imprisonment for 14 years and, on summary conviction, the maximum sentence is imprisonment for 6 months or a fine not exceeding the statutory maximum or both (s 34(3) and s 35(3)).

6.3.2.2 *Sentence for ss 36 and 37*
Where A is convicted of an offence contrary to s 36 or s 37, a substantial maximum sentence is still available, but these offences are less serious and so there is no possibility of a life sentence, and the maximum on indictment is lower. In all cases, the offence is triable either way and, on conviction on indictment, the maximum sentence is imprisonment for 10 years and, on summary conviction, the maximum sentence is imprisonment for 6 months or a fine not exceeding the statutory maximum or both (s 36(2) and s 37(2)).

6.4 THE CARE WORKER OFFENCES

6.4.1 Introduction

Sadly, it has to be acknowledged that care workers have been the perpetrators of sexual abuse against people with mental disorders (*Setting the Boundaries*, at para 4.8.1). It is proper to introduce laws to deter this behaviour and to set an expected standard of behaviour. Care workers should not have sexual relationships with those for whom they care as the power imbalance is such that exploitation and abuse cannot be avoided. The only specific example of this approach in the old law was to be found in the Mental Health Act 1959, s 128, which was limited to men working in hospitals and mental nursing homes or who had a formal relationship of responsibility with them through various pieces of legislation. The introduction of a new comprehensive set of offences, building upon those with regard to children that were introduced by the Sexual Offences (Amendment) Act 2000, is to be welcomed.

6.4.2 General issues

The offences, to be found in ss 38–41, draw on many of the elements from the first set of offences. They are distinguishable by requiring that the defendant, A, is a care worker as defined by s 42. It is important to emphasize that consent and capacity have no role to play in these offences. This is not, however, a set of simplistic status offences. Within certain relationships, sexual activity should not take place. There is always the option of the care relationship ending and a sexual relationship then taking place, if lawful. In order to achieve an appropriate balance between the right to express one's sexuality and the right of vulnerable people to be protected from exploitation and abuse, it would appear that this approach achieves that balance properly.

6.4.3 Interpretation of 'care worker'

'Care worker' is not used in the offences themselves, but appears in the offence headings. Who to include was much discussed in Parliament as there was a desire and commitment to get it right so as to catch those who need to be caught. A person is a care worker or, rather, 'involved in the care of another person (B)' if they fall within s 42(2) to (4) (s 42(1)). One common feature of each of these definitions is the requirement for A to have 'regular face-to-face contact with B'. It is an interesting phrase to have used. It is also used in those offences concerned with those in a position of trust who look after persons on an individual basis (see ch 5). It must fully and accurately describe the care relationship so that it covers all desired situations. The interpretation in s 42 first identifies the relationship between A and B by examining the context in which they come across each other, whether in the course of A's employment (the first two) or not (the last) and then moves to whether there is sufficient contact between them, that is whether there is 'regular face-to-face contact with B'.

6.4.3.1 *Residential accommodation*

Section 42(2) provides that a person is involved in the care of another person where

(a) B is accommodated and cared for in a care home, community home, voluntary home or children's home, and

(b) A has functions to perform in the home in the course of employment which have brought him or are likely to bring him into regular face-to-face contact with B, (s 42(2)(a), (b)).

'Care home', 'community home', 'voluntary home', and 'children's home' are all defined in s 42(5). In combination, the full range of social care accommodation in which a person with a mental disorder might find themselves living when not at home or in a hospital is covered. There is no lower age limit on the application of these offences, so it is appropriate for residents with mental disorder in children's homes to be included. 'Employment' is defined in s 42(5).

6.4.3.2 *Receiving medical services*
Section 42(3) provides that a person is involved in the care of another person where

B is a patient for whom services are provided

    (a) by a National Health Service body or an independent medical agency or

    (b) in an independent clinic or an independent hospital,

and A has functions to perform for the body or agency or in the clinic or hospital in the course of employment which have brought him or are likely to bring him into regular face-to-face contact with B.

'National Health Service body' is defined in s 42(5). Section 42(5) also defines 'independent medical agency', 'independent clinic', and 'independent hospital' by reference to the Care Standards Act 2000, s 2 which provides as follows:

[a] hospital which is not a health service hospital is an independent hospital (Care Standards Act 2000, s 2(2));

'independent clinic' means an establishment of a prescribed kind not being a hospital in which services are provided by medical practitioners (whether or not any services are also provided for the purposes of the establishment or elsewhere). But an establishment in which, or for the purposes of which, services are provided by medical practitioners in pursuance of the National Health Service Act 1977 is not an independent clinic (Care Standards Act 2000, s 2(4)). The following kinds of establishments are prescribed:

    (a) a walk-in centre, in which one or more medical practitioners provide services of a kind which, if provided in pursuance of the NHS Act, would be provided as general medical services under Part II of that Act; and

    (b) a surgery or consulting room in which a medical practitioner who provides no services in pursuance of the NHS Act provides medical services of any kind (including psychiatric treatment) otherwise than under arrangements made on behalf of the patients by their employer or another person (The Private and Voluntary Health Care (England) Regulations 2001, SI 2001 No 3968, reg 4(1)).

'independent medical agency, means an undertaking (not being an independent clinic) which consists of or includes the provision of services by medical practitioners. But if any of the services are provided for the purposes of an independent clinic, or by medical practitioners in pursuance of the National Health Service Act 1977, it is not an independent medical agency (Care Standards Act 2000, s 2(5)).

Many people with mental disorders are accommodated in privately-run accommodation, which has many of the characteristics of a hospital. These range from institutions that provide the same type of environment as an ordinary hospital offering facilities to care and treat people with mental disorders to specialized accommodation meeting the needs of particular clients, including those who need fairly high levels of security. People with mental disorders may also regularly access other care environments that are not run by the NHS and these are also captured by the definitions above. The coverage is not limited to residential accommodation but includes private and NHS surgeries and out-patient clinics, etc.

6.4.3.3 *Provision of care, assistance, or services*
Section 42(4) provides that a person cares for another person as follows.

[I]f A, (a) is, whether or not in the course of employment, a provider of care, assistance, or services to B in connection with B's mental disorder, and (b) as such, has had or is likely to have regular face-to-face contact with B.

In the first two definitions, there was a requirement that A be an employee. That is not a requirement here. So, non-paid carers are covered by the legislation. Also included are those working with homeless people in a hostel and those providing day-care services (Lord Falconer, HL Debs 28 April 2003, col 548). The words 'assistance' and 'services' mean that a wide range of helpers will be covered and will include advocates and supervisors (Lord Falconer, HL Debs 28 April 2003, col 548). It should, though, exclude such people as taxi drivers as they do not provide their services normally 'in connection with B's mental disorder'.

6.4.3.4 *Regular face-to-face contact*
It is a factual question for the jury or magistrates to decide as to whether A has 'regular face-to-face contact with B'. If cleaners and caretakers have no face-to-face contact with B on a regular basis, then they are excluded. But cleaners and caretakers will work in different ways in different places, and many will have regular face-to-face contact, and so may, in this context, be covered by the legislation. It is not unknown for persons in such roles to be abusers. Thus, the range of care workers is not limited to professionals and others providing direct care to a person with a mental disorder. Further, the phrasing makes it clear that it is sufficient if A is likely to be in regular face-to-face contact. This was introduced to ensure that care workers abusing their position on the first time of meeting would be caught by these offences (Lord Falconer, HL Debs 28 April 2003, col 547).

6.4.4 Knowledge of mental disorder

A must also '[know] or could reasonably be expected to know that B has a mental disorder' (s 38(1)(d), s 39(1)(d), s 40(1)(e), and s 41(1)(d)). This provision must be read in conjunction with the following provision which appears in each offence.

Where in proceedings for an offence under this section it is proved that the other person had a mental disorder, it is to be taken that the defendant knew or could reasonably have been expected to know that that person had a mental disorder unless sufficient evidence is adduced to raise an issue as to whether he knew or could reasonably have been expected to know it (s 38(2), s 39(2), s 40(2), and s 41(2)).

Thus, the defendant will not be guilty if he has no knowledge of B's mental disorder. This is appropriate given the wide range of persons who may be care workers. Also, it ensures that persons such as taxi-drivers and shopkeepers will not ordinarily be caught by these offences. The imposition of the evidential burden upon the defendant is appropriate. It will involve the raising of evidence to challenge the presumption of knowledge. This will rarely be successfully achieved where the defendant is a professional carer, since he will know B's diagnosis. The most likely case where there will be a successful claim is where the care worker is a non-professional and especially where he is providing voluntary services. The Government took the view that this approach would be consistent with the European Convention on Human Rights and its concerns about reverse burdens of proof, including the use of presumptions that might lead to guilt, at least with respect to one or more element of an offence (see, e.g., Lord Falconer at HL Debates 28 April 2003, col 529).

6.4.5 Other elements of the offences

Otherwise, the actus reus elements of the offences, i.e, engaging in sexual activity, causing or inciting sexual activity, sexual activity in the presence of a person with a mental disorder, and causing a person to watch a sexual act, mirror those considered in the first set of offences in terms of the activity undertaken by A.

6.4.6 Sentence

The maxima take one of two approaches.

(a) For the offences contrary to s 38 and s 39 and where penetration occurs, a maximum of 14 years imprisonment is available in the most serious cases (s 38(3), s 39(3)). Otherwise, the offence is triable either way and, on summary conviction, imprisonment for a term not exceeding 6 months or a fine not exceeding the statutory maximum, or both, or, on conviction on indictment, imprisonment for a term not exceeding 10 years (s 38(4) and s 39(4)),

(b) The offences contrary to s 40 and s 41 are triable either way and, on summary conviction, imprisonment for a term not exceeding 6 months or a fine not exceeding the statutory maximum, or both, or, on conviction on indictment, imprisonment for a term not exceeding 7 years (s 40(3) and s 41(3)).

The explanation for the difference is a perceived greater level of harm where the care worker's activity is either sexual activity involving penetration with a person with mental disorder (s 38) or causing or inciting another in sexual activity with a person with mental disorder (s 39) than where the care worker engages in sexual activity in the presence of a person with a mental disorder (s 40) or causes a person with a mental disorder to watch a sexual act (s 41).

6.4.7 Exceptions to the offences

There are two sets of circumstances in which no care worker offence is committed which reflect the defences available in relation to abuse of position of trust (see ch 5).

6.4.7.1 *The marriage exception*

No offence under ss 38–41 can be committed by A where he is lawfully married to B and the burden of proving that marriage is on A (s 43(1),(2)). As the offences can cover voluntary care arrangements, it is not surprising that this provision appears. Of course, any offence that can be committed within marriage can be committed by A. The difference is that the care worker offences apply regardless of the consent or capacity of B, whereas the within marriage offences, such as rape, rely upon establishing that B did not consent.

6.4.7.2 *The pre-existing relationship exception*

A commits no offence 'if, immediately before A became involved in B's care . . ., a sexual relationship existed between A and B' (s 44(1)), but that cannot apply where 'sexual intercourse between A and B would have been unlawful' (s 44(2)). The most likely examples would be where one of an unmarried couple or sexual partners acquires a mental illness or becomes senile. A has the burden of establishing that such a relationship existed at the time (s 44(3)). The burdens imposed by both exceptions on the defendant are likely to be able to withstand challenge under Article 6(2) of the European Convention on Human Rights primarily on the basis that the evidence is peculiarly within the knowledge of and is easily proved by the defendant (though proof of the second exception is much harder than the first and so might less easily sustain a challenge), and also that the policy issue of protecting those vulnerable people within care from sexual abuse demands that the burden in this part of the offence be upon the defendant.

6.5 CONCLUSION

In combination with the recent reforms in the law of evidence and changes introduced in practice and procedure through training and education, these substantive offences are likely to produce a much better balance of the need to protect the rights of vulnerable persons to understand and exercise their sexuality with their right to be protected by the law from sexual abuse and exploitation.

7

FAMILIAL SEXUAL OFFENCES

7.1 INTRODUCTION

Sexual intercourse between close relatives has long been regarded as taboo in our society. In fact, most societies disapprove of such behaviour but surprisingly incest was not made a criminal offence in this country until 1908. Prior to that date it was dealt with by the canon law and ecclesiastical courts as a moral issue, the punishment for which was normally a penance. Before the SOA 2003 was enacted, the crime of incest was set out in ss 10–11 SOA 1956 but was little used. Few prosecutions took place and the number of prosecutions was falling. Home Office figures quoted in the Review show that in 1987 184 males were proceeded against but by 1997 this figure had fallen to 25. Prosecutions against females were even rarer. The figure for 1987 was only six and in 1997 just one (*Setting the Boundaries*, para 5.2.3). This was partly because the consent of the Director of Public Prosecutions was needed before a prosecution could be commenced but also because other charges, such as rape or USI, could be laid instead. Nevertheless, the charge of incest was sometimes useful to prosecutors. It could be used in child abuse situations where there were problems of proof in relation to other offences because consent was irrelevant to incest.

However, there were a number of problems relating to the old law, which was seriously in need of updating. In fact, the Review considered whether such an offence was needed at all and this is even more an issue now that the Act has created a number of new child sex offences, which have been outlined in Chapters 4 to 5. The arguments for retaining the offence of incest fall into three main categories. The first is the eugenics argument. This argument relies on the biological risks of inbreeding but it is doubtful whether this reason in itself would justify criminalization. After all, it is not illegal for people who carry genetic defects to have children. The Review concluded that the eugenic argument was not significant when considering whether an offence of incest should be retained. The reasons preferred by the Review were twofold; that the offence constitutes a breach of trust and an abuse of power by one family member over a more vulnerable member and that there is a need to express society's disapproval of certain behaviour within families. Nevertheless, it was acknowledged that the existing offences needed to be updated to reflect in particular the looser structures of modern families. The result is that the old incest offences contained in ss 10–11 SOA 1956 have been repealed and replaced with a number of new offences, some dealing specifically with children and some with adults.

The Review also recommended that the word 'incest' should not be used in any new offence because of the stigma attached to it. This was because of the perception that the behaviour was consensual and the parties complicit, whereas in reality, there was often a victim who was being abused by another. This recommendation has been followed and the word 'incest' does not appear anywhere in the Act. However, it is doubtful whether the word will fall out of use, since the alternative expressions used in the Act are too long-winded to be used easily in conversation or writing.

7.2 EXISTING PROVISIONS

The SOA 1956 contained two offences relating to incest. The first in s 10 made it an offence for a man to have sexual intercourse with a woman he knows to be his granddaughter, daughter, sister, or mother. The second in s 11 made it an offence for a woman of the age of 16 or over to permit a man whom she knows to be her grandfather, father, brother, or son to have sexual intercourse with her. The first thing, which is immediately obvious, is that these offences made no distinction between sexual intercourse with children or with adults. A 45 year-old father who had sexual intercourse with his 14 year-old daughter would be guilty of the same offence as a brother and sister in their 20s (although the father could also be charged with USI). The maximum penalty in each case was 7 years imprisonment (life if a girl was under 13).

Another problem was that certain relationships were not criminalized. It was not an offence under s 10 for a male to have sexual intercourse with his grandmother and it was not an offence under s11 for a woman to have sexual intercourse with her grandson. The reasons for this are unclear but are generally perceived to be related to a woman's capacity to conceive. If, however, the reason for the offence was to control abuse of power rather than eugenics, there is no logical reason why these relationships should not be prohibited. The old offences only dealt with vaginal sexual intercourse, not other forms of sexual behaviour. This meant that homosexual behaviour was not covered at all. Again, if the reason for the offence is abuse of trust and power it would make more sense to cover a wider range of sexual activity. In both the old offences the words 'brother' and 'sister' were defined to include half-brothers and sisters but not adopted children, or step-children.

The first major difference between the new law and the old is that the Act introduces completely separate offences dealing with children and adults and there are substantial differences between them. The new law also attempts to reflect the changing nature of family structures by including, in the offences relating to children, some more distant relatives who are likely to be in a position of control or trust in relation to the child. Finally, the new law is much wider in application than the old in that a wide range of sexual behaviour is covered, not just vaginal sexual intercourse. For the purposes of the new offences a child is someone under 18, not 16 years.

7.3 OFFENCES RELATING TO CHILDREN

Sections 25 to 26 create two new offences, sexual activity with a child family member and inciting a child family member to engage in sexual activity.

7.3.1 Sexual activity with a child family member

Section 25 provides that:

A commits an offence if—

he intentionally touches another person B

the touching is sexual

the relation of A to B is within section 27

A knows or could reasonably be expected to know that his relation to B falls within that section and

B is under 18 and A does not reasonably believe that B is 18 or over or

B is under 13.

The maximum penalty depends on the age of the offender and the type of sexual touching (see below). The offence is completely gender-neutral and can therefore be committed by a woman or a man with a boy or a girl. It would cover all forms of sexual activity involving physical contact. 'Touching' is widely defined in s 79(8) to include touching 'with any part of the body, with anything else, through anything' and specifically includes penetration. 'Sexual' is defined in s 78, as has already been discussed in Chapter 3. It is therefore immediately obvious that this offence is much wider than the old incest offences, which only dealt with vaginal sexual intercourse and made no provision for same sex contact at all. Consent is still irrelevant.

There is a question of whether this offence is necessary, bearing in mind the range of new offences relating to child sexual abuse which have been discussed in Chapter 4.

Consent is also irrelevant to those offences and so it is difficult to see why an additional offence of sexual activity with a child family member is necessary. The Review considered that an offence relating to incest was needed in addition to the child sex offences in order to express society's disapproval of certain sexual relationships within a family. It should also be noted that the offences in ss 25 to 26 can be committed until the child is 18 years old, whereas the child sex offences discussed in Chapter 4 relate to children under the age of 16 years.

The existence of the offence under s 25 also raises the question of how someone who has engaged in sexual intercourse with a child family member under the age of 13 should be charged. In relation to abuse of such a child by someone who was not a family member, statutory rape would have to be charged under s 5 as there is no alternative offence. But in the case of a family member the lesser offence of sexual intercourse with a child family member could be charged instead. The Review envisaged that rape would always be charged where a child under the age of 13 is concerned and the perpetrator is an adult but the Act does not expressly specify this. It is therefore possible that the lesser offence under s 25 could be charged instead, particularly where the offender is a young person. For example, if a 13 year-old boy had sexual intercourse with his 12 year-old sister and there was factual consent, would he be charged with rape or with sexual activity with a child family member? The maximum penalty for rape of a child under 13 years-old under s 5 is life imprisonment but under s 25 the maximum penalty for an offender under the age of 18 years is 5 years imprisonment.

7.3.2 Relevant family relationships

Section 27 sets out the relevant relationships for this offence and again, they are much wider than under the old law of incest. Close blood relatives are included but people who are not related by blood to the child are also covered in specific circumstances. The family members specified are parents, grandparents, brothers, sisters, half-brothers and sisters, aunts, or uncles (s 27(2)). The inclusion of aunt or uncle reflects the recommendation of the Review, which noted that relationships between uncles and nieces are not uncommon (NSPCC submission to the Review, March 1999). 'Aunt' and 'uncle' are defined to be blood relatives, not aunts and uncles by marriage (s 27(5)). If the Review's reason for keeping and extending this offence was not eugenic, but a matter of abuse of family power, it is difficult to see why aunts or uncles by marriage should not also be included. However, the Review did make the comment that blood relatives 'are in a particular position of trust to their nieces and nephews' and this seems to be the reason for including them while excluding aunts and uncles related by marriage only (*Setting the Boundaries,* para 5.5.13).

In addition to more distant relatives, foster parents are included for the first time (s 27(2)(b)). Anyone who is or *has been* a foster parent of the child is included, so while the child is under 18 no sexual touching may take place, even if A is no longer

B's foster parent. There are no time limits, so even temporary foster carers would be included.

Section 27(3) widens the pool of potential family members who can commit an offence even more: step-parents, cousins (the child of an aunt or uncle), step-brothers and sisters, and foster siblings all come within the prohibited degree of relationship 'if A or B live or have lived in the same household, or A has been regularly involved in caring for, training, supervising, or being in sole charge of B'. Cousins would therefore commit an offence if they had at any time lived in the same household together but not if they had not. The Act does not specify any length of time for which they must have lived in the same household so on the face of it, if two cousins lived together when they were very young, even temporarily, an offence would be committed if they later engaged in a sexual relationship while one was under the age of 18 years. This would be the case even if they had not lived together for some time. Cousins can legally marry and there is a defence of marriage (see below) but if they had lived in the same household *before* marriage, they would have to refrain from sexual intercourse to avoid committing an offence, even after they were engaged, and until such time as they were legally married. Step-parent is defined to include a parent's partner and a person is another's partner if they 'live together as partners in an enduring family relationship' (s 27(5)(d), (e)). The phrase 'enduring family relationship' is not defined anywhere in the Act and so raises the question of how long a relationship has to last for it to be regarded as enduring. Would a few months be enough, or would it depend not on time but on an intention that the relationship should be permanent? The purpose of including such people is obviously to cover cohabitees who are not married. Same-sex relationships are expressly included by s 27(5)(d).

Adoptive relationships are also covered by s 27 since an adopted child is regarded as a child of their adopted parents under s 74 Adoption and Children Act 2002 but s 27(1)(b) goes further and provides that the adoptive child's biological family relationships are also covered by the offence. For example, the brother of an adopted child's biological mother would be regarded as an uncle and so is within the prohibited degrees of relationship.

Section 27(4) goes on to widen the categories of people who may commit an offence under this section even more by providing that A will commit the offence if

A and B live in the same household and

A is regularly involved in caring for, training, supervising, or being in sole charge of B.

This provision is wide enough to cover not only more distant family members (including aunts and uncles by marriage) but also carers such as nannies or au pairs who are looking after the child, provided they live in the same household. The Explanatory Notes to the Act specifically mention that this is in fact the intention of the section. In this case, however, the relationship would no longer be 'relevant' once the carer left the household or ceased to be involved in the care of the child. This means that an au pair who has a sexual relationship with a 17 year-old male member of the family she is working for could be guilty of an offence, even if she is the same age as he is (the offence may be committed by those under 18 years, as well as adults). The prosecution would need to show that she was regularly involved in caring for him but neither the Act nor the Explanatory Notes give any indication of what is meant by this phrase. Would she be regularly involved in his care if she cooked for him, washed and ironed his clothes, and cleaned his bedroom, for example?

7.3.3 Inciting a child family member to engage in sexual activity

Section 26 makes it an offence for a person to intentionally incite a child family member to touch or allow himself to be touched where the touching is sexual. This section replaces s 54 Criminal Law Act 1977 (inciting a girl under 16 to have incestuous sexual intercourse). Section 26 provides that

A commits an offence if

he intentionally incites another person B to touch, or allows himself to be touched by A

the touching is sexual

the relation of A to B is within section 27

A knows or could reasonably be expected to know that his relation to B is of a description falling within that section, and

either B is under 18 and A does not reasonably believe that B is 18 or over, or

B is under 13.

This offence is also completely gender-neutral and the prohibited family relationships are the same as for the offence under s 25. This offence is intended to cover a situation where, for example, a child is encouraged to masturbate a family member or where a child is persuaded to engage in sexual activity with a family member but the actual activity does not take place, perhaps because a third person enters the room and intervenes. The mens rea is the intention to incite the other person to touch. No actual touching has to take place for the offence to be complete. The other elements of the offence are the same as the s 25 offence. Again, it should be noted that this offence can be committed by an adult or a child who is over the age of criminal responsibility. Consent is again irrelevant. Penalties, which depend on the age of the offender, are discussed below.

7.3.4 Presumptions

The burden of proof is on the prosecution to prove all the elements of both ss 25 and 26. However, in both cases there are presumptions that can be rebutted by D adducing sufficient evidence. The first concerns the age of the child. Sections 25(2) and 26(2) provide that where the prosecution proves the child was under 18 years, D is taken not to have reasonably believed that the child was over 18 years unless he adduces sufficient evidence to this effect. In other words, there is a presumption that he did not reasonably believe the child was over 18 years that can be rebutted by evidence adduced by D. This could apply where an adult family member has lost touch with the family and has not seen the child for many years and so may not know the child's exact age. There is no question of reasonable belief if the child is under 13 years.

There is also a presumption that D knew, or could reasonably be expected to know, of the relevant relationship between the parties unless D can adduce sufficient evidence to rebut that presumption (ss 25(3) and 26(3)). This could apply in a situation where an adoptive child does not know their biological family and enters into a sexual relationship with someone who they later find out is actually related to them.

7.3.5 Defences

There are two potential defences to the offences contained in ss 25 and 26, which are similar to the defences relating to abuse of position of trust (ch 5). The first relates to marriage and the second to sexual relationships which pre-date family relationships.

7.3.5.1 *Defence of lawful marriage*
D may claim a defence where A and B were lawfully married at the time of the conduct which would otherwise be an offence (s 28). This is a defence that could not have applied under the old law on incest as the prohibited relationships under the SOA 1956 were also prohibited for the purpose of marriage because of consanguinity. However, now that the offence covers a much wider range of relationships it is not surprising that a defence of marriage should be included. For example, adoptive siblings can marry, as can cousins. The burden of proof is on the defendant to show that the parties were lawfully married at the time.

7.3.5.2 *Relationships that pre-date position of trust*
The defence of a sexual relationship which pre-dates the familial relationship is set out in s 29. The relevant relationships included in s 27 are so wide that it is not difficult to imagine situations arising where someone could have a pre-existing sexual relationship with another person who later became a member of their family through marriage or cohabitation. The defence does not apply to the family relationships set out in s 27(2) (whether the relationships are by blood or adoption). It is therefore confined to situations of more distant family relationships where the parties lived in the same household or one party was involved in the care of the other. For example, a man who had a sexual relationship with his 16 year-old female cousin would not be guilty of an offence under s 25 if he later moved into the family home and therefore came within the prohibited relationships in s 27(3). The Explanatory Notes also give the example of two divorced adults whose 16 and 17 year-old children are having a sexual relationship. If the adults

meet and subsequently marry so that they all live in the same household the young people would not be guilty of an offence, even though they become step-siblings and live in the same household. The defence is limited to situations where the pre-existing sexual relationship was lawful, so it would not apply if the female cousin was under 16 years at the time of the pre-existing sexual relationship (s 27(2)). The burden of proof is on the defendant to show on a balance of probabilities that the elements of the defence are made out.

7.3.6 Penalties

The penalties are the same for the two offences of sexual activity with a child family member and inciting a child family member to engage in sexual activity. In each case, a person guilty of an offence who is aged 18 years or over is liable to 14 years imprisonment on indictment where the sexual activity involves penetration. Where the activity does not involve penetration the offence is triable summarily or on indictment, again with a maximum penalty of 14 years on indictment and only 6 months if tried summarily. A person who is under 18 years is liable on summary conviction to a fine or a term of imprisonment of up to 6 months or on conviction on indictment to imprisonment for a term not exceeding 5 years.

The maximum penalty for the old incest offences was 7 years imprisonment (life if a girl was under 13 years) and so the sentencing guidelines will need to be reviewed. However, the principles established in the cases on sentencing for incest will no doubt still be relevant. In *AG's Reference (No 4 of 1989)* [1990] 1 WLR 41 the Court of Appeal had to consider a sentence of 18 months imprisonment suspended for 2 years which had been imposed on a father who had pleaded guilty to incest and indecent assault on his daughter, who was aged 13 and 15 at the time of the offences. The court quashed the sentence and replaced it with a probation order for 3 years. Although this seems lenient in the light of more recent cases (see, for example, *R v H (Colin L)* [2002] EWCA Crim 2149 and *R v ITD* [2003] EWCA Crim 805) the court did emphasize that the case was exceptional and that the probation order was in the best interests of the offender and the whole family. The matters which the court thought it proper to take into account were:

(a) the age of the child when the offences were committed,

(b) the family relationships, which the court described as 'far from conducive to normal emotional development',

(c) the interest of the victim; a more severe sentence could further alienate the victim from her family,

(d) mitigating factors such as a guilty plea, the offender's good conduct and character,

(e) the risk of repetition of the offence, which was considered unlikely in the case before the court.

These guidelines may have to be revisited in the light of the new offences but the broad principles considered by the court will probably still be appropriate.

7.4 OFFENCES RELATING TO ADULTS

Different considerations apply to related adults who engage in a sexual relationship. It could be argued that adults are less likely to be abused by other family members since they are far more able to reject pressure for sexual activity in a situation where a child would find this difficult. The eugenics argument would still apply, however, but as already pointed out the Review did not regard this argument as crucial to the debate. There have been many arguments put forward by academics that an offence relating to incest among adults is not necessary. Most of these have revolved around the idea that adults should be able to indulge in consensual sexual activity without the interference of the criminal law. In addition, generally such activity is not harmful to society as a whole and is no threat to anyone else (for a comprehensive review of the arguments see J. Temkin, 'Do we need the crime of incest?', *Current Legal Problems* (1991), vol 44, 185). The Criminal Law Revision Committee considered the issue in 1984 and although it concluded that the crime of incest was still needed it did recommend that sibling incest should cease to be an offence once the parties were over the age of 21 years (Fifteenth Report, Sexual Offences (1984), Cmnd 9213, para 8.22). The Review, however, rejected this view, pointing out that many of these relationships begin when one of the parties is a child and that they often reflect a long term abuse of power within a family. Many adult incestuous relationships arise as a result of grooming and pressure from an older family member during childhood and therefore cannot be regarded as genuinely consensual. For example, in August 2003 it was reported that a man who had fathered six children by his own daughter was jailed. The daughter was aged 31 when the case was heard and had her first child when she was 19 years-old. She was reported as saying that her father had started indecently assaulting her when she was 8 years-old and that he had used emotional blackmail to continue the abuse when she became an adult. She was also worried that her father would leave home if she revealed the abuse, thus highlighting the invidious position of such individuals (BBC News website, 19 August 2003). The Act therefore includes two offences relating to adult family members, although they are substantially different from the offences relating to children.

7.4.1 Offences involving adult relatives

Sections 64 to 65 create two new offences, the first relating to penetrative sex with an adult relative and the second dealing with consensual penetration by an adult relative.

Section 64 provides that A commits an offence if:

he intentionally penetrates another person's vagina or anus with a part of his body or anything else, or penetrates another person's mouth with his penis,

the penetration is sexual

the other person B is aged 18 or over

A is related to B in a way mentioned in subsection (2), and

A knows or could reasonably be expected to know that he is related to B in that way.

Section 65 provides that:

A, aged 16 or over commits an offence if

another person, B penetrates A's vagina or anus with a part of B's body or anything else, or penetrates A's mouth with B's penis

A consents to the penetration

the penetration is sexual

B is aged 18 or over

A is related to B in a way mentioned in subsection (2) and

A knows or could reasonably be expected to know that he is related to B in that way.

Consent is not a defence to either offence. Both sections are gender-neutral, which means that the offences can cover homosexual as well as heterosexual acts, provided the sexual activity falls within the required penetrative acts. The Review expressed some concern at the possibility that making the passive partner criminally liable under s 65 would discourage victims from coming forward. Potentially, a woman who was sexually abused in childhood could be later prosecuted for continuing that relationship into adulthood. However, the Review acknowledged that it must be for the police and the CPS to examine the facts of each case and exercise their discretion in order to determine who was the instigator of an act and who should therefore be prosecuted.

7.4.2 The prohibited degrees of relationship

The prohibited degrees of relationship are the same for both offences. 'A' may be related to 'B' as parent, grandparent, child, grandchild, brother, sister, half-brother, half-sister, uncle, aunt, nephew, or niece (ss 64(2), 65(2)). 'Aunt' and 'uncle' are defined to mean the sister or brother of a parent (ss 64(3), 65(3)). The offence therefore applies to blood relatives only, not relatives by marriage. This is understandable if the reason for the offence is eugenic. If, however, the reason for creating the offence is to address long-term abuse of power within a family, then surely aunts and uncles by marriage should also be included. Under the old law of incest, uncles and aunts were not included at all but the Marriage Act 1949 does not allow uncles and aunts to marry their nieces and nephews. This meant that under the old law an uncle could have a sexual relationship with a niece who was over 16 years without committing an offence but he could not marry her. Thus these new offences are at least consistent with our marriage laws.

Unlike the offences relating to children in ss 25 and 26, adopted relationships are not included within the prohibited relationships. Sch 6, para 47 of the Act amends the Adoption and Children Act 2002 to exclude these relationships. Again, there seems to be some confusion here about the underlying rationale for the offence. Excluding adoptive relationships seems to recognize the eugenic arguments only and not those based on abuse of power within a family.

7.4.3 Acts of penetration

Unlike the offences relating to children these adult offences deal only with penetrative acts. However, their ambit is much wider than just vaginal or anal sexual intercourse. Oral sex is included, as is penetration of the anus or vagina with an object or any part of the body, such as a finger, or tongue (reflecting the s 2 offence of assault by penetration, see ch 3). Sexual acts that do not involve penetration are not caught by the provision. For example, an adult woman who masturbates her adult son will not be guilty of an offence. If, however, they engage in oral sex, both will be guilty of an offence; the man by virtue of s 64 because he penetrates her mouth with his penis, the woman under s 65 because she allows her mouth to be penetrated by his penis. The penetration does have to be sexual (defined in s 78) so an offence would not be committed where a family member had to help another with a medical procedure which involved penetration, such as inserting a pessary.

7.4.4 Age requirements

Both offences can be committed by anyone who is aged 16 years or over. The other person involved in the act must be over 18 years. If the 'offender' is under 16 years then s/he cannot be charged with either of these two offences. The purpose here is to make the older party liable and the assumption is that the younger party is in the more vulnerable position. It is also to ensure that where those under the age of 18 years are involved the more serious offences relating to children are charged. For example, if a 16 year-old girl agrees to have sexual intercourse with her 18 year-old brother, she will be guilty of an offence under s 65, for which the maximum penalty is 2 years imprisonment. She would commit no offence if aged under 16 years. He will not be guilty of an offence under s 64, but he will be guilty of the much more serious offence of sexual activity with a child family member under s 25, which is punishable by up to 14 years imprisonment because he is over 18 years-old. If she was aged 16 years and he was aged 17 years, both would commit an offence under s 25 (sexual activity with a child family member) since both are under 18 years and there is no age requirement for an offender under that section. These age requirements therefore give rise to the strange effect that those aged under 16 years cannot be charged with sex with an adult relative but can be charged with the more serious offences relating to children provided in ss 25 to 26, which also cover a much wider range of sexual activity.

7.4.5 Knowledge of relationship

The prosecution must prove that A knew, or could reasonably be expected to know, that he is related to B in the proscribed way. It is presumed that A does know, or could reasonably be expected to know, that B is a relative, unless he adduces sufficient evidence to show otherwise. This might arise in a situation where A and B were siblings who were separated at an early age (and perhaps adopted by different families) and they did not discover that they were related until after they had entered into a sexual relationship. Once they discover the truth, however, they will be committing an offence if the relationship continues. This could be criticized as unduly harsh if by this time A and B had established a committed relationship. In 1997, The Times reported the story of a Spanish couple who were brother and sister but had been brought up separately. They met and fell in love as adults and had been living together with their two children for 18 years. When they found out about their relationship they said that they found it impossible to part (The Times, 4 April 1997). Such relationships are obviously rare but for a couple in this situation the combined result of ss 64 and 65 appears to be that their family must separate once they know that they are related.

7.4.6 Penalties

The penalties for the offences under ss 64 to 65 are substantially lower than those for the offences relating to children. Both offences are punishable by a fine or 6 months imprisonment if there is summary conviction and up to 2 years imprisonment on indictment.

7.5 CONCLUSION

The new offences relating to sex with a child family member are far more wide-ranging than the old offences of incest. The penalties are also more severe. By extending the definition of a family to include more distant relatives, and even those who are not related to the child, the Act has fulfilled the stated objective of the Review, which was to take into account the looser structure of modern families. The separation of offences relating to adults and children is to be welcomed. However, the various age requirements contained in these offences can be confusing and sometimes give rise to illogical results. There also seems to be some confusion about the underlying purpose of the offences, especially the ones relating to adult family members, which sometimes seem to be based on the eugenics arguments but on occasion are more concerned with the abuse of power within a family. Nevertheless, the new offences are an improvement on the old law relating to incest, which failed to address a number of serious issues of sexual abuse within families.

8

SEXUAL EXPLOITATION:
CHILD PORNOGRAPHY, TRAFFICKING,
AND PROSTITUTION

8.1 INTRODUCTION

This chapter will deal with offences relating to certain aspects of sexual exploitation, primarily the control of prostitution relating to adults and children, and child pornography. The Act deals with these two separate types of exploitation in the same part and, in some cases, regarding the offences relating to child pornography and prostitution, within the same sections, so it is difficult to separate them without much repetition of information. The justification for dealing with these two different types of behaviour together in this way is that the basic philosophy of the Act, i.e., to protect the vulnerable from exploitation, applies in both cases. In addition, the same elements apply to what in practice would be very different offences. The Act also amends the law relating to adult prostitution, creating a number of new offences which are similar, but subtly different, from the child prostitution offences.

8.2 INDECENT PHOTOGRAPHS OF CHILDREN

Public concern about, and media coverage of, the availability of child pornography on the Internet made it inevitable that the law would be amended. The National

Criminal Intelligence Service (NCIS), which works on behalf of all UK law enforcement agencies, has been involved in a number of high profile international child pornography operations in the last few years. One of the most infamous of these was Operation Cathedral, which culminated in a number of convictions of members of 'The Wonderland Club', an international paedophile ring. Police forces in the United States, the UK and other European countries worked together, resulting in the arrest of 107 people, eight of whom were British. Each member of the club was personally required to contribute 10,000 indecent photographs of children, which were then encrypted and exchanged on the Internet. Detective Superintendent Peter Spindler of NCIS stated that three quarters of a million paedophilic images had been retrieved (BBC News website,10 January 2001). The NSPCC has recently published a review of child pornography, which found that 140,000 images of child sexual abuse were posted on the Internet in one six-week period. Christine Atkinson, NSPCC Policy Advisor, has said that 'child pornography is instrumental in the sexual abuse of children within prostitution, sex rings and trafficking' (see The Devastating Impact of Child Pornography, 8 October 2003, www.nspcc.org.uk).

Rather than repealing the existing law and replacing it with a range of new offences, the Act amends existing statutory provisions, mainly by raising the age at which someone is considered to be a child. A child is now considered to be anyone up to the age of 18 years. This is presumably in recognition of the fact that those over the age of 16 years can still be vulnerable to abuse but this could also be said to be something of an over-reaction to public concern about paedophilia.

8.2.1 Existing provisions

The existing provisions are contained in the Protection of Children Act 1978 (PCA 1978) and the Criminal Justice Act 1988 (CJA 1988). The SOA 2003 amends both of these Acts, rather than replacing them, hence it is necessary to look at several of these statutory provisions in order to examine the new law relating to indecent photographs of children.

Section 1 PCA 1978 provides that:

1(1) It is an offence for a person—

(a) to take, or permit to be taken, or to make any indecent photograph or pseudo-photograph of a child; or

(b) to distribute or show such indecent photographs or pseudo-photographs; or

(c) to have in his possession such indecent photographs, or pseudo-photographs with a view to their being distributed or shown by himself or others; or

(d) to publish or cause to be published any advertisement likely to be understood as conveying that the advertiser distributes or shows such indecent photographs or pseudo-photographs, or intends to do so.

A 'pseudo-photograph' is defined in s 7 PCA 1978 as 'an image, whether made by computer-graphics or otherwise howsoever which appears to be a photograph'.

'Photograph' includes 'data stored on a computer disc or by other electronic means which is capable of conversion into a photograph'.

For the purposes of the PCA 1978 a child was originally a person under the age of 16 years. Section 7(8) PCA 1978 provides that where the impression conveyed by a pseudo-photograph is that the person is a child, then it is deemed to be a child even if some of the characteristics shown are those of an adult. In *R v Land* [1998] Crim LR 70 the Court of Appeal held that it was a matter for the jury to decide whether an unknown person depicted in an indecent photograph was a child. The PCA 1978 did not provide for an offence of possession and so was reinforced by s 160 CJA 1988 which provides that

It is an offence for a person to have any indecent photograph of a child in his possession.

Mere possession of an indecent photograph of a child is therefore an offence, although knowledge is an essential element of the mens rea, see *Atkins v DPP* [2000] 2 All ER 425. Again, under the CJA 1988 a child originally meant a person under the age of 16 years.

8.2.2 The meaning of 'indecent'

There has been some ambiguity in the past concerning the meaning of 'indecent' for the purposes of both the PCA 1978 and the CJA 1988 but it is now clear that it is not construed as having the same meaning as the word 'obscene' for the purpose of the Obscene Publications Act 1959. In *R v Stanley* [1965] 2 QB 327 Lord Parker CJ said that the words 'indecent' and 'obscene' 'convey one idea, namely offending against the recognized standards of propriety, indecent being at the lower end of the scale and obscene at the upper end of the scale'. It is also clear that the question of whether a photograph of a child is indecent is a matter for the jury (*R v Graham Kerr* [1988] 1 WLR 1098). The jury will of course know the age of the child, as age is an essential element of the offence, and in *R v Owen* [1988] 1WLR 134 it was held that the age of the child is something the jury is entitled to take into account when deciding the question 'is this an indecent photograph of a child?'. That case concerned a professional photographer who took a series of photographs of a 14 year-old girl who wanted to be a model. A few of the photographs showed her with bare breasts. At the trial the photographer originally pleaded not guilty, arguing that the photograph was not indecent per se. However, when the judge ruled that the jury were entitled to take into account the age of the girl, he changed his plea to guilty, apparently accepting that such a photograph of a 14 year-old would be indecent even though such a photograph of an adult would not.

8.2.3 Changes to the existing law

Section 45 SOA 2003 amends both the PCA 1978 and the CJA 1988 in a number of ways while retaining the basic provisions. The main change is that the age under which someone is regarded as a child is raised from 16 to 18 years thus extending the law's remit to situations not previously prohibited. This raises some interesting questions. The age at which both boys and girls can consent to sexual intercourse is generally 16 but this change in the law effectively means that they cannot consent to an indecent photograph being taken (subject to the defences mentioned below). This means that 16 or 17 year-old models would not be able to work in the so-called 'glamour' industry without their photographer or distributor running the risk of prosecution, as happened in *Owen*. Of course, any photograph taken would have to be indecent, which raises a further question about whether a jury would regard a semi-nude photograph of a 16 year-old 'child' as indecent in circumstances where such a photograph of someone over the age of 18 years would not be deemed indecent. For example, would a jury regard a topless photograph of a 16 year-old girl as indecent, bearing in mind that the Act now regards a girl of that age as a child? Since the jury is entitled to take into account the age of the child when deciding this issue, it is not only possible but perhaps probable that glamour photographs of 16 year-olds may be deemed to be indecent. The objective of the change, to protect children from exploitation, is admirable but it seems curious that it is regarded as more harmful for a 16 year-old to have a photograph taken than for her to have sexual intercourse.

8.2.4 The defences

There are two different types of defences contained in the Act. The first, contained in s 45 applies in the case of marriage and other relationships and the second, in s 46 relates to criminal proceedings and investigations.

8.2.4.1 *Marriage and other relationships*
Section 45 provides a defence to some of the offences contained in s 1 PCA 1978 and to the offence contained in s 160 CJA 1988. The wording of the section is difficult to follow but the main defence is basically one of consent, or of reasonable belief in consent, but it only applies if the defendant can prove that certain conditions are satisfied. The conditions are:

(i)   that the child was over 16 at the time the photograph was taken and

(ii)   that at the time of the offence the child and he were married or living as partners in an enduring family relationship and

(iii)   that the photograph showed the child alone or with the defendant but not with anyone else.

It should be noted that although the SOA 2003 uses the word 'child', for the purpose of the defences in ss 45 and 46, a child is someone who is at least 16 years old but under 18 years. Provided that the three conditions above are satisfied, D is not guilty of an offence under s 1(1)(a) PCA 1978 (taking or making an indecent photograph of a child) or s 160 CJA (possession of an indecent photograph of a child) if he can raise sufficient evidence to show that the child consented, or he reasonably believed the child consented. This means that if the relevant relationship exists (see below) but there is no consent then D is guilty. On the other hand, if there is consent but there is no relevant relationship between D and the child, D is also guilty of an offence. Therefore a man who takes an indecent photograph of his 17 year-old girl-friend would be guilty of an offence even if she consented if he is unable to prove an enduring family relationship. Glamour photographers who take photographs of someone under the age of 18 will obviously be guilty of an offence even if the child fully consents.

As is the case in relation to adult familial sex offences (see ch 7) the Act contains no definition of the phrase 'partners in an enduring family relationship'. However, this would clearly cover lesbian and gay relationships as well as heterosexual ones. It is not clear what the word 'enduring' means. Would six months cohabitation be sufficient? Would the defendant have to prove an intention that the relationship be long term? This may prove to be a difficult burden to discharge and perhaps this is the intention. Provided D can prove the requisite conditions and can adduce suffi-cient evidence to show consent, or reasonable belief in consent, he will not be guilty of an offence unless the prosecution can prove that the child did not in fact consent or there was no reasonable belief in consent.

In the case of the offence under s 1(1)(b) PCA 1978 (distributing or showing the indecent photographs) there is no defence of consent or reasonable belief in consent available. However, provided that the three conditions above are satisfied, no offence is committed if the photograph of the child is shown only to that child. Again, it should be noted that a 'child' for these purposes is someone at least 16 years-old but under 18 years. The defendant will be guilty of an offence if the photo-graph is shown to someone else as this will constitute distribution.

In the case of an offence under s 1(1)(c) PCA 1978 (possession of indecent photo-graph of a child with a view to distribution of the photographs) there is also a defence of consent, or reasonable belief in consent, provided the same three condi-tions mentioned above are fulfilled. However, in this case there is an additional element in that D must also adduce evidence to show that there was no intention to distribute the photograph. The onus is then on the prosecution to show that the child did not in fact consent, or there was no reasonable belief in consent, and that D did intend to distribute the photograph.

8.2.4.2 *Criminal investigations or proceedings*
The second type of defence (contained in s 46) concerns criminal investigations or proceedings and authorizes the 'making' of indecent images of children by those involved in such cases, such as policemen or lawyers. Section 46 provides a defence to the offence of making an indecent photograph contrary to s 1(1)(a) PCA 1978. There is already a defence of *legitimate reason* to the possession offence in s 160 CJA 1988. In *Atkins* this was held to include academic research into pornography but it would also cover appropriate possession in the course of an investigation.

However, the PCA 1978 did not originally include such a defence and it is therefore now amended so that the making of an indecent photograph of a child, for example by downloading from an Internet site, is not an offence provided that D can prove one of the following three grounds:

(a) that it was necessary for the prevention, detection or investigation of crime or criminal proceedings;

(b) that at the time of the offence he was a member of the Security Service and it was necessary for the exercise of the functions of the service; or

(c) that at the time of the offence he was a member of GCHQ and it was necessary for the exercise of any of the functions of GCHQ.

This defence would therefore cover the situation where a police officer copied or downloaded an image from a computer or the Internet as evidence or to analyse it or perhaps investigate its source, as in Operation Cathedral.

8.2.5 Penalties and sentencing

The maximum penalty for offences committed under the PCA 1978 remains at 10 years imprisonment. This was increased from 3 years by the Criminal Justice and Court Services Act 2000, s 41. For the offence of possession under the CJA 1988 the maximum penalty remains at 5 years.

In November 2002 the Court of Appeal set out comprehensive guidelines for sentencing those found guilty of child pornography offences, *R v Oliver* [2003] 1 Cr App R 28. These guidelines replaced previous judicial guidelines that were set out before the maximum penalties were increased and to a large extent followed the advice of the Sentencing Advisory Panel. The two main factors which should be taken into account when sentencing are the nature of the indecent material and the extent of the offender's involvement in it.

8.2.5.1 *The nature of the indecent material*
The court in *Oliver* divided the activities portrayed in the relevant material into five different levels. These partly followed the COPINE Project's (NSPCC, 2003) description of images, but with some amendments. The relevant levels referred to by the court are:

Level 1: images depicting erotic posing with no sexual activity

Level 2: sexual activity between children, or solo masturbation by a child

Level 3: non-penetrative sexual activity between adults and children

Level 4: penetrative sexual activity between children and adults

Level 5: sadism or bestiality.

The way these levels relate to sentencing is discussed below.

8.2.5.2 *The extent of the offender's involvement*

An offender's proximity to, and responsibility for, the original abuse will be relevant to sentencing as will any element of commercial gain. The court regarded swapping of images as a commercial activity, even if there was no financial gain, because it fuels demand for such material. Wide-scale distribution is regarded as more harmful than distribution between two or three individuals. On the whole, the court advised that merely locating an image on the Internet should be viewed less seriously than downloading it, which in turn is to be regarded less seriously than taking an original film or photograph.

8.2.5.3 *Sentencing thresholds*

The Court of Appeal specified that where an offender is found to be in possession of material for his own personal use, there is no evidence of actual abuse of children and only a small quantity of level 1 material, then a fine would be appropriate. A community sentence would be appropriate where there is a large amount of material at level 1 and a small amount of level 2 material, provided the material has not been distributed to others. A community rehabilitation order with a sex offender programme would be appropriate for some offenders. The custody threshold would normally be passed where the material has been shown to, or distributed to, others or where there is a large amount of material at level 2 or a small amount at level 3 or above. Up to 6 months imprisonment would be appropriate in such a case, but this would increase to 12 months where a large number of images at level 2 or 3 had been distributed or where the offender was in possession of a small number of images at levels 4 or 5. A sentence of between 12 months and 3 years would apply where an offender

(i)   possesses a large quantity of material at levels 4 or 5 (even if it was not shown to others)

(ii)   shows or distributes a large number of images at level 3 or

(iii)   produces or trades in material at levels 1 to 3.

Where an offender distributes images at levels 4 or 5, or is actively involved in the production or commissioning of such images (especially where there is a breach of trust) then a sentence of over 3 years should be handed down. The maximum sentence should be reserved for cases where the offender has a previous similar conviction or has a conviction for sexually abusing children or using violence against them.

Within these guidelines there are a number of aggravating factors which can increase the sentence, e.g., whether the images have been shown to a child, the number of images distributed, involvement in the actual abuse of the child (especially if in a position of trust over that child) and the age of the child. These guidelines were decided at a time when the definition of a child for these offences was someone under the age of 16 years. Now that the age has been increased to 18 some adjustment to the guidelines may be necessary.

8.3 ABUSE OF CHILDREN THROUGH PROSTITUTION
AND PORNOGRAPHY

Sections 47 to 51 of the Act deal with the exploitation of children, whether through prostitution or pornography. Rather than dealing with the two issues separately the Act creates a number of offences that apply to both types of exploitation. The elements of the offences are the same and so they are dealt with together although each offence could actually be split into two completely separate offences. In the Review the emphasis of the recommendations in relation to prostitution was laid squarely on the question of sexual exploitation, especially of children. The report pointed out that the law lacked coherence, being made up of piecemeal legislation with a lack of statutory definitions (*Setting the Boundaries*, para 7.6.1).

One of the main issues facing enforcement authorities is whether a child prostitute should be treated as an offender or as a victim who is being exploited by adults (e.g., pimps or clients). The Review mentions the fact that men who use child prostitutes are rarely charged with anything more than kerb crawling, although they could be charged with USI or a number of other offences. Many police forces have now taken the decision to treat young prostitutes as victims (e.g., Nottinghamshire Police and West Midlands Police) and changed their law enforcement practices accordingly. As a result the Review reported that the numbers of cautions and convictions of girls under the age of 18 years for prostitution offences is relatively small in comparison with the total number of cautions and convictions for such offences. Children can still be charged with the same prostitution offences as adults but this part of the Act concentrates on those adults who exploit such children.

8.3.1 Paying for sexual services of a child

Section 47 creates an entirely new offence of paying for the sexual services of a child. A person commits an offence if he intentionally obtains for himself the sexual services of someone under the age of 18. Section 47 provides that

A commits an offence if

he intentionally obtains for himself the sexual services of another person B

before obtaining those services, he has made or promised payment for those services to B or a third person, or knows that another person has made or promised such a payment, and

either B is under 18, and B does not reasonably believe that B is 18 or over or B is under 13.

A child can therefore consent to sexual intercourse at the age of 16 but cannot be paid for it until s/he is 18. The justification for this is the desire to protect young people from exploitation. To be guilty of the offence the person must have made or promised payment to the child or a third person (e.g., the child's pimp) or know that someone else has promised to pay. There is no definition of 'sexual services' in the Act but the word 'sexual' is defined in s 78 and so it is presumed that this definition should be used here (see chs 3 and 4).

8.3.2 Payment

'Payment' is defined to mean any financial advantage, including the discharge of an obligation or the provision of goods and services gratuitously or at a discount (s 51(3)). This could cover the waiver of a debt or the supply of drugs to the child or the child's pimp. Rather curiously, the definition of payment also includes the provision of sexual services. It seems that this is meant to cover a situation where someone provides sexual services to a pimp in order to obtain the sexual services of the child in return but the wording is not very specific. As the wording stands an offence would be committed by someone who 'pays' for the sexual services of a 17 year-old by providing that 17 year-old with sexual services, either from himself or someone else. A person will not commit an offence under this section if he reasonably believes that the child is 18 or over but if the child is under 13 no such defence is available. It will be for the prosecution to prove that the person does not reasonably believe that the child is 18 or over (s 47(1)(c)(i)).

Section 47 makes no mention of the word 'prostitute' or 'prostitution' although it is clearly intended to apply to child prostitutes. The section merely refers to payment. It is therefore wide enough to cover a situation where a child is not actually a prostitute but is paid for a one-off sexual act. In the case of *R v Pickup* (1993) 14 Cr App R (S) 271 a 34 year-old man was found guilty of indecent assault committed on a 14 year-old girl because he paid her to come to his home and she let him insert his finger into her vagina. He would clearly be guilty of an offence under s 47. On the face of it the definition of payment is also wide enough to apply to an adult man who 'paid' his 17 year-old girlfriend for sex by means of gifts to her (e.g., I will buy you a new car/dress/dinner if you have sex with me). No doubt the prosecuting authorities will formulate their own guidelines on prosecution in these circumstances.

8.3.3 Penalties

The penalties for this offence vary according to the age of the child and the type of sexual services obtained. Where the child is under 13 years and the sexual activity involves a penetrative act the offence carries a maximum penalty of life imprisonment on indictment. Section 47(6) lists those acts of penetration that are relevant for the purpose of sentencing. The section not only covers the penetration of the child's anus or vagina with *any* part of the offender's body or anything else but also covers the penetration of the *offender's* anus or vagina by any part of the child's body or by an implement used by the child. In addition, the penetration of the child's mouth by the offender's penis is included as is the penetration of the offender's mouth by the child's penis. Thus the offence is committed even if the child is the active and the offender the passive participant in the sexual services provided.

Where the child is 13 years or over but under 16 (17 in Northern Ireland) or where the child is under 13 years but there is no penetration, the maximum penalty on indictment is 14 years imprisonment. Where the child is 16 years or over, the offence is punishable by a maximum of 6 months on summary conviction or 7 years on indictment.

8.3.4 Exploitation of children through prostitution or pornography

There are three other offences in this Part of the Act that deal specifically with child (as opposed to adult) prostitution (ss 48 to 50). All three also deal with the issue of child pornography and are dealt with together because the elements of the offences are the same and would otherwise need much repetition of information. The three offences replace various prostitution offences in the SOA 1956 but so far as they relate to pornography, they are entirely new.

8.3.5 The definition of prostitution and pornography

The word 'prostitute' is defined in s 51(2) as 'a person (A) who on at least one occasion and whether or not compelled to do so, offers or provides sexual services to another person in return for payment or a promise of payment to A or a third person'. This is the first time that there has been a statutory definition of the word prostitute. Common law definitions have in the past concentrated on the meaning of the word in the context of the offence of soliciting as contained in s 1 Street Offences Act 1959. In *R v Morris Lowe* [1985] 1 All ER 400, a single act of prostitution was not deemed sufficient for someone to be regarded as a 'common prostitute'. The Act makes it clear that a single act is sufficient for the purposes of these offences. Payment is defined in the same way as it is in s 47.

For the purposes of the other strand of these offences, that relating to pornography, s 51 states that a person is involved in pornography if an 'indecent image' of the person is recorded and s 79(4) defines 'image' to include a moving or still image, produced by any means. There is no requirement that the image be distributed, it just has to be *recorded*. This is also the first time that a legal definition of the word 'pornography' has been formulated and it is suggested that this definition may prove to be less than satisfactory in practice as discussed below.

8.3.6 Causing or inciting child prostitution or pornography

Section 28 SOA 1956 made it an offence for a person who was responsible for a girl under 16 years to cause or encourage her prostitution. Persons treated as responsible included parents, legal guardians or those with custody, charge or care of the girl. The section did not apply to someone who was not responsible for the girl but still actively encouraged her prostitution, although in most cases this would be a pimp who would be charged with other offences. The offence only applied to girls, not boys. A further offence was provided by s 23 SOA 1956 (procuring a girl under the age of 21 years to have USI anywhere in the world). Both these offences are now replaced by s 48 of the Act which states that

A person (A) commits an offence if—

he intentionally causes or incites another person (B) to become a prostitute, or to be involved in pornography, in any part of the world and either

B is under 18, and A does not reasonably believe that B is 18 or over, or

B is under 13.

Thus for the purpose of this offence a child is someone (of either sex) who is under the age of 18 years but where the child is 13 years or over the offence will not be committed where the defendant *reasonably believes* that the child is 18 years or over. Reasonable belief is irrelevant if the child is under 13 years. The burden of proof is on the prosecution to prove that D does not reasonably believe that the child is over 18 years. In relation to pornography, this again raises the question of young people involved in the glamour industry. The image has to be merely indecent to be caught by this section, not obscene. The question of reasonable belief could arise where a photographer takes an indecent photograph of a young model who is below the age of 18 years but who is wearing make up which makes her look older. It would be for the jury to decide whether his belief that she was over 18 was reasonable in these circumstances.

The offender does not have to be someone who is responsible for the child, as was the case under s 28 SOA 1956, so the scope for convictions has been considerably widened. There is also no requirement in s 48 that the defendant be motivated by gain (as there is in relation to the adult equivalent offence in s 52). This would mean that anyone who encouraged a 17 year-old into prostitution or pornography (perhaps because they thought it was a good career move) would be guilty of this offence even if they had no motivation of personal gain. In relation to the pornography strand of the offence this lack of requirement of gain, together with the definition of pornography in s 51 has a curious effect. If a man persuaded his 17 year-old wife to let him take some indecent photographs of her, which he intended to keep for his personal use only, he would not be guilty of an offence under the PCA 1978 or CJA 1988 because he could plead the defence of consent under s 45 of the SOA 2003. However, it seems he would be guilty of the offence of causing or inciting child pornography under s 48 because there is no requirement that he be motivated by gain and the definition of pornography merely requires the *recording* of an indecent image, not its distribution. This cannot be the intention of the legislature and it seems unlikely that a prosecution would be brought in these circumstances but that remains to be seen. This offence is punishable summarily by a maximum of 6 months imprisonment and on indictment by 14 years imprisonment. The meaning of causing and inciting is dealt with in Chapters 3 and 4.

123

8.3.7 Controlling a child prostitute or a child involved in pornography

Section 49 creates a new offence in so far as it specifically relates to children. Prior to this Act a pimp or a madam could have been charged under ss 30 or 31 SOA 1956 which failed to make any distinction between child and adult prostitution (for further discussion of these sections see below). Under s 49 of the Act a person commits an offence if he intentionally controls a child's involvement in pornography or prostitution in any part of the world. Section 49 provides that

A person (A) commits an offence if—

he intentionally controls any of the activities of another person (B) relating to B's prostitution or involvement in pornography in any part of the world, and either

B is under 18, and A does not reasonably believe that B is 18 or over, or

B is under 13.

As in s 48, a child is someone of either sex who is under the age of 18 years but where the child is 13 years or over the offence will not be committed where D reasonably believes that the child is 18 years or over. The penalty for this offence is a maximum of 6 months imprisonment on summary conviction and 14 years on indictment.

8.3.7.1 *The meaning of control*
There is no statutory definition of control but the Explanatory Notes to the Act suggest that a person who 'requires or directs' the child to charge a certain price or to use a particular hotel for the sexual services would be controlling the child. It could be argued that this is rather less than control. Under the old law, a woman could be guilty of an offence under s 30 SOA 1956 if she exercised 'control, direction or influence' over a prostitute but there was very little authority on the meaning of those words. Such authority as did exist concentrated more on the word 'influence' rather than 'control' (the word influence does not appear in the Act) e.g., *R v O* [1983] Crim LR 401 held that simple encouragement was not enough and some element of compulsion or persuasion was necessary. However, in *AG's Reference (No 2 of 1995)* (1997) 1 Cr App R 72 the Court of Appeal stated that compulsion or persuasion may well be a necessary ingredient of control and possibly direction (although the meaning of influence was wider). It will be interesting to see whether the courts will develop a different interpretation of the word 'control' in relation to a child and an adult. After all, the type of behaviour needed to control a child may be entirely different from that required to control an adult, especially if the child is anxious to please the adult or perhaps is offered a reward by the adult.

8.3.8 Arranging or facilitating child prostitution or pornography

Section 50 makes it an offence to intentionally arrange or facilitate the involvement of a child in prostitution or pornography in any part of the world and provides that

A person (A) commits an offence if—

he intentionally arranges or facilitates the prostitution or involvement in pornography in any part of the world of another person (B), and

either B is under 18, and A does not reasonably believe that B is 18 or over, or

B is under 13.

The penalties are the same as the offences under ss 48 and 49, i.e., a maximum of 6 months imprisonment on summary conviction and 14 years on indictment. There is no definition of 'arranging or facilitating' in the Act but the Explanatory Notes suggest it would include delivering the child to a place where they will be used to make pornography or making arrangements for prostitution to take place, such as a particular hotel room or other pre-arranged location.

8.4 OFFENCES RELATING TO ADULT PROSTITUTION

Sections 52 to 56 deal with offences relating to adult prostitution. The Act does not specifically use the words 'adult prostitution' but this is implied by the fact that the sections referred to above relate specifically to child prostitution. Two offences are created, causing or inciting prostitution for gain (s 52) and controlling prostitution for gain (s 53) but there are other important changes to the law relating to prostitution which are contained in Sch 1 of the Act.

The Review recommended that the law relating to prostitution should concentrate on the issue of exploitation of individuals without criminalizing sex workers and their personal relationships in a way that denies them respect for their private life. The legislation therefore concentrates on those who exploit prostitutes for gain. Prostitution is not in itself illegal, but there are more than 35 provisions relating to the trade. The old law contained a number of anomalies, particularly relating to the unequal treatment of the sexes. For example, s 30 SOA 1956 made it an offence for a man knowingly to live wholly or partly on the earnings of prostitution and such a man was presumed to be doing so if he lived with the prostitute or was habitually in her company. Section 31 SOA 1956, on the other hand, made it an offence for a woman for the purposes of gain to exercise control, direction, or influence over a prostitute. Only a man could be charged under s 30 and only a woman under s 31. The elements of the offences were different, sometimes giving rise to strange results, e.g., in *R v O* the lesbian lover of the prostitute was acquitted under s 31 in circumstances where a male partner would undoubtedly have been found guilty under s 30. Another example of gender differences related to the question of soliciting, as formerly only a *female* prostitute could be guilty of soliciting under s 1 Street Offences Act 1959 (*DPP v Bull* [1994] 4 All ER 411). Male prostitutes had to be charged under s 32 SOA 1956 (persistently soliciting or importuning in a public place for immoral purposes), an offence that did not mention prostitution and was originally intended to criminalize homosexual behaviour irrespective of payment or involvement in prostitution.

Under the old law the act of prostitution itself, i.e., the acceptance of money for sex, was not illegal and that remains the case. In some ways it seems curious that *causing or inciting* an adult to become a prostitute should be an offence when the actual prostitution itself is not. However, the purpose of the two offences under ss 52 and 53 is to discourage the recruitment of others into prostitution by force or otherwise.

8.4.1 Causing or inciting prostitution and controlling prostitution for gain

Sections 30 and 31 SOA 1956 are repealed and replaced by new offences that are gender-neutral. Both the offences under ss 52 and 53 are punishable summarily by 6 months imprisonment and on indictment by a maximum of 7 years (equivalent to the child prostitution offences when the child is over 16 years). Section 52 provides that

A person commits an offence if—

he intentionally causes or incites another person to become a prostitute in any part of the world, and

he does so for or in the expectation of gain for himself or a third person.

Section 53 provides that

A person commits an offence if—

he intentionally controls any of the activities of another person relating to that person's prostitution in any part of the world, and

he does so for or in the expectation of gain for himself or a third person.

There is no offence of arranging or facilitating the prostitution of an adult (as there is with a child). In both ss 52 and 53 there is a further element not contained in the child offences and that is that the person only commits an offence if he does so for, or in the expectation of, gain for himself or a third person. Gain is defined in s 54 to mean

any financial advantage, including the discharge of an obligation to pay or the provision of goods or services (including sexual services) gratuitously or at a discount; or

the goodwill of any person which is or appears likely, in time, to bring financial advantage.

This definition is wider than the definition of 'payment' for the purpose of the offence of paying for the sexual services of a child under s 47 in that it also includes the goodwill of any person, which is or appears likely, in time, to bring financial advantage.

8.4.2 Penalties for keeping a brothel

Section 55 amends s 33 SOA 1956 which provides that it is an offence for a person to keep, or to manage, or act or assist in the management of, a brothel. The word brothel was not defined in s 33 SOA 1956 but a common law definition was provided by Lord Parker CJ in *Gorman v Standen* [1964] 1 QB 294 when he described a brothel as 'a house resorted to or used by more than one woman for the purposes of fornication'. This definition is archaic and ambiguous and so s 55 attempts to clarify what is meant by a brothel by adding to s 33 SOA 1956 the words 'to which people resort for practices involving prostitution (whether or not also for other practices)'. Section 55 also amends the penalty for the offence of keeping a brothel which was triable summarily only with a maximum sentence of 6 months imprisonment. The offence can now also be tried on indictment and carries a maximum penalty of 7 years imprisonment, which is consistent with the penalties for causing or inciting prostitution or controlling prostitution under ss 52 and 53.

8.4.3 Extension of gender-specific prostitution offences

Section 56 brings into effect Sch 1 of the Act that amends four offences relating to prostitution which under the old law were gender-specific.

The first is 'permitting premises to be used for prostitution'. Whereas s 36 SOA 1956 related only to female prostitution it is now an offence whether the prostitute is male or female. The offence is otherwise unchanged.

The second offence is the offence of soliciting under s 1 Street Offences Act 1959. In *DPP v Bull* [1994] 4 All E R 411 the court made it clear that only a woman could be a 'common prostitute' for the purposes of this offence. Mann LJ stating 'it is plain that the mischief that the Act was intended to remedy was a mischief created by women' (at 416d). Male prostitutes therefore had to be charged under s 32 SOA 1956 that is repealed by this Act. The Act now amends s 1 Street Offences Act 1959 to make clear that a prostitute can be either male or female. This is the only change to the offence of soliciting.

Finally, Sch 1 amends the two offences of kerb-crawling and persistent soliciting for the purpose of prostitution under ss 1–2 SOA 1985. These offences were introduced to deal with the problem of men looking for prostitutes. Such men often create a nuisance for local residents and are seen as a threat to women who are not prostitutes but who are constantly approached by them. However, the existence of the offences has not successfully dealt with the problem because the SOA 1985 requires proof of *persistent* kerb-crawling or soliciting by the man. In practice, this means that men who are stopped by the police on one occasion cannot be said to be persistently soliciting and so are not charged. This could have been remedied by the removal of the word 'persistent' from the offence but the Act has not done this. Instead it merely amends ss 1–2 SOA 1985 to make both offences gender-neutral. The amended offences now relate to all people, irrespective of gender, so would cover a man who is kerb-crawling in order to find a gay male prostitute or even a woman looking for a male/female prostitute. It remains to be seen whether many women will be charged with this offence!

8.5 TRAFFICKING FOR SEXUAL EXPLOITATION

8.5.1 The problem

In 2000 the Home Office produced a report on trafficking (*Stopping Traffic*, HO 2000) which examined the nature and extent of trafficking in women for the purposes of sexual exploitation in the UK. The report stated that there are no accurate figures available and that finding reliable information proved problematic. However, the Review described trafficking for sexual exploitation as 'a growing area of transnational organized crime' and pointed out that the Internal Office of Migration estimated that in 1995 half a million women were trafficked into the UK (*Setting the Boundaries*, para 7.1.4). It is also estimated that up to 4 million are annually victims of trafficking worldwide. It is most acute in South East Asia and the former Soviet Union and changes in political systems and economies in Eastern Europe, together with the relative ease of transportation between countries, have exacerbated the problem. It appears that women who are trafficked into the EU are often misled as to the type of work they will be doing and are often too frightened to give evidence against their traffickers. It is also the case that some women know that they are being recruited into the sex industry and use this as a way to illegally enter a country where they hope to earn a better living than they can at home. In both circumstances they are reluctant to give evidence making the job of the investigating authorities extremely difficult. In March 2003, the Home Office announced a new scheme to give counselling and accommodation to women trying to escape their traffickers but many are so terrified that they prefer to be deported rather than give evidence to the police (BBC News website, 10 March 2003).

Prior to this Act traffickers could be charged with a number of different offences including living on the earnings of prostitution (s 30 SOA 1956) and immigration offences. This can be illustrated by the story of a 26 year-old man who was jailed for 10 years on 22 December 2003 for smuggling kidnapped women into Britain to work as prostitutes. It was reported that he was head of a gang of traffickers who made more than £1 million. He admitted facilitating the illegal entry into the UK of between 50 and 60 young women. He was convicted of kidnap, incitement to rape, and living on the earnings of prostitution (BBC News website, 22 December 2003). The offences of causing the prostitution of women (s 22 SOA 1956) and detention of a woman in a brothel (s 24) could also be used but these carry a maximum of 2 years imprisonment and were largely ineffective to stop the traffickers. The Home Office Report recommended that the adequacy of existing legislation should be examined and the Review came to the conclusion that there should be a specific trafficking offence. In fact the Act creates three offences, each dealing with a different aspect of trafficking but containing similar elements and with the same penalties, which are a maximum of 6 months imprisonment if tried summarily, or 14 years on indictment.

8.5.2 Trafficking into the UK for sexual exploitation

Section 57 provides that

A person commits an offence if he intentionally arranges or facilitates the arrival in the UK of another person (B) and either—

he intends to do anything to or in respect of B, after B's arrival but in any part of the world, which if done will involve the commission of a relevant offence, or

he believes that another person is likely to do something to or in respect of B, after B's arrival but in any part of the world, which if done will involve the commission of a relevant offence

This section replaces s 145 Nationality, Asylum and Immigration Act 2002. The section is designed to cover the situation where someone is trafficked into the UK as an interim destination as well as for the sex trade in this country. The mens rea is the intention to arrange or facilitate the arrival of the person, for example by arranging travel documents, so D would be guilty even if the person trafficked never actually worked as a prostitute.

8.5.3 Trafficking within the UK for sexual exploitation

Section 58 creates a very similar offence of intentionally arranging or facilitating travel *within* the UK which would apply to UK nationals who are moved from one part of the country to another as well as foreign nationals who are brought into the UK and then moved around.

8.5.4 Trafficking out of the UK for sexual exploitation

Section 59 creates another very similar offence of intentionally arranging or facilitating the *departure* from the UK for the purposes of a relevant offence. This would apply to UK residents who are trafficked out of the country or to foreign nationals who are trafficked here and then moved on to another country.

8.5.5 The meaning of 'relevant offence'

'Relevant offence' is defined in s 60 and includes any offence under this part of the Act e.g., causing or inciting prostitution, but also includes taking or making an indecent photograph of a child under the PCA 1978. It is also clear that it covers anything done outside the UK that would be an offence if committed here, even if it is not an offence in that country. This could, for example, include trafficking a child to a country where sex with children is not an offence. Section 60 also sets out who these offences will apply to, including British citizens and UK companies. The offence will apply to actions that take place in any part of the world (not just within the UK). The offences are widely drawn and appear to give the prosecuting authorities plenty of scope to charge and effectively punish traffickers. However, given the problems encountered in persuading the victims of this trade to give evidence, they may be less effective in practice than they appear to be on paper.

8.5.6 Seizing assets

The Review also recommended that any offence of trafficking should trigger financial powers to trace assets similar to those used in drug trafficking and this recommendation has found its way into the Act. Sch 6 amends the Proceeds of Crime Act 2002 to include any of the prostitution or trafficking offences contained in the Act (see *Blackstone's Guide to the Proceeds of Crime Act 2002*).

8.6 CONCLUSION

This part of the Act has succeeded in clarifying the law on prostitution and has ensured that the law is gender-neutral. However, given the Home Office's announcement of its intention in December 2003 to conduct a review of the law relating to prostitution, and in particular to consider the possible legislation of brothels, some of these offences may be short-lived. The new trafficking offences establish a framework that should help to discourage the international sex trade. However, the provisions may not be as successful in practice as hoped, given the problems in obtaining evidence in situations where the victims are too frightened to testify. The law relating to the abuse of children through prostitution and pornography has been strengthened. However, it could be argued that in places the Act has gone too far. This is especially true of the child pornography offences, where the definition of a child now includes 16 and 17 year-olds. This may well cause problems in practice for those young people who wish to consent to indecent photographs being taken and is perhaps an over-reaction to the problem of child pornography. On the other hand the potential problems created by these provisions may well be outweighed by the benefits to be gained from providing adequate safeguards against those who would exploit children and young people.

9

PREPARATORY AND OTHER SEXUAL OFFENCES

9.1 INTRODUCTION

Part 1 of the SOA 2003 contains a number of offences that are grouped under the headings, *Preparatory Offences* and *Other Offences*. The Act attempts to fill gaps in the present law by replacing some existing offences but also by creating some entirely new ones, the necessity for which is questionable. Some of these changes seem to arise from the motivation to categorize offenders as sex offenders, since most, but not all, of the offences give rise to registration as a sex offender under Part 2 of the Act. There was some controversy about certain of these offences during the passage of the Bill through Parliament. Nudists objected to the new offence of exposure and there were also objections relating to the offence of having sex in a public lavatory, which appears to exist in order to control the activity of gay men who use public lavatories for sexual encounters, although the offence is not confined to gay men.

9.2 PREPARATORY OFFENCES

There are three preparatory offences all of which criminalize behaviour entered into with the intention of committing a sexual offence. The first, administering a substance with intent (s 61), is intended to deal with the use of 'date rape' drugs, such as Rohypnol, which may render a victim unable to refuse sex and replaces the offence under s 4 SOA 1956. The second is contained in a very widely drafted section, which is intended to cover any situation where someone commits an offence with the intention to commit a sexual offence (s 62), and the third deals with trespassing with intent to commit a sexual offence (s 63).

9.2.1 Administering a substance with intent

The Review regarded this as an important offence, pointing out that there is very real concern about the use of drugs and alcohol to enable rape to take place. The drug Rohypnol, a prescription-only drug that is part of the Valium family, has been implicated in several date rape cases in the US. Its use has also been confirmed in the UK in sexual assault cases and publicity about its potential led the manufacturer to revise its formula in 1998 to ensure that if placed in a drink, a blue dye will appear, making it less likely to be consumed by an unsuspecting victim. When combined with alcohol, Rohypnol can make users shed their inhibitions, feel disorientated and suffer from memory loss. There are other similar drugs that could be used by a potential rapist, such as GHB (gamma-hydroxybutryate), known to clubbers as liquid ecstasy. The use of this drug seems to have increased in recent years. For example, in May 2003 a satellite TV installer from Carmarthen who tricked a woman into drinking cider laced with GHB was jailed for 10 years for indecent assault and grievous bodily harm. When he was arrested he was found to be in possession of a substantial amount of GHB, which he kept in his car in a Lucozade bottle (BBC News website, 23 May 2003). The offence is wide enough to cover any substance, not just controlled drugs, and therefore includes alcohol, which remains the most commonly used substance that is associated with sexual assault.

Section 61 provides that:

A person commits an offence if he intentionally administers a substance to, or causes a substance to be taken by, another person B

knowing that B does not consent, and

with the intention of stupefying or overpowering B, so as to enable any person to engage in a sexual activity that involves B.

9.2.1.1 *The existing law*
Section 61 replaces s 4 SOA 1956 which provided that it was an offence for a person to administer any drug to a *woman* to enable any man to have unlawful sexual intercourse with her. The new offence in s 61 is similar to the old offence but there are some very important changes. Firstly, the old offence applied only to sexual intercourse whereas the new offence is much wider and applies to 'any sexual activity'. The phrase 'sexual activity' is not defined but the word sexual is defined in s 78 of the Act (as discussed in ch 3). Secondly, the new offence is completely gender-neutral. The offence can be committed by a man or a woman with either a male or female victim. The reported cases are generally about men who drug women but police in Edinburgh have recently warned gay men in the city that they are being

targeted by a man who spikes drinks and then subjects his victims to serious sexual assaults (BBC News website, 11 November 2002). Such an offender could not be charged under s 4 SOA 1956 because that offence related only to female victims (although he could have been charged with indecent assault, or rape) but he will be guilty of an offence under s 61.

9.2.1.2 *The elements of the offence*

It is clear that the offence would be committed even if no actual sexual activity takes place since the prosecution only has to prove the administering of the substance, without consent, with the relevant intention. However, in the absence of actual sexual activity, proving such an intention may be difficult. It could perhaps be shown by the perpetrator carrying items such as condoms, or sex aids. If a sexual assault did actually take place, D would of course be charged with the appropriate offence, e.g., rape or sexual assault and it should be noted that s 75(1)(f) provides that lack of consent is presumed for the purpose of rape or sexual assault where D administers a substance which stupefied or overpowered the victim (see ch 2). The significance of the offence under s 61 is that D would be guilty even if no actual assault took place.

The lack of consent by the victim applies to the administering of the substance, not the sexual activity, although clearly the assumption is that the victim would not have consented to the sexual activity without having taken the drug. This means that the offence would not be committed where, for example, someone was rendered more amenable to sexual activity through drinking alcohol when she knew it was alcohol she was consuming. If, however, she believed she was drinking orange juice which had been spiked with alcohol, then D would be guilty of the offence, provided the necessary intention to stupefy in order to engage in sexual activity could be shown. The penalty for this offence is 6 months on summary conviction and 10 years on indictment. A convicted offender is liable to be registered as a sex offender under Part 2 of the Act.

9.2.2 Committing an offence with intent to commit a sexual offence

Section 62 creates an entirely new offence which has no previous equivalent:

A person commits an offence under this section if he commits an offence with the intention of committing a relevant sexual offence.

'Relevant sexual offence' is defined to mean any offence under Part 1 of the Act, including aiding, abetting, counselling, or procuring such an offence. Section 62 could cover situations such as kidnapping or false imprisonment with the intention of committing a sexual offence but the section is so widely drafted that it would cover the commission of *any* offence committed with the intention of committing a sexual offence. This could include theft of a motor vehicle, a physical assault of someone while trying to snatch a child, criminal damage or even common assault, such as a threat to inflict violence. It would also cover serious crimes such as murder if D's objective was to engage in sexual activity with the victim's body once they were killed, the relevant sexual assault in this case being an offence under s 70 (sexual penetration of a corpse). A defendant would be guilty even if the sexual act never took place but there is the problem of proving the requisite intention where no such act is actually carried out. Liberty, in their briefing to the House of Commons, stated that this offence is so wide that it will be impossible to police and will be unfair to defendants (Liberty, July 2003). In some ways, it is difficult to see why this offence is necessary, bearing in mind that the offences of kidnapping and false imprisonment already exist and that if someone actually commits a sexual offence, such as rape, they will be charged with that offence. However, it could be argued that the real purpose of this offence is to categorize the offender as a sex offender who is liable to be placed on the Sex Offender's Register (see ch 11). In the case of a murderer who murders in order to commit a sexual offence, D would be seen not only as a murderer but also a sex offender and similarly in the case of someone who stole a vehicle in order to commit a sexual offence, D would be seen as a sex offender and not just a thief.

In addition, this offence could be charged in a situation where someone *attempted* to commit a sexual offence but the prosecution are unable to prove D's actions are more than preparatory, as required by the Criminal Attempts Act 1981. For example, if D intends to rape a woman but is disturbed before any sexual contact takes place, he could be charged under s 62 if he committed an assault with the intention of raping her. This of course assumes that the prosecution can show evidence of his intention, which could perhaps be shown by something he said to the intended victim or by items found in his possession, such as condoms.

The penalty for this offence depends on the type of offence committed. Subsection (3) provides that where the offence involves kidnapping or false imprisonment, the maximum penalty on indictment is life imprisonment. In the case of any other type of offence, the maximum penalty is 6 months for a summary conviction and 10 years on indictment.

9.2.3 Trespass with intent to commit a sexual offence

Section 63 provides that

A person commits an offence if—

> he is a trespasser on any premises,

> he intends to commit a relevant sexual offence on the premises and

> he knows that, or is reckless as to whether, he is a trespasser.

This offence replaces and extends the offence under s 9(1)(a) Theft Act 1968, whereby a defendant was guilty of burglary if he entered a building as a trespasser with intent to rape any woman.

9.2.3.1 *The existing law relating to burglary*

There were various problems with the wording of the offence of burglary in s 9 Theft Act 1968 in relation to those who intended to commit rape. Firstly, the offence was committed only where D entered a *building*, which was defined to include an 'inhabited vehicle or vessel' such as a caravan or houseboat but this definition would not include a garden, or a yard because it is not part of a building. The second problem was with the word *'enters'*. To be guilty of an offence under s 9 the offender had to enter as a trespasser and had to have formed the intention to rape at that point. The case of *R v Collins* [1973] QB 100 illustrates the problem. D climbed up a ladder, naked except for his socks, intending to enter a young woman's bedroom. While he was on the window sill the young woman woke up and (apparently mistaking him for her boyfriend) invited him in, following which they had sexual intercourse. She later realized that he was not her boyfriend and he was charged with burglary under s 9. He won his appeal against conviction because the jury had not been properly directed to consider whether he had *entered* as a trespasser, which depended on where exactly he was on the window sill when she invited him in. Finally, the offence under s 9 only applied to an intention to rape, other forms of sexual assault were not included in the offence.

9.2.3.2 *The elements of the offence*

The Review considered whether such an offence should be treated as an aggravated burglary or as a sex offence. One of the issues was whether an offender should be required to register as a sex offender (burglary is not registrable). The conclusion was that the essence of the offence was sexual and therefore should be regarded as a sex crime. The recommendation was also that it should cover all serious sex offences, not just rape.

Section 63 has removed the word 'enters' from the offence, thus avoiding the problems encountered in *Collins*. A person would now be guilty of an offence if he was a trespasser and at any time while he was a trespasser he formed the intention to commit a relevant sexual offence. For example, if a burglar entered premises with the intention to steal from the owner but whilst on the premises noticed a woman in bed and then decided to commit a sexual offence against her, he would be guilty under s 63, even though he did not enter the premises with that intention. Such an intention could be inferred by what he says or does to the intended victim or by the surrounding circumstances, e.g., by removing his clothing or by items in his possession at the time of the trespass.

The defendant must know that, or be reckless as to whether, he is a 'trespasser'. Trespass is a civil concept and so civil cases on the meaning of the word are as relevant as cases on burglary. Someone is a trespasser on premises if he is there without the permission of the owner or occupier or without a right to be there. Consent of the owner or occupier may be express or implied (e.g., postmen have implied permission to enter property to deliver mail). However, even a general permission to enter premises (e.g., for members of the public to enter a shop) can be limited to certain areas of the premises or to entry for a particular purpose. Scrutton LJ illustrated this in the case of *T v Calgarth* [1926] P 93 by saying 'when you invite a person into your house to use the staircase you do not invite him to slide down the banisters'. Someone who enters premises lawfully but then exceeds the permission given by going into other areas that he had not been given permission to enter, or who is on the premises for an unlawful purpose will be a trespasser. In *R v Walkington* [1979] 2 ALL ER 716 a man who entered the area behind the counter of a shop (probably to steal from the till) was regarded as a trespasser, even though members of the public were given general permission to enter the shop. In the context of the offence under s 63, someone who enters premises with permission but, once there, forms the intent to commit a sexual offence would at that point become a trespasser. As referred to above, s 63 does not require D to *enter* as a trespasser. He merely has to know or be reckless as to whether he *is* a trespasser. For example, if a delivery man lawfully entered premises to deliver goods but while there decided to commit a sexual assault, then he would be a trespasser once he had exceeded his permission by remaining there for an unlawful purpose. No actual sexual offence need be committed provided the intention to commit such an offence can be shown.

Section 63 uses the word 'premises' rather than 'building'. The word 'premises' is defined in s 63(2) to include 'a structure or part of a structure' but its application is clearly much wider than that. There is no suggestion that it is limited to private or residential premises. It could therefore include gardens or yards, perhaps even fields or parks (the defendant would be a trespasser after the gates had been locked). 'Structure' is defined to include a tent (there was some doubt about whether the old offence covered this), vehicle or vessel or other temporary or moveable structure. There is no requirement that the vehicle or vessel be inhabited and therefore cars parked in a drive or in a car park would be included, as would portacabins. The defendant must intend to commit a 'relevant sexual offence' and again this means any offence in Part 1 of the Act.

The maximum penalty for this offence is 6 months on summary conviction, or 10 years on indictment. This is actually less than the maximum sentence for burglary which is 14 years but, unlike burglary, D will be registrable as a sex offender (see ch 11).

9.3 OTHER OFFENCES

Sections 66 to 71 of the Act are grouped together under the heading 'Other Offences' and comprise a variety of provisions, including exposure (s 66), voyeurism (s 67), and intercourse with an animal (s 69). Some of the offences have no previous equivalent e.g., voyeurism and sexual penetration of a corpse (s 70), while some update existing offences. The offence prohibiting sexual activity in a public lavatory (s 71) is controversial and is intended to deal with the perceived problem of gay men engaging in 'cottaging', although in fact the offence is gender-neutral. For the purposes of s 24 PACE, the offences are specific arrestable offences.

9.3.1 Exposure

Section 66 makes it an offence for a person intentionally to expose his genitals where he intends that someone will see them and be caused alarm or distress. The old law on exposure was very out of date (and rather quaintly worded). Under the Vagrancy Act 1824 a man was guilty of an offence if he 'wilfully openly lewdly and obscenely' exposed his 'person' with intent to insult any female. The penalty for this offence was up to 3 months imprisonment or a fine.

A similar offence in the Town Police Clauses Act 1847 concerned 'wilfully or indecently exposing the person in a street to the obstruction annoyance or danger of the residents and passers by'. In this case the penalty was a fine or 14 days imprisonment. Both of these relatively minor offences could only be committed by a man. In addition to these two offences, the common law offence of outraging public decency could be charged and in this case, a woman could also be guilty.

The Review considered whether these offences were needed at all, pointing out that many regard 'flashers' as pathetic and inadequate men who need not be taken seriously. However, it was pointed out that research indicates that victims of this offence are often seriously affected, experiencing shock, disgust, and a fear of rape or even death. In addition, there is evidence that those convicted of serious sex offences often started by committing 'nuisance' offences such as exposure. The Review therefore recommended keeping an offence of exposure but updating it.

The Act therefore repeals the provisions in the Vagrancy Act 1824 and the Town Police Clauses Act 1847 and replaces them with the new offence of exposure contained in s 66.

9.3.1.1 *The elements of the offence*
Section 66 provides that

A person commits an offence if

> he intentionally exposes his genitals and
>
> he intends that someone will see them and be caused alarm or distress.

This offence is completely gender-neutral, which means that for the first time women can be guilty of exposure. It also means that a man or a boy can be a victim as well as a woman or a girl. The offence only applies to exposure of the genitals, not the buttocks, so the great British tradition of mooning will probably continue. A woman who exposes her breasts will not be guilty of an offence under s 66, although she could still be charged with a public order offence.

During the passage of the Bill through Parliament nudist groups became very concerned about this new offence, fearing that they would be charged with exposure. However, the way the offence is phrased seems to rule this out since there must be the intention to cause alarm or distress. This requirement would probably also mean that streakers at sporting or other events would not be guilty since they could plead that their intention was to entertain or amuse, or perhaps gain publicity for a cause, but not to alarm or distress. The test seems to be a subjective one and raises the question of how the relevant intention could be proved. In a threatening situation the circumstances themselves may be sufficient, for example where a man exposes himself to a lone woman or child in an isolated place. The section does not require there to have been any *actual* alarm or distress caused, just the intention to cause alarm or distress. There is also no requirement that the offender exposes himself for sexual gratification, the intention to alarm or distress is sufficient. This is a more serious offence than the old offences under the Vagrancy Act 1824 or the Town Police Clauses Act 1847, carrying a maximum penalty of 6 months imprisonment if tried summarily or 2 years on indictment.

9.3.2 Voyeurism

Section 67 creates an entirely new offence, which will apply in situations where one person observes another doing a private act for the purpose of sexual gratification. It would probably come as a surprise to most people that, prior to this Act being passed, there was no such offence in this country. The kind of activity this new offence would cover is illustrated by the story of a hotel owner in mid-Wales who drilled a hole through the ceiling of the hotel bathroom and used a camera to film guests while they were in the bathroom (BBC News website, 11 July 2003). In the past, people who observed others in these circumstances could perhaps be charged with offences relating to obscenity if they recorded and published images obtained through voyeurism, or perhaps with child pornography offences if someone under the age of 16 was observed and then recorded (this was the case with the hotel owner). However, in classic 'peeping tom' activities such as peeping through someone's curtains into their home, there was nothing they could be charged with. The only remedy would have been under the civil law of trespass. In the case of landlords who spy on tenants, or perhaps individuals in public changing rooms or toilets even an action for trespass may not have been a remedy, although the tort of private nuisance could have been an option.

It could be argued that the reason the law has not recognized such an offence in the past is that it is not serious behaviour and is merely a nuisance, rather than threatening. Liberty, in their response to the House of Commons on this offence, stated that they did not accept that this behaviour should be a matter for the criminal law (Liberty, July 2003). However, the guests who were observed by the hotel owner may disagree. The Review pointed out that there are links between such behaviour and more serious sexual offences, e.g., in one study mentioned by the Review 14 per cent of child molesters and 20 per cent of rapists had engaged in voyeurism (Abel, Mittleman and Becker in Clinical Criminology: the assessment and treatment of criminal behaviour, Ben-Aron et al, Toronto, *Setting the Boundaries*, para 8.3.7). In addition to this finding, there is the matter of the sense of violation experienced by victims, who often feel threatened by such behaviour. This may be sufficient reason in itself to criminalize such conduct. Section 67 actually creates four separate offences, all punishable by 6 months imprisonment on summary conviction or 2 years on indictment.

9.3.2.1 *Observing another*

The first offence is the offence of observing another person doing a private act for the purpose of sexual gratification. Section 67(1) provides

A person commits an offence if

for the purpose of obtaining sexual gratification, he observes another person doing a private act, and

he knows that the other person does not consent to being observed for his sexual gratification.

This would obviously cover the situation where someone looks into a home through a gap in the curtains or looks through a peephole at someone doing a private act. The meaning of 'private act' is carefully defined in s 68(1) which provides

A person is doing a private act if the person is in a place which, in the circumstances, would reasonably be expected to provide privacy, and

the person's genitals, buttocks or breasts are exposed or covered only with underwear,

the person is using a lavatory, or

the person is doing a sexual act that is not of a kind ordinarily done in public.

The first point to note is that the person doing the private act must be in a place that would reasonably be expected to provide privacy. This would include someone's home or even a hotel room but would exclude observations in public places such as on beaches or even in private gardens if they were exposed to public view. If, however, a garden was surrounded by a high fence, it could be argued that it is a place where privacy could reasonably be expected. Tents, caravans, boats, mobile homes, and perhaps cars would be covered by the section as would the sort of temporary portacabin toilets often used at outdoor events such as concerts. To be guilty of an offence, the observer must *know* that the person doing the private act does not consent to being observed. This raises the issue of how this would be proved, especially as recklessness is not mentioned.

A person is deemed to be doing a private act if their genitals, buttocks, or breasts are exposed or covered only with underwear. What if they are trying on a bikini? It could be argued that a swimsuit is a garment intended to be worn in public but in terms of the amount of coverage, it could be indistinguishable from underwear.

The observation must be for the purpose of sexual gratification. If someone peeps through a keyhole to ascertain whether someone is home and then notices them wandering about naked, it could easily be argued that the observation was not for the purpose of sexual gratification but if the observer then continues to watch for sexual gratification, he would be guilty of an offence, although there would be a problem of proving such an intention, unless he admits it.

Section 79(7) provides that references to 'observation' are to 'observation whether direct or by looking at an image'. It is not clear how this would apply in relation to this first offence, it is perhaps irrelevant because a separate offence of recording an image is created (see below) but could perhaps apply to a situation where someone is observed through a camera lens even though an image is not recorded, or via a periscope, or perhaps where an image is projected onto a wall but not recorded.

9.3.2.2 *Operating equipment*
Section 67(2) makes it an offence to operate equipment with the intention of enabling *another person* to observe a third person doing a private act without their consent, for sexual gratification. Section 67(2) provides that

A person commits an offence if

he operates equipment with the intention of enabling another person to observe, for the purpose of obtaining sexual gratification, a third person (B) doing a private act, and

he knows that B does not consent to his operating equipment with that intention.

This could cover someone who operates a webcam and then makes the images available over the Internet to others. It is clear that it is the sexual gratification of the viewers, not the operator of the equipment, which is relevant. The definition of 'private act' is the same as for s 67(1).

9.3.2.3 *Recording another person doing a private act*
Section 67(3) makes it an offence to record an image of another person doing a private act, for the purpose of sexual gratification without consent. Section 67(3) provides that

A person commits an offence if

he records another person (B) doing a private act,

he does so with the intention that he or a third person will, for the purpose of obtaining sexual gratification, look at an image of B doing the act, and

he knows that B does not consent to his recording the act with that intention.

This would obviously include the taking of photographs, or video recordings. In this case, the offence is committed if the intention is for the viewer to enable himself or another to obtain sexual gratification by looking at the image. 'Image' is defined in s 79(7) and means a 'moving or still image and includes an image produced by any means'. It is irrelevant whether the other people who view the image know whether or not consent was given, only the defendant has to know that the person who is observed did not consent for the purpose of sexual gratification.

9.3.2.4 *Installing equipment*

The final offence contained in s 67(4) is that of installing equipment, or constructing or adapting a structure with the intention of enabling the observer or another to commit an offence under s 67(1). This would include drilling a spy hole or installing a two-way mirror. The Welsh hotel owner mentioned above would have been guilty of this offence even if no images had been recorded as he had constructed an elaborate system of observation in the roof of his hotel. However, the intention to observe someone for sexual gratification or to enable others to do so is an essential part of the offence. A workman who is asked to install a mirror would not be guilty of an offence if he did not know the purpose for which it would be used.

9.3.2.5 *Observations for purposes other than sexual gratification*

All the offences in s 67 require that the observation should be for sexual gratification. The question of security cameras in changing rooms or other buildings needs to be considered in relation to these new offences. Someone who tries clothes on in a shop, for example, would normally expect privacy. However, for an offence to be committed there must be an intention to provide sexual gratification, either the viewer's sexual gratification, or another's. It is difficult to see how the elements of any of the offences could be fulfilled when cameras are used for security reasons only. In addition, if a shop put up notices in the changing rooms saying that a security camera was in use then it could also be argued that the customer was not in a place where there was an expectation of privacy. It would be difficult to prove that a camera operator observed private acts for his own sexual gratification in a situation where the primary purpose of the camera was security, even if it is suspected that a secondary purpose of sexual gratification exists.

There have been reported cases of people being videoed in lifts, or offices whilst engaging in sexual activities and it remains to be seen whether those who use such images for entertainment or gain (and not for 'sexual gratification') will be charged with any of these offences. The better view may be that in those situations, the participants are not in a place where there is an expectation of privacy and are therefore not engaging in a private act under this section but it could be argued that if it is not clear that security cameras are in use then such privacy is expected.

9.3.3 Intercourse with an animal

Section 69 creates two new offences relating to sexual penetration of or by an animal, which replaces the old offence of buggery. It has long been an offence under the common law to have sexual intercourse with an animal but it is interesting to consider why we should have such an offence at all. One of the arguments for retaining the offence is that sexual activity should be consensual and since animals cannot consent, the activity should be criminal. However, it does not take much thought to regard this argument as inadequate because we kill and eat animals without ever obtaining their consent and this is not illegal. There is another argument that such behaviour should be dealt with as a matter of animal cruelty rather than as a sex crime because this kind of behaviour is not a threat to people or to society as a whole (see Liberty, July 2003). However, this argument seems to miss the point. The Review considered whether this offence should still exist and came to the conclusion that it should, based on a 'suggestion' of a link between the abuse of animals and other sexual offending but also because of the 'profound abhorrence' society feels for this kind of behaviour. The reasons for the existence of the offence therefore seem to be firstly, that someone who engages in this kind of behaviour may later become a threat to people, and secondly, that society has a right to decide that certain behaviour is so unacceptable that it should be criminal. The Review regarded sexual intercourse with an animal as 'a sex offence reflecting some profoundly disturbed behaviour', which raises the question of whether treatment of such people would be perhaps more appropriate than criminalization.

9.3.3.1 *The existing offence of buggery*
Section 12(1) SOA 1956 provided:

It is an offence for a person to commit buggery with another person or with an animal.

Buggery was never defined in statute and so its interpretation relied on the common law. At common law it consisted of anal intercourse between a man and a woman, or between two men, or intercourse with an animal, either vaginal or anal. Sexual intercourse between a woman and an animal was recognized (see *R v Bourne* (1952) 36 Cr App R 125). This lack of distinction between human intercourse and intercourse with an animal was offensive to some and coincidentally also makes it impossible to tell how common sexual intercourse with animals is, since the crime statistics did not separate out the different types of behaviour covered by this offence. The maximum penalty was life imprisonment, which now seems rather excessive by modern standards. Section 12 SOA 1956 is repealed by the Act and replaced by a number of new offences of assault by penetration (see chs 3 and 4) and by the offences relating to animals in s 69.

9.3.3.2 *Elements of the offences*
The first offence is contained in s 69(1) which provides

A person commits an offence if

> he intentionally performs an act of penetration with his penis,
>
> what is penetrated is the vagina or anus of a living animal and
>
> he knows that, or is reckless as to whether, that is what is penetrated.

The second is contained in s 69(2) which provides

A person (A) commits an offence if

> A intentionally causes, or allows, A's vagina or anus to be penetrated,
>
> the penetration is by the penis of a living animal, and
>
> A knows or is reckless as to whether, that is what A is being penetrated by.

Both offences are confined to penile penetration, so if someone engages in some other kind of sexual activity with an animal (e.g., causing or allowing an animal to lick a person's genitals), no offence is committed, which begs the question as to why penetration of an animal is seen to be criminal behaviour when other kinds of sexual behaviour with animals is not. In addition, the animal must be living for an offence to be committed. If someone killed an animal and then penetrated its carcass, no offence would be committed although it is submitted that this behaviour is at least, if not more, disturbed than any sexual penetration of a living animal. The inclusion of recklessness as an element of the offence is curious in that it is difficult to imagine how one could be reckless as to whether or not it is an animal that is being penetrated. Following the case of *R v G and another* [2003] UKHL 50, the court would presumably apply a subjective test of recklessness for this offence but it is still difficult to imagine how an individual could be less than fully aware that it is an animal that is being penetrated.

Both offences are punishable by 6 months imprisonment if tried summarily and up to 2 years imprisonment on indictment, significantly less than the former maximum of life imprisonment. Both offences give rise to registration requirements under Part 2 of the Act.

9.3.4 Sexual penetration of a corpse

There is anecdotal evidence that necrophilia takes place from time to time, and that sometimes it is connected with other very serious offending such as murder. However, until this Act was passed sexual activity with a corpse was not illegal, a fact which came as a surprise to most members of the Review panel. The reasons for creating such an offence were examined and the Review came to the conclusion that a new offence of sexual interference with human remains should be enacted. The justification for this view is partly the distress that relatives would feel if they knew that the remains of their loved ones were treated in this way and partly the belief that society should be able to provide that some kinds of behaviour are so unacceptable that they should be criminal. In addition, the Review felt that those who kill and then have sex with the bodies of their victims should be treated as sex offenders as well as murderers. Other common law countries have specific statutory provisions to deal with interference with human remains, e.g., Canada and New Zealand, but in both these cases the offence is not confined to sexual acts but would also cover other damage to, or improper activity with, a dead body.

9.3.4.1 *Elements of the offence*
It is an offence under s 70 for a person to intentionally penetrate a part of a body of a dead person where that penetration is sexual. The penetration can be either with a part of the offender's body or with anything else but as the penetration must be sexual, activities carried out by medical staff, funeral parlour staff or during an autopsy would not be an offence. It is difficult to see why this offence should be

confined to penetrative acts only and it is suggested that a wider offence of interference with human remains would seem to be preferable. The desire to categorize offenders as sex offenders is probably the reason for limiting the offence to penetrative sexual acts. This is a registrable offence under Part 2 of the Act. As with the offence of intercourse with an animal (see above) one of the elements of the offence is that the offender must know *or be reckless* as to whether it is a corpse that is being penetrated. Again, it is difficult to imagine how someone could be reckless about such an issue, unless perhaps their partner died during sexual intercourse and the offender chose to carry on with the activity while aware of a risk that they were dead. However, the Explanatory Notes to the Act state that the offence will not be committed where someone unexpectedly dies during intercourse and no doubt the prosecuting authorities would choose not to prosecute in those circumstances. The decision in *R v G*, means that the court would probably apply a subjective test of recklessness. The question of recklessness could arise in the case of a serious physical assault carried out for the purpose of sexual pleasure, where D was aware of a risk that the other party was dead and unreasonably took that risk. In those circumstances, D would obviously be charged with the assault but being guilty of the offence of sexual penetration of a corpse gives rise to registration under Part 2 of the Act and so D would be categorized as a sex offender. The maximum penalty for this offence is 6 months imprisonment on summary conviction or 2 years on indictment.

9.3.5 Sexual activity in a public lavatory

Although this is in effect a new offence, it has a long history. The basic prohibition clearly arises from the desire to control the activity of gay men who use public lavatories for sexual encounters (which became known as 'cottaging'). Under the old law (s 32 SOA 1956) it was an offence for a *man* to persistently solicit or importune in a public place for an immoral purpose. The phrase *immoral purpose* was clearly meant to cover homosexual acts and the existence of this offence was a source of discontent amongst the gay community as it criminalized behaviour that was not criminal if carried out by heterosexuals or lesbians. In addition to this section, the offences of buggery and gross indecency under ss 12–13 SOA 1956 (both now repealed and replaced with other offences) were also committed if the activity took place in a public lavatory, even if the parties were both consenting adults. Again, there was no specific heterosexual equivalent, although public order offences could be charged (e.g., ss 4–5 Public Order Act 1986). One of the objectives of this Act was to remove any gender bias in the law, so that people are treated fairly irrespective of gender or sexuality. The Review recommended the abolition of the offences of buggery, gross indecency and soliciting for an immoral purpose and this has been achieved (see Sch 7). However, it was recognized that there is genuine public concern about sexual activity taking place in public and the original draft of the Bill contained an offence of 'sexual activity in a public place'. This provoked dismay in the media who delighted in pointing out that in future we would all be unable to have sex on a beach or in our gardens (see, for example, 'Outdoor lovers face jail under new sex laws', The Times, 30 January 2003). As a result, the offence was reconsidered and re-drafted as the offence of sexual activity in a public lavatory contained in s 71.

9.3.5.1 *Elements of the offence*
Section 71 provides that

A person commits an offence if—

he is in a lavatory to which the public or a section of the public has or is permitted to have access, whether on payment or otherwise,

he intentionally engages in an activity and

the activity is sexual.

The offence is gender-neutral, applying to all persons who engage in sexual activities, whether gay or heterosexual.

'Sexual' is defined in s 71(2) as follows:

an activity is sexual if a reasonable person would in all the circumstances, *but regardless of any person's purpose*, consider it to be sexual.

This definition is different from the general definition of the word 'sexual' in s 78, specifically because it excludes the purpose for which someone carries out the activity. It is obvious that a wide range of activities would potentially come within this definition, including sexual intercourse, oral sex and masturbation but any activity that is not actually sexual will not be covered. Therefore, any intimate medical procedure taking place in a public lavatory would not fall within the definition, nor would the exercise of normal bodily functions. The inclusion of the phrase 'regardless of any person's purpose' in the definition of 'sexual' appears to be an attempt to exclude invitations to engage in sexual activity from being criminalized, as they were under s 32 SOA 1956. For example, if while in a public lavatory a gay man invites another to indulge in sexual activity with him, he does not commit any offence, provided that the sexual activity takes place elsewhere. It is only if the sexual activity takes place in the lavatory that an offence is committed. If, however, a man tacitly invites another man to engage in sexual activity with him by doing an act which could be construed as sexual, for example, by masturbating at a urinal, then it is submitted that he would be committing an offence, since the reasonable person would regard masturbation as sexual, even if the purpose of the act is disregarded. With regard to any potential Article 8 issue, the Employment Appeal Tribunal has recently declared that any transitory sexual encounter between consenting male adults in public lavatories does not fall within the right to respect for private life, *X v Y* (2003) Employment Appeal Tribunal, 11 June 2003.

It should be noted that this offence is gender-neutral so heterosexuals or lesbians who engage in sexual activity in a lavatory would also commit the offence. This is a relatively minor offence, triable summarily only, the penalty being a fine, or a maximum of 6 months imprisonment.

9.4 CONCLUSION

One of the main purposes of the offences discussed in this chapter seems to be the desire to categorize offenders as sex offenders by ensuring that a conviction gives rise to registration on the Sex Offenders Register. Another objective is to make existing offences gender-neutral and to recognize that both men and women can be perpetrators and victims of sexual offences. However, the Act goes further than this by criminalizing behaviour that has not been regarded as criminal before, as with the new offence of voyeurism. The preparatory offences of administering a substance with intent to engage in sexual activity and trespass with intent to commit a sexual offence are an improvement on the existing law. However, the offence of committing an offence with intent to commit a sexual offence in s 62 is so widely drafted that it could be criticized as unfair. The practical need for some of the offences, such as sex with an animal, and sex with a corpse, is questionable and the Act's emphasis on penetration in relation to those offences is difficult to defend. There may be problems of proof relating to certain offences, which may mean that there are very few convictions, but this is not in itself sufficient reason to remove them. On the whole, these offences seem to recognize and acknowledge public concern about certain types of sexual behaviour thereby reflecting society's intolerance of sexual deviance.

10

EVIDENTIAL PROVISIONS

10.1 INTRODUCTION

Historically the exclusionary rules of evidence governing the competency and credibility of children and vulnerable persons to give evidence in cases of sexual offences, and the manner in which it was given, was the subject of much legal confusion and public criticism. In the aftermath of controversies in the 1980s such as the Cleveland and Rochdale child sexual abuse scandals concerning the inappropriate use of interview and diagnostic techniques by childcare professionals, guidelines for inter-agency cooperation were produced and initiatives to facilitate child testimonies such as video links and video recordings introduced. The rules regarding the requirements of corroborating evidence and corroborative warnings were relaxed; and, in response to concerns about the humiliating and distressing cross-examination of some rape victims, restrictions were imposed limiting the extent of questioning in certain circumstances. In 1998 an Inter-departmental Working Group commissioned to investigate the treatment of vulnerable and intimidated witnesses and victims in the criminal justice system made a number of recommendations to facilitate the delivery of their testimonies and soften the court environment. Their report, *Speaking up for Justice* (HO June 1998) formed the basis of the subsequent Youth Justice and Criminal Evidence Act 1999 (YJCEA), which provides measures for assisting vulnerable witnesses. The aim of this chapter is to provide a brief summary of the current provisions governing the admissibility and manner of delivery of testimonies to serve as a reference point in the context of the substantive sexual offences discussed in this book (for further detail on these provisions see *Blackstone's Criminal Practice 2004*). For guidance on the provision of therapy for victims of sexual offences and whether this might prejudice their evidence see *Provision of Therapy for Child Witnesses Prior to a Criminal Trial*, Practice Guidance for the CPS and Police (HO 2001); and *Provision of Therapy for Vulnerable or Intimidated Witnesses prior to a Criminal Trial*, Practice Guidance for the CPS and Police (HO 2001). Also, in light of the current reforms to the criminal trial process see R. Taylor, M.Wasik and R. Leng, *Blackstone's Guide to the Criminal Justice Act 2003*, particularly in relation to the admissibility in evidence of the defendant's previous bad conduct.

10.2 COMPETENCY TO GIVE EVIDENCE

Primarily all persons are competent to give evidence at every stage in criminal proceedings unless it appears to the court that they cannot understand any questions put to them by a witness and give answers to them which can be understood (s 53 YJCEA). The court shall determine, in camera, any question as to the competency of a witness and may receive expert evidence on the issue. It is up to the party calling the witness to satisfy the court on a balance of probabilities that the witness is competent and, where a Special Measures Direction is authorized, to treat the witness as having the benefit of such direction (s 54).

A witness may not be permitted to give sworn evidence unless he has attained the age of 14 years and has a sufficient appreciation of the solemnity of the occasion and the particular responsibility to tell the truth which is involved in taking an oath (s 55). If the witness understands questions put and is able to give comprehensible answers she will be presumed to have sufficient appreciation. Children under 14 years may give unsworn evidence provided they are competent.

10.3 SPECIAL MEASURES

Chapter I of Pt II YJCEA provides for the authorization of Special Measures in relation to vulnerable or intimidated witnesses called to give evidence in criminal proceedings. The provisions, except ss 28 and 29 relating to cross-examination outside the presence of the accused and the use of an interpreter, came into force on 24 July 2002. The objective is to allow special concessions to be made to facilitate the delivery of evidence where the witness is vulnerable or may feel threatened or distressed. The provisions apply equally to all witnesses whether giving evidence for the prosecution or defence. For information for potential witnesses see *Witness in Court* leaflet (HO 2002).

10.3.1 Special Measures Direction

Where the court is satisfied that specific special measures should be made available for the assistance of a particular witness it must make a Special Measures Direction (SMD).

10.3.1.1 *Eligibility for Special Measures Direction*

There are two categories of potential witnesses eligible for assistance, those who are accepted as being vulnerable due to age or incapacity and those who may feel vulnerable on the grounds of experiencing fear or distress. Section 16 YJCEA encompasses the former, i.e., those aged under 17 years at the time of the hearing; and those aged over 17 years but where the quality of their evidence is likely to be diminished because the witness is suffering from a mental or physical disorder, or other significant impairment of intelligence and social functioning. In determining whether or not such a witness is eligible the court must consider any views they express (ss 16(1), (2), and (5)).

Section 17 permits assistance for witnesses of all ages where, at the time of the hearing, the court is satisfied that the quality of their evidence is likely to be diminished by fear or distress. In determining whether or not such a witness is eligible the court must take into account:

(i) the nature and circumstances of the offence

(ii) the age of the witness

(iii) other relevant factors such as their social, cultural and ethnic background, domestic and employment circumstances, religious and political beliefs

(iv) any behaviour towards the witness instigated by the accused, members of his family or associates, or person likely to be an accused

(v) any views the witness expresses (ss 17(1), (2)).

Where the witness is a complainant in a sexual offence she is automatically eligible for assistance unless she informs the court to the contrary.

10.3.1.2 *Procedure*

Either a party to the proceedings can apply for a SMD or the court can raise the possibility of a SMD of its own volition. An application should be made to the Magistrates' Courts under the Magistrates' Courts (Special Measures Direction) Rules 2002 (SI 1687/2002) and to the Crown Court under the Crown Court (Special Measures Directions and Directions Prohibiting Cross-Examination) Rules 2002 (SI 1688/2002)). Guidance for police officers and the CPS on making an application is provided in *Early Special Measures Meetings: Practice Guidance for the CPS and Police* (HO 2001). Where the court is satisfied that a witness is eligible it must:

(i) determine whether any of the special measures available would, in its opinion, be likely to improve the quality of evidence given by the witness, and if so

(ii) determine which measure, or combination of measures, would be likely to maximize so far as practicable the quality of such evidence and

(iii) give such a direction (ss 19(1), (2)).

In making this decision the court should take into account any views expressed by the witness and whether any measures might tend to inhibit the effective testing by a party of the evidence given (s 19(3)). A SMD is binding from the time it is made until the relevant proceedings are either determined or abandoned (s 20(1)). Where evidence is given in accordance with a SMD the jury must be given such warning (if any), as the judge considers necessary to ensure that the SMD itself does not prejudice the accused (s 32).

10.3.2 Special provisions relating to child witnesses

Where a child under 17 years is eligible for assistance by virtue of s 16 they may also warrant the application of special provisions under s 21 where they are deemed to be in need of special protection because they are a 'child witness'. Three types of case are covered: sexual offences (defined in s 35(3)(a)), an offence of violence, child cruelty, kidnapping, false imprisonment or assault (ss 35(3)(b), (c)); or any other case (s 35(3)(d)). Section 21 imposes, as a primary rule, that in all three types of cases the court must allow any 'relevant recording' i.e., a video-recorded interview as evidence-in-chief, to be admitted as evidence in accordance with s 27 (unless inadmissible in the interests of justice), and any further evidence, whether in-chief or otherwise, to be received by live link in accordance with s 24. In addition where a sexual offence is involved any subsequent cross-examination or re-examination of the child must be pre-recorded unless the witness declares otherwise (s 21(6)). In cases of violence any further evidence-in-chief, cross-examination, or re-examination is to be admitted by live video link. In making such directions the court must then consider s 19(2) to determine whether any other additional measures should be made available. The primary rule is held in abeyance where the special measure is not available (e.g., non-provision or failure of technical equipment), is not in the interests of justice, or is not likely to maximize the quality of the witness's evidence because a SMD has already been imposed by another section. Except that where a child witness is in need of special protection, the primary rule stands together with any other SMD authorized under another section, i.e. s 16 (s 21(5)). The primary rule also stands where child witnesses give evidence against their peers or other young persons. *R v D and others* [2003] 2 Cr App R 16 involved two different cases where child witnesses aged 12–16 years old gave evidence in cases of robbery and assault against child defendants aged 14–16 years old. The justices in one were advised that they had no discretion but to make SMDs in respect of the child witnesses, whereas the trial judge in the other refused on the grounds that this would raise a substantial inequality between prosecution and defence in violation of Articles 6(1) and 6(3)(d)—the right to cross-examine witnesses under the same conditions as witnesses against the defendant. The Divisional Court held that s 21(5), which requires a timely SMD in relation to child witnesses in need of special protection, did not breach Article 6. The court confirmed that vulnerable witnesses as well as defendants have rights and need protection. Neither a live link nor video recording of evidence-in-chief infringe the right to cross-examine witnesses provided the defendant's lawyers could see as well as hear the witness.

The provisions in s 21 also apply to persons aged under 17 years at the time of the offence but who are aged over 17 when called as a 'qualifying witness' during the criminal proceedings thereby permitting any video-recorded interview to be admitted and any other evidence to be given by live link (s 22).

10.3.3 Special Measures available

The forerunner to the availability of facilities such as video recordings and live links was Judge Pigot's permission in the case of *R v XYZ* (1990) 91 Cr App R 128 to allow a 13 year-old girl to give her evidence against her father and three other men from behind a screen and sitting next to a social worker. The use of live links and video recordings was subsequently authorized under the Criminal Justice Acts 1988 and 1991. The YJCEA consolidated these provisions together with other concessions. Currently video link and video recording equipment are available in all Crown Court centres and video link equipment in 154 Magistrates' Courts, temporary facilities may be made available where there is no existing equipment.

10.3.3.1 *Screens*
Section 23 allows the witness to be physically screened from the accused so that the witness is prevented from seeing the accused but the witness can see, and be seen by, the judge and jury, legal representatives and any interpreter present. If two or more legal representatives are acting for a party to the proceedings then it is sufficient that the witness is seen by, and can see, just one of them. The imposition of screens was challenged in *Stanford v UK* Case No 50/1992/395/473 on the grounds that their presence might prejudice the jury into assuming that the accused must have committed the crime alleged but the ECtHR held that this did not infringe Article 6(1), the right to a fair trial.

10.3.3.2 *Evidence by video link*
Section 24 allows a SMD to be given in respect of the delivery and reception of testimony and cross-examination by live video link where it is in the interests of justice to do so. Here the witness is physically removed from the court and gives their evidence and testimony from another room by means of a closed-circuit live TV link. There is a presumption that a witness who gives evidence by live link for part of the proceedings will continue to give evidence in this manner. Criticism has been made that despite the availability of this measure there are still issues about the manner in which questions are posited by the defence in that barristers sometimes

fail to acknowledge and accommodate the child's knowledge of language and sexual understanding and often adopt an inappropriate and confusing linguistic style (*An Evaluation of the Live Link for Child Witnesses*, HO 1991).

10.3.3.3 *Privacy*
Section 25 allows for evidence to be given in private without the presence of any person described in the SMD except for the accused, legal representatives, or interpreter. This exclusion can extend to members of the public and media representatives except that one member only of the press will be allowed to attend on behalf of all interested news gathering and reporting organizations. This concession applies only in the case of a sexual offence or where the court is satisfied that a witness is at risk of, or has been, intimidated by a person or persons other than the accused.

10.3.3.4 *Wigs*
Section 26 permits the removal of wigs and gowns, which may be dispensed with during the giving of evidence. This applies to both members of the judiciary and legal representatives.

10.3.3.5 *Video recordings*
Section 27 governs the admissibility and use of video recordings. A video recording of an interview with a witness may be admitted as evidence-in-chief both at trial and for the purposes of committal proceedings provided that it is in the interests of justice. The court has a discretion not to admit any part of a recording thus allowing an edited version but in making this decision must consider whether any subsequent prejudice to the accused is outweighed by the desirability of showing the whole, or substantial whole, of the recorded interview (s 27(3)). A video recording may be refused if the witness is not available for cross-examination and the parties have not agreed that there is no need for the witness to be available, or any rules requiring the disclosure of the circumstances in which the recording was made have not been complied with (s 27(4)). The video recording forms the whole of the evidence-in-chief unless the witness is asked about matters not covered, or matters not covered adequately, in the recorded interview. Further questioning of the witness may be conducted via live link. Guidelines for joint agency interviews (primarily police and social services) conducted by video recordings were outlined in the *Memorandum of Good Practice 1992*, but this has now been superseded by *Achieving Best Evidence in Criminal Proceedings* (HO 2002). The guidance describes best practice procedures when interviewing vulnerable or intimidated witnesses, whether adults or children, to ensure that they are able to give their best evidence. Where any question arises as to the disclosure of the existence or contents of a video interview and its transcript to another interested party; such as where a local authority is required to reveal such in the context of any civil proceedings, that authority must promptly submit the question to a court for its determination as any delay which adversely affects the family rights of an individual could violate Article 8, see *TP and KM v UK* App No 28945/95 ECHR [2001] Times LR May 31.

10.3.3.6 *Pre-trial video recorded cross-examination*

Section 28, which is not yet in force, makes provision for any cross-examination or re-examination of the witness undertaken subsequent to their video recorded evidence-in-chief to also be recorded by means of a video recording. This may be undertaken outside the physical presence of the accused provided he can see and hear such cross-examination and can communicate with any legal representative. Where there are two or more legal representatives acting for one of the parties, it is sufficient that the witness is seen by, and can see, just one of them.

10.3.3.7 *Intermediaries*

Section 29, which is also not yet in force, allows for the examination of a witness to be conducted through an interpreter or other approved person who will communicate questions to the witness asked by the prosecution and defence, and communicate back the answers the witness gives in reply. The intermediary may explain the questions and answers where a witness has difficulty understanding them if this will facilitate the communication between the witness and the court. An intermediary must be someone approved by the court and will normally have received specialist training, specialist skills such as in the case of interpreting for deaf witnesses, or specialist knowledge of the witness. The judge or magistrates and at least one legal representative for each party must be able to see and hear the witness giving evidence and be able to communicate with the intermediary. The evidence may be video recorded in which case the jury will not see it until the recording is shown to them later. Intermediaries may be called upon to assist in the early stages of an investigation or proceedings, in which case the court's approval to receive the video recording of an interview must be gained retrospectively. If any false or misleading statements are wilfully made to the witness or the court an offence under the Perjury Act 1911 is committed.

10.4 CROSS-EXAMINATION BY THE ACCUSED

Formerly under the Criminal Procedure Act 1865 defendants were permitted to personally cross-examine their accuser. After *R v Ralston Edwards* (1996) Old Bailey, unreported, 23 August 1996, where the complainant, Julia Mason, was subjected to six days personal cross-examination about her 16-hour rape ordeal with the accused who wore the same jumper and jeans as he did at the time of committing the offence; and *R v Brown (Milton)* [1998] Times LR 7 May where the accused unjustifiably intimidated and humiliated the complainant, this provision was rescinded. Sections 34 to 40 YJCEA now prohibit unrepresented defendants from personally cross-examining adult and child witnesses in respect of certain specified offences. Section 34 provides that no person charged with a sexual offence may cross-examine the complainant in person as regards that offence or any other offence with which the accused is charged. Section 35 makes special provision for 'protected witnesses' i.e., child witnesses, prohibiting the personal cross-examination of any child witness, not just the complainant, in respect of any charge for an offence under Part 1 Sexual Offences Act 2003. Further judicial discretion is allowed under s 36 to cover any other situations not governed by ss 34 and 35. In order to avoid any incompatibility with Article 6, where a defendant wishes to represent himself s 38 requires the court to invite him to arrange for a legal representative to act on his behalf solely for the purpose of cross-examination. If the accused refuses to nominate a legal representative and the court believes this is necessary in the interests of justice the court must appoint a suitably qualified person to cross-examine the witness in the interests of the accused (ss 38(3)–(8)). Finally, as with a SMD, there is a statutory duty on the judge to ensure that the accused is not prejudiced in the eyes of the jury by any inferences that might be drawn from the application of these sections (s 39).

10.5 CROSS-EXAMINATION ON PREVIOUS SEXUAL HISTORY

In 1975, the Report of the Advisory Group on the Law of Rape (the Heilbron Committee) recommended that there should be some restrictions on the right of the defendant to cross-examine the complainant on her previous sexual history. Section 2 SO(A)A 1976 addressed this by requiring that a defendant apply for permission from the judge who should give leave, if and only if, it would be unfair not to allow such questions. Much criticism was targeted at the judiciary and the Court of Appeal for interpreting this provision too generously. As a result s 41 YJCEA introduced a new rape shield provision, which in effect stipulated a virtual blanket ban on any cross-examination about previous sexual history unless denial would lead to an unsafe conclusion by the jury or the court about any 'relevant issue', i.e., one that either the prosecution or defence must prove/disprove. The section applies in respect of all sexual offences under Part 1 of the SOA 2003 and so is not restricted to complainants giving evidence in rape cases as was previously the case (s 62 YJCEA as amended by Sch 6 SOA 2003). The starting point is that except with the leave of the court, no evidence may be adduced, and no question may be asked in cross-examination, by or on behalf of the accused, about *any* sexual behaviour of the complainant. Sexual behaviour means any sexual behaviour or other sexual experience whether or not it involves the accused (s 42(1)(c)). Where it is claimed that the complainant has made former false allegations of rape this would not normally constitute 'sexual behaviour' because such evidence goes more towards the credibility of the complainant and whether she has a history of making unproven complaints. Such evidence therefore falls outside s 42 but should only be elicited by the defence where it is proper to do so and not as a deliberate means of trying to reveal previous sexual experience, especially where there is nothing to suggest any previous complaints were in fact false (see *R v T (Complainant's Sexual History)* [2001] EWCA Crim 1877; *R v H (Stephan)* [2003] EWCA Crim 2367 and J. Temkin, *Rape and the Legal Process*, (Oxford University Press 2002, pp 208–9).

Leave may be given permitting cross-examination in three situations provided that it is clear that the purpose is not to impugn the credibility of the witness (s 41(4)). Any application made by the accused or on his behalf is heard in private and in the absence of the complainant. The court must be satisfied that one of the following three conditions are met.

(i) The issue is a relevant issue that is not an issue of consent (s 41(3)(a)). Section 42(1)(b) expressly provides that a defence of belief in consent is not an 'issue of consent' and therefore potentially the defence could adduce any evidence of previous sexual behaviour to discharge their burden. Thus prior to the SOA 2003 the defendant's honest but mistaken belief in consent fell into this category but in light of the new reasonableness requirement in relation to rape (s 1(2)) a defendant should only be granted permission where any previous sexual conduct is relevant, for example, where there have been previous sexual relations in the past. The point is not that he must show he reasonably believed that she might consent because of any knowledge he has about the complainant's previous sexual behaviour but that he reasonably believed she did in fact consent. Where the defendant disputes that he was actually the perpetrator and so identity is at issue then evidence may be adduced which may prove the identity of the individual responsible, this might involve, for example, questions about previous sexual relations resulting in pregnancy. Section 41(3)(a) could also permit questioning about the victim's motives in alleging a sexual offence or in the case say of young children where knowledge of previous sexual activity might be needed to explain the context of the present charge, such as in a case of familial abuse.

(ii) It is an issue of consent and the sexual behaviour of the complainant was alleged to have taken place at the time or about the same time as the event charged (s 41(3)(b)). This allows the court to consider the context of the alleged offence and any circumstances involving the complainant in a sexual activity that occurred before or at the same time. The section is silent as to any time-frames within which the previous sexual behaviour must have occurred but the Home Office Guidance Notes suggested 24 hours and the courts have proven unwilling to extend the interpretation to cover events occurring days, weeks, or more beforehand, see *R v A* [2001] 1 All ER 1.

(iii) It is an issue of consent and the sexual behaviour of the complainant is alleged to have been so similar to that which occurred as part of the event charged or took place at or about the same time, and that that similarity cannot be explained by coincidence (s 41(3)(c)). A literal interpretation of this provision suggests that where the complainant has had a previous relationship with the accused he could not adduce this in evidence as it would be automatically excluded. It quickly became apparent that there was therefore a fundamental tension between the aims of s 41 in seeking to protect rape complainants and the defendant's rights under Article 6 to a fair trial. This was tested in the leading case of *R v A (No 2)* [2002] 1 AC 45 where the House of Lords held that s 41(3)(c) was not compatible and in effect 'read down' the section to construe it as allowing the admission of evidence so relevant to the issue of consent that to not do so would prejudice the defendant. Thus the major factor is relevance and so not all previous relationships or sexual behaviour with the accused will be susceptible to cross-examination.

Finally the court will also be justified in lifting the shield where evidence is adduced by the prosecution and any cross-examination of the witness would, in the opinion of the court, go no further than is necessary to be rebutted or explained by the accused (s 41(5)). Here the prosecution may introduce previous sexual history evidence but it must relate to a specific instance or series of specific instances of alleged sexual behaviour on the part of the complainant (s 41(5)). Thus where the prosecution introduce details of a previous sexual relationship the defence may only cross-examine the complainant on the details of this inasmuch as it will help clear up any misunderstandings or ambiguities. It is up to the trial judge to exercise discretion in this respect, *R v Peter Rooney* [2001] EWCA Crim 2844.

10.6 CORROBORATION

Historically where a child gave unsworn evidence, as a matter of law, independent corroborating evidence was required in order for the accused to be convicted and, in addition, the judge had to give a corroboration warning about the dangers of convicting on any uncorroborated evidence. Section 34 CJA 1988 removed any such requirements in relation to both the sworn and unsworn testimonies of children. As well as historical obstacles requiring the corroboration of child testimonies, an additional corroboration requirement existed where an allegation of a sexual offence was made. A corroboration warning was required as a matter of law and, as a matter of practice, corroborating evidence was usually required to obtain a conviction. Thus the judiciary still retained discretion to give an appropriate warning in certain sexual offences. Section 34 was therefore amended by s 32 CJPOA 1994 which removed all requirements as a matter of law for corroboration warnings to be given either because it is a child who is giving unsworn evidence or the offence is a sexual one. However, in *R v Makanjuola and Easton* [1995] 1 WLR 1348 the Court of Appeal confirmed that the judiciary may still consider it 'necessary to urge caution' and administer an appropriate warning to the jury of the dangers of convicting on the evidence of an unreliable or 'suspect' witness in certain cases, but not just because it is a sexual offence or the witness is a child (see also *R v Gilbert* [2002] 2 WLR 1498, and *Blackstone's Criminal Practice 2004*, para F5.6).

10.7 INFERENCES AND PRESUMPTIONS

Although there is no legal requirement on a person accused of rape or any other sexual offence to explain or justify their actions, Parliament has seen fit to allow the court the opportunity to make any adverse inferences that it considers proper in certain circumstances. Primarily such inferences may arise in two contexts in relation to sexual offences; the refusal to give consent to intimate samples and the failure to disclose any information or facts to the police which the accused may later wish to rely on in court. The drawing of such inferences will not infringe Article 6 but the trial judge should follow the specimen directions as confirmed in *Beckles v UK* [2003] 36 EHRR 13 as any possible contravention must be determined in the light of all the circumstances of the case and in this respect the trial judge's direction to the jury will be of particular relevance. Here the trial judge had given insufficient weight to the defendant's explanation for his silence, allowing the jury to draw an adverse inference where it might have been satisfied with his explanation.

Section 62 PACE authorizes a police officer above the rank of Inspector to seek consent from a person detained at a police station and suspected of a sexual offence for an intimate sample to be taken in order to confirm, for example by forensic analysis, that sexual intercourse occurred and, where the evidence can show this, that it occurred between the complainant and the accused. Such intimate samples include the provision of any samples of blood, tissue, semen, urine or pubic hair, or dental impressions and swabs taken from an orifice other than the mouth. If appropriate permission is refused without good cause then in relation to any associated proceedings the court or jury, in order to determine guilt, may draw any such inferences as may appear proper (s 62(10)).

Sections 34 to 38 CJPOA 1994 limit an accused's absolute right to silence in certain circumstances. If, in his defence, D wishes to rely on any evidence or facts that he has not previously mentioned to the police in the course of their investigation and interview, the court may draw such inferences, including a general inference of guilt, as may appear proper in the circumstances. A person cannot be convicted solely on the drawing of an adverse inference. Section 34 applies where a person is either being interviewed under caution or charged with an offence and fails to mention any fact the circumstance of which he could reasonably have been expected to mention. The Court of Appeal, in respect of a case where D was charged with a number of counts of rape and indecent assault committed upon his daughters between 1977 and 1985, stressed that s 34 was a 'minefield', *R v B* CACD (unreported, 23 October 2003) and confirmed that the judge must identify and specify the relevant facts on which the jury may draw an adverse inference (see also *R v Argent* (1997) 2 Cr App R 27). D's refusal, on legal advice, to answer any questions put by the police in relation to the alleged offences and his subsequent responses at trial where he gave, according to the trial judge, evidence of 'umpteen facts' as to why no abuse had occurred or why his daughters had made the allegations they did, were not specific enough to form the basis of an adverse inference direction. Similarly in *R v Phillip Knight* [2003] EWCA Crim 1977 where the defendant was convicted of indecently assaulting a 10 year-old girl by putting his hand down her trousers, a statement of denial and subsequent 'no comment' interview from which he did not depart in the witness box was not sufficient to draw an adverse inference. The Court of

Appeal stated that the true purpose of s 34 was no more than early disclosure of a suspect's account and not, separately and distinctly, the subjection of that account to the test of police cross-examination. As D had already given a full account in a prepared statement and had mentioned all the facts on which he later relied it was not appropriate to draw any adverse inference. Section 35 relates to specific situations regarding silence at trial whereby the accused chooses not to give evidence, or refuses without good cause to answer any questions put to him. In such cases the court must make it clear that any defendant who opts not to give evidence is aware of any likely consequences. Section 36 deals with the accused's failure to account for any objects, substances, or marks found on his person or in his possession at the time of arrest. Where the police reasonably believe that the presence of such items and factors might be attributable to the defendant's role in committing the alleged offence, and are therefore entitled to ask for an explanation about them, any failure on his part to so respond again opens up the possibility of adverse inferences being drawn. For example, if he is unwilling to explain how certain injuries or recent bite marks were obtained or he has in his possession any sex aids or items for procuring sex. Section 37 deals with situations where the accused fails to satisfactorily explain his presence at any particular location at the time of arrest or states to the police that he is in one location but during the trial negates this and states he was somewhere else. For further detail and explanation on these provisions see *Blackstone's Criminal Practice 2004* F19.5.

10.8 CONCLUSION

A considerable range of initiatives and reforms have been introduced in recent years to ease as far as possible the experience of victims of sexual offences called as witnesses in criminal proceedings. These provisions serve to mitigate the somewhat harsh and unforgiving environment of the trial process and facilitate the delivery of testimony whether by child or adult. In terms of the future application of the SOA 2003, and the desired success in terms of increasing the conviction rates for sexual offences, the overriding issue is the extent to which the very nature of the adversarial process can accommodate and balance the interests and needs of all those involved in such cases, whether victims or defendants. From the perspective of the victim, the harsh edges of the criminal process have been considerably softened and it is unlikely that any further reforms will be forthcoming; for the defendant the provisions of the ECHR and particularly Article 6 act as an effective means of protection, thus it remains to be seen what impact the combined application of the new substantive statutory provisions underpinned by these evidential changes will secure.

11

SEX OFFENDERS:
NOTIFICATION REQUIREMENTS

11.1 INTRODUCTION

The Sex Offenders Register (SOR) was first introduced in Part 1 of the Sex Offenders Act 1997 (SOA 1997) in response to public concern about the whereabouts of sex offenders, particularly paedophiles, and tracking their release from custody. The Register was justified on the basis of administrative necessity and is not designed to be a punitive measure. At the time it was estimated that there were some 110,000 convicted paedophiles and a total of 260,000 convicted sex offenders. The Register is maintained by the police and currently holds information on nearly 22,000 individuals with approximately another 3,000 added annually. The SOA 1997 did not apply retrospectively therefore individuals could only be entered subsequent to arrest and conviction so many escaped monitoring. National outrage about the Sarah Payne murder in July 2000 and the subsequent 'outing paedophiles' campaign led by the *News of the World* fired public fears and concerns. As a result the Criminal Justice and Court Services Act 2000 made a number of changes to notification procedures and increased the penalty for failure to register, initially designated a summary offence, to 5 years once it became apparent that a 6 month sentence was an insufficient deterrent. The Act also laid down the framework for the creation of Multi-Agency Public Protection Panels (MAPPS) to ensure a more effective monitoring process to allay public fears.

The Home Office conducted a review five years after the implementation of the SOR and concluded that it should be further strengthened to increase its effectiveness and improve public safety through better monitoring, thereby reducing offences and increasing detection rates (*Protecting the Public*). These changes are incorporated into Part 2 of the Act, ss 80–93, which virtually re-enact Part 1 of the 1997 Act but with some amendments. For example, anyone already registered must re-register annually instead of the five-yearly intervals allowed under the SOA 1997. Persons convicted of sex offences abroad, whether British citizens or foreign nationals now resident in the UK, are also made subject to the same requirements.

While the introduction of the Register went some way towards allaying public concern it has not been universally accepted in all quarters. The main criticism is that the Register is not just limited to the inclusion of paedophiles and sex offenders who present a genuine threat to society. Virtually anyone convicted of a sexual offence is subject to the notification requirements, there is no risk assessment as to the likely threat they pose. Controversially men convicted of consensual homosexual sex under ss 12 and 13 SOA 1956 (because it was not in private or prior to the SO(A)A 2000 one party may have been 16 or 17 years-old) were included. This infuriated groups such as Liberty and Outrage. Now that such homosexual activities are decriminalized an amendment was inserted at the Common's Committee Stage to enable those individuals entered on the Register under the SOA 1997 to apply to the Secretary of State for removal, provided their offence did not involve anyone aged under 16 (see Sch 4). Secondly, no concessions are made as regards juveniles and young persons convicted or cautioned for a sexual offence except that the length of time they are required to remain subject to notification requirements is one half that of an equivalent adult. The press have regularly published details of the 'youngest person' to be entered and there are now a number of 10–14 year-olds on the Register, some for fairly minor offences. The Register is unable to provide any breakdown of statistics according to e.g., age, gender, or ethnicity and there is no review process as such. But surely there is a difference between the 13 year-old boy found to have 326 pornographic images of young children and babies on his computer and the two 15 year-olds who confessed to putting their hands up a girl's skirt or pinging her bra straps? The former was sentenced to an 18 month Supervision Order, required to attend a rehabilitation course and remains on the Register for 2½ years (BBC News website, 14 May 2001); the latter were given a police warning and also entered on the Register for 2½ years (BBC News website, 12 November 2002, 29 November 2002). The opportunity afforded by the new Act to make some distinction between these types of examples has not been seized.

11.2 RELEVANT OFFENDERS

Individuals subject to Part 2 notification requirements are known as *relevant offenders* for the duration of their notification period. Section 80(1) defines those who are subject to notification requirements as including all persons convicted of, or cautioned for, a specified offence as listed in Sch 3 of the Act. Conviction includes a finding by a court martial and exceptionally a conditional or absolute discharge by virtue of s 134, hence specifically excluding this provision from the normal rule that such discharges do not constitute a conviction. A caution means a caution administered by a police officer where an admission is made and also includes a reprimand or warning given to a young person under s 65 CDA 1998 (s 133). Where a finding is made that a person did the act charged but was found not guilty by reason of insanity or disability then they are deemed to be relevant offenders. Guidance on whether a finding in respect of a mentally disordered person constitutes a conviction can be found in s 135. Provided the verdict is stated in open court and the conviction or finding for the offence in question is one to which Part 2 applies, the court's certification, either at the time or subsequently, is evidence of those facts, as is the certification by a police officer where a person has been cautioned (s 92).

11.2.1 Schedule 3 offences

Schedule 3 lists those offences commonly acknowledged as sexual offences whether committed in England/Wales, Scotland, or Northern Ireland, and includes virtually all offences created by the Act together with their former counterparts under the SOA 1956. The structure of the schedule reflects its 1997 predecessor incorporating those offences previously listed in Sch 1 SOA 1997 (all serious sexual crimes and particularly sexual offences involving children) together with all the new provisions relating to offences committed against children, rape, sexual assault, and assault by penetration.

Formerly the list only covered certain sexual offences, primarily those committed against children, but even then there were some omissions. For example, Luke Sadowski, a 19 year-old trainee teacher, was sentenced to 18 months in August 2003 for trying to buy a 9 year-old girl over the Internet for sexual purposes (BBC News website, 20 August 2003). He was charged with inciting another person to procure the girl under s 28 SOA 1956, an offence not included on the original list but which has now been added. Sch 3 is a more extensive list of some 35 sexual offences (plus their Scottish and Northern Irish equivalents) but does not cover other sexually motivated crimes such as murder, kidnapping, or false imprisonment. However, the offence, in s 62, of committing an offence with intent to commit a sexual offence would encompass such sexually motivated 'non-sexual' offences making them registrable as specifically indicated in the Explanatory Notes (see ch 9). The schedule is very comprehensive and catches those convicted of offences that might be perceived as less serious, at least in the sense that they may not involve children or violence, such as voyeurism, exposure, sex with an adult relative or with an animal. This is a fairly heavy-handed approach. It seems that one of the overriding objectives of the whole Act is to get as many people as possible on the Register irrespective of whether they present a real risk to the public. The fact that some people abhor certain sexual practices as deviant does not necessarily justify universal monitoring. Albeit the schedule covers most of the offences in the SOA 2003 and other Acts, reference needs to be made in respect of any particular offence, as many stipulate additional criteria to be fulfilled in respect of the sentence imposed based on age and sentence thresholds. For example, previously a person convicted of indecent assault only attracted notification requirements if sentenced to 30 months imprisonment or more. For an equivalent conviction for sexual assault (s 3) a person becomes a relevant offender if he is (Sch 3(18)):

(i)   *under* 18 the imposition of a sentence of imprisonment for at least 12 months,

(ii)   *over 18* and any victim or intended *victim was under* 18, or

(iii) *over 18* and any custodial sentence, community sentence of at least 12 months (involving the offender being subject to a community rehabilitation order, community punishment, supervision order, or electronic monitoring), or period of hospital detention was imposed.

The same criteria apply to the offences committed by care workers against persons with a mental disorder (ss 38–41), committing an offence or trespassing with intent to commit a sexual offence (ss 62–63), exposure (s 67) and voyeurism (s 68) for example; but the community sentence aspect in respect of a conviction for intercourse with an animal (s 69) or penetration of a corpse (s 70) is not a condition. Care needs to be taken therefore to ensure that any conviction satisfies the relevant criteria.

11.2.2 Persons convicted of sexual offences before implementation of the Act

The new notification requirements apply equally to those offenders already on the SOR by virtue of Part 1 SOA 1997 and whose notification period has not yet expired i.e., those convicted of an offence listed in Sch 1 SOA 1997 *after* 1 September 1997 and before Part 2 of the Act comes into operation (s 81). However, some individuals who committed offences *before* 1 September 1997 may still be susceptible to the notification requirements as relevant offenders. These include anyone who has not yet been arrested and dealt with for an offence committed before that date and, to catch any 'oddball' cases of offenders convicted prior to September 1 1997, who were unlawfully at large, absent without leave, in hospital detention, on bail pending appeal, or otherwise not physically in custody on that day (s 81(3)–(6)).

Irrespective of whether a relevant offender is subject to notification requirements associated with his actual conviction if he is also currently subject to a Sexual Offences Restraining Order (s 5A SOA 1997), or Sex Offences Prevention Order (s 2 CDA, now ss 104, 109 SOA 2003), or Risk of Sexual Harm Order (s 123 see ch 12) he automatically becomes subject to notification requirements for the duration of these orders (s 81(7)).

11.3 NOTIFICATION PERIOD

The notification period is the length of time a relevant offender is required to remain on the Register and comply with the notification requirements stipulated in Part 2. It is commensurate with the severity of sentence imposed. Registration is compulsory. The notification periods are statutory and apply automatically though critics, including Liberty, have suggested that judicial discretion to impose such restrictions might be fairer. The imposition of a notification period is not an additional penalty or sentence. In *Ibbotson v UK* (1999) Crim LR 153 the European Commission declared the applicant's claim, that the requirement to register was a heavier penalty than that applicable to the offence committed, inadmissible. The requirement was deemed not to be a 'penalty' within Article 7(1) ECHR but a preventative measure. Notification periods remain the same as in Part 1 SOA 1997 but relevant offenders convicted under the equivalent Scottish law are also included.

Section 82 tabulates the notification periods as below:

Relevant Offender	Notification Period beginning with the relevant date	Relevant Offender under 18
Sentenced to life imprisonment or 30 months	Indefinite period	
Scottish order for lifelong restriction s 210F Criminal Procedure (Scotland) Act 1995	Indefinite period	
Admitted to hospital subject to a restriction order	Indefinite period	
Sentenced to 6 months but less than 30 months	10 years	Half
Sentenced to 6 months or less	7 years	Half
Admitted to hospital but not subject to a restriction order	7 years	Half
Cautioned	2 years	Half
Conditional discharge (Scottish probation order)	Period of conditional discharge (or Scottish probation order)	
Person of any other description	5 years	Half

11.3.1 Indefinite period or notification for life

Offenders sentenced to 30 months or more imprisonment for a relevant offence remain subject to all notification requirements indefinitely, in other words for life. There are no provisions in the Act for such indefinite requirements, or for that matter requirements for specified periods, to be terminated or reduced. As these are not sentences as such there are no provisions for appeal. However, where the initial sentence that attracted the indefinite period is subject of an appeal and the appellate court allows the appeal then the court is obliged to substitute a fixed term of years as the notification period commensurate with the reduced sentence if that falls below 30 months. In *R v David H* [2001] EWCA Crim 2753 where the defendant had indecently assaulted his sisters when drunk, the Court of Appeal replaced the original custodial sentence of 30 months detention in a young offenders institution with a 2 year community rehabilitation order because of his full admission and positive progress. The court respectively reduced the notification requirements from life to 5 years. Conversely when the Court of Appeal increases a sentence on application from the Attorney General then the notification period will automatically increase commensurately as in *AG's Reference (No 134 of 2002)* [2003] EWCA Crim 1211. As LJ Kay confirmed, notification periods are not sentences but any variation is an *automatic consequence* of any increase or reduction in sentence.

11.3.2 Definite notification period

Offenders sentenced to a term of imprisonment of less than 30 months but more than 6 months are subject to a 10 year notification period and for those sentenced to less than 6 months the period is 7 years. The catch-all 5 year period for 'a person of any other description' remains but a specific reduction to 2 years appears in respect of persons cautioned, minimizing the potential for excessive tariffs. Similarly where a conditional discharge is made the notification period runs concurrently to the period of discharge. In the case of young offenders under 18 the specific periods of 10, 7, 5 and 2 years are halved but there is no concession for a young person sentenced to 30 months or more, his notification period will remain for life (s 82(2)). Carl Higgins, 17 years, who broke into a 92 year-old woman's house, smothered her with a pillow and indecently assaulted her, was ordered to remain on the SOR for life after being sentenced to 2 years imprisonment (BBC News website, 2 October 2003). However, entries made on to the Register as a result of the Final Warning Scheme for young offenders authorized under ss 65 and 66 CDA 1998 have been held to be incompatible with the ECHR. In *R v MPC, ex parte U, R v Durham Constabulary, ex parte R* [2002] EWHC 2486 (Admin) two 15 year-old boys who were given final warnings in respect of indecent assaults committed on girls at their school and ordered to remain on the Register for two years, won their appeal because there was no obligation on them to give their informed consent as a precondition to a warning being administered by the police. The Administrative Court therefore ordered that their names be removed from the SOR.

To avoid any confusion as to when the notification period commences 'beginning with the relevant date' means the date of conviction or date of caution. In cases where an individual is found to be under a disability but it is ascertained that he did the act alleged, the relevant date is the date of that finding and the notification period ends at the conclusion of the trial (s 82(5)).

Where a relevant offender is convicted of two or more offences listed in Sch 3 and has been sentenced either to consecutive terms of imprisonment or terms which are partly concurrent then the notification period is aggregated (s 82(4)).

Example: A is sentenced to 15 months each for two offences of sexual assault. If the sentences run concurrently, or if he had only been convicted of one offence, his notification period would be 10 years. If the sentences run consecutively both are aggregated meaning that his total sentence is 30 months lifting him into the top band where the notification period is indefinite. If one sentence was for 15 months and the other 9 months to run partly concurrent then the calculation is 9+15 = 24 minus the overlapping period of 9 giving a total of 15 months and so the notification period would remain at 10 years. If sentenced to a third offence for 9 months the calculation is 9+9+15 = 33 minus the overlapping period of 9 which would increase the time to be taken into account to 24 months but again the notification period would remain at 10 years.

11.4 NOTIFICATION REQUIREMENTS

Where a sex offender is released from prison he must notify the police of his name and main residential address within three days from the relevant date i.e., his release date, excluding any time spent in custody, service, or hospital detention, or outside the UK (s 83). If he is already subject to notification requirements by virtue of a previous conviction either under this Act or s 2(1) SOA 1997 there is no obligation to re-notify provided he has complied with all existing requirements.

11.4.1 Initial notification—information to be provided

More personal information must be provided than was previously required under the SOA 1997. The information and personal details that must be supplied are listed in s 83(5) and failure to supply just one of them leaves a person open to a charge of failure to comply. As before, date of birth, name and any other aliases used either at the relevant date or date of notification must be provided by the relevant offender to the police. Similarly a relevant offender's home address on the relevant date and, if different, on the date of notification, must be declared. Home address means either his sole or main residence in the UK. Those who have no permanent address, who are peripatetic, homeless, or live in hostels, are no longer permitted to nominate a place they regularly visit as previously allowed. Instead the wording has been subtly altered requiring the nomination of a place where the person can 'be regularly found' thereby shifting the responsibility to the offender to ensure the police can easily find him. This is to ensure released offenders who choose to have no fixed abode can be tracked. The Explanatory Notes suggest this could be a shelter or even a park bench. The issue was highlighted in July 2003 over concerns about the release on licence of Christopher Davies, convicted in 1995 for raping two former prostitutes who brought successful private prosecutions. Davies had previously failed to report to a hostel while on parole (The Times, 31 July 2003).

    In addition any addresses of other premises where a person regularly resides or stays must be volunteered such as relatives, estranged wives/partners, children, or close friends. Offenders must also now provide their national insurance number as a further means of identification (s 83(5)(b)).

11.4.1.1 Subsequent periodic notification

After initial notification the relevant offender must again notify the police of all the above information required under s 83(5) within one year of first supplying it and annually thereafter (s 85(1)). Persons already subject to notification periods prior to the commencement of Part 2 of the Act are also required to notify the police within 12 months of all the information required, which, given the numbers involved could cause some administrative headaches for some police forces.

11.4.2 Method of notification

A relevant offender required to make an initial notification must present himself in person at a police station (designated by the Home Secretary) in his local police area and give an oral notification to any police officer or person authorized to receive that information by the officer in charge of the station (s 87(1)). The requisite police station in his local area is either the police area covering his home address, or in the absence of any current home address his last notified previous address. If there are no such addresses the police area is the one where the court last dealt with him in relation to the Sch 3 offence or that made any Sexual Offender Order, Sexual Offences Prevention Order, or any such interim order. Written acknowledgement of the relevant offender's attendance and information must be made by the recording officer. On the first, and any subsequent, occasion a person is required to register, the police have authority to take and check his fingerprints and take a current photograph of any part of him in order to verify his correct identity (s 87(4)). 'Photographs' may include any process by means of which an image may be produced so would include digital and computerized images. In *Hellewell v CC Derbyshire* [1995] 4 All ER 473 the court held that the police would have a public interest defence to any action for breach of confidence where a photograph was used reasonably in relation to the prevention or detection of crime. 'Reasonably' means that its circulation is restricted to those who have a reasonable need to make use of it.

11.4.3 Notification of any changes to personal details or circumstances

Section 84(1) imposes a duty to notify any change of personal details and wherever possible offenders are encouraged to notify such changes in circumstance or address in advance. If a person decides to use another name not previously notified to the police or changes his home address then he may give that information in advance specifying the date when the event is expected to occur, but in any case he must inform the police of such changes within three days of adoption. If for any reason this change in personal circumstances in fact occurs more than two days *before* the date anticipated by the offender the duty under s 84(1) supersedes any advance notice given. If the proposed change in circumstances fails to occur within three days *after* the anticipated date then again the duty to notify any change supersedes any advance notice. It is then incumbent on the relevant offender to notify the police within six days of the anticipated date that the change of personal circumstances failed to occur. As failure to comply with any of these requirements is an offence individuals offered promises of housing or accommodation that are then let down at the last minute need to be aware of these implications.

If a relevant offender temporarily stays at any premises not declared as his home address or as an address that he visits regularly then if he stays there for a qualifying period the police must be informed (s 84(1)(c)). 'Qualifying period' means seven or more days, either consecutively or taken on a number of occasions, within one calendar year. This could include holiday addresses, residential courses or treatment programmes of more than a week, and other work-related commitments.

11.4.3.1 *Subsequent periodic notification*

Where a person gives notification under s 84(1) the next subsequent 12 month periodic notification is counted from that date, not the initial date of notification. If a person provides information of a change of circumstance or personal detail more than once in a 12 month period from initial notification then the annual periodic notifications recommence from the last s 84(1) notification within that 12 month period (s 85(1)(c)). This could cause some confusion and it remains to be seen whether both relevant offenders and the authorities can keep track of the requisite date changes and maintain accurate records.

Example: A is released from prison having been convicted of USI with a girl under 16 to a hostel address in Nottingham on 1 May 2004. He has three days to comply with s 83(1) initial notification so must supply the police in that force area of all the information listed in s 83(5). At the time his partner refuses to have anything to do with him so he decides not to declare this address. In July 2004 A secures short-term summer contract work as a cook in a hotel in Blackpool with accommodation provided. He informs the Nottingham police two weeks in advance of taking up the position (s 84(2)), which starts 21 July, but on 23 July having worked for two days is told that the work is no longer available as the manager has heard about his conviction. He must now inform the police that he will no longer be living in the hotel within six days from 21 July. A is unable to return to the Nottingham hostel but arranges to stay with his ex-partners' brother for a week in Blackpool while finding suitable alternative accommodation. He would need to inform either the Nottingham or Blackpool police if he stays more than seven days between 1 May 2004–1 May 2005 as this would count as a qualifying period (s 84(1)(c)). On 5 August his ex-partner permits him to return to their family home; again he must notify the police within three days of moving back (s 84(1)(b)), he does so on 7 August. His subsequent annual periodic notification would then be within three days of 7 August 2005, not 1 May 2005. Any failure to notify any of the above could render A liable to an offence of failure to comply.

11.4.4 Notification of travel abroad

Relevant offenders who leave the UK to travel or work abroad may be required to notify the police beforehand of all countries, including territories and destinations, they intend to visit and the date when they will leave the country. Section 86 makes provision for this duty and gives the Secretary of State discretion to enforce it through further regulations exercisable by statutory instrument. This provision will not come into effect immediately but when further consideration has been given to the nature and content of any accompanying regulations. For example regulations may be drafted requiring the individual to present himself at foreign police stations or UK embassies and to give a detailed itinerary of where he is or intends to stay. The full implications of the nature of such further potential restrictions is therefore not yet apparent.

11.4.5 Failure to comply with requirements

Failure to comply with any of the stipulated requirements regarding initial and periodic notification, supply of and changes to information, travel arrangements etc., is a criminal offence (s 91(1)(a)). The section permits a defence of reasonable excuse, for example where a person is suddenly taken ill or incapacitated or in the case of a young person (see below) where the responsible parent has been unable to persuade him to attend the police station despite all reasonable efforts. The offence is committed on the first day the person fails to comply without reasonable excuse and the offence is a continuing one for the duration in which the failure continues. Only one charge may be brought however and any continued omission should be reflected in the sentence. If an offender is convicted of failing to comply and then fails to comply again in respect of the same provision then this should be treated as a new offence. It is also an offence for a relevant offender to give any information to the police that he knows to be fraudulent (s 91(1)(b)). Genuine errors or mistakes about accommodation addresses are therefore not punishable. Proceedings may be brought in any court having jurisdiction where the offender resides or is found.

On summary conviction a person may be sentenced to 6 months imprisonment or a fine not exceeding the statutory maximum, or both. On indictment the maximum penalty is 5 years. This was increased under the CJCSA 2000 in response to criticism about the leniency and disincentives created by a summary only offence. The Home Office asserts that this tough sanction ensures a high compliancy rate of 97% and justifies refusing the public access to the Register. In *R v James Clark* [2003] 1 Cr App R(S) 2 the Court of Appeal held that a 3 month sentence for failing to notify change of address when D was forced to move from Derby to Skegness because associates discovered his previous conviction for abduction and indecent assault on a young girl was 'perfectly proper and proportionate to the offence'.

11.4.6 Young persons—parental responsibilities

Where a relevant offender is under 18, (or in the case of a person convicted in Scotland under 16), at the time he is dealt with by the court then in addition to the notification period being halved the court also has the power to impose obligations upon his parents or individuals having parental responsibility (s 89(1)). A direction under this section means that any notification requirements imposed on the young offender under ss 83 to 86 are instead to be treated as obligations upon the parent who must ensure that when s/he attends the police station to give the notification the young offender also attends. Such directions take immediate effect and apply until the young offender attains the age of 18, in which case he takes full responsibility as an adult, or terminate where the court has directed that a shorter period apply. Chief Constables also have the power under s 89(4) to seek a direction of parental responsibility by complaint to the Magistrates' Court where a young offender under 18 is living, or is intending to come to his police area. The young offender, his parent, or Chief Constable in the circumstances above, may all apply to the appropriate court (Crown Court or by way of complaint) for an order to renew, vary, or discharge a parental direction. The court may make a new order on hearing the application from the applicant and must also hear any of the other individuals entitled to make an application if they wish to be heard. For example, a variation or discharge might be sought where it is no longer appropriate for the responsible parent to notify on their son's behalf because either they are estranged, no longer resident in the UK, or are unable to control the young person.

The Secretary of State also has powers to make regulations regarding any individual responsible for a relevant offender who is serving a term of imprisonment or service or hospital detention to notify any specified person of the date of the relevant offender's release or of any changes to the person/s responsible for him. Thus prison governors, hospital, and military managers, and other associated professionals such as psychiatrists and probation officers should be aware of this potential (s 96).

11.5 NOTIFICATION ORDERS

In addition to the above automatic notification requirements which are activated on conviction, s 97 also provides the Chief Officer of Police with the power to apply for a notification order, or interim notification order, in respect of any defendant who he believes is in, or is intending to come to, his police area. This provision is aimed at catching offenders who have been convicted abroad and intend to return to the UK or are deported back to the UK on release from prison. The Chief Officer may make a complaint to any Magistrates' Court covering his police area where it appears to him that the following three conditions are met.

(i) The defendant has been convicted (but not necessarily punished for), cautioned, or dealt with in a way equivalent to a finding of insanity or disability, of an offence under the law in another country that is equivalent to a relevant offence in Sch 3 howsoever described or framed. The defendant may challenge an application where he believes that any offence he was convicted of abroad does not, in his opinion, equate to a relevant offence listed in Sch 3. He must serve a notice to this effect on the applicant requiring the applicant to prove that the condition is met and show grounds for belief (s 97(2)). For example, it is possible that some of the older and more bizarre provisions, that have not yet been removed from certain statute books in some American states, or that exist in more fundamentalist religious regimes, would not constitute a relevant offence.

(ii) The conviction, finding, or caution occurred on or after 1 September 1997, or the offence was committed before that date but the offender was detained or imprisoned or undertaking any other form of sentence in that country on 1 September 1997, or was not dealt with until after 1 September 1997 or has yet to be dealt with (s 97(3)). This latter implies that a notification order could be sought in the UK in respect of a defendant who has not yet been found guilty by a court of law in the foreign jurisdiction where the offence alleged was committed, raising the spectre of possible human rights implications.

(iii) The notification period in respect of the relevant offence has not expired (s 97(4)). For example, if A was convicted abroad of a minor sexual offence for which he received, or would have received if he had committed the offence in the UK, a caution or the equivalent thereof, the notification period is 2 years from the date of the caution administered in that country. If A remains in that country for 2 years or more before returning to the UK no notification order could be sought as the 2 year notification period would have expired. Similarly if convicted of an offence for which the notification period is 7 years and he remains abroad another 4 years after conviction, on his return he would only be subject to notification requirements for the remaining 3 years. If A had been convicted abroad of an offence of sexually abusing children then it is more likely that he would have received a sentence commensurate with indefinite notification for life and sensibly this is what the provision aims to secure though in a rather convoluted and confusing way.

Pending the determination of any application for a notification order the applicant may seek an interim order either appended to the main complaint or submitted subsequently. The court may make such interim order if it considers it just to do so. Such an order may be required pending the receipt of papers confirming the conviction abroad. The order must be for a fixed period but can be varied, renewed or discharged by complaint from either the applicant or the defendant and will terminate automatically when the main application has been determined (s 100). An appeal lies to the Crown Court against the making of either a full or interim notification order.

11.6 DISCLOSURE OF INFORMATION

Despite a 700,000 signature petition handed to Home Secretary Jack Straw in September 2000 by the parents of Sarah Payne, murdered by Roy Whiting, and supported by a *News of the World* campaign, the Government refused to allow any controlled public, i.e., parental, access to the SOR equivalent to Megan's law in the USA. David Blunkett later promised to 'clamp down on the evil around us' but would not allow the register to be open to vigilantes who 'cannot understand the difference between a paediatrician and a paedophile'. (BBC News website, 2 October 2002). Like the SOA 1997 the Act fails to address and provide guidance on the circumstances in which information on sex offenders may be made available and to whom. An amendment was inserted at the Commons Committee Stage authorizing the supply, to the Secretary of State, of information notified to the police for the purposes of crime prevention, investigation, and detection; and vice versa from the Secretary of State to a Chief Constable or the Director Generals of the National Criminal Intelligence Service (NCIS) and National Crime Squad (ss 94–5).

11.6.1 Police responsibilities in relation to the Register

The Police are required to identify, locate, monitor, and assess the risks posed by sex offenders but surprisingly there is no actual SOR as such. When offenders notify their details to the police they are entered on the Police National Computer, thus forces need to communicate with each other to obtain and check information. A national database is currently being developed to provide a more comprehensive and efficient resource. Many forces now have dedicated units (such as Dangerous Persons Unit or equivalent) with specific responsibilities to collate and check the accuracy of information and disseminate intelligence.

The police may use information to assist in the prevention and detection of crime and may share it with other agencies. Managing information on the SOR is a complex business given the number of agencies involved and potential for any disclosure to be counter-productive. Individuals may be placed at risk, which could cause them to 'disappear' so any release of information to third parties must be carefully assessed, particularly if it involves the media. The CJCSA 2000, s 67, imposes a duty on the police and probation services to work together and take the lead in managing sex offenders and to share information and decision-making with other agencies through Multi-Agency Public Protection Panels (MAPPS). The two lead agencies are required to establish local policies and procedures to assess and manage the risks posed by relevant sex offenders considered to be a potential harm to the public.

11.6.2 When is disclosure justified?

The disclosure of inaccurate information affecting a person's reputation may not only place them at personal risk but could also lead to possible defamation proceedings unless justified or made in good faith. Section 115 Crime and Disorder Act 1998 provides a power to disclose when it is necessary in relation to any provision in that Act. The provisions of the Data Protection Act 1998 may also be relevant and the Rehabilitation of Offenders Act 1974 is currently under review. The Association of Chief Police Officers (ACPO) have adopted a general policy of confidentiality, a presumption that any decision to disclose must be based on strong legal and moral grounds, and the disclosure itself to be properly managed. Details of those registered can only be disclosed by the police in exceptional circumstances, essentially where there is the likelihood of danger or risk of serious harm occurring unless disclosed. In *R v CC North Wales Police and Others ex parte Thorpe and another* [1999] QB 396 a married couple released from prison who had committed serious sexual offences on children went to live on a caravan site in North Wales. North Wales Police received information from Northumbria Police that they presented a substantial risk to children and so asked them to leave by the Easter holidays. The couple refused and so the police informed the site owner of their convictions, he then requested them to leave. They sought a judicial review of the decision to release their identity on the grounds of irrationality and that they had not had the opportunity to challenge the decision. The Court of Appeal held that although the convictions were in the public domain the police should only disclose the identity of former sex offenders if they reasonably concluded, having taken into account the interests of the applicants, that there is a pressing need to do so. In making the decision to disclose they must gather as much information as possible and the individuals concerned must be given an opportunity to respond to that information.

In a case involving social workers it was held that as they had a statutory duty (s 17 CA 1989) to protect children the disclosure of allegations that the applicant had previously sexually abused a child in one household to two other households where he subsequently moved was justified. Even though he had not been convicted their genuine belief based on reasonable grounds that he was likely to abuse other children meant that they were right to inform the other families. In balancing the competing interests of the children and their right to protection with the rights of the applicant his came second (*R v Devon County Council ex parte L* [1991] 2 FLR 541). Further in *R(o/a A) v Chief Constable of C* [2001] 1 WLR 461 the release by one Chief Constable to another of sensitive non-conviction information which was then divulged to a local education authority in relation to the vetting of A who applied for a headmaster's post was not unlawful albeit the disclosure was in breach of HO Circular 9/93. The failure to comply with a government circular was not actionable on the basis of illegality though could be relied upon as evidence of unlawfulness in respect of other administrative functions performed by a public body. The LEA had a lawful interest in the information and a pressing need to receive it; the police had an obligation to pass it between themselves in the exercise of their law enforcement function. Finally the former Data Protection Act 1984 was inapplicable as although the information was sensitive data it was manually and not electronically processed. This is now covered by the Data Protection Act 1998 which authorizes the disclosure of information kept electronically or on paper except where non-disclosure is justified in the public interest or disclosure is likely to lead to harm being caused to an individual: see also *R(o/a A) v Chief Constable of C.*

11.7 CONCLUSION

While the Government's objective in seeking to effectively monitor sex offenders who present a real and imminent risk to society is entirely justifiable, and the Act should appease critics of inappropriate entries in relation to those convicted of certain homosexual acts, it is still not clear exactly what the real purpose is behind such an all-encompassing administrative catalogue. Is it really necessary that so many individuals, some of whom pose no serious threat, should be monitored by the state so intrusively? Especially when it is not always possible to seek any process of review or individual risk assessment? Notification requirements may be deemed civil in legal status but it is unlikely that all can appreciate this fine distinction between 'administrative necessity' and the more popular perception of the Register as a punitive measure. Conversely, the need to keep and maintain certain information about alleged sex offenders, even where it does not relate to any convictions, was tragically highlighted after Ian Huntley's convictions for the murders of Holly Wells and Jessica Chapman. At the time of going to press, the Chief Constable of Humberside was facing increasing pressure to resign over the destruction of information relating to previous allegations of rape and sexual assault made against Huntley. If the information had been available Huntley would probably not have been offered the caretaker's job at Soham School. Humberside Police erroneously believed that they had to destroy the information under the Data Protection Acts. (See generally, Policing and Reducing Crime Unit, *Risk Assessment and Management of Known Sexual and Violent Offenders: A Review of Current Issues* (HO 2001) and *Risk Management of Sexual and Violent Offenders: The Work of Public Protection Panels* (HO 2001); ACPO, *Media Group Advisory Guidelines No. 5—Sex Offenders* (www.acpo.police.uk/policies/index.html).

12

SEX OFFENDER ORDERS

12.1 INTRODUCTION

Sex Offender Orders (SOOs) are civil restraining orders designed to protect the public from serious harm and comprise two types; Sex Offences Prevention Orders (SOPOs) and Risk of Sexual Harm Orders (RSHOs). SOPOs replace and amend the former restraining orders introduced under s 5A SOA 1997 and which first came into force 1 December 1998, and Sex Offender Orders, ss 2–4 CDA 1998. They are an enhanced version of the original SOOs, their ambit is broadened to cover not just persons convicted of sexual offences but anyone convicted of a violent or specified offence who may also present a risk of causing serious sexual harm. RSHOs are new and are specifically targeted at persons aged 18 or over to prohibit them from engaging in any sexual activities with children. The minimum duration of both orders is 5 years but they can be renewed and remain in operation indefinitely. Registration, by way of a marker, on the Sex Offenders Register (SOR) is automatic when either order is made enabling more offenders to be entered on the Register.

SOOs were first introduced in response to concerns about the 100,000 sex offenders who could not be registered on the SOR as they had been convicted before 1997. These orders were designed to operate as 'community protection orders' as part of the management and monitoring of potentially dangerous sex offenders to allay public fears and concerns and to act as a preventative measure to curb the commission of further offences. The Police Reform Act 2002 subsequently enacted a number of changes to increase the flexibility of these orders and strengthen their effectiveness. Their jurisdiction was extended beyond England and Wales making these orders mutually applicable in Scotland and Northern Ireland. Though initially slow to take off, less than 100 orders were applied for by police forces in England and Wales up to February 2002 and just over 200 to date, recent Home Office research based on a sample survey suggests that the success rate for applications is high (94%), and that nearly 50% are breached suggesting they are being targeted at appropriate individuals (*The Police Perspective on Sex Offender Orders*, HO May 2003). The two types of SOOs authorized under the new Act are extremely wide-ranging and, for example, can be used to prohibit persons from making any contact with children, typically by preventing them going near schools, children's events, or residing in any premises where children live or visit. Because of the possible infringements on civil liberties their use is limited to those sex offenders who present a risk of serious sexual harm to the public.

12.2 LEGAL STATUS AND STANDARD OF PROOF

SOOs are a form of *civil order* that can be imposed directly within the court's discretion or by the court on application from the police. In both cases the court must be satisfied that such an order is necessary to protect the public from serious sexual harm. SOOs are intended to operate in a similar way to injunctions and breach of an order is a *criminal offence*. The orders are not criminal convictions and must not be recorded as such, neither do they constitute a criminal record but details will be placed on the Police National Computer (PNC); a marker will also appear on the Sex Offenders Register. When first introduced the Government recognized the potential non-compliance with Article 8 ECHR and possible invasion of an individual's privacy rights. By making them civil orders a compromise was achieved avoiding the stricter provisions and safeguards associated with criminal proceedings necessitated by Article 6. Even so *Liberty* have attacked the Government's justification of their use as administrative risk-prevention measures claiming that they are tantamount to a criminal punishment (*Liberty's Second Reading Briefing on the Sex Offences (Amendment) Bill in the House of Commons,* July 2003).

As civil orders it might be expected that the standard of proof to be satisfied when making an application would be the civil standard of a balance of probabilities. Parliament intended to create civil orders determinable by civil proceedings but if the order is breached then that breach precipitates a criminal matter, in effect retrospectively criminalizing the conduct prohibited by the order. Hence this caused problems in respect of the applicable standard of proof. The House of Lords sought to clarify any confusion in *R(McCann and Others) v Crown Court at Manchester* [2003] 1 AC 787 in relation to two applications for Anti-Social Behaviour Orders (ASBOs) under s 1 CDA 1998. The court was asked to consider whether the standard of proof in determining if a case had been made out to grant an ASBO preventing three brothers from entering a part of Manchester, was the civil or criminal standard. If the proceedings for making such orders were civil and so not subject to the rules of evidence that apply in criminal proceedings, then the associated protection afforded by Article 6(2) could not be utilized. The judge at first instance adopted a more stringent standard of proof than that of the balance of probabilities—the court must be 'satisfied so that it was sure' that the orders should be made. The Court of Appeal confirmed that the criminal standard of proof was 'likely to be appropriate' in the majority of applications for ASBOs. In the House of Lords, Lord Steyn, following *B v CC Avon & Somerset Constabulary* [2001] 1 WLR 340 agreed that ASBOs are civil in character but given the *seriousness* of the matters involved at least some reference to the heightened civil standard of proof would usually be necessary. As this is virtually indistinguishable from the criminal standard of beyond all reasonable doubt he advised that pragmatism therefore dictates that magistrates should universally apply the criminal standard of proof with respect to all s 1 ASBO applications. There are clear implications from this decision as regards the standard of proof to be achieved in respect of applications for SOOs. The standard of evidence required must now be assumed to be the *criminal* standard of proof thus in making their risk assessment magistrates will need to be convinced beyond all reasonable doubt that an order is necessary to protect the public from serious sexual harm.

12.3 SEX OFFENCES PREVENTION ORDERS

12.3.1 Relationship with previous provisions

12.3.1.1 *Sex Offender Orders*
When SOOs were first introduced it was incumbent on the police to initiate an application as the court had no original discretion to make such orders. Under s 2 CDA 1998 the Chief Officer of Police could apply to the Magistrates' Court for a SOO with respect to anyone living in his police area where two conditions were satisfied. Firstly, that the person was a sex offender meaning that he had been convicted of, or cautioned for, a sexual offence either in the UK or for an act committed elsewhere that would constitute a sexual offence if committed in the UK. Secondly, that the person had acted, since the relevant date, in such a way as to give reasonable cause to believe an order was necessary to protect the public from serious sexual harm. Thus the court had to be convinced that he was both a sex offender and a risk to the public.

12.3.1.2 *Restraining Orders*
In addition Sch 5 Criminal Justice and Courts Services Act 2000 inserted a new clause, s 5A, into the Sex Offenders Act 1997 enabling the Crown Court to make restraining orders in respect of persons convicted of sexual or violent offences and sentenced to 12 months or more imprisonment. The same criteria regarding the need

to protect the public from serious sexual harm also applied. Such orders became live when the person was released on licence and conditions could be attached disqualifying him, for example, from working with children.

This parallel system meant that public protection was somewhat unpredictable since if a person was sentenced by the Crown Court s 5A would activate, whereas if the case was heard at the Magistrates' Court or the defendant received a non-custodial sentence then any imposition of a SOO was reliant on the police making an initial application. The Act removes this inconsistency and repeals all previous provisions relating to both SOOs and Restraining Orders incorporating both types of order as a single Sex Offences Prevention Order (s 104).

12.3.2 General provisions and effect

SOPOs may be imposed by a court on any person aged 10 or over (the age of criminal responsibility) on application from the police (s 104(1)(a)) or acting within its own discretion (s 104(1)(b)). In both cases the court must be satisfied that the public, or particular members of the public, need to be protected from serious sexual harm occasioned by the defendant, not by any other person. The court may be satisfied of this either by the circumstances of the offence or from any other evidence of D's behaviour. Where a Chief Officer of Police makes an application for a SOPO the court must be satisfied that D is a 'qualifying offender' as defined in s 106 i.e., that he has been convicted of, or cautioned for, a Sch 3 or Sch 5 offence, or found to have committed the offence while under a disability, or found not guilty by reason of insanity. A person will also be a qualifying offender if convicted etc. of a relevant offence abroad. It is not necessary to identify an individual member of the public or potential victim. 'Serious sexual harm' was not defined in the previous statutory provisions but was accepted as meaning either serious physical or psychological harm. This is now formalized in s 106(3) as meaning 'protecting the public in the UK, or any particular members of it, from any serious physical or psychological harm caused by the defendant committing one or more offences listed in Schedule 3'. Thus orders may be made prohibiting D from entering general areas such as public spaces or shopping centres, specific localities such as universities, schools, or children's parks or making contact with particular individuals or groups, such as children of a certain age, or prostitutes. Any assessment of risk must be based on the threat that the defendant currently poses to the community. For example, in July 2002, Steven Callaghan, a convicted sex offender who was allowed to referee children's football matches was banned by Blackburn Magistrates from entering any park or recreational ground, allowing anybody under 18 into his home, and taking up any activity, paid, voluntary, or recreational, which could bring him into regular contact with persons under 18. The court was satisfied that a psychiatric assessment of Callaghan confirmed he still represented a serious physical risk (thisislancashire.co.uk/lancashire/archive/2002/07/19/NEWSBBN0ZM.html). In *R v Trevor Anthony Norkett* [2003] EWCA Crim 2083 an order was made prohibiting a

Church of England vicar from possessing or wearing any clerical clothing that showed he was an ordained minister as he had previously deceived others as to his profession, had been convicted of gross indecency with a child, and posed a risk to vulnerable people.

The effect of a SOPO is to prohibit D from doing anything described in the order and such prohibitions must be identifiable as necessary to protect the public from serious sexual harm (s 107(2)). The minimum duration of an order is 5 years and its imposition automatically triggers a marker onto the SOR. Where a second SOPO is made in relation to a person who is already the subject of a former SOPO, or equivalent SOO imposed before the implementation of this Act, then the first order ceases to have effect. An offender cannot be made subject to more than one SOPO at any one time (s 107(6)). In all cases the notification period, once a SOPO has been imposed, runs from the date of the service of the order, not the date of conviction or application. A person subject to an order will then have three days to comply with the notification requirements and initially register at a police station (s 107(5) see ch 11).

12.3.3 Discretionary court orders

12.3.3.1 *Against whom may an order be made?*
The Crown Court or the Magistrates' Court may make a SOPO where it deals with the defendant in respect of any conviction listed in Sch 3 or 5 of the Act and is satisfied that it is necessary to make such an order for the purpose of protecting the public or any particular members of the public from serious sexual harm from the defendant (s 104(1)(b)). The section applies where D is convicted of the offence or is found guilty by reason of insanity or is under a disability (e.g., learning disorder or hyperglycaemia) but has been found to have done the act. Just because D is a persistent offender may not automatically mean that the public requires protection from *serious* sexual harm. This will depend on the circumstances of each case including, the nature and seriousness of any sexual violation, where the offence occurred, the defendant's intent and whether the victim was known to him, see *R v Osman* [2000] 2 Cr App R(S) 112. Consideration should also be given to the accuracy of any information relied on and the extent to which D has complied with any previous orders or licence conditions.

12.3.3.2 *Where convicted of a sexual offence*
Schedule 3 lists those offences commonly acknowledged as sexual offences whether committed in England/Wales, Scotland, or Northern Ireland, and includes all offences created by the Act and their former counterparts under the SOA 1956. As is the case with notification requirements certain offences which might be perceived as 'less serious' because no penetration or direct sexual assault occurred, such as voyeurism, exposure and trespassing with intent, or because there might be a wide range of severity and culpability, such as sexual assault and sex with an adult relative, require additional criteria to apply. Generally these are:

179

(i)   that any victim or intended victim was under 18 (see e.g., Sch 3(8), (18)), or

(ii)   if the offender was under 18 a sentence of at least 12 months imprisonment was imposed (Sch 3(18)), or

(iii) where the offender was over 18 a custodial sentence, community sentence of at least 12 months, or a period of hospital detention was imposed (Sch 3(18), (25), (28)).

In respect of any former charges under ss 12 and 13 SOA 1956 regarding offences relating to homosexual acts these require D to be 20 years or over and his victim under 18 years to count (Sch 3(5),(6)).

Example: A is convicted by the Crown Court for a series of sexual assaults on male adult prostitutes under s 3 SOA 2003 committed in the early evening in a local-ized area and receives a custodial sentence of 3 years. As he is over 18 and sentenced to more than 12 months imprisonment he is eligible. If the court is satisfied by proof to a criminal standard, i.e., there is evidence of other previous convictions/cautions or psychiatric/probation reports, that on his release he may resume this activity, it may make a SOPO prohibiting him from visiting that locality at certain times in order to protect particular members of the public—male adult prostitutes. Such order would become live on his release and remain in force for 5 years from the date it was made. A marker would also be made on the SOR.

If A had been sentenced by the Magistrates' Court, a community sentence of at least 12 months must have been imposed for an accompanying SOPO to be made.

If A was under 18 years he must have been sentenced to a custodial term of imprisonment of at least 12 months for the same to apply (Sch 3(18)).

12.3.3.3 *Where convicted of a non-sexual offence*
Schedule 5 is much broader, listing some 63 (mainly indictable) offences relating to violence to persons or property including murder, the majority of offences under the OAPA 1861, most firearms offences, public order offences, and a miscellaneous mix including harassment, racially-aggravated offences, causing death by dangerous/reckless driving, and female circumcision. Clearly the intention is to permit the court to make an order where D has been convicted of a non-sexual offence but there is sufficient evidence to justify the imposition of a SOPO because of his previous character and sexual propensities. It would also cover situations where for some reason a charge of physical violence is preferred either because of the severity of the violence perpetrated in committing a sexual offence i.e., murder or GBH, or a crime of violence is easier to prove, or plea-bargaining has occurred. Sch 5 also includes a range of offences directed at combating terrorist acts and orga-nized crime, such as endangering aircraft, hijacking ships, the taking of hostages, and the commission of crimes against humanity as defined by the International Criminal Court (e.g., gang rape in a warfare context). The inclusion of these seem-ingly unrelated offences means that theoretically SOPOs could be imposed on those

involved in organized crime, global prostitution, and people-trafficking provided they present a current threat and risk of serious harm to the public or members of it. Such individuals could then be monitored as they would be automatically entered on the SOR even though not convicted of a sexual offence.

Example: A, a doctor, is convicted of unlawfully circumcising teenage girls brought to his surgery by their parents. The court might consider a SOPO necessary to prohibit him from undertaking any future operations. A has not committed a sexual offence but the risk of serious sexual harm could be made out (Sch 5(44)).

12.3.4 On application by the police

12.3.4.1 *Against whom may an order be made?*
The Chief Officer of Police may, by complaint to the Magistrates' Court acting in its civil capacity, apply for an order in respect of a person who he believes is in, or is intending to come to, his police area if it appears that:

(i)   the person is a qualifying offender, and

(ii)   has acted in such a way as to give reasonable cause to believe it is necessary for such an order to be made (s 104(5)).

The person does not need to be habitually resident in the police area and so potentially an order could be sought for someone visiting or who is a vagrant or transient. They would then become subject to notification requirements and residential details would need to be registered on the SOR. A 'qualifying offender' is anyone convicted of, or cautioned for, an offence listed in Sch 3 or 5, or found not guilty of such an offence by reason of insanity or other disability, or convicted of an equivalent offence committed overseas (unless he can prove the contrary s 106(5)–(7)). The police would be expected to liaise with other appropriate agencies and where the person is under 18 should consult the relevant social services department and youth offending team (see Home Office guidance www.homeoffice.gov.uk).

Example: D receives a 9 month Community Order at the Magistrates' Court for indecently exposing himself to female students on a university campus under s 67. Under Sch 3 the court may only impose a SOPO if the victim was under 18 or he was sentenced to at least 12 months imprisonment or community sentence. He would therefore not be eligible for a SOPO under s 104(1). However, if he has previous convictions for sexually assaulting other female students and had been detained in hospital for a short period and the police can satisfy the court to the criminal standard that he is currently a serious risk to all or some female students an application could be made under s 104(5). If he has previously been cautioned for indecently exposing himself to young schoolgirls under 18 then he also becomes a qualifying offender.

12.3.4.2 *What conduct may be taken into account?*

In determining whether it is necessary to make an order and the extent of the risk of sexual harm presented to the public, the court must base its decision on the nature of the defendant's behaviour since the 'appropriate date' (s 104(5)(b)). This replaces the term 'relevant date' (CDA 1998, s 3(2)) which meant either the date on which D was convicted, or if convicted before 1 December 1998, that date—whichever was the later. Previously if the police wished to make an application they needed to get their timing right as illustrated in *Hopson v CC North Wales Police* [2002] EWHC 2430. Hopson had a number of previous convictions for rape and indecent assault on young girls dating back to 1994. On 3 October 2001 he was convicted of USI with a girl under 16 and the Crown Court adjourned the case for sentence. On 19 November the Chief Officer of Police applied to the Magistrates' Court seeking a SOO on the basis that the relevant date should be 1 December 1998 thereby catching his previous convictions as well as his behaviour, the subject of the present conviction. On 23 November he was sentenced and on 13 December the magistrates made the SOO. D appealed by way of case-stated that the relevant date was the date of his last conviction—3 October, and that he had not done anything between then and the date the application was made—19 November, that could justify an order being imposed. The Administrative Court confirmed that where a person had committed a sexual offence *prior* to 1 December 1998 then that became the relevant date subject to any subsequent conviction date. Here the relevant date was the date Hopson *was convicted*—3 October 2001, and as no relevant acts had occurred since, no SOO should have been made. The Chief Officer of Police should have made his application *before* the conviction on 3 October or obtained an Interim Order in the meantime.

The replacement of relevant date with *appropriate date* means that if an application was sought now Hopson's conduct dating back to 1994 could be taken into account by the court as 1 December 1998 no longer acts as a cut-off date. 'Appropriate date' therefore means the date or (as the case may be) the *first* date on which a qualifying offender was convicted, found not guilty by reason of insanity/disability, cautioned, or punished for any offence under Sch 3 or 5 (s 106(8)). Thus the court can consider any past behaviour/conduct dating back to the first time a person was convicted for any sexual/violent offence provided it can be shown that he currently presents a serious risk to the public.

12.3.5 Procedural aspects

Copies of the application form and other relevant documents are published in SI 2782/2002 Magistrates' Courts (Sex Offender Orders) Rules 2002 and any application must be made in accordance with ss 51–7 Magistrates' Courts Act 1980. Where a defendant is under 18 years any application for an order should only be considered where there are exceptional circumstances. In any case where the person is under 16 years the court will require the attendance of a parent or guardian, including the local authority social services department (s 34A CYPA 1933). It should also be expected that magistrates with relevant experience be assigned to such hearings.

12.3.6 Interim Sex Offences Prevention Orders

These first appeared in s 68 Police Reform Act 2002 which inserted a new clause s 2A into the CDA 1998 whereby interim SOOs could be made pending the magistrates' determination of the principal application. Interim SOPOs prohibit the defendant from doing anything described in the order and may be imposed where the court considers it just to do so (s 109(3)). An application may be made at the same time as the complaint for the main application is made, or if the main application has already been made a further application for an Interim SOPO may only be made by the same person who initially applied (s 109(2)). Under the CDA 1998 magistrates were permitted a wide discretion and could make an order where they considered it 'appropriate'. The language has now been changed to the slightly more stringent 'considers it just to do so'. An Interim Order must be made for a fixed period and ceases to have effect on determination of the main application.

Interim SOPOs can be enforced by a criminal penalty if breached (s 113(1)(b)) unless D can show, on a balance of probabilities, that he had a reasonable excuse for doing something that the Interim Order prohibited. For example, he needed to pass by a school entrance in order to carry out an authorized errand ordered by his employer. Breach of an Interim Order is punishable on summary conviction by imprisonment not exceeding 6 months or a fine not exceeding the statutory maximum, or both; or a maximum penalty on indictment of 5 years (s 113(2)).

12.4 RISK OF SEXUAL HARM ORDERS

12.4.1 General provisions and effect

RSHOs are similar to those SOPOs issued via police applications in that only a Chief Officer of Police may apply but there are two main differences. RSHOs can only be made in respect of a person *aged 18 or over* and an order may only be made where *necessary to protect a child, or children, under 16 from harm* (under 17 in Northern Ireland). Clearly RSHOs are only intended to apply to paedophiles and child sex abusers. A condition is attached that before a RSHO can be made it must be shown that the person named has engaged in sexually explicit conduct or communication with or towards a child on at least two occasions. In addition the court must have reasonable cause to believe that the order is necessary to prevent any harm to children arising from D's future acts (s 123). Harm includes both physical and psychological harm as stressed by the trial judge in *R v Britton* [2002] EWCA Crim 1860 'assaults upon young children result in serious damage, often physical, but almost invariably psychological' and this is confirmed in s 124(2).

12.4.2 Against whom may an order be made?

As with SOPOs, a Chief Officer of Police may apply to the Magistrates' Court in respect of anyone he believes 'is in, or is intending to come to his police area' (s 123(1)). Thus D need not be a permanent resident but must be 18 or over and, on at least two occasions, whether before or after the commencement of the Act, have done a sexual act or act with sexual connotations as specified in s 123. This is reminiscent of the two cautions required to prove a 'common' prostitute but its reach is much broader as 'two occasions' would cover incidents for which a person has not been formally cautioned or convicted. Issues raised in the context of custody disputes and social inquiry reports for example could constitute such acts. The circumstances surrounding Ian Huntley could also be a case in point. Under the new law, Cambridgeshire Police might now be justified in applying for a RSHO once they were aware that Huntley was coming to their force area and provided that they had been informed of the previous intelligence kept on him by Humberside Police. Unfortunately this information was destroyed by Humberside Police, but the intelligence suggested that Huntley was suspected of sexually abusing young girls on at least two occasions. Thus there will now be more onus on the police to keep this type of information.

No time limit is stipulated within which these acts must have taken place and the section therefore applies to incidents committed before and after the commencement of the Act. An order prohibits D from doing anything specified within it and must be imposed for a fixed period of not less than two years (s 123(5)). Where an order is made against a person already subject to a RSHO the former ceases to have effect and is rolled into the new order. The only controlling mechanism is that the police must have reasonable cause to believe that an order is necessary and that the court is satisfied it is necessary, not that it considers it just to do so as with SOPOs (s 123(4)). Thus there is considerable potential for exercising discretion.

12.4.3 What conduct may be taken into account?

The acts listed in s 123(3) which constitute the 'trigger behaviour' for an order all require some form of explicit sexual behaviour or communication with or towards a child. The conduct may also equate to a criminal offence such as in ss 9 to 12 but does not have to meet this threshold.

12.4.3.1 engaging in sexual activity involving a child or in the presence of a child
Sexual activity is defined as an activity which a reasonable person would in all the circumstances but regardless of motive or any person's purpose consider to be sexual (s 124(5)). The test to apply is therefore an objective one similar to that applied in relation to sexual activity with a child under ss 7 and 9. Masturbating in front of a child or having sexual intercourse with a child would suffice, see *R v JT*

[2001] 1 Cr App R(S) 60 for some examples of acts that would be perceived as such.

12.4.3.2 *causing/inciting a child to watch a person engaging in sexual activity or to look at a moving or still image that is sexual*

An image may be produced by any means, whether a real or imaginary subject so would include composite and pseudo-sexual computer images. An image is sexual if any part of it relates to sexual activity or a reasonable person would, in all the circumstances, but regardless of purpose, consider any part of it to be sexual. Making a child watch while adults have sexual intercourse, showing the child videos, printed material, websites etc. with sexual content or perhaps showing them an ambiguous adult advertisement such as those found in glossy fashion magazines simulating sexual acts would fit under this category.

12.4.3.3 *giving a child anything that relates to sexual activity or contains a reference to such*

Items here include giving a child a condom, vibrator, sex toy, pornographic magazine or book etc.

12.4.3.4 *communicating with a child where any part of the communication is sexual*

Whether a communication, or part of it, is sexual is to be construed in the same manner as an image based on what a reasonable person would think looking at all the circumstances. The Explanatory Notes suggest that where double entendres are deployed, motive may be relevant. Otherwise engaging in sexual dialogue orally, pictorially, or via electronic means including the sending of pornographic images or text over the Internet would suffice.

Example: A and B are convicted of offences of child cruelty and neglect under s 1 CYPA 1933 and during the proceedings it transpires that they have been downloading images of child pornography and created Internet chatrooms to talk to children about these. As they have not been convicted of a sexual offence under Sch 3 the court cannot impose a SOPO; potentially a SOPO could be imposed as they have been convicted of a Sch 5 offence (child cruelty) but the court would have to consider it just to do so and this may depend on how strong the evidence is and to what extent it is an order which is necessary to protect the public from serious sexual harm, which may be debatable. Alternatively an application could be made pending further enquiries into their conduct for a RSHO provided the court is satisfied that on two or more occasions they have engaged in Internet communications with children about sexual activities. Such an order could prohibit them from communicating, or attempting to communicate, in this manner.

The procedural requirements as regards applications made by the police are the same as in respect of SOPOs in that an application may be made to any Magistrates' Court whose commission area includes the person's local police area or any place where it is alleged that he acted in a way that would satisfy one of the four forms of sexually explicit behaviour (see s 123(2)). Interim RSHOs may also be applied for pending any determination of the main application as per Interim SOPOs where the court considers it just to do so (s 126).

12.5 ENFORCEMENT AND BREACH

Once a SOPO has been obtained it automatically activates the SOR notification requirements for the duration of the order (s 107(4)) but there is no equivalent notification requirement for RSHOs as there is no associated conviction. It is only when a RSHO or Interim RSHO is breached and D is convicted under s 128 that he becomes subject to notification requirements. Breach of both main and Interim SOPOs and RSHOs without reasonable excuse is a criminal offence triable either way with a maximum penalty on indictment of 5 years or summarily 6 months/fine (ss 113 and 128). The standard of proof is the criminal one of beyond all reasonable doubt. Breach of an order is an arrestable offence (s 24(1)(b) PACE) though breach of any registration requirement is not. In the case of SOPOs where the defendant is a juvenile the case will be heard at the Youth Court. If it appears that a person in breach of a SOO suffers from a mental disorder then consideration should be given to disposal under Part III Mental Health Act 1983.

12.5.1 Determining the appropriate length of sentence for breach

The Court of Appeal considered this in *R v Terry John Wilcox* [2002] EWCA Crim 1430. Wilcox ran a part-time business providing equipment (bouncy castles and the like) for children's parties. In 1998 he was convicted of indecently assaulting a girl under 14 and sentenced to a 3-year probation order. In May 2001 the Chief Constable of Gwent successfully applied for a SOO (SOPO), which was varied a month later to take into account his business and the need to attend functions and set up equipment. The Variation Order prohibited D from remaining at any event up to an hour beforehand and afterwards to minimize any contact with young children. Wilcox breached the order on six separate occasions—five of which were after it had been varied. He pleaded guilty at the Crown Court and was sentenced to 2 years imprisonment to run concurrently. The Court of Appeal confirmed this was a flagrant and continued breach of the court order but in light of the defendant's background reduced the sentence to 12 months. Similarly in *R v James Clark* [2003] 1 Cr App R(S) 2 the Court of Appeal reduced a sentence of 3 years imprisonment for breach to 18 months. Clark, 59 years, and 'a man with a perverted interest in prepubescent girls' was seen seeking the company of young girls. With previous convictions for attempting to abduct a child and impersonating a police officer an order was made restricting his movements and prohibiting him from residing in any place where persons under 16 resided or might be present. He complied with the order for 12 months but then moved into a house where two young children lived and failed to notify this change of address. There was no suggestion of any impropriety or interference towards the children. The Court of Appeal confirmed that this was not a case of immediate and purposeful contempt of the order and, as there was no suggestion of any further targeting of the young girls he had previously displayed an improper sexual interest in, the circumstances did not justify such a high tariff.

Similarly in *Trevor Anthony Norkett* the Court of Appeal held that a sentence of 2 years imprisonment for breach of the condition that the defendant, a vicar, must not wear any clerical clothing was manifestly excessive where he admitted to having dressed as a vicar twice a week for 12 months but with no intent to gain access to any vulnerable young persons. Norkett had previously breached his SOO twice for which he received 4 months imprisonment but as his behaviour on this occasion was devoid of any sexual element a reduced sentence of 12 months was held to be more appropriate.

12.5.2 Public identification

Although SOOs are intended to deter and limit public reaction to the knowledge of offenders residing in a particular area, the court has no power to ban the publication of a qualifying sex offender's name and address. In May 2003 the *Banbury Guardian* challenged Banbury Magistrates' decision to ban the publication of the address of convicted sex offender Martin Smith. This would have effectively barred the publication and identification of his name because of the danger of confusing his (relatively common) name with others in the area. Such a restriction was held to be unlawful because the provisions were not intended to protect defendants and in any case all applications are heard in public (Banbury Today, 8 May 2003). Section 115 CDA 1998 allowed the lawful disclosure of information, for the purposes of the Act, to the police, local authorities, probation services, or health authority in line with the common law provisions regarding confidentiality and statutory provisions regarding data protection. Thus it would appear that persons made subject to a SOO have no automatic right to confidentiality which in the context of SOPOs is arguably justifiable as they will normally have been convicted but in relation to RSHOs this is not necessarily the case.

12.5.3 Mutual applicability

The mutual applicability of SOOs across the jurisdictions of the United Kingdom is retained. Section 70 Police Reform Act 2002, which makes it an offence to do anything prohibited by an order issued in Scotland, remains unchanged but s 69 which covered Northern Ireland is expressly repealed and replaced by implication by Part 2 of the Act which applies equally to England, Wales, and Northern Ireland.

12.6 VARIATIONS AND APPEALS

12.6.1 Variations and renewals

SOPOs endure for five years but can be renewed indefinitely provided this is justi-fied. They may not be discharged by the magistrates before the expiry of that five years without the consent of the defendant, or where an application was made by the police under s 104(5) the consent of the Chief Officer of Police who made the appli-cation, or in any other case the Chief Officer of Police for the area in which D now resides. Similarly in the case of RSHOs the court must not discharge an order before the 2 years is up without the consent of the defendant and relevant Chief Officer of Police (s 125(5)).

Applications for renewals and variations in respect of both SOPOs and RSHOs may be made to the appropriate court by complaint in respect of the Magistrates' Court and in accordance with the Rules of Court in respect of the Crown Court by the:

(i)   defendant,

(ii)   Chief Officer of Police on whose application the original order was made,

(iii) Chief Officer of Police for the area in which D resides,

(iv)   Chief Officer of Police who believes D is in, or is intending to come, to his police area (ss 108(2), 125(2)).

For SOPOs the 'appropriate court' is the Crown Court where the Crown Court or Court of Appeal originally made the order, or where the Magistrates' or Youth Court made the original order, the Magistrates' or Youth Court for the area in which D resides or where an application was made by the police, whose commission area includes that police area (s 108(7)). The 'appropriate court' in the case of RSHOs is either the court that made the original order or the Magistrates' Court for the area in which D resides or, where an application was made by the police, the relevant court for that police area (s 125(7)).

Where the appropriate court considers it necessary, it may renew or vary the order so as to impose additional prohibitions on D provided these are justified only where it is necessary for the purpose of protecting the public from serious sexual harm (s 108(5)), or a child or children generally from harm (s 125(4)).

12.6.2 Appeals

Provisions for appeals against the making of either order can be found in ss 110 and 127. Reference should also be made to Rules 74 and 75 Magistrates' Courts Rules 1981 and Rules 6–11 Crown Court Rules 1982. Appeals against the original order, interim order, or variations/renewals are to the Crown Court (or the Court of Appeal where the order was originally made by the Crown Court) which has the power to make further orders where necessary including the making of incidental or consequential orders. Any subsequent order made by the Crown Court shall be regarded as the original order in respect of any further application for discharge or variation. A defendant may also appeal against the refusal to make a variation or discharge order.

Appeals are conducted by way of re-hearing and the Crown Court should have before it a copy of the original application, the full order, and the notice of appeal. Further challenges against a decision of the Crown Court lie to the High Court either by way of case-stated or by application for judicial review as in the case of *Hopson* above (ss 28–29 Supreme Court Act 1981).

12.7 CONCLUSION

The variety of orders—SOPOs, RSHOs, Notification Orders, and Disqualification Orders—now available to the courts to deal with sex offenders, mean that all convicted offenders, adult or juvenile, including those cautioned, and in some cases those not yet convicted, can be monitored, supervised, and tracked with a view to preventing them committing further offences. But in issuing such orders and in exercising their discretion the courts must be certain that any restrictions or requirements limiting a person's conduct or behaviour are justified on the basis that he presents a serious and ongoing risk to the public. Individuals convicted of sexual offences face significant social stigma and often have to deal with being ostracized from their communities and family. The imposition of additional obligations and incursions can serve to reinforce such censure placing these individuals in a marginalized and invidious position. The combination of orders that may be imposed also requires that information is properly managed and controlled in terms of ensuring it is accurate and up to date. Again, in the light of recent events, it remains to be seen whether those responsible for managing such administrative systems are able to meet the requisite standards of best practice.

13

CONCLUSION

There is no question that the Sexual Offences Act 2003 is a key feature and flagship in the Government's armada of programmes to control and reduce crime; its success is crucial not only in terms of this objective but to restore public faith and confidence in a criminal justice system generally perceived to work against, rather than in the interests of, victims of sex crimes. In seeking to both codify the criminal law relating to sexual offences and to provide a comprehensive set of measures designed to protect the public and prevent sex offenders from re-offending there is a lot at stake. And it is not just the reputation of a government willing to tackle difficult and often controversial matters that is at issue here. This Act is unique in terms of its broad and genuine consultation with all interested parties, feminine involvement, and sponsorship by a Home Secretary who, in a break with convention, has no legal credentials or practitioner experience. It needs to work and be effective in practice, not only in recognition of those who contributed to its formation but also to those who were entrusted to protect the most personal and intimate violations of all.

Has the Act therefore achieved its stated objectives of being coherent, non-discriminatory and more appropriate for modern society? Certainly this enactment strives to achieve a balance and close the gap between two extremes: a prescriptive and particularized approach whereby the number of offences incorporated and the attention to detail are intended to cover all potential loopholes and possibilities, and a more generalized and pragmatic stance allowing the courts some discretion, particularly as regards reasonableness. In order to draw together these two approaches it is evident that there has been a genuine effort in trying to secure a more protectionist approach counter-balanced with the recognition of a more liberal attitude towards sexuality. There is some justified criticism that in places the Act has gone too far, particularly in its apparent criminalization of teenage sex and in respect of certain offences enacted in the laudable interest of protecting children, but where the age at which someone is now considered to be a child has been raised to 18 years. The policies adopted by the prosecuting authorities will therefore be crucial in some circumstances. A number of new offences might also be perceived as unnecessary, and some are so widely drafted that their application could be seen to be unfair to defendants. Problems associated with the securing of proof and evidence in relation to a number of these also mean that in practice it may be difficult to secure a conviction.

Yes, there are shortcomings and those responsible for securing the Act's passage have had to bite the bullet on occasion in terms of lobbying to focus on the more important and achievable objectives. Yes, there is a tendency towards over-specificity resulting in an amount of overlap and there may possibly be some loop-holes yet to be revealed. However, in a more positive light, the Act is almost entirely gender-neutral, recognizing that both women and men can be perpetrators and victims of sexual offences; and the belated removal of the indefensible and discrimi-natory provisions relating to homosexual acts finally signals a more universal public acceptance of sexual diversity.

Appendix 1
Sexual Offences Act 2003

CONTENTS

PART 1
SEXUAL OFFENCES

PART 3

GENERAL

Sexual Offences Act 2003

PART 1
SEXUAL OFFENCES

Rape

1. Rape

(1) A person (A) commits an offence if—

    (a) he intentionally penetrates the vagina, anus or mouth of another person (B) with his penis,

    (b) B does not consent to the penetration, and

    (c) A does not reasonably believe that B consents.

(2) Whether a belief is reasonable is to be determined having regard to all the circumstances, including any steps A has taken to ascertain whether B consents.

(3) Sections 75 and 76 apply to an offence under this section.

(4) A person guilty of an offence under this section is liable, on conviction on indictment, to imprisonment for life.

Assault

2. Assault by penetration

(1) A person (A) commits an offence if—

    (a) he intentionally penetrates the vagina or anus of another person (B) with a part of his body or anything else,

    (b) the penetration is sexual,

    (c) B does not consent to the penetration, and

    (d) A does not reasonably believe that B consents.

(2) Whether a belief is reasonable is to be determined having regard to all the circumstances, including any steps A has taken to ascertain whether B consents.

(3) Sections 75 and 76 apply to an offence under this section.

(4) A person guilty of an offence under this section is liable, on conviction on indictment, to imprisonment for life.

3. Sexual assault

(1) A person (A) commits an offence if—

    (a) he intentionally touches another person (B),

    (b) the touching is sexual,

    (c) B does not consent to the touching, and

    (d) A does not reasonably believe that B consents.

(2) Whether a belief is reasonable is to be determined having regard to all the circumstances, including any steps A has taken to ascertain whether B consents.

(3) Sections 75 and 76 apply to an offence under this section.

(4) A person guilty of an offence under this section is liable—

    (a) on summary conviction, to imprisonment for a term not exceeding 6 months or a fine not exceeding the statutory maximum or both;

    (b) on conviction on indictment, to imprisonment for a term not exceeding 10 years.

Causing sexual activity without consent

4. Causing a person to engage in sexual activity without consent

(1) A person (A) commits an offence if—

(a) he intentionally causes another person (B) to engage in an activity,

(b) the activity is sexual,

(c) B does not consent to engaging in the activity, and

(d) A does not reasonably believe that B consents.

(2) Whether a belief is reasonable is to be determined having regard to all the circumstances, including any steps A has taken to ascertain whether B consents.

(3) Sections 75 and 76 apply to an offence under this section.

(4) A person guilty of an offence under this section, if the activity caused involved—

(a) penetration of B's anus or vagina,

(b) penetration of B's mouth with a person's penis,

(c) penetration of a person's anus or vagina with a part of B's body or by B with anything else, or

(d) penetration of a person's mouth with B's penis,

is liable, on conviction on indictment, to imprisonment for life.

(5) Unless subsection (4) applies, a person guilty of an offence under this section is liable—

(a) on summary conviction, to imprisonment for a term not exceeding 6 months or to a fine not exceeding the statutory maximum or both;

(b) on conviction on indictment, to imprisonment for a term not exceeding 10 years.

Rape and other offences against children under 13

5. Rape of a child under 13

(1) A person commits an offence if—

(a) he intentionally penetrates the vagina, anus or mouth of another person with his penis, and

(b) the other person is under 13.

(2) A person guilty of an offence under this section is liable, on conviction on indictment, to imprisonment for life.

6. Assault of a child under 13 by penetration

(1) A person commits an offence if—

(a) he intentionally penetrates the vagina or anus of another person with a part of his body or anything else,

(b) the penetration is sexual, and

(c) the other person is under 13.

(2) A person guilty of an offence under this section is liable, on conviction on indictment, to imprisonment for life.

7. Sexual assault of a child under 13

(1) A person commits an offence if—

(a) he intentionally touches another person,

(b) the touching is sexual, and

(c) the other person is under 13.

(2) A person guilty of an offence under this section is liable—

(a) on summary conviction, to imprisonment for a term not exceeding 6 months or a fine not exceeding the statutory maximum or both;

(b) on conviction on indictment, to imprisonment for a term not exceeding 14 years.

8. Causing or inciting a child under 13 to engage in sexual activity

(1) A person commits an offence if—

(a) he intentionally causes or incites another person (B) to engage in an activity,

(b) the activity is sexual, and

(c) B is under 13.

(2) A person guilty of an offence under this section, if the activity caused or incited involved—

(a) penetration of B's anus or vagina,

(b) penetration of B's mouth with a person's penis,

(c) penetration of a person's anus or vagina with a part of B's body or by B with anything else, or

(d) penetration of a person's mouth with B's penis,

is liable, on conviction on indictment, to imprisonment for life.

(3) Unless subsection (2) applies, a person guilty of an offence under this section is liable—

(a) on summary conviction, to imprisonment for a term not exceeding 6 months or to a fine not exceeding the statutory maximum or both;

(b) on conviction on indictment, to imprisonment for a term not exceeding 14 years.

Child sex offences

9. Sexual activity with a child

(1) A person aged 18 or over (A) commits an offence if—

(a) he intentionally touches another person (B),

(b) the touching is sexual, and

(c) either—

(i) B is under 16 and A does not reasonably believe that B is 16 or over, or

(ii) B is under 13.

(2) A person guilty of an offence under this section, if the touching involved—

(a) penetration of B's anus or vagina with a part of A's body or anything else,

(b) penetration of B's mouth with A's penis,

(c) penetration of A's anus or vagina with a part of B's body, or

(d) penetration of A's mouth with B's penis,

is liable, on conviction on indictment, to imprisonment for a term not exceeding 14 years.

(3) Unless subsection (2) applies, a person guilty of an offence under this section is liable—

(a) on summary conviction, to imprisonment for a term not exceeding 6 months or to a fine not exceeding the statutory maximum or both;

(b) on conviction on indictment, to imprisonment for a term not exceeding 14 years.

10. Causing or inciting a child to engage in sexual activity

(1) A person aged 18 or over (A) commits an offence if—

(a) he intentionally causes or incites another person (B) to engage in an activity,

    (b) the activity is sexual, and

    (c) either—

        (i)   B is under 16 and A does not reasonably believe that B is 16 or over, or

        (ii) B is under 13.

(2) A person guilty of an offence under this section, if the activity caused or incited involved—

    (a) penetration of B's anus or vagina,

    (b) penetration of B's mouth with a person's penis,

    (c) penetration of a person's anus or vagina with a part of B's body or by B with anything else, or

    (d) penetration of a person's mouth with B's penis,

is liable, on conviction on indictment, to imprisonment for a term not exceeding 14 years.

   (3) Unless subsection (2) applies, a person guilty of an offence under this section is liable—

    (a) on summary conviction, to imprisonment for a term not exceeding 6 months or to a fine not exceeding the statutory maximum or both;

    (b) on conviction on indictment, to imprisonment for a term not exceeding 14 years.

11. Engaging in sexual activity in the presence of a child

   (1) A person aged 18 or over (A) commits an offence if—

    (a) he intentionally engages in an activity,

    (b) the activity is sexual,

    (c) for the purpose of obtaining sexual gratification, he engages in it—

        (i)   when another person (B) is present or is in a place from which A can be observed, and

        (ii) knowing or believing that B is aware, or intending that B should be aware, that he is engaging in it, and

    (d) either—

        (i)   B is under 16 and A does not reasonably believe that B is 16 or over, or

        (ii) B is under 13.

   (2) A person guilty of an offence under this section is liable—

    (a) on summary conviction, to imprisonment for a term not exceeding 6 months or a fine not exceeding the statutory maximum or both;

    (b) on conviction on indictment, to imprisonment for a term not exceeding 10 years.

12. Causing a child to watch a sexual act

   (1) A person aged 18 or over (A) commits an offence if—

    (a) for the purpose of obtaining sexual gratification, he intentionally causes another person (B) to watch a third person engaging in an activity, or to look at an image of any person engaging in an activity,

    (b) the activity is sexual, and

    (c) either—

        (i)   B is under 16 and A does not reasonably believe that B is 16 or over, or

        (ii) B is under 13.

   (2) A person guilty of an offence under this section is liable—

    (a) on summary conviction, to imprisonment for a term not exceeding 6 months or a fine not exceeding the statutory maximum or both;

    (b) on conviction on indictment, to imprisonment for a term not exceeding 10 years.

13. Child sex offences committed by children or young persons

(1) A person under 18 commits an offence if he does anything which would be an offence under any of sections 9 to 12 if he were aged 18.

(2) A person guilty of an offence under this section is liable—

(a) on summary conviction, to imprisonment for a term not exceeding 6 months or a fine not exceeding the statutory maximum or both;

(b) on conviction on indictment, to imprisonment for a term not exceeding 5 years.

14. Arranging or facilitating commission of a child sex offence

(1) A person commits an offence if—

(a) he intentionally arranges or facilitates something that he intends to do, intends another person to do, or believes that another person will do, in any part of the world, and

(b) doing it will involve the commission of an offence under any of sections 9 to 13.

(2) A person does not commit an offence under this section if—

(a) he arranges or facilitates something that he believes another person will do, but that he does not intend to do or intend another person to do, and

(b) any offence within subsection (1)(b) would be an offence against a child for whose protection he acts.

(3) For the purposes of subsection (2), a person acts for the protection of a child if he acts for the purpose of—

(a) protecting the child from sexually transmitted infection,

(b) protecting the physical safety of the child,

(c) preventing the child from becoming pregnant, or

(d) promoting the child's emotional well-being by the giving of advice,

and not for the purpose of obtaining sexual gratification or for the purpose of causing or encouraging the activity constituting the offence within subsection (1)(b) or the child's participation in it.

(4) A person guilty of an offence under this section is liable—

(a) on summary conviction, to imprisonment for a term not exceeding 6 months or a fine not exceeding the statutory maximum or both;

(b) on conviction on indictment, to imprisonment for a term not exceeding 14 years.

15. Meeting a child following sexual grooming etc.

(1) A person aged 18 or over (A) commits an offence if—

(a) having met or communicated with another person (B) on at least two earlier occasions, he—

(i)   intentionally meets B, or

(ii)   travels with the intention of meeting B in any part of the world,

(b) at the time, he intends to do anything to or in respect of B, during or after the meeting and in any part of the world, which if done will involve the commission by A of a relevant offence,

(c) B is under 16, and

(d) A does not reasonably believe that B is 16 or over.

(2) In subsection (1)—

(a) the reference to A having met or communicated with B is a reference to A having met B in any part of the world or having communicated with B by any means from, to or in any part of the world;

(b) 'relevant offence' means—

(i)   an offence under this Part,

(ii) an offence within any of paragraphs 61 to 92 of Schedule 3, or

(iii) anything done outside England and Wales and Northern Ireland which is not an offence within sub-paragraph (i) or (ii) but would be an offence within sub-paragraph (i) if done in England and Wales.

(3) In this section as it applies to Northern Ireland—

(a) subsection (1) has effect with the substitution of '17' for '16' in both places;

(b) subsection (2)(b)(iii) has effect with the substitution of 'sub-paragraph (ii) if done in Northern Ireland' for 'sub-paragraph (i) if done in England and Wales'.

(4) A person guilty of an offence under this section is liable—

(a) on summary conviction, to imprisonment for a term not exceeding 6 months or a fine not exceeding the statutory maximum or both;

(b) on conviction on indictment, to imprisonment for a term not exceeding 10 years.

Abuse of position of trust

16. Abuse of position of trust: sexual activity with a child

(1) A person aged 18 or over (A) commits an offence if—

(a) he intentionally touches another person (B),

(b) the touching is sexual,

(c) A is in a position of trust in relation to B,

(d) where subsection (2) applies, A knows or could reasonably be expected to know of the circumstances by virtue of which he is in a position of trust in relation to B, and

(e) either—

(i)   B is under 18 and A does not reasonably believe that B is 18 or over, or

(ii) B is under 13.

(2) This subsection applies where A—

(a) is in a position of trust in relation to B by virtue of circumstances within section 21(2), (3), (4) or (5), and

(b) is not in such a position of trust by virtue of other circumstances.

(3) Where in proceedings for an offence under this section it is proved that the other person was under 18, the defendant is to be taken not to have reasonably believed that that person was 18 or over unless sufficient evidence is adduced to raise an issue as to whether he reasonably believed it.

(4) Where in proceedings for an offence under this section—

(a) it is proved that the defendant was in a position of trust in relation to the other person by virtue of circumstances within section 21(2), (3), (4) or (5), and

(b) it is not proved that he was in such a position of trust by virtue of other circumstances,

it is to be taken that the defendant knew or could reasonably have been expected to know of the circumstances by virtue of which he was in such a position of trust unless sufficient evidence is adduced to raise an issue as to whether he knew or could reasonably have been expected to know of those circumstances.

(5) A person guilty of an offence under this section is liable—

(a) on summary conviction, to imprisonment for a term not exceeding 6 months or a fine not exceeding the statutory maximum or both;

(b) on conviction on indictment, to imprisonment for a term not exceeding 5 years.

17. Abuse of position of trust: causing or inciting a child to engage in sexual activity

(1) A person aged 18 or over (A) commits an offence if—

    (a) he intentionally causes or incites another person (B) to engage in an activity,

    (b) the activity is sexual,

    (c) A is in a position of trust in relation to B,

    (d) where subsection (2) applies, A knows or could reasonably be expected to know of the circumstances by virtue of which he is in a position of trust in relation to B, and

    (e) either—

        (i)   B is under 18 and A does not reasonably believe that B is 18 or over, or

        (ii) B is under 13.

(2) This subsection applies where A—

    (a) is in a position of trust in relation to B by virtue of circumstances within section 21(2), (3), (4) or (5), and

    (b) is not in such a position of trust by virtue of other circumstances.

(3) Where in proceedings for an offence under this section it is proved that the other person was under 18, the defendant is to be taken not to have reasonably believed that that person was 18 or over unless sufficient evidence is adduced to raise an issue as to whether he reasonably believed it.

(4) Where in proceedings for an offence under this section—

    (a) it is proved that the defendant was in a position of trust in relation to the other person by virtue of circumstances within section 21(2), (3), (4) or (5), and

    (b) it is not proved that he was in such a position of trust by virtue of other circumstances,

it is to be taken that the defendant knew or could reasonably have been expected to know of the circumstances by virtue of which he was in such a position of trust unless sufficient evidence is adduced to raise an issue as to whether he knew or could reasonably have been expected to know of those circumstances.

(5) A person guilty of an offence under this section is liable—

    (a) on summary conviction, to imprisonment for a term not exceeding 6 months or a fine not exceeding the statutory maximum or both;

    (b) on conviction on indictment, to imprisonment for a term not exceeding 5 years.

18. Abuse of position of trust: sexual activity in the presence of a child

(1) A person aged 18 or over (A) commits an offence if—

    (a) he intentionally engages in an activity,

    (b) the activity is sexual,

    (c) for the purpose of obtaining sexual gratification, he engages in it—

        (i)   when another person (B) is present or is in a place from which A can be observed, and

        (ii) knowing or believing that B is aware, or intending that B should be aware, that he is engaging in it,

    (d) A is in a position of trust in relation to B,

    (e) where subsection (2) applies, A knows or could reasonably be expected to know of the circumstances by virtue of which he is in a position of trust in relation to B, and

    (f) either—

        (i)   B is under 18 and A does not reasonably believe that B is 18 or over, or

        (ii) B is under 13.

(2) This subsection applies where A—

(a) is in a position of trust in relation to B by virtue of circumstances within section 21(2), (3), (4) or (5), and

(b) is not in such a position of trust by virtue of other circumstances.

(3) Where in proceedings for an offence under this section it is proved that the other person was under 18, the defendant is to be taken not to have reasonably believed that that person was 18 or over unless sufficient evidence is adduced to raise an issue as to whether he reasonably believed it.

(4) Where in proceedings for an offence under this section—

(a) it is proved that the defendant was in a position of trust in relation to the other person by virtue of circumstances within section 21(2), (3), (4) or (5), and

(b) it is not proved that he was in such a position of trust by virtue of other circumstances,

it is to be taken that the defendant knew or could reasonably have been expected to know of the circumstances by virtue of which he was in such a position of trust unless sufficient evidence is adduced to raise an issue as to whether he knew or could reasonably have been expected to know of those circumstances.

(5) A person guilty of an offence under this section is liable—

(a) on summary conviction, to imprisonment for a term not exceeding 6 months or a fine not exceeding the statutory maximum or both;

(b) on conviction on indictment, to imprisonment for a term not exceeding 5 years.

19. Abuse of position of trust: causing a child to watch a sexual act

(1) A person aged 18 or over (A) commits an offence if—

(a) for the purpose of obtaining sexual gratification, he intentionally causes another person (B) to watch a third person engaging in an activity, or to look at an image of any person engaging in an activity,

(b) the activity is sexual,

(c) A is in a position of trust in relation to B,

(d) where subsection (2) applies, A knows or could reasonably be expected to know of the circumstances by virtue of which he is in a position of trust in relation to B, and

(e) either—

(i) B is under 18 and A does not reasonably believe that B is 18 or over, or

(ii) B is under 13.

(2) This subsection applies where A—

(a) is in a position of trust in relation to B by virtue of circumstances within section 21(2), (3), (4) or (5), and

(b) is not in such a position of trust by virtue of other circumstances.

(3) Where in proceedings for an offence under this section it is proved that the other person was under 18, the defendant is to be taken not to have reasonably believed that that person was 18 or over unless sufficient evidence is adduced to raise an issue as to whether he reasonably believed it.

(4) Where in proceedings for an offence under this section—

(a) it is proved that the defendant was in a position of trust in relation to the other person by virtue of circumstances within section 21(2), (3), (4) or (5), and

(b) it is not proved that he was in such a position of trust by virtue of other circumstances, it is to be taken that the defendant knew or could reasonably have been expected to know of the circumstances by virtue of which he was in such a position of trust unless sufficient evidence is adduced to raise an issue as to whether he knew or could reasonably have been expected to know of those circumstances.

(5) A person guilty of an offence under this section is liable—

(a) on summary conviction, to imprisonment for a term not exceeding 6 months or a fine not exceeding the statutory maximum or both;

(b) on conviction on indictment, to imprisonment for a term not exceeding 5 years.

20. Abuse of position of trust: acts done in Scotland

Anything which, if done in England and Wales or Northern Ireland, would constitute an offence under any of sections 16 to 19 also constitutes that offence if done in Scotland.

21. Positions of trust

(1) For the purposes of sections 16 to 19, a person (A) is in a position of trust in relation to another person (B) if—

(a) any of the following subsections applies, or

(b) any condition specified in an order made by the Secretary of State is met.

(2) This subsection applies if A looks after persons under 18 who are detained in an institution by virtue of a court order or under an enactment, and B is so detained in that institution.

(3) This subsection applies if A looks after persons under 18 who are resident in a home or other place in which—

(a) accommodation and maintenance are provided by an authority under section 23(2) of the Children Act 1989 (c. 41) or Article 27(2) of the Children (Northern Ireland) Order 1995 (S.I. 1995/755 (N.I. 2)), or

(b) accommodation is provided by a voluntary organisation under section 59(1) of that Act or Article 75(1) of that Order,

and B is resident, and is so provided with accommodation and maintenance or accommodation, in that place.

(4) This subsection applies if A looks after persons under 18 who are accommodated and cared for in one of the following institutions—

(a) a hospital,

(b) an independent clinic,

(c) a care home, residential care home or private hospital,

(d) a community home, voluntary home or children's home,

(e) a home provided under section 82(5) of the Children Act 1989, or

(f) a residential family centre,

and B is accommodated and cared for in that institution.

(5) This subsection applies if A looks after persons under 18 who are receiving education at an educational institution and B is receiving, and A is not receiving, education at that institution.

(6) This subsection applies if A is appointed to be the guardian of B under Article 159 or 160 of the Children (Northern Ireland) Order 1995 (S.I. 1995/755 (N.I. 2)).

(7) This subsection applies if A is engaged in the provision of services under, or pursuant to anything done under—

(a) sections 8 to 10 of the Employment and Training Act 1973 (c. 50), or

(b) section 114 of the Learning and Skills Act 2000 (c. 21),

and, in that capacity, looks after B on an individual basis.

(8) This subsection applies if A regularly has unsupervised contact with B (whether face to face or by any other means)—

(a) in the exercise of functions of a local authority under section 20 or 21 of the Children Act 1989 (c. 41), or

(b) in the exercise of functions of an authority under Article 21 or 23 of the Children (Northern Ireland) Order 1995.

(9) This subsection applies if A, as a person who is to report to the court under section 7 of the Children Act 1989 or Article 4 of the Children (Northern Ireland) Order 1995 on matters relating to the welfare of B, regularly has unsupervised contact with B (whether face to face or by any other means).

(10) This subsection applies if A is a personal adviser appointed for B under—

(a) section 23B(2) of, or paragraph 19C of Schedule 2 to, the Children Act 1989, or

(b) Article 34A(10) or 34C(2) of the Children (Northern Ireland) Order 1995,

and, in that capacity, looks after B on an individual basis.

(11) This subsection applies if—

(a) B is subject to a care order, a supervision order or an education supervision order, and

(b) in the exercise of functions conferred by virtue of the order on an authorised person or the authority designated by the order, A looks after B on an individual basis.

(12) This subsection applies if A—

(a) is an officer of the Service appointed for B under section 41(1) of the Children Act 1989,

(b) is appointed a children's guardian of B under rule 6 or rule 18 of the Adoption Rules 1984 (S.I. 1984/265), or

(c) is appointed to be the guardian ad litem of B under rule 9.5 of the Family Proceedings Rules 1991 (S. I. 1991/1247) or under Article 60(1) of the Children (Northern Ireland) Order 1995,

and, in that capacity, regularly has unsupervised contact with B (whether face to face or by any other means).

(13) This subsection applies if—

(a) B is subject to requirements imposed by or under an enactment on his release from detention for a criminal offence, or is subject to requirements imposed by a court order made in criminal proceedings, and

(b) A looks after B on an individual basis in pursuance of the requirements.

22. Positions of trust: interpretation

(1) The following provisions apply for the purposes of section 21.

(2) Subject to subsection (3), a person looks after persons under 18 if he is regularly involved in caring for, training, supervising or being in sole charge of such persons.

(3) A person (A) looks after another person (B) on an individual basis if—

(a) A is regularly involved in caring for, training or supervising B, and

(b) in the course of his involvement, A regularly has unsupervised contact with B (whether face to face or by any other means).

(4) A person receives education at an educational institution if—

(a) he is registered or otherwise enrolled as a pupil or student at the institution, or

(b) he receives education at the institution under arrangements with another educational institution at which he is so registered or otherwise enrolled.

(5) In section 21—

'authority'—

(a) in relation to England and Wales, means a local authority;

(b) in relation to Northern Ireland, has the meaning given by Article 2(2) of the Children (Northern Ireland) Order 1995 (S.I. 1995/755 (N.I. 2));

'care home' means an establishment which is a care home for the purposes of the Care Standards Act 2000 (c. 14);

'care order' has—

(a) in relation to England and Wales, the same meaning as in the Children Act 1989 (c. 41), and

(b) in relation to Northern Ireland, the same meaning as in the Children (Northern Ireland) Order 1995;

'children's home' has—

(a) in relation to England and Wales, the meaning given by section 1 of the Care Standards Act 2000, and

(b) in relation to Northern Ireland, the meaning that would be given by Article 9 of the Health and Personal Social Services (Quality, Improvement and Regulation) (Northern Ireland) Order 2003 (S.I. 2003/431 (N.I. 9)) ('the 2003 Order') if in paragraph (4) of that Article sub-paragraphs (d), (f) and (g) were omitted;

'community home' has the meaning given by section 53 of the Children Act 1989;

'education supervision order' has—

(a) in relation to England and Wales, the meaning given by section 36 of the Children Act 1989, and

(b) in relation to Northern Ireland, the meaning given by Article 49(1) of the Children (Northern Ireland) Order 1995;

'hospital'—

(a) in relation to England and Wales, means a hospital within the meaning given by section 128(1) of the National Health Service Act 1977 (c. 49), or any other establishment which is a hospital within the meaning given by section 2(3) of the Care Standards Act 2000 (c. 14);

(b) in relation to Northern Ireland, means a hospital within the meaning given by Article 2(2) of the Health and Personal Social Services (Northern Ireland) Order 1972 (S.I. 1972/1265 (N.I. 14)), or any other establishment which is a hospital within the meaning given by Article 2(2) of the 2003 Order;

'independent clinic' has—

(a) in relation to England and Wales, the meaning given by section 2 of the Care Standards Act 2000;

(b) in relation to Northern Ireland, the meaning given by Article 2(2) of the 2003 Order;

'private hospital' has the meaning given by Article 90(2) of the Mental Health (Northern Ireland) Order 1986 (S.I. 1986/595 (N.I. 4));

'residential care home' means an establishment which is a residential care home for the purposes of the 2003 Order;

'residential family centre' has the meaning given by section 22 of the Health and Personal Social Services Act (Northern Ireland) 2001 (c. 3);

'supervision order' has—

(a) in relation to England and Wales, the meaning given by section 31(11) of the Children Act 1989 (c. 41), and

(b) in relation to Northern Ireland, the meaning given by Article 49(1) of the Children (Northern Ireland) Order 1995 (S.I. 1995/ 755 (N.I. 2));

'voluntary home' has—

(a) in relation to England and Wales, the meaning given by section 60(3) of the Children Act 1989, and

(b) in relation to Northern Ireland, the meaning given by Article 74(1) of the Children (Northern Ireland) Order 1995.

23. Sections 16 to 19: marriage exception

(1) Conduct by a person (A) which would otherwise be an offence under any of sections 16 to 19 against another person (B) is not an offence under that section if at the time—

(a) B is 16 or over, and

(b) A and B are lawfully married.

(2) In proceedings for such an offence it is for the defendant to prove that A and B were lawfully married at the time.

24. Sections 16 to 19: sexual relationships which pre-date position of trust

(1) Conduct by a person (A) which would otherwise be an offence under any of sections 16 to 19 against another person (B) is not an offence under that section if, immediately before the position of trust arose, a sexual relationship existed between A and B.

(2) Subsection (1) does not apply if at that time sexual intercourse between A and B would have been unlawful.

(3) In proceedings for an offence under any of sections 16 to 19 it is for the defendant to prove that such a relationship existed at that time.

Familial child sex offences

25. Sexual activity with a child family member

(1) A person (A) commits an offence if—

(a) he intentionally touches another person (B),

(b) the touching is sexual,

(c) the relation of A to B is within section 27,

(d) A knows or could reasonably be expected to know that his relation to B is of a description falling within that section, and

(e) either—

(i) B is under 18 and A does not reasonably believe that B is 18 or over, or

(ii) B is under 13.

(2) Where in proceedings for an offence under this section it is proved that the other person was under 18, the defendant is to be taken not to have reasonably believed that that person was 18 or over unless sufficient evidence is adduced to raise an issue as to whether he reasonably believed it.

(3) Where in proceedings for an offence under this section it is proved that the relation of the defendant to the other person was of a description falling within section 27, it is to be taken that the defendant knew or could reasonably have been expected to know that his relation to the other person was of that description unless sufficient evidence is adduced to raise an issue as to whether he knew or could reasonably have been expected to know that it was.

(4) A person guilty of an offence under this section, if aged 18 or over at the time of the offence, is liable—

(a) where subsection (6) applies, on conviction on indictment to imprisonment for a term not exceeding 14 years;

(b) in any other case—

    (i) on summary conviction, to imprisonment for a term not exceeding 6 months or a fine not exceeding the statutory maximum or both;

    (ii) on conviction on indictment, to imprisonment for a term not exceeding 14 years.

(5) Unless subsection (4) applies, a person guilty of an offence under this section is liable—

(a) on summary conviction, to imprisonment for a term not exceeding 6 months or a fine not exceeding the statutory maximum or both;

(b) on conviction on indictment, to imprisonment for a term not exceeding 5 years.

(6) This subsection applies where the touching involved—

(a) penetration of B's anus or vagina with a part of A's body or anything else,

(b) penetration of B's mouth with A's penis,

(c) penetration of A's anus or vagina with a part of B's body, or

(d) penetration of A's mouth with B's penis.

26. Inciting a child family member to engage in sexual activity

(1) A person (A) commits an offence if—

(a) he intentionally incites another person (B) to touch, or allow himself to be touched by, A,

(b) the touching is sexual,

(c) the relation of A to B is within section 27,

(d) A knows or could reasonably be expected to know that his relation to B is of a description falling within that section, and

(e) either—

    (i) B is under 18 and A does not reasonably believe that B is 18 or over, or

    (ii) B is under 13.

(2) Where in proceedings for an offence under this section it is proved that the other person was under 18, the defendant is to be taken not to have reasonably believed that that person was 18 or over unless sufficient evidence is adduced to raise an issue as to whether he reasonably believed it.

(3) Where in proceedings for an offence under this section it is proved that the relation of the defendant to the other person was of a description falling within section 27, it is to be taken that the defendant knew or could reasonably have been expected to know that his relation to the other person was of that description unless sufficient evidence is adduced to raise an issue as to whether he knew or could reasonably have been expected to know that it was.

(4) A person guilty of an offence under this section, if he was aged 18 or over at the time of the offence, is liable—

(a) where subsection (6) applies, on conviction on indictment to imprisonment for a term not exceeding 14 years;

(b) in any other case—

    (i) on summary conviction, to imprisonment for a term not exceeding 6 months or a fine not exceeding the statutory maximum or both;

    (ii) on conviction on indictment, to imprisonment for a term not exceeding 14 years.

(5) Unless subsection (4) applies, a person guilty of an offence under this section is liable—

(a) on summary conviction, to imprisonment for a term not exceeding 6 months or a fine not exceeding the statutory maximum or both;

(b) on conviction on indictment, to imprisonment for a term not exceeding 5 years.

(6) This subsection applies where the touching to which the incitement related involved—

(a) penetration of B's anus or vagina with a part of A's body or anything else,

(b) penetration of B's mouth with A's penis,

(c) penetration of A's anus or vagina with a part of B's body, or

(d) penetration of A's mouth with B's penis.

27. Family relationships

(1) The relation of one person (A) to another (B) is within this section if—

(a) it is within any of subsections (2) to (4), or

(b) it would be within one of those subsections but for section 67 of the Adoption and Children Act 2002 (c. 38) (status conferred by adoption).

(2) The relation of A to B is within this subsection if—

(a) one of them is the other's parent, grandparent, brother, sister, half-brother, half-sister, aunt or uncle, or

(b) A is or has been B's foster parent.

(3) The relation of A to B is within this subsection if A and B live or have lived in the same household, or A is or has been regularly involved in caring for, training, supervising or being in sole charge of B, and—

(a) one of them is or has been the other's step-parent,

(b) A and B are cousins,

(c) one of them is or has been the other's stepbrother or stepsister, or

(d) the parent or present or former foster parent of one of them is or has been the other's foster parent.

(4) The relation of A to B is within this subsection if—

(a) A and B live in the same household, and

(b) A is regularly involved in caring for, training, supervising or being in sole charge of B.

(5) For the purposes of this section—

(a) 'aunt' means the sister or half-sister of a person's parent, and 'uncle' has a corresponding meaning;

(b) 'cousin' means the child of an aunt or uncle;

(c) a person is a child's foster parent if—

(i) he is a person with whom the child has been placed under section 23(2)(a) or 59(1)(a) of the Children Act 1989 (c. 41) (fostering for local authority or voluntary organisation), or

(ii) he fosters the child privately, within the meaning given by section 66(1)(b) of that Act;

(d) a person is another's partner (whether they are of different sexes or the same sex) if they live together as partners in an enduring family relationship;

(e) 'step-parent' includes a parent's partner and 'stepbrother' and 'stepsister' include the child of a parent's partner.

28. Sections 25 and 26: marriage exception

(1) Conduct by a person (A) which would otherwise be an offence under section 25 or 26 against another person (B) is not an offence under that section if at the time—

(a) B is 16 or over, and

(b) A and B are lawfully married.

(2) In proceedings for such an offence it is for the defendant to prove that A and B were lawfully married at the time.

29. Sections 25 and 26: sexual relationships which pre-date family relationships

(1) Conduct by a person (A) which would otherwise be an offence under section 25 or 26 against another person (B) is not an offence under that section if—

(a) the relation of A to B is not within subsection (2) of section 27,

(b) it would not be within that subsection if section 67 of the Adoption and Children Act 2002 (c. 38) did not apply, and

(c) immediately before the relation of A to B first became such as to fall within section 27, a sexual relationship existed between A and B.

(2) Subsection (1) does not apply if at the time referred to in subsection (1)(c) sexual intercourse between A and B would have been unlawful.

(3) In proceedings for an offence under section 25 or 26 it is for the defendant to prove the matters mentioned in subsection (1)(a) to (c).

Offences against persons with a mental disorder impeding choice

30. Sexual activity with a person with a mental disorder impeding choice

(1) A person (A) commits an offence if—

(a) he intentionally touches another person (B),

(b) the touching is sexual,

(c) B is unable to refuse because of or for a reason related to a mental disorder, and

(d) A knows or could reasonably be expected to know that B has a mental disorder and that because of it or for a reason related to it B is likely to be unable to refuse.

(2) B is unable to refuse if—

(a) he lacks the capacity to choose whether to agree to the touching (whether because he lacks sufficient understanding of the nature or reasonably foreseeable consequences of what is being done, or for any other reason), or

(b) he is unable to communicate such a choice to A.

(3) A person guilty of an offence under this section, if the touching involved—

(a) penetration of B's anus or vagina with a part of A's body or anything else,

(b) penetration of B's mouth with A's penis,

(c) penetration of A's anus or vagina with a part of B's body, or

(d) penetration of A's mouth with B's penis,

is liable, on conviction on indictment, to imprisonment for life.

(4) Unless subsection (3) applies, a person guilty of an offence under this section is liable—

(a) on summary conviction, to imprisonment for a term not exceeding 6 months or to a fine not exceeding the statutory maximum or both;

(b) on conviction on indictment, to imprisonment for a term not exceeding 14 years.

31. Causing or inciting a person, with a mental disorder impeding choice, to engage in sexual activity

(1) A person (A) commits an offence if—

(a) he intentionally causes or incites another person (B) to engage in an activity,

213

(b) the activity is sexual,

(c) B is unable to refuse because of or for a reason related to a mental disorder, and

(d) A knows or could reasonably be expected to know that B has a mental disorder and that because of it or for a reason related to it B is likely to be unable to refuse.

(2) B is unable to refuse if—

(a) he lacks the capacity to choose whether to agree to engaging in the activity caused or incited (whether because he lacks sufficient understanding of the nature or reasonably foreseeable consequences of the activity, or for any other reason), or

(b) he is unable to communicate such a choice to A.

(3) A person guilty of an offence under this section, if the activity caused or incited involved—

(a) penetration of B's anus or vagina,

(b) penetration of B's mouth with a person's penis,

(c) penetration of a person's anus or vagina with a part of B's body or by B with anything else, or

(d) penetration of a person's mouth with B's penis,

is liable, on conviction on indictment, to imprisonment for life.

(4) Unless subsection (3) applies, a person guilty of an offence under this section is liable—

(a) on summary conviction, to imprisonment for a term not exceeding 6 months or to a fine not exceeding the statutory maximum or both;

(b) on conviction on indictment, to imprisonment for a term not exceeding 14 years.

32. Engaging in sexual activity in the presence of a person with a mental disorder impeding choice

(1) A person (A) commits an offence if—

(a) he intentionally engages in an activity,

(b) the activity is sexual,

(c) for the purpose of obtaining sexual gratification, he engages in it—

(i) when another person (B) is present or is in a place from which A can be observed, and

(ii) knowing or believing that B is aware, or intending that B should be aware, that he is engaging in it,

(d) B is unable to refuse because of or for a reason related to a mental disorder, and

(e) A knows or could reasonably be expected to know that B has a mental disorder and that because of it or for a reason related to it B is likely to be unable to refuse.

(2) B is unable to refuse if—

(a) he lacks the capacity to choose whether to agree to being present (whether because he lacks sufficient understanding of the nature of the activity, or for any other reason), or

(b) he is unable to communicate such a choice to A.

(3) A person guilty of an offence under this section is liable—

(a) on summary conviction, to imprisonment for a term not exceeding 6 months or a fine not exceeding the statutory maximum or both;

(b) on conviction on indictment, to imprisonment for a term not exceeding 10 years.

33. Causing a person, with a mental disorder impeding choice, to watch a sexual act

(1) A person (A) commits an offence if—

(a) for the purpose of obtaining sexual gratification, he intentionally causes another person (B) to watch a third person engaging in an activity, or to look at an image of any person engaging in an activity,

(b) the activity is sexual,

(c) B is unable to refuse because of or for a reason related to a mental disorder, and

(d) A knows or could reasonably be expected to know that B has a mental disorder and that because of it or for a reason related to it B is likely to be unable to refuse.

(2) B is unable to refuse if—

(a) he lacks the capacity to choose whether to agree to watching or looking (whether because he lacks sufficient understanding of the nature of the activity, or for any other reason), or

(b) he is unable to communicate such a choice to A.

(3) A person guilty of an offence under this section is liable—

(a) on summary conviction, to imprisonment for a term not exceeding 6 months or a fine not exceeding the statutory maximum or both;

(b) on conviction on indictment, to imprisonment for a term not exceeding 10 years.

Inducements etc. to persons with a mental disorder

34. Inducement, threat or deception to procure sexual activity with a person with a mental disorder

(1) A person (A) commits an offence if—

(a) with the agreement of another person (B) he intentionally touches that person,

(b) the touching is sexual,

(c) A obtains B's agreement by means of an inducement offered or given, a threat made or a deception practised by A for that purpose,

(d) B has a mental disorder, and

(e) A knows or could reasonably be expected to know that B has a mental disorder.

(2) A person guilty of an offence under this section, if the touching involved—

(a) penetration of B's anus or vagina with a part of A's body or anything else,

(b) penetration of B's mouth with A's penis,

(c) penetration of A's anus or vagina with a part of B's body, or

(d) penetration of A's mouth with B's penis,

is liable, on conviction on indictment, to imprisonment for life.

(3) Unless subsection (2) applies, a person guilty of an offence under this section is liable—

(a) on summary conviction, to imprisonment for a term not exceeding 6 months or a fine not exceeding the statutory maximum or both;

(b) on conviction on indictment, to imprisonment for a term not exceeding 14 years.

35. Causing a person with a mental disorder to engage in or agree to engage in sexual activity by inducement, threat or deception

(1) A person (A) commits an offence if—

(a) by means of an inducement offered or given, a threat made or a deception practised by him for this purpose, he intentionally causes another person (B) to engage in, or to agree to engage in, an activity,

(b) the activity is sexual,

215

(c) B has a mental disorder, and

(d) A knows or could reasonably be expected to know that B has a mental disorder.

(2) A person guilty of an offence under this section, if the activity caused or agreed to involved—

(a) penetration of B's anus or vagina,

(b) penetration of B's mouth with a person's penis,

(c) penetration of a person's anus or vagina with a part of B's body or by B with anything else, or

(d) penetration of a person's mouth with B's penis,

is liable, on conviction on indictment, to imprisonment for life.

(3) Unless subsection (2) applies, a person guilty of an offence under this section is liable—

(a) on summary conviction, to imprisonment for a term not exceeding 6 months or a fine not exceeding the statutory maximum or both;

(b) on conviction on indictment, to imprisonment for a term not exceeding 14 years.

36. Engaging in sexual activity in the presence, procured by inducement, threat or deception, of a person with a mental disorder

(1) A person (A) commits an offence if—

(a) he intentionally engages in an activity,

(b) the activity is sexual,

(c) for the purpose of obtaining sexual gratification, he engages in it—

(i)   when another person (B) is present or is in a place from which A can be observed, and

(ii) knowing or believing that B is aware, or intending that B should be aware, that he is engaging in it,

(d) B agrees to be present or in the place referred to in paragraph (c)(i) because of an inducement offered or given, a threat made or a deception practised by A for the purpose of obtaining that agreement,

(e) B has a mental disorder, and

(f) A knows or could reasonably be expected to know that B has a mental disorder.

(2) A person guilty of an offence under this section is liable—

(a) on summary conviction, to imprisonment for a term not exceeding 6 months or a fine not exceeding the statutory maximum or both;

(b) on conviction on indictment, to imprisonment for a term not exceeding 10 years.

37. Causing a person with a mental disorder to watch a sexual act by inducement, threat or deception

(1) A person (A) commits an offence if—

(a) for the purpose of obtaining sexual gratification, he intentionally causes another person (B) to watch a third person engaging in an activity, or to look at an image of any person engaging in an activity,

(b) the activity is sexual,

(c) B agrees to watch or look because of an inducement offered or given, a threat made or a deception practised by A for the purpose of obtaining that agreement,

(d) B has a mental disorder, and

(e) A knows or could reasonably be expected to know that B has a mental disorder.

(2) A person guilty of an offence under this section is liable—

 (a) on summary conviction, to imprisonment for a term not exceeding 6 months or a fine not exceeding the statutory maximum or both;

 (b) on conviction on indictment, to imprisonment for a term not exceeding 10 years.

Care workers for persons with a mental disorder

38. Care workers: sexual activity with a person with a mental disorder

(1) A person (A) commits an offence if—

 (a) he intentionally touches another person (B),

 (b) the touching is sexual,

 (c) B has a mental disorder,

 (d) A knows or could reasonably be expected to know that B has a mental disorder, and

 (e) A is involved in B's care in a way that falls within section 42.

(2) Where in proceedings for an offence under this section it is proved that the other person had a mental disorder, it is to be taken that the defendant knew or could reasonably have been expected to know that that person had a mental disorder unless sufficient evidence is adduced to raise an issue as to whether he knew or could reasonably have been expected to know it.

(3) A person guilty of an offence under this section, if the touching involved—

 (a) penetration of B's anus or vagina with a part of A's body or anything else,

 (b) penetration of B's mouth with A's penis,

 (c) penetration of A's anus or vagina with a part of B's body, or

 (d) penetration of A's mouth with B's penis,

is liable, on conviction on indictment, to imprisonment for a term not exceeding 14 years.

(4) Unless subsection (3) applies, a person guilty of an offence under this section is liable—

 (a) on summary conviction, to imprisonment for a term not exceeding 6 months or a fine not exceeding the statutory maximum or both;

 (b) on conviction on indictment, to imprisonment for a term not exceeding 10 years.

39. Care workers: causing or inciting sexual activity

(1) A person (A) commits an offence if—

 (a) he intentionally causes or incites another person (B) to engage in an activity,

 (b) the activity is sexual,

 (c) B has a mental disorder,

 (d) A knows or could reasonably be expected to know that B has a mental disorder, and

 (e) A is involved in B's care in a way that falls within section 42.

(2) Where in proceedings for an offence under this section it is proved that the other person had a mental disorder, it is to be taken that the defendant knew or could reasonably have been expected to know that that person had a mental disorder unless sufficient evidence is adduced to raise an issue as to whether he knew or could reasonably have been expected to know it.

(3) A person guilty of an offence under this section, if the activity caused or incited involved—

(a) penetration of B's anus or vagina,

(b) penetration of B's mouth with a person's penis,

(c) penetration of a person's anus or vagina with a part of B's body or by B with anything else, or

(d) penetration of a person's mouth with B's penis,

is liable, on conviction on indictment, to imprisonment for a term not exceeding 14 years.

(4) Unless subsection (3) applies, a person guilty of an offence under this section is liable—

(a) on summary conviction, to imprisonment for a term not exceeding 6 months or a fine not exceeding the statutory maximum or both;

(b) on conviction on indictment, to imprisonment for a term not exceeding 10 years.

40. Care workers: sexual activity in the presence of a person with a mental disorder

(1) A person (A) commits an offence if—

(a) he intentionally engages in an activity,

(b) the activity is sexual,

(c) for the purpose of obtaining sexual gratification, he engages in it—

(i) when another person (B) is present or is in a place from which A can be observed, and

(ii) knowing or believing that B is aware, or intending that B should be aware, that he is engaging in it,

(d) B has a mental disorder,

(e) A knows or could reasonably be expected to know that B has a mental disorder, and

(f) A is involved in B's care in a way that falls within section 42.

(2) Where in proceedings for an offence under this section it is proved that the other person had a mental disorder, it is to be taken that the defendant knew or could reasonably have been expected to know that that person had a mental disorder unless sufficient evidence is adduced to raise an issue as to whether he knew or could reasonably have been expected to know it.

(3) A person guilty of an offence under this section is liable—

(a) on summary conviction, to imprisonment for a term not exceeding 6 months or a fine not exceeding the statutory maximum or both;

(b) on conviction on indictment, to imprisonment for a term not exceeding 7 years.

41. Care workers: causing a person with a mental disorder to watch a sexual act

(1) A person (A) commits an offence if—

(a) for the purpose of obtaining sexual gratification, he intentionally causes another person (B) to watch a third person engaging in an activity, or to look at an image of any person engaging in an activity,

(b) the activity is sexual,

(c) B has a mental disorder,

(d) A knows or could reasonably be expected to know that B has a mental disorder, and

(e) A is involved in B's care in a way that falls within section 42.

(2) Where in proceedings for an offence under this section it is proved that the other person had a mental disorder, it is to be taken that the defendant knew or could reasonably have been expected to know that that person had a mental disorder unless sufficient evidence is adduced to raise an issue as to whether he knew or could reasonably have been expected to know it.

(3) A person guilty of an offence under this section is liable—

(a) on summary conviction, to imprisonment for a term not exceeding 6 months or a fine not exceeding the statutory maximum or both;

(b) on conviction on indictment, to imprisonment for a term not exceeding 7 years.

42. Care workers: interpretation

(1) For the purposes of sections 38 to 41, a person (A) is involved in the care of another person (B) in a way that falls within this section if any of subsections (2) to (4) applies.

(2) This subsection applies if—

(a) B is accommodated and cared for in a care home, community home, voluntary home or children's home, and

(b) A has functions to perform in the home in the course of employment which have brought him or are likely to bring him into regular face to face contact with B.

(3) This subsection applies if B is a patient for whom services are provided—

(a) by a National Health Service body or an independent medical agency, or

(b) in an independent clinic or an independent hospital,

and A has functions to perform for the body or agency or in the clinic or hospital in the course of employment which have brought him or are likely to bring him into regular face to face contact with B.

(4) This subsection applies if A—

(a) is, whether or not in the course of employment, a provider of care, assistance or services to B in connection with B's mental disorder, and

(b) as such, has had or is likely to have regular face to face contact with B.

(5) In this section—

'care home' means an establishment which is a care home for the purposes of the Care Standards Act 2000 (c. 14);

'children's home' has the meaning given by section 1 of that Act;

'community home' has the meaning given by section 53 of the Children Act 1989 (c. 41);

'employment' means any employment, whether paid or unpaid and whether under a contract of service or apprenticeship, under a contract for services, or otherwise than under a contract;

'independent clinic', 'independent hospital' and 'independent medical agency' have the meaning given by section 2 of the Care Standards Act 2000;

'National Health Service body' means—

(a) a Health Authority,

(b) a National Health Service trust,

(c) a Primary Care Trust, or

(d) a Special Health Authority;

'voluntary home' has the meaning given by section 60(3) of the Children Act 1989.

43. Sections 38 to 41: marriage exception

(1) Conduct by a person (A) which would otherwise be an offence under any of sections 38 to 41 against another person (B) is not an offence under that section if at the time—

(a) B is 16 or over, and

(b) A and B are lawfully married.

(2) In proceedings for such an offence it is for the defendant to prove that A and B were lawfully married at the time.

44. Sections 38 to 41: sexual relationships which pre-date care relationships

(1) Conduct by a person (A) which would otherwise be an offence under any of sections 38 to 41 against another person (B) is not an offence under that section if, immediately before A became involved in B's care in a way that falls within section 42, a sexual relationship existed between A and B.

(2) Subsection (1) does not apply if at that time sexual intercourse between A and B would have been unlawful.

(3) In proceedings for an offence under any of sections 38 to 41 it is for the defendant to prove that such a relationship existed at that time.

Indecent photographs of children

45. Indecent photographs of persons aged 16 or 17

(1) The Protection of Children Act 1978 (c. 37) (which makes provision about indecent photographs of persons under 16) is amended as follows.

(2) In section 2(3) (evidence) and section 7(6) (meaning of 'child'), for '16' substitute '18'.

(3) After section 1 insert—

'1A Marriage and other relationships

(1) This section applies where, in proceedings for an offence under section 1(1)(a) of taking or making an indecent photograph of a child, or for an offence under section 1(1)(b) or (c) relating to an indecent photograph of a child, the defendant proves that the photograph was of the child aged 16 or over, and that at the time of the offence charged the child and he—

(a) were married, or

(b) lived together as partners in an enduring family relationship.

(2) Subsections (5) and (6) also apply where, in proceedings for an offence under section 1(1)(b) or (c) relating to an indecent photograph of a child, the defendant proves that the photograph was of the child aged 16 or over, and that at the time when he obtained it the child and he—

(a) were married, or

(b) lived together as partners in an enduring family relationship.

(3) This section applies whether the photograph showed the child alone or with the defendant, but not if it showed any other person.

(4) In the case of an offence under section 1(1)(a), if sufficient evidence is adduced to raise an issue as to whether the child consented to the photograph being taken or made, or as to whether the defendant reasonably believed that the child so consented, the defendant is not guilty of the offence unless it is proved that the child did not so consent and that the defendant did not reasonably believe that the child so consented.

(5) In the case of an offence under section 1(1)(b), the defendant is not guilty of the offence unless it is proved that the showing or distributing was to a person other than the child.

(6) In the case of an offence under section 1(1)(c), if sufficient evidence is adduced to raise an issue both—

(a) as to whether the child consented to the photograph being in the defendant's possession, or as to whether the defendant reasonably believed that the child so consented, and

(b) as to whether the defendant had the photograph in his possession with a view to its being distributed or shown to anyone other than the child, the defendant is not guilty of the offence unless it is proved either that the child did not so consent and that the defendant did not reasonably believe that the child so consented, or that the defendant had the photograph in his possession with a view to its being distributed or shown to a person other than the child.'

(4) After section 160 of the Criminal Justice Act 1988 (c. 33) (possession of indecent photograph of child) insert—

'160A Marriage and other relationships

(1) This section applies where, in proceedings for an offence under section 160 relating to an indecent photograph of a child, the defendant proves that the photograph was of the child aged 16 or over, and that at the time of the offence charged the child and he—

(a) were married, or

(b) lived together as partners in an enduring family relationship.

(2) This section also applies where, in proceedings for an offence under section 160 relating to an indecent photograph of a child, the defendant proves that the photograph was of the child aged 16 or over, and that at the time when he obtained it the child and he—

(a) were married, or

(b) lived together as partners in an enduring family relationship.

(3) This section applies whether the photograph showed the child alone or with the defendant, but not if it showed any other person.

(4) If sufficient evidence is adduced to raise an issue as to whether the child consented to the photograph being in the defendant's possession, or as to whether the defendant reasonably believed that the child so consented, the defendant is not guilty of the offence unless it is proved that the child did not so consent and that the defendant did not reasonably believe that the child so consented.'

46. Criminal proceedings, investigations etc.

(1) After section 1A of the Protection of Children Act 1978 (c. 37) insert—

'1B Exception for criminal proceedings, investigations etc.

(1) In proceedings for an offence under section 1(1)(a) of making an indecent photograph or pseudo-photograph of a child, the defendant is not guilty of the offence if he proves that—

(a) it was necessary for him to make the photograph or pseudo-photograph for the purposes of the prevention, detection or investigation of crime, or for the purposes of criminal proceedings, in any part of the world,

(b) at the time of the offence charged he was a member of the Security Service, and it was necessary for him to make the photograph or pseudo-photograph for the exercise of any of the functions of the Service, or

(c) at the time of the offence charged he was a member of GCHQ, and it was necessary for him to make the photograph or pseudo-photograph for the exercise of any of the functions of GCHQ.

(2) In this section 'GCHQ' has the same meaning as in the Intelligence Services Act 1994.'

(2) After Article 3 of the Protection of Children (Northern Ireland) Order 1978 (S.I. 1978/1047 (N.I. 17)) insert—

'3A. Exception for criminal proceedings, investigations etc.

(1) In proceedings for an offence under Article 3(1)(a) of making an indecent photograph or pseudo-photograph of a child, the defendant is not guilty of the offence if he proves that—

(a) it was necessary for him to make the photograph or pseudo-photograph for the purposes of the prevention, detection or investigation of crime, or for the purposes of criminal proceedings, in any part of the world,

(b) at the time of the offence charged he was a member of the Security Service, and it was necessary for him to make the photograph or pseudo-photograph for the exercise of any of the functions of the Service, or

(c) at the time of the offence charged he was a member of GCHQ, and it was necessary for him to make the photograph or pseudo-photograph for the exercise of any of the functions of GCHQ.

(2) In this Article 'GCHQ' has the same meaning as in the Intelligence Services Act 1994.'

Abuse of children through prostitution and pornography

47. Paying for sexual services of a child

(1) A person (A) commits an offence if—

(a) he intentionally obtains for himself the sexual services of another person (B),

(b) before obtaining those services, he has made or promised payment for those services to B or a third person, or knows that another person has made or promised such a payment, and

(c) either—

(i) B is under 18, and A does not reasonably believe that B is 18 or over, or

(ii) B is under 13.

(2) In this section, 'payment' means any financial advantage, including the discharge of an obligation to pay or the provision of goods or services (including sexual services) gratuitously or at a discount.

(3) A person guilty of an offence under this section against a person under 13, where subsection (6) applies, is liable on conviction on indictment to imprisonment for life.

(4) Unless subsection (3) applies, a person guilty of an offence under this section against a person under 16 is liable—

(a) where subsection (6) applies, on conviction on indictment, to imprisonment for a term not exceeding 14 years;

(b) in any other case—

(i) on summary conviction, to imprisonment for a term not exceeding 6 months or a fine not exceeding the statutory maximum or both;

(ii) on conviction on indictment, to imprisonment for a term not exceeding 14 years.

(5) Unless subsection (3) or (4) applies, a person guilty of an offence under this section is liable—

(a) on summary conviction, to imprisonment for a term not exceeding 6 months or a fine not exceeding the statutory maximum or both;

(b) on conviction on indictment, to imprisonment for a term not exceeding 7 years.

(6) This subsection applies where the offence involved—

(a) penetration of B's anus or vagina with a part of A's body or anything else,

(b) penetration of B's mouth with A's penis,

(c) penetration of A's anus or vagina with a part of B's body or by B with anything else, or

(d) penetration of A's mouth with B's penis.

(7) In the application of this section to Northern Ireland, subsection (4) has effect with the substitution of '17' for '16'.

48. Causing or inciting child prostitution or pornography

(1) A person (A) commits an offence if—

(a) he intentionally causes or incites another person (B) to become a prostitute, or to be involved in pornography, in any part of the world, and

(b) either—

  (i) B is under 18, and A does not reasonably believe that B is 18 or over, or

  (ii) B is under 13.

 (2) A person guilty of an offence under this section is liable—

  (a) on summary conviction, to imprisonment for a term not exceeding 6 months or a fine not exceeding the statutory maximum or both;

  (b) on conviction on indictment, to imprisonment for a term not exceeding 14 years.

49. Controlling a child prostitute or a child involved in pornography

 (1) A person (A) commits an offence if—

  (a) he intentionally controls any of the activities of another person (B) relating to B's prostitution or involvement in pornography in any part of the world, and

  (b) either—

   (i) B is under 18, and A does not reasonably believe that B is 18 or over, or

   (ii) B is under 13.

 (2) A person guilty of an offence under this section is liable—

  (a) on summary conviction, to imprisonment for a term not exceeding 6 months or a fine not exceeding the statutory maximum or both;

  (b) on conviction on indictment, to imprisonment for a term not exceeding 14 years.

50. Arranging or facilitating child prostitution or pornography

 (1) A person (A) commits an offence if—

  (a) he intentionally arranges or facilitates the prostitution or involvement in pornography in any part of the world of another person (B), and

  (b) either—

   (i) B is under 18, and A does not reasonably believe that B is 18 or over, or

   (ii) B is under 13.

 (2) A person guilty of an offence under this section is liable—

  (a) on summary conviction, to imprisonment for a term not exceeding 6 months or a fine not exceeding the statutory maximum or both;

  (b) on conviction on indictment, to imprisonment for a term not exceeding 14 years.

51. Sections 48 to 50: interpretation

 (1) For the purposes of sections 48 to 50, a person is involved in pornography if an indecent image of that person is recorded; and similar expressions, and 'pornography', are to be interpreted accordingly.

 (2) In those sections 'prostitute' means a person (A) who, on at least one occasion and whether or not compelled to do so, offers or provides sexual services to another person in return for payment or a promise of payment to A or a third person; and 'prostitution' is to be interpreted accordingly.

 (3) In subsection (2), 'payment' means any financial advantage, including the discharge of an obligation to pay or the provision of goods or services (including sexual services) gratuitously or at a discount.

Exploitation of prostitution

52. Causing or inciting prostitution for gain

 (1) A person commits an offence if—

(a) he intentionally causes or incites another person to become a prostitute in any part of the world, and

(b) he does so for or in the expectation of gain for himself or a third person.

(2) A person guilty of an offence under this section is liable—

(a) on summary conviction, to imprisonment for a term not exceeding 6 months or a fine not exceeding the statutory maximum or both;

(b) on conviction on indictment, to imprisonment for a term not exceeding 7 years.

53. Controlling prostitution for gain

(1) A person commits an offence if—

(a) he intentionally controls any of the activities of another person relating to that person's prostitution in any part of the world, and

(b) he does so for or in the expectation of gain for himself or a third person.

(2) A person guilty of an offence under this section is liable—

(a) on summary conviction, to imprisonment for a term not exceeding 6 months or a fine not exceeding the statutory maximum or both;

(b) on conviction on indictment, to imprisonment for a term not exceeding 7 years.

54. Sections 52 and 53: interpretation

(1) In sections 52 and 53, 'gain' means—

(a) any financial advantage, including the discharge of an obligation to pay or the provision of goods or services (including sexual services) gratuitously or at a discount; or

(b) the goodwill of any person which is or appears likely, in time, to bring financial advantage.

(2) In those sections 'prostitute' and 'prostitution' have the meaning given by section 51(2).

Amendments relating to prostitution

55. Penalties for keeping a brothel used for prostitution

(1) The Sexual Offences Act 1956 (c. 69) is amended as follows.

(2) After section 33 insert—

'33A Keeping a brothel used for prostitution

(1) It is an offence for a person to keep, or to manage, or act or assist in the management of, a brothel to which people resort for practices involving prostitution (whether or not also for other practices).

(2) In this section 'prostitution' has the meaning given by section 51(2) of the Sexual Offences Act 2003.'

(3) In Schedule 2 (mode of prosecution, punishment etc.), after paragraph 33 insert (as a paragraph with no entry in the fourth column)—

| '33A | Keeping a brothel used for prostitution (section 33A). | (i) on indictment | Seven years |
| | | (ii) summarily | Six months, or the statutory maximum, or both.' |

56. Extension of gender-specific prostitution offences

Schedule 1 (extension of gender-specific prostitution offences) has effect.

Trafficking

57. Trafficking into the UK for sexual exploitation

(1) A person commits an offence if he intentionally arranges or facilitates the arrival in the United Kingdom of another person (B) and either—

(a) he intends to do anything to or in respect of B, after B's arrival but in any part of the world, which if done will involve the commission of a relevant offence, or

(b) he believes that another person is likely to do something to or in respect of B, after B's arrival but in any part of the world, which if done will involve the commission of a relevant offence.

(2) A person guilty of an offence under this section is liable—

(a) on summary conviction, to imprisonment for a term not exceeding 6 months or a fine not exceeding the statutory maximum or both;

(b) on conviction on indictment, to imprisonment for a term not exceeding 14 years.

58. Trafficking within the UK for sexual exploitation

(1) A person commits an offence if he intentionally arranges or facilitates travel within the United Kingdom by another person (B) and either—

(a) he intends to do anything to or in respect of B, during or after the journey and in any part of the world, which if done will involve the commission of a relevant offence, or

(b) he believes that another person is likely to do something to or in respect of B, during or after the journey and in any part of the world, which if done will involve the commission of a relevant offence.

(2) A person guilty of an offence under this section is liable—

(a) on summary conviction, to imprisonment for a term not exceeding 6 months or a fine not exceeding the statutory maximum or both;

(b) on conviction on indictment, to imprisonment for a term not exceeding 14 years.

59. Trafficking out of the UK for sexual exploitation

(1) A person commits an offence if he intentionally arranges or facilitates the departure from the United Kingdom of another person (B) and either—

(a) he intends to do anything to or in respect of B, after B's departure but in any part of the world, which if done will involve the commission of a relevant offence, or

(b) he believes that another person is likely to do something to or in respect of B, after B's departure but in any part of the world, which if done will involve the commission of a relevant offence.

(2) A person guilty of an offence under this section is liable—

(a) on summary conviction, to imprisonment for a term not exceeding 6 months or a fine not exceeding the statutory maximum or both;

(b) on conviction on indictment, to imprisonment for a term not exceeding 14 years.

60. Sections 57 to 59: interpretation and jurisdiction

(1) In sections 57 to 59, 'relevant offence' means—

(a) an offence under this Part,

(b) an offence under section 1(1)(a) of the Protection of Children Act 1978 (c. 37),

(c) an offence listed in Schedule 1 to the Criminal Justice (Children) (Northern Ireland) Order 1998 (S.I. 1998/1504 (N.I. 9)),

(d) an offence under Article 3(1)(a) of the Protection of Children (Northern Ireland) Order 1978 (S.I. 1978/1047 (N.I. 17)), or

(e) anything done outside England and Wales and Northern Ireland which is not an offence within any of paragraphs (a) to (d) but would be if done in England and Wales or Northern Ireland.

(2) Sections 57 to 59 apply to anything done—

(a) in the United Kingdom, or

(b) outside the United Kingdom, by a body incorporated under the law of a part of the United Kingdom or by an individual to whom subsection (3) applies.

(3) This subsection applies to—

(a) a British citizen,

(b) a British overseas territories citizen,

(c) a British National (Overseas),

(d) a British Overseas citizen,

(e) a person who is a British subject under the British Nationality Act 1981 (c. 61),

(f) a British protected person within the meaning given by section 50(1) of that Act.

Preparatory offences

61. Administering a substance with intent

(1) A person commits an offence if he intentionally administers a substance to, or causes a substance to be taken by, another person (B)—

(a) knowing that B does not consent, and

(b) with the intention of stupefying or overpowering B, so as to enable any person to engage in a sexual activity that involves B.

(2) A person guilty of an offence under this section is liable—

(a) on summary conviction, to imprisonment for a term not exceeding 6 months or a fine not exceeding the statutory maximum or both;

(b) on conviction on indictment, to imprisonment for a term not exceeding 10 years.

62. Committing an offence with intent to commit a sexual offence

(1) A person commits an offence under this section if he commits any offence with the intention of committing a relevant sexual offence.

(2) In this section, 'relevant sexual offence' means any offence under this Part (including an offence of aiding, abetting, counselling or procuring such an offence).

(3) A person guilty of an offence under this section is liable on conviction on indictment, where the offence is committed by kidnapping or false imprisonment, to imprisonment for life.

(4) Unless subsection (3) applies, a person guilty of an offence under this section is liable—

(a) on summary conviction, to imprisonment for a term not exceeding 6 months or a fine not exceeding the statutory maximum or both;

(b) on conviction on indictment, to imprisonment for a term not exceeding 10 years.

63. Trespass with intent to commit a sexual offence

(1) A person commits an offence if—

(a) he is a trespasser on any premises,

(b) he intends to commit a relevant sexual offence on the premises, and

(c) he knows that, or is reckless as to whether, he is a trespasser.

(2) In this section—

'premises' includes a structure or part of a structure;

'relevant sexual offence' has the same meaning as in section 62;

'structure' includes a tent, vehicle or vessel or other temporary or movable structure.

(3) A person guilty of an offence under this section is liable—

(a) on summary conviction, to imprisonment for a term not exceeding 6 months or a fine not exceeding the statutory maximum or both;

(b) on conviction on indictment, to imprisonment for a term not exceeding 10 years.

Sex with an adult relative

64. Sex with an adult relative: penetration

(1) A person aged 16 or over (A) commits an offence if—

(a) he intentionally penetrates another person's vagina or anus with a part of his body or anything else, or penetrates another person's mouth with his penis,

(b) the penetration is sexual,

(c) the other person (B) is aged 18 or over,

(d) A is related to B in a way mentioned in subsection (2), and

(e) A knows or could reasonably be expected to know that he is related to B in that way.

(2) The ways that A may be related to B are as parent, grandparent, child, grandchild, brother, sister, half-brother, half-sister, uncle, aunt, nephew or niece.

(3) In subsection (2)—

(a) 'uncle' means the brother of a person's parent, and 'aunt' has a corresponding meaning;

(b) 'nephew' means the child of a person's brother or sister, and 'niece' has a corresponding meaning.

(4) Where in proceedings for an offence under this section it is proved that the defendant was related to the other person in any of those ways, it is to be taken that the defendant knew or could reasonably have been expected to know that he was related in that way unless sufficient evidence is adduced to raise an issue as to whether he knew or could reasonably have been expected to know that he was.

(5) A person guilty of an offence under this section is liable—

(a) on summary conviction, to imprisonment for a term not exceeding 6 months or a fine not exceeding the statutory maximum or both;

(b) on conviction on indictment, to imprisonment for a term not exceeding 2 years.

65. Sex with an adult relative: consenting to penetration

(1) A person aged 16 or over (A) commits an offence if—

(a) another person (B) penetrates A's vagina or anus with a part of B's body or anything else, or penetrates A's mouth with B's penis,

(b) A consents to the penetration,

(c) the penetration is sexual,

(d) B is aged 18 or over,

(e) A is related to B in a way mentioned in subsection (2), and

(f) A knows or could reasonably be expected to know that he is related to B in that way.

(2) The ways that A may be related to B are as parent, grandparent, child, grandchild, brother, sister, half-brother, half-sister, uncle, aunt, nephew or niece.

(3) In subsection (2)—

(a) 'uncle' means the brother of a person's parent, and 'aunt' has a corresponding meaning;

(b) 'nephew' means the child of a person's brother or sister, and 'niece' has a corresponding meaning.

(4) Where in proceedings for an offence under this section it is proved that the defendant was related to the other person in any of those ways, it is to be taken that the defendant knew or could reasonably have been expected to know that he was related in that way unless sufficient evidence is adduced to raise an issue as to whether he knew or could reasonably have been expected to know that he was.

(5) A person guilty of an offence under this section is liable—

(a) on summary conviction, to imprisonment for a term not exceeding 6 months or a fine not exceeding the statutory maximum or both;

(b) on conviction on indictment, to imprisonment for a term not exceeding 2 years.

Other offences

66. Exposure

(1) A person commits an offence if—

(a) he intentionally exposes his genitals, and

(b) he intends that someone will see them and be caused alarm or distress.

(2) A person guilty of an offence under this section is liable—

(a) on summary conviction, to imprisonment for a term not exceeding 6 months or a fine not exceeding the statutory maximum or both;

(b) on conviction on indictment, to imprisonment for a term not exceeding 2 years.

67. Voyeurism

(1) A person commits an offence if—

(a) for the purpose of obtaining sexual gratification, he observes another person doing a private act, and

(b) he knows that the other person does not consent to being observed for his sexual gratification.

(2) A person commits an offence if—

(a) he operates equipment with the intention of enabling another person to observe, for the purpose of obtaining sexual gratification, a third person (B) doing a private act, and

(b) he knows that B does not consent to his operating equipment with that intention.

(3) A person commits an offence if—

(a) he records another person (B) doing a private act,

(b) he does so with the intention that he or a third person will, for the purpose of obtaining sexual gratification, look at an image of B doing the act, and

(c) he knows that B does not consent to his recording the act with that intention.

(4) A person commits an offence if he instals equipment, or constructs or adapts a structure or part of a structure, with the intention of enabling himself or another person to commit an offence under subsection (1).

(5) A person guilty of an offence under this section is liable—

(a) on summary conviction, to imprisonment for a term not exceeding 6 months or a fine not exceeding the statutory maximum or both;

(b) on conviction on indictment, to imprisonment for a term not exceeding 2 years.

68. Voyeurism: interpretation

(1) For the purposes of section 67, a person is doing a private act if the person is in a place which, in the circumstances, would reasonably be expected to provide privacy, and—

(a) the person's genitals, buttocks or breasts are exposed or covered only with underwear,

(b) the person is using a lavatory, or

(c) the person is doing a sexual act that is not of a kind ordinarily done in public.

(2) In section 67, 'structure' includes a tent, vehicle or vessel or other temporary or movable structure.

69. Intercourse with an animal

(1) A person commits an offence if—

(a) he intentionally performs an act of penetration with his penis,

(b) what is penetrated is the vagina or anus of a living animal, and

(c) he knows that, or is reckless as to whether, that is what is penetrated.

(2) A person (A) commits an offence if—

(a) A intentionally causes, or allows, A's vagina or anus to be penetrated,

(b) the penetration is by the penis of a living animal, and

(c) A knows that, or is reckless as to whether, that is what A is being penetrated by.

(3) A person guilty of an offence under this section is liable—

(a) on summary conviction, to imprisonment for a term not exceeding 6 months or a fine not exceeding the statutory maximum or both;

(b) on conviction on indictment, to imprisonment for a term not exceeding 2 years.

70. Sexual penetration of a corpse

(1) A person commits an offence if—

(a) he intentionally performs an act of penetration with a part of his body or anything else,

(b) what is penetrated is a part of the body of a dead person,

(c) he knows that, or is reckless as to whether, that is what is penetrated, and

(d) the penetration is sexual.

(2) A person guilty of an offence under this section is liable—

(a) on summary conviction, to imprisonment for a term not exceeding 6 months or a fine not exceeding the statutory maximum or both;

(b) on conviction on indictment, to imprisonment for a term not exceeding 2 years.

71. Sexual activity in a public lavatory

(1) A person commits an offence if—

(a) he is in a lavatory to which the public or a section of the public has or is permitted to have access, whether on payment or otherwise,

(b) he intentionally engages in an activity, and,

(c) the activity is sexual.

(2) For the purposes of this section, an activity is sexual if a reasonable person would, in all the circumstances but regardless of any person's purpose, consider it to be sexual.

(3) A person guilty of an offence under this section is liable on summary conviction, to imprisonment for a term not exceeding 6 months or a fine not exceeding level 5 on the standard scale or both.

Offences outside the United Kingdom

72. Offences outside the United Kingdom

(1) Subject to subsection (2), any act done by a person in a country or territory outside the United Kingdom which—

    (a) constituted an offence under the law in force in that country or territory, and

    (b) would constitute a sexual offence to which this section applies if it had been done in England and Wales or in Northern Ireland,

constitutes that sexual offence under the law of that part of the United Kingdom.

(2) Proceedings by virtue of this section may be brought only against a person who was on 1st September 1997, or has since become, a British citizen or resident in the United Kingdom.

(3) An act punishable under the law in force in any country or territory constitutes an offence under that law for the purposes of this section, however it is described in that law.

(4) Subject to subsection (5), the condition in subsection (1)(a) is to be taken to be met unless, not later than rules of court may provide, the defendant serves on the prosecution a notice—

    (a) stating that, on the facts as alleged with respect to the act in question, the condition is not in his opinion met,

    (b) showing his grounds for that opinion, and

    (c) requiring the prosecution to prove that it is met.

(5) The court, if it thinks fit, may permit the defendant to require the prosecution to prove that the condition is met without service of a notice under subsection (4).

(6) In the Crown Court the question whether the condition is met is to be decided by the judge alone.

(7) Schedule 2 lists the sexual offences to which this section applies.

Supplementary and general

73. Exceptions to aiding, abetting and counselling

(1) A person is not guilty of aiding, abetting or counselling the commission against a child of an offence to which this section applies if he acts for the purpose of—

    (a) protecting the child from sexually transmitted infection,

    (b) protecting the physical safety of the child,

    (c) preventing the child from becoming pregnant, or

    (d) promoting the child's emotional well-being by the giving of advice,

and not for the purpose of obtaining sexual gratification or for the purpose of causing or encouraging the activity constituting the offence or the child's participation in it.

(2) This section applies to—

    (a) an offence under any of sections 5 to 7 (offences against children under 13);

    (b) an offence under section 9 (sexual activity with a child);

    (c) an offence under section 13 which would be an offence under section 9 if the offender were aged 18;

    (d) an offence under any of sections 16, 25, 30, 34 and 38 (sexual activity) against a person under 16.

(3) This section does not affect any other enactment or any rule of law restricting the

circumstances in which a person is guilty of aiding, abetting or counselling an offence under this Part.

74. 'Consent'

For the purposes of this Part, a person consents if he agrees by choice, and has the freedom and capacity to make that choice.

75. Evidential presumptions about consent

(1) If in proceedings for an offence to which this section applies it is proved—

    (a) that the defendant did the relevant act,

    (b) that any of the circumstances specified in subsection (2) existed, and

    (c) that the defendant knew that those circumstances existed,

the complainant is to be taken not to have consented to the relevant act unless sufficient evidence is adduced to raise an issue as to whether he consented, and the defendant is to be taken not to have reasonably believed that the complainant consented unless sufficient evidence is adduced to raise an issue as to whether he reasonably believed it.

(2) The circumstances are that—

    (a) any person was, at the time of the relevant act or immediately before it began, using violence against the complainant or causing the complainant to fear that immediate violence would be used against him;

    (b) any person was, at the time of the relevant act or immediately before it began, causing the complainant to fear that violence was being used, or that immediate violence would be used, against another person;

    (c) the complainant was, and the defendant was not, unlawfully detained at the time of the relevant act;

    (d) the complainant was asleep or otherwise unconscious at the time of the relevant act;

    (e) because of the complainant's physical disability, the complainant would not have been able at the time of the relevant act to communicate to the defendant whether the complainant consented;

    (f) any person had administered to or caused to be taken by the complainant, without the complainant's consent, a substance which, having regard to when it was administered or taken, was capable of causing or enabling the complainant to be stupefied or overpowered at the time of the relevant act.

(3) In subsection (2)(a) and (b), the reference to the time immediately before the relevant act began is, in the case of an act which is one of a continuous series of sexual activities, a reference to the time immediately before the first sexual activity began.

76. Conclusive presumptions about consent

(1) If in proceedings for an offence to which this section applies it is proved that the defendant did the relevant act and that any of the circumstances specified in subsection (2) existed, it is to be conclusively presumed—

    (a) that the complainant did not consent to the relevant act, and

    (b) that the defendant did not believe that the complainant consented to the relevant act.

(2) The circumstances are that—

(a) the defendant intentionally deceived the complainant as to the nature or purpose of the relevant act;

(b) the defendant intentionally induced the complainant to consent to the relevant act by impersonating a person known personally to the complainant.

77. Sections 75 and 76: relevant acts

In relation to an offence to which sections 75 and 76 apply, references in those sections to the relevant act and to the complainant are to be read as follows—

Offence	Relevant Act
An offence under section 1 (rape).	The defendant intentionally penetrating, with his penis, the vagina, anus or mouth of another person ('the complainant').
An offence under section 2 (assault by penetration).	The defendant intentionally penetrating, with a part of his body or anything else, the vagina or anus of another person ('the complainant'), where the penetration is sexual.
An offence under section 3 (sexual assault).	The defendant intentionally touching another person ('the complainant'), where the touching is sexual.
An offence under section 4 (causing a person to engage in sexual activity without consent).	The defendant intentionally causing another person ('the complainant') to engage in an activity, where the activity is sexual.

78. 'Sexual'

For the purposes of this Part (except section 71), penetration, touching or any other activity is sexual if a reasonable person would consider that—

(a) whatever its circumstances or any person's purpose in relation to it, it is because of its nature sexual, or

(b) because of its nature it may be sexual and because of its circumstances or the purpose of any person in relation to it (or both) it is sexual.

79. Part 1: general interpretation

(1) The following apply for the purposes of this Part.

(2) Penetration is a continuing act from entry to withdrawal.

(3) References to a part of the body include references to a part surgically constructed (in particular, through gender reassignment surgery).

(4) 'Image' means a moving or still image and includes an image produced by any means and, where the context permits, a three-dimensional image.

(5) References to an image of a person include references to an image of an imaginary person.

(6) 'Mental disorder' has the meaning given by section 1 of the Mental Health Act 1983 (c. 20).

(7) References to observation (however expressed) are to observation whether direct or by looking at an image.

(8) Touching includes touching—

(a) with any part of the body,

(b) with anything else,

(c) through anything,

and in particular includes touching amounting to penetration.

(9) 'Vagina' includes vulva.

(10) In relation to an animal, references to the vagina or anus include references to any similar part.

PART 2
NOTIFICATION AND ORDERS

Notification requirements

80. Persons becoming subject to notification requirements

(1) A person is subject to the notification requirements of this Part for the period set out in section 82 ('the notification period') if—

(a) he is convicted of an offence listed in Schedule 3;

(b) he is found not guilty of such an offence by reason of insanity;

(c) he is found to be under a disability and to have done the act charged against him in respect of such an offence; or

(d) in England and Wales or Northern Ireland, he is cautioned in respect of such an offence.

(2) A person for the time being subject to the notification requirements of this Part is referred to in this Part as a 'relevant offender'.

81. Persons formerly subject to Part 1 of the Sex Offenders Act 1997

(1) A person is, from the commencement of this Part until the end of the notification period, subject to the notification requirements of this Part if, before the commencement of this Part—

(a) he was convicted of an offence listed in Schedule 3;

(b) he was found not guilty of such an offence by reason of insanity;

(c) he was found to be under a disability and to have done the act charged against him in respect of such an offence; or

(d) in England and Wales or Northern Ireland, he was cautioned in respect of such an offence.

(2) Subsection (1) does not apply if the notification period ended before the commencement of this Part.

(3) Subsection (1)(a) does not apply to a conviction before 1st September 1997 unless, at the beginning of that day, the person—

(a) had not been dealt with in respect of the offence;

(b) was serving a sentence of imprisonment or a term of service detention, or was subject to a community order, in respect of the offence;

(c) was subject to supervision, having been released from prison after serving the whole or part of a sentence of imprisonment in respect of the offence; or

(d) was detained in a hospital or was subject to a guardianship order, following the conviction.

(4) Paragraphs (b) and (c) of subsection (1) do not apply to a finding made before 1st September 1997 unless, at the beginning of that day, the person—

(a) had not been dealt with in respect of the finding; or

(b) was detained in a hospital, following the finding.

(5) Subsection (1)(d) does not apply to a caution given before 1st September 1997.

(6) A person who would have been within subsection (3)(b) or (d) or (4)(b) but for the fact that at the beginning of 1st September 1997 he was unlawfully at large or absent without leave, on temporary release or leave of absence, or on bail pending an appeal, is to be treated as being within that provision.

(7) Where, immediately before the commencement of this Part, an order under a provision within subsection (8) was in force in respect of a person, the person is subject to the notification requirements of this Part from that commencement until the order is discharged or otherwise ceases to have effect.

(8) The provisions are—

(a) section 5A of the Sex Offenders Act 1997 (c. 51) (restraining orders);

(b) section 2 of the Crime and Disorder Act 1998 (c. 37) (sex offender orders made in England and Wales);

(c) section 2A of the Crime and Disorder Act 1998 (interim orders made in England and Wales);

(d) section 20 of the Crime and Disorder Act 1998 (sex offender orders and interim orders made in Scotland);

(e) Article 6 of the Criminal Justice (Northern Ireland) Order 1998 (S.I. 1998/2839 (N.I. 20)) (sex offender orders made in Northern Ireland);

(f) Article 6A of the Criminal Justice (Northern Ireland) Order 1998 (interim orders made in Northern Ireland).

82. The notification period

(1) The notification period for a person within section 80(1) or 81(1) is the period in the second column of the following Table opposite the description that applies to him.

TABLE

Description of relevant offender	Notification period
A person who, in respect of the offence, is or has been sentenced to imprisonment for life or for a term of 30 months or more	An indefinite period beginning with the relevant date
A person who, in respect of the offence, has been made the subject of an order under section 210F(1) of the Criminal Procedure (Scotland) Act 1995 (order for lifelong restriction)	An indefinite period beginning with that date
A person who, in respect of the offence or finding, is or has been admitted to a hospital subject to a restriction order	An indefinite period beginning with that date

Description of relevant offender	Notification period
A person who, in respect of the offence, is or has been sentenced to imprisonment for a term of more than 6 months but less than 30 months	10 years beginning with that date
A person who, in respect of the offence, is or has been sentenced to imprisonment for a term of 6 months or less	7 years beginning with that date
A person who, in respect of the offence or finding, is or has been admitted to a hospital without being subject to a restriction order	7 years beginning with that date
A person within section 80(1)(d)	2 years beginning with that date
A person in whose case an order for conditional discharge or, in Scotland, a probation order, is made in respect of the offence	The period of conditional discharge or, in Scotland, the probation period
A person of any other description	5 years beginning with the relevant date

(2) Where a person is under 18 on the relevant date, subsection (1) has effect as if for any reference to a period of 10 years, 7 years, 5 years or 2 years there were substituted a reference to one-half of that period.

(3) Subsection (4) applies where a relevant offender within section 80(1)(a) or 81(1)(a) is or has been sentenced, in respect of two or more offences listed in Schedule 3—

(a) to consecutive terms of imprisonment; or

(b) to terms of imprisonment which are partly concurrent.

(4) Where this subsection applies, subsection (1) has effect as if the relevant offender were or had been sentenced, in respect of each of the offences, to a term of imprisonment which—

(a) in the case of consecutive terms, is equal to the aggregate of those terms;

(b) in the case of partly concurrent terms (X and Y, which overlap for a period Z), is equal to X plus Y minus Z.

(5) Where a relevant offender the subject of a finding within section 80(1)(c) or 81(1)(c) is subsequently tried for the offence, the notification period relating to the finding ends at the conclusion of the trial.

(6) In this Part, 'relevant date' means—

(a) in the case of a person within section 80(1)(a) or 81(1)(a), the date of the conviction;

(b) in the case of a person within section 80(1)(b) or (c) or 81(1)(b) or (c), the date of the finding;

(c) in the case of a person within section 80(1)(d) or 81(1)(d), the date of the caution;

(d) in the case of a person within section 81(7), the date which, for the purposes of Part 1 of the Sex Offenders Act 1997 (c. 51), was the relevant date in relation to that person.

83. Notification requirements: initial notification

(1) A relevant offender must, within the period of 3 days beginning with the relevant date (or, if later, the commencement of this Part), notify to the police the information set out in subsection (5).

(2) Subsection (1) does not apply to a relevant offender in respect of a conviction, finding or caution within section 80(1) if—

(a) immediately before the conviction, finding or caution, he was subject to the notification requirements of this Part as a result of another conviction, finding or caution or an order of a court ('the earlier event'),

(b) at that time, he had made a notification under subsection (1) in respect of the earlier event, and

(c) throughout the period referred to in subsection (1), he remains subject to the notification requirements as a result of the earlier event.

(3) Subsection (1) does not apply to a relevant offender in respect of a conviction, finding or caution within section 81(1) or an order within section 81(7) if the offender complied with section 2(1) of the Sex Offenders Act 1997 in respect of the conviction, finding, caution or order.

(4) Where a notification order is made in respect of a conviction, finding or caution, subsection (1) does not apply to the relevant offender in respect of the conviction, finding or caution if—

(a) immediately before the order was made, he was subject to the notification requirements of this Part as a result of another conviction, finding or caution or an order of a court ('the earlier event'),

(b) at that time, he had made a notification under subsection (1) in respect of the earlier event, and

(c) throughout the period referred to in subsection (1), he remains subject to the notification requirements as a result of the earlier event.

(5) The information is—

(a) the relevant offender's date of birth;

(b) his national insurance number;

(c) his name on the relevant date and, where he used one or more other names on that date, each of those names;

(d) his home address on the relevant date;

(e) his name on the date on which notification is given and, where he uses one or more other names on that date, each of those names;

(f) his home address on the date on which notification is given;

(g) the address of any other premises in the United Kingdom at which, at the time the notification is given, he regularly resides or stays.

(6) When determining the period for the purpose of subsection (1), there is to be disregarded any time when the relevant offender is—

(a) remanded in or committed to custody by an order of a court;

(b) serving a sentence of imprisonment or a term of service detention;

(c) detained in a hospital; or

(d) outside the United Kingdom.

(7) In this Part, 'home address' means, in relation to any person—

(a) the address of his sole or main residence in the United Kingdom, or

(b) where he has no such residence, the address or location of a place in the United Kingdom where he can regularly be found and, if there is more than one such place, such one of those places as the person may select.

84. Notification requirements: changes

(1) A relevant offender must, within the period of 3 days beginning with—

(a) his using a name which has not been notified to the police under section 83(1), this subsection, or section 2 of the Sex Offenders Act 1997 (c. 51),

(b) any change of his home address,

(c) his having resided or stayed, for a qualifying period, at any premises in the United Kingdom the address of which has not been notified to the police under section 83(1), this subsection, or section 2 of the Sex Offenders Act 1997, or

(d) his release from custody pursuant to an order of a court or from imprisonment, service detention or detention in a hospital,

notify to the police that name, the new home address, the address of those premises or (as the case may be) the fact that he has been released, and (in addition) the information set out in section 83(5).

(2) A notification under subsection (1) may be given before the name is used, the change of home address occurs or the qualifying period ends, but in that case the relevant offender must also specify the date when the event is expected to occur.

(3) If a notification is given in accordance with subsection (2) and the event to which it relates occurs more than 2 days before the date specified, the notification does not affect the duty imposed by subsection (1).

(4) If a notification is given in accordance with subsection (2) and the event to which it relates has not occurred by the end of the period of 3 days beginning with the date specified—

(a) the notification does not affect the duty imposed by subsection (1), and

(b) the relevant offender must, within the period of 6 days beginning with the date specified, notify to the police the fact that the event did not occur within the period of 3 days beginning with the date specified.

(5) Section 83(6) applies to the determination of the period of 3 days mentioned in subsection (1) and the period of 6 days mentioned in subsection (4)(b), as it applies to the determination of the period mentioned in section 83(1).

(6) In this section, 'qualifying period' means—

(a) a period of 7 days, or

(b) two or more periods, in any period of 12 months, which taken together amount to 7 days.

85. Notification requirements: periodic notification

(1) A relevant offender must, within the period of one year after each event within subsection (2), notify to the police the information set out in section 83(5), unless within that period he has given a notification under section 84(1).

(2) The events are—

(a) the commencement of this Part (but only in the case of a person who is a relevant offender from that commencement);

(b) any notification given by the relevant offender under section 83(1) or 84(1); and

(c) any notification given by him under subsection (1).

(3) Where the period referred to in subsection (1) would (apart from this subsection) end whilst subsection (4) applies to the relevant offender, that period is to be treated as continuing until the end of the period of 3 days beginning when subsection (4) first ceases to apply to him.

(4) This subsection applies to the relevant offender if he is—

(a) remanded in or committed to custody by an order of a court,

(b) serving a sentence of imprisonment or a term of service detention,

(c) detained in a hospital, or

(d) outside the United Kingdom.

86. Notification requirements: travel outside the United Kingdom

(1) The Secretary of State may by regulations make provision requiring relevant offenders who leave the United Kingdom, or any description of such offenders—

(a) to give in accordance with the regulations, before they leave, a notification under subsection (2);

(b) if they subsequently return to the United Kingdom, to give in accordance with the regulations a notification under subsection (3).

(2) A notification under this subsection must disclose—

(a) the date on which the offender will leave the United Kingdom;

(b) the country (or, if there is more than one, the first country) to which he will travel and his point of arrival (determined in accordance with the regulations) in that country;

(c) any other information prescribed by the regulations which the offender holds about his departure from or return to the United Kingdom or his movements while outside the United Kingdom.

(3) A notification under this subsection must disclose any information prescribed by the regulations about the offender's return to the United Kingdom.

(4) Regulations under subsection (1) may make different provision for different categories of person.

87. Method of notification and related matters

(1) A person gives a notification under section 83(1), 84(1) or 85(1) by—

(a) attending at such police station in his local police area as the Secretary of State may by regulations prescribe or, if there is more than one, at any of them, and

(b) giving an oral notification to any police officer, or to any person authorised for the purpose by the officer in charge of the station.

(2) A person giving a notification under section 84(1)—

(a) in relation to a prospective change of home address, or

(b) in relation to premises referred to in subsection (1)(c) of that section,

may give the notification at a police station that would fall within subsection (1) above if the change in home address had already occurred or (as the case may be) if the address of those premises were his home address.

(3) Any notification under this section must be acknowledged; and an acknowledgment under this subsection must be in writing, and in such form as the Secretary of State may direct.

(4) Where a notification is given under section 83(1), 84(1) or 85(1), the relevant offender must, if requested to do so by the police officer or person referred to in subsection (1)(b), allow the officer or person to—

(a) take his fingerprints,

(b) photograph any part of him, or

(c) do both these things.

(5) The power in subsection (4) is exercisable for the purpose of verifying the identity of the relevant offender.

(6) Regulations under subsection (1) may make different provision for different categories of person.

88. Section 87: interpretation

(1) Subsections (2) to (4) apply for the purposes of section 87.

(2) 'Photograph' includes any process by means of which an image may be produced.

(3) 'Local police area' means, in relation to a person—

(a) the police area in which his home address is situated;

(b) in the absence of a home address, the police area in which the home address last notified is situated;

(c) in the absence of a home address and of any such notification, the police area in which the court which last dealt with the person in a way mentioned in subsection (4) is situated.

(4) The ways are—

(a) dealing with a person in respect of an offence listed in Schedule 3 or a finding in relation to such an offence;

(b) dealing with a person in respect of an offence under section 128 or a finding in relation to such an offence;

(c) making, in respect of a person, a notification order, interim notification order, sexual offences prevention order or interim sexual offences prevention order;

(d) making, in respect of a person, an order under section 2, 2A or 20 of the Crime and Disorder Act 1998 (c. 37) (sex offender orders and interim orders made in England and Wales or Scotland) or Article 6 or 6A of the Criminal Justice (Northern Ireland) Order 1998 (S.I. 1998/2839 (N.I. 20)) (sex offender orders and interim orders made in Northern Ireland);

and in paragraphs (a) and (b), 'finding' in relation to an offence means a finding of not guilty of the offence by reason of insanity or a finding that the person was under a disability and did the act or omission charged against him in respect of the offence.

(5) Subsection (3) applies as if Northern Ireland were a police area.

89. Young offenders: parental directions

(1) Where a person within the first column of the following Table ('the young offender') is under 18 (or, in Scotland, 16) when he is before the court referred to in the second column of the Table opposite the description that applies to him, that court may direct that subsection (2) applies in respect of an individual ('the parent') having parental responsibility for (or, in Scotland, parental responsibilities in relation to) the young offender.

TABLE

Description of person	Court which may make the direction
A relevant offender within section 80(1)(a) to (c) or 81(1)(a) to (c)	The court which deals with the offender in respect of the offence or finding
A relevant offender within section 129(1)(a) to (c)	The court which deals with the offender in respect of the offence or finding
A person who is the subject of a notification order, interim notification order, sexual offences prevention order or interim sexual offences prevention order	The court which makes the order

Description of person	Court which may make the direction
A relevant offender who is the defendant to an application under subsection (4) (or, in Scotland, the subject of an application under subsection (5))	The court which hears the application

(2) Where this subsection applies—

(a) the obligations that would (apart from this subsection) be imposed by or under sections 83 to 86 on the young offender are to be treated instead as obligations on the parent, and

(b) the parent must ensure that the young offender attends at the police station with him, when a notification is being given.

(3) A direction under subsection (1) takes immediate effect and applies—

(a) until the young offender attains the age of 18 (or, where a court in Scotland gives the direction, 16); or

(b) for such shorter period as the court may, at the time the direction is given, direct.

(4) A chief officer of police may, by complaint to any magistrates' court whose commission area includes any part of his police area, apply for a direction under subsection (1) in respect of a relevant offender ('the defendant')—

(a) who resides in his police area, or who the chief officer believes is in or is intending to come to his police area, and

(b) who the chief officer believes is under 18.

(5) In Scotland, a chief constable may, by summary application to any sheriff within whose sheriffdom lies any part of the area of his police force, apply for a direction under subsection (1) in respect of a relevant offender ('the subject')—

(a) who resides in that area, or who the chief constable believes is in or is intending to come to that area, and

(b) who the chief constable believes is under 16.

90. Parental directions: variations, renewals and discharges

(1) A person within subsection (2) may apply to the appropriate court for an order varying, renewing or discharging a direction under section 89(1).

(2) The persons are—

(a) the young offender;

(b) the parent;

(c) the chief officer of police for the area in which the young offender resides;

(d) a chief officer of police who believes that the young offender is in, or is intending to come to, his police area;

(e) in Scotland, where the appropriate court is a civil court—

(i) the chief constable of the police force within the area of which the young offender resides;

(ii) a chief constable who believes that the young offender is in, or is intending to come to, the area of his police force,

and in any other case, the prosecutor;

(f) where the direction was made on an application under section 89(4), the chief officer of police who made the application;

(g) where the direction was made on an application under section 89(5), the chief constable who made the application.

(3) An application under subsection (1) may be made—

(a) where the appropriate court is the Crown Court (or in Scotland a criminal court), in accordance with rules of court;

(b) in any other case, by complaint (or, in Scotland, by summary application).

(4) On the application the court, after hearing the person making the application and (if they wish to be heard) the other persons mentioned in subsection (2), may make any order, varying, renewing or discharging the direction, that the court considers appropriate.

(5) In this section, the 'appropriate court' means—

(a) where the Court of Appeal made the order, the Crown Court;

(b) in any other case, the court that made the direction under section 89(1).

91. Offences relating to notification

(1) A person commits an offence if he—

(a) fails, without reasonable excuse, to comply with section 83(1), 84(1), 84(4)(b), 85(1), 87(4) or 89(2)(b) or any requirement imposed by regulations made under section 86(1); or

(b) notifies to the police, in purported compliance with section 83(1), 84(1) or 85(1) or any requirement imposed by regulations made under section 86(1), any information which he knows to be false.

(2) A person guilty of an offence under this section is liable—

(a) on summary conviction, to imprisonment for a term not exceeding 6 months or a fine not exceeding the statutory maximum or both;

(b) on conviction on indictment, to imprisonment for a term not exceeding 5 years.

(3) A person commits an offence under paragraph (a) of subsection (1) on the day on which he first fails, without reasonable excuse, to comply with section 83(1), 84(1) or 85(1) or a requirement imposed by regulations made under section 86(1), and continues to commit it throughout any period during which the failure continues; but a person must not be prosecuted under subsection (1) more than once in respect of the same failure.

(4) Proceedings for an offence under this section may be commenced in any court having jurisdiction in any place where the person charged with the offence resides or is found.

92. Certificates for purposes of Part 2

(1) Subsection (2) applies where on any date a person is—

(a) convicted of an offence listed in Schedule 3;

(b) found not guilty of such an offence by reason of insanity; or

(c) found to be under a disability and to have done the act charged against him in respect of such an offence.

(2) If the court by or before which the person is so convicted or found—

(a) states in open court—

(i) that on that date he has been convicted, found not guilty by reason of insanity or found to be under a disability and to have done the act charged against him, and

(ii) that the offence in question is an offence listed in Schedule 3, and

(b) certifies those facts, whether at the time or subsequently,

the certificate is, for the purposes of this Part, evidence (or, in Scotland, sufficient evidence) of those facts.

(3) Subsection (4) applies where on any date a person is, in England and Wales or Northern Ireland, cautioned in respect of an offence listed in Schedule 3.

(4) If the constable—

(a) informs the person that he has been cautioned on that date and that the offence in question is an offence listed in Schedule 3, and

(b) certifies those facts, whether at the time or subsequently, in such form as the Secretary of State may by order prescribe,

the certificate is, for the purposes of this Part, evidence (or, in Scotland, sufficient evidence) of those facts.

93. Abolished homosexual offences

Schedule 4 (procedure for ending notification requirements for abolished homosexual offences) has effect.

Information for verification

94. Part 2: supply of information to Secretary of State etc. for verification

(1) This section applies to information notified to the police under—

(a) section 83, 84 or 85, or

(b) section 2(1) to (3) of the Sex Offenders Act 1997 (c. 51).

(2) A person within subsection (3) may, for the purposes of the prevention, detection, investigation or prosecution of offences under this Part, supply information to which this section applies to—

(a) the Secretary of State,

(b) a Northern Ireland Department, or

(c) a person providing services to the Secretary of State or a Northern Ireland Department in connection with a relevant function,

for use for the purpose of verifying the information.

(3) The persons are—

(a) a chief officer of police (in Scotland, a chief constable),

(b) the Police Information Technology Organisation,

(c) the Director General of the National Criminal Intelligence Service,

(d) the Director General of the National Crime Squad.

(4) In relation to information supplied under subsection (2) to any person, the reference to verifying the information is a reference to—

(a) checking its accuracy by comparing it with information held—

(i) where the person is the Secretary of State or a Northern Ireland Department, by him or it in connection with the exercise of a relevant function, or

(ii) where the person is within subsection (2)(c), by that person in connection with the provision of services referred to there, and

(b) compiling a report of that comparison.

(5) Subject to subsection (6), the supply of information under this section is to be taken not to breach any restriction on the disclosure of information (however arising or imposed).

(6) This section does not authorise the doing of anything that contravenes the Data Protection Act 1998 (c. 29).

(7) This section does not affect any power existing apart from this section to supply information.

(8) In this section—

'Northern Ireland Department' means the Department for Employment and Learning, the Department of the Environment or the Department for Social Development;
'relevant function' means—

(a) a function relating to social security, child support, employment or training,

(b) a function relating to passports,

(c) a function under Part 3 of the Road Traffic Act 1988 (c. 52) or Part 2 of the Road Traffic (Northern Ireland) Order 1981 (S.I. 1981/154 (N.I. 1)).

95. Part 2: supply of information by Secretary of State etc.

(1) A report compiled under section 94 may be supplied by—

(a) the Secretary of State,

(b) a Northern Ireland Department, or

(c) a person within section 94(2)(c),

to a person within subsection (2).

(2) The persons are—

(a) a chief officer of police (in Scotland, a chief constable),

(b) the Director General of the National Criminal Intelligence Service,

(c) the Director General of the National Crime Squad.

(3) Such a report may contain any information held—

(a) by the Secretary of State or a Northern Ireland Department in connection with the exercise of a relevant function, or

(b) by a person within section 94(2)(c) in connection with the provision of services referred to there.

(4) Where such a report contains information within subsection (3), the person within subsection (2) to whom it is supplied—

(a) may retain the information, whether or not used for the purposes of the prevention, detection, investigation or prosecution of an offence under this Part, and

(b) may use the information for any purpose related to the prevention, detection, investigation or prosecution of offences (whether or not under this Part), but for no other purpose.

(5) Subsections (5) to (8) of section 94 apply in relation to this section as they apply in relation to section 94.

Information about release or transfer

96. Information about release or transfer

(1) This section applies to a relevant offender who is serving a sentence of imprisonment or a term of service detention, or is detained in a hospital.

(2) The Secretary of State may by regulations make provision requiring notice to be given by the person who is responsible for that offender to persons prescribed by the regulations, of any occasion when the offender is released or a different person becomes responsible for him.

(3) The regulations may make provision for determining who is to be treated for the purposes of this section as responsible for an offender.

Notification orders

97. Notification orders: applications and grounds

(1) A chief officer of police may, by complaint to any magistrates' court whose commission area includes any part of his police area, apply for an order under this section (a 'notification order') in respect of a person ('the defendant') if—

(a) it appears to him that the following three conditions are met with respect to the defendant, and

(b) the defendant resides in his police area or the chief officer believes that the defendant is in, or is intending to come to, his police area.

(2) The first condition is that under the law in force in a country outside the United Kingdom—

(a) he has been convicted of a relevant offence (whether or not he has been punished for it),

(b) a court exercising jurisdiction under that law has made in respect of a relevant offence a finding equivalent to a finding that he is not guilty by reason of insanity,

(c) such a court has made in respect of a relevant offence a finding equivalent to a finding that he is under a disability and did the act charged against him in respect of the offence, or

(d) he has been cautioned in respect of a relevant offence.

(3) The second condition is that—

(a) the first condition is met because of a conviction, finding or caution which occurred on or after 1st September 1997,

(b) the first condition is met because of a conviction or finding which occurred before that date, but the person was dealt with in respect of the offence or finding on or after that date, or has yet to be dealt with in respect of it, or

(c) the first condition is met because of a conviction or finding which occurred before that date, but on that date the person was, in respect of the offence or finding, subject under the law in force in the country concerned to detention, supervision or any other disposal equivalent to any of those mentioned in section 81(3) (read with sections 81(6) and 131).

(4) The third condition is that the period set out in section 82 (as modified by subsections (2) and (3) of section 98) in respect of the relevant offence has not expired.

(5) If on the application it is proved that the conditions in subsections (2) to (4) are met, the court must make a notification order.

(6) In this section and section 98, 'relevant offence' has the meaning given by section 99.

98. Notification orders: effect

(1) Where a notification order is made—

(a) the application of this Part to the defendant in respect of the conviction, finding or caution to which the order relates is subject to the modifications set out below, and

(b) subject to those modifications, the defendant becomes or (as the case may be) remains subject to the notification requirements of this Part for the notification period set out in section 82.

(2) The 'relevant date' means—

(a) in the case of a person within section 97(2)(a), the date of the conviction;

(b) in the case of a person within section 97(2)(b) or (c), the date of the finding;

(c) in the case of a person within section 97(2)(d), the date of the caution.

(3) In section 82—

(a) references, except in the Table, to a person (or relevant offender) within any provision of section 80 are to be read as references to the defendant;

(b) the reference in the Table to section 80(1)(d) is to be read as a reference to section 97(2)(d);

(c) references to an order of any description are to be read as references to any corresponding disposal made in relation to the defendant in respect of an offence or finding by reference to which the notification order was made;

(d) the reference to offences listed in Schedule 3 is to be read as a reference to relevant offences.

(4) In sections 83 and 85, references to the commencement of this Part are to be read as references to the date of service of the notification order.

99. Sections 97 and 98: relevant offences

(1) 'Relevant offence' in sections 97 and 98 means an act which—

(a) constituted an offence under the law in force in the country concerned, and

(b) would have constituted an offence listed in Schedule 3 (other than at paragraph 60) if it had been done in any part of the United Kingdom.

(2) An act punishable under the law in force in a country outside the United Kingdom constitutes an offence under that law for the purposes of subsection (1) however it is described in that law.

(3) Subject to subsection (4), on an application for a notification order the condition in subsection (1)(b) is to be taken as met unless, not later than rules of court may provide, the defendant serves on the applicant a notice—

(a) stating that, on the facts as alleged with respect to the act concerned, the condition is not in his opinion met,

(b) showing his grounds for that opinion, and

(c) requiring the applicant to prove that the condition is met.

(4) The court, if it thinks fit, may permit the defendant to require the applicant to prove that the condition is met without service of a notice under subsection (3).

100. Interim notification orders

(1) This section applies where an application for a notification order ('the main application') has not been determined.

(2) An application for an order under this section ('an interim notification order')—

(a) may be made in the complaint containing the main application, or

(b) if the main application has been made, may be made by the person who has made that application, by complaint to the court to which that application has been made.

(3) The court may, if it considers it just to do so, make an interim notification order.

(4) Such an order—

(a) has effect only for a fixed period, specified in the order;

(b) ceases to have effect, if it has not already done so, on the determination of the main application.

(5) While such an order has effect—

(a) the defendant is subject to the notification requirements of this Part;

(b) this Part applies to the defendant, subject to the modification set out in subsection (6).

(6) The 'relevant date' means the date of service of the order.

(7) The applicant or the defendant may by complaint apply to the court that made the interim notification order for the order to be varied, renewed or discharged.

101. Notification orders and interim notification orders: appeals

A defendant may appeal to the Crown Court against the making of a notification order or interim notification order.

102. Appeals in relation to notification orders and interim notification orders: Scotland
In Scotland—

(a) an interlocutor granting or refusing a notification order or interim notification order is an appealable interlocutor; and

(b) where an appeal is taken against an interlocutor so granting such an order the order shall, without prejudice to any power of the court to vary or recall it, continue to have effect pending the disposal of the appeal.

103. Sections 97 to 100: Scotland
(1) Sections 97 to 100 apply to Scotland with the following modifications—

(a) references to a chief officer of police and to his police area are to be read, respectively, as references to a chief constable and to the area of his police force;

(b) references to the defendant are to be read as references to the person in respect of whom the order is sought or has effect;

(c) an application for a notification order or interim notification order is made by summary application to any sheriff within whose sheriffdom lies any part of the area of the applicant's police force (references to 'the court' being construed accordingly).

(2) A record of evidence shall be kept on any summary application made by virtue of subsection (1)(c) above.

(3) The clerk of the court by which, by virtue of that subsection, a notification order or interim notification order is made, varied, renewed or discharged shall cause a copy of, as the case may be—

(a) the order as so made, varied or renewed; or

(b) the interlocutor by which discharge is effected,

to be given to the person named in the order or sent to him by registered post or by the recorded delivery service (an acknowledgement or certificate of delivery of a copy so sent, issued by the Post Office, being sufficient evidence of the delivery of the copy on the day specified in the acknowledgement or certificate).

Sexual offences prevention orders

104. Sexual offences prevention orders: applications and grounds
(1) A court may make an order under this section in respect of a person ('the defendant') where any of subsections (2) to (4) applies to the defendant and—

(a) where subsection (4) applies, it is satisfied that the defendant's behaviour since the appropriate date makes it necessary to make such an order, for the purpose of protecting the public or any particular members of the public from serious sexual harm from the defendant;

(b) in any other case, it is satisfied that it is necessary to make such an order, for the purpose of protecting the public or any particular members of the public from serious sexual harm from the defendant.

(2) This subsection applies to the defendant where the court deals with him in respect of an offence listed in Schedule 3 or 5.

(3) This subsection applies to the defendant where the court deals with him in respect of a finding—

(a) that he is not guilty of an offence listed in Schedule 3 or 5 by reason of insanity, or

(b) that he is under a disability and has done the act charged against him in respect of such an offence.

(4) This subsection applies to the defendant where—

(a) an application under subsection (5) has been made to the court in respect of him, and

(b) on the application, it is proved that he is a qualifying offender.

(5) A chief officer of police may by complaint to a magistrates' court apply for an order under this section in respect of a person who resides in his police area or who the chief officer believes is in, or is intending to come to, his police area if it appears to the chief officer that—

(a) the person is a qualifying offender, and

(b) the person has since the appropriate date acted in such a way as to give reasonable cause to believe that it is necessary for such an order to be made.

(6) An application under subsection (5) may be made to any magistrates' court whose commission area includes—

(a) any part of the applicant's police area, or

(b) any place where it is alleged that the person acted in a way mentioned in subsection (5)(b).

105. SOPOs: further provision as respects Scotland

(1) A chief constable may apply for an order under this section in respect of a person who he believes is in, or is intending to come to, the area of his police force if it appears to the chief constable that—

(a) the person has been convicted of, found not guilty by reason of insanity of or found to be under a disability and to have done the act charged against him in respect of—

(i) an offence listed in paragraph 60 of Schedule 3; or

(ii) before the commencement of this Part, an offence in Scotland other than is mentioned in paragraphs 36 to 59 of that Schedule if the chief constable considers that had the conviction or finding been after such commencement it is likely that a determination such as is mentioned in paragraph 60 would have been made in relation to the offence; and

(b) the person has since the conviction or finding acted in such a way as to give reasonable cause to believe that it is necessary for such an order to be made.

(2) An application under subsection (1) may be made by summary application to a sheriff within whose sheriffdom lies—

(a) any part of the area of the applicant's police force; or

(b) any place where it is alleged that the person acted in a way mentioned in subsection (1)(b).

(3) The sheriff may make the order where satisfied—

(a) that the person's behaviour since the conviction or finding makes it necessary to make such an order, for the purposes of protecting the public or any particular members of the public from serious sexual harm from the person; and

(b) where the application is by virtue of subsection (1)(a)(ii), that there was a significant sexual aspect to the person's behaviour in committing the offence.

(4) Subsection (3) of section 106 applies for the purposes of this section as it applies for the purposes of section 104 and subsections (2) and (3) of section 112 apply in relation to a summary application made by virtue of subsection (1) as they apply in relation to one made by virtue of subsection (1)(g) of that section.

106. Section 104: supplemental

(1) In this Part, 'sexual offences prevention order' means an order under section 104 or 105.

(2) Subsections (3) to (8) apply for the purposes of section 104.

(3) 'Protecting the public or any particular members of the public from serious sexual harm from the defendant' means protecting the public in the United Kingdom or any particular members of that public from serious physical or psychological harm, caused by the defendant committing one or more offences listed in Schedule 3.

(4) Acts, behaviour, convictions and findings include those occurring before the commencement of this Part.

(5) 'Qualifying offender' means a person within subsection (6) or (7).

(6) A person is within this subsection if, whether before or after the commencement of this Part, he—

(a) has been convicted of an offence listed in Schedule 3 (other than at paragraph 60) or in Schedule 5,

(b) has been found not guilty of such an offence by reason of insanity,

(c) has been found to be under a disability and to have done the act charged against him in respect of such an offence, or

(d) in England and Wales or Northern Ireland, has been cautioned in respect of such an offence.

(7) A person is within this subsection if, under the law in force in a country outside the United Kingdom and whether before or after the commencement of this Part—

(a) he has been convicted of a relevant offence (whether or not he has been punished for it),

(b) a court exercising jurisdiction under that law has made in respect of a relevant offence a finding equivalent to a finding that he is not guilty by reason of insanity,

(c) such a court has made in respect of a relevant offence a finding equivalent to a finding that he is under a disability and did the act charged against him in respect of the offence, or

(d) he has been cautioned in respect of a relevant offence.

(8) 'Appropriate date', in relation to a qualifying offender, means the date or (as the case may be) the first date on which he was convicted, found or cautioned as mentioned in subsection (6) or (7).

(9) In subsection (7), 'relevant offence' means an act which—

(a) constituted an offence under the law in force in the country concerned, and

(b) would have constituted an offence listed in Schedule 3 (other than at paragraph 60) or in Schedule 5 if it had been done in any part of the United Kingdom.

(10) An act punishable under the law in force in a country outside the United Kingdom constitutes an offence under that law for the purposes of subsection (9), however it is described in that law.

(11) Subject to subsection (12), on an application under section 104(5) the condition in subsection (9)(b) (where relevant) is to be taken as met unless, not later than rules of court may provide, the defendant serves on the applicant a notice—

(a) stating that, on the facts as alleged with respect to the act concerned, the condition is not in his opinion met,

(b) showing his grounds for that opinion, and

(c) requiring the applicant to prove that the condition is met.

(12) The court, if it thinks fit, may permit the defendant to require the applicant to prove that the condition is met without service of a notice under subsection (11).

107. SOPOs: effect

(1) A sexual offences prevention order—

(a) prohibits the defendant from doing anything described in the order, and

(b) has effect for a fixed period (not less than 5 years) specified in the order or until further order.

(2) The only prohibitions that may be included in the order are those necessary for the purpose of protecting the public or any particular members of the public from serious sexual harm from the defendant.

(3) Where—

(a) an order is made in respect of a defendant who was a relevant offender immediately before the making of the order, and

(b) the defendant would (apart from this subsection) cease to be subject to the notification requirements of this Part while the order (as renewed from time to time) has effect,

the defendant remains subject to the notification requirements.

(4) Where an order is made in respect of a defendant who was not a relevant offender immediately before the making of the order—

(a) the order causes the defendant to become subject to the notification requirements of this Part from the making of the order until the order (as renewed from time to time) ceases to have effect, and

(b) this Part applies to the defendant, subject to the modification set out in subsection (5).

(5) The 'relevant date' is the date of service of the order.

(6) Where a court makes a sexual offences prevention order in relation to a person already subject to such an order (whether made by that court or another), the earlier order ceases to have effect.

(7) Section 106(3) applies for the purposes of this section and section 108.

108. SOPOs: variations, renewals and discharges

(1) A person within subsection (2) may apply to the appropriate court for an order varying, renewing or discharging a sexual offences prevention order.

(2) The persons are—

(a) the defendant;

(b) the chief officer of police for the area in which the defendant resides;

(c) a chief officer of police who believes that the defendant is in, or is intending to come to, his police area;

(d) where the order was made on an application under section 104(5), the chief officer of police who made the application.

(3) An application under subsection (1) may be made—

(a) where the appropriate court is the Crown Court, in accordance with rules of court;

(b) in any other case, by complaint.

(4) Subject to subsections (5) and (6), on the application the court, after hearing the person making the application and (if they wish to be heard) the other persons mentioned in subsection (2), may make any order, varying, renewing or discharging the sexual offences prevention order, that the court considers appropriate.

(5) An order may be renewed, or varied so as to impose additional prohibitions on the defendant, only if it is necessary to do so for the purpose of protecting the public or any particular members of the public from serious sexual harm from the defendant (and any renewed or varied order may contain only such prohibitions as are necessary for this purpose).

(6) The court must not discharge an order before the end of 5 years beginning with the day on which the order was made, without the consent of the defendant and—

(a) where the application is made by a chief officer of police, that chief officer, or

(b) in any other case, the chief officer of police for the area in which the defendant resides.

(7) In this section 'the appropriate court' means—

(a) where the Crown Court or the Court of Appeal made the sexual offences prevention order, the Crown Court;

(b) where a magistrates' court made the order, that court, a magistrates' court for the area in which the defendant resides or, where the application is made by a chief officer of police, any magistrates' court whose commission area includes any part of the chief officer's police area;

(c) where a youth court made the order, that court, a youth court for the area in which the defendant resides or, where the application is made by a chief officer of police, any youth court whose commission area includes any part of the chief officer's police area.

(8) This section applies to orders under—

(a) section 5A of the Sex Offenders Act 1997 (c. 51) (restraining orders),

(b) section 2 or 20 of the Crime and Disorder Act 1998 (c. 37) (sex offender orders made in England and Wales or Scotland), and

(c) Article 6 of the Criminal Justice (Northern Ireland) Order 1998 (S.I. 1998/2839 (N.I. 20)) (sex offender orders made in Northern Ireland),

as it applies to sexual offences prevention orders.

109. Interim SOPOs

(1) This section applies where an application under section 104(5) or 105(1) ('the main application') has not been determined.

(2) An application for an order under this section ('an interim sexual offences prevention order')—

(a) may be made by the complaint by which the main application is made, or

(b) if the main application has been made, may be made by the person who has made that application, by complaint to the court to which that application has been made.

(3) The court may, if it considers it just to do so, make an interim sexual offences prevention order, prohibiting the defendant from doing anything described in the order.

(4) Such an order—

(a) has effect only for a fixed period, specified in the order;

(b) ceases to have effect, if it has not already done so, on the determination of the main application.

(5) Section 107(3) to (5) apply to an interim sexual offences prevention order as if references to an order were references to such an order, and with the omission of 'as renewed from time to time' in both places.

(6) The applicant or the defendant may by complaint apply to the court that made the interim sexual offences prevention order for the order to be varied, renewed or discharged.

(7) Subsection (6) applies to orders under—

(a) section 2A or 20(4)(a) of the Crime and Disorder Act 1998 (c. 37) (interim orders made in England and Wales or Scotland), and

(b) Article 6A of the Criminal Justice (Northern Ireland) Order 1998 (S.I. 1998/2839 (N.I. 20)) (interim orders made in Northern Ireland),

as it applies to interim sexual offences prevention orders.

110. SOPOs and interim SOPOs: appeals

(1) A defendant may appeal against the making of a sexual offences prevention order—

(a) where section 104(2) applied to him, as if the order were a sentence passed on him for the offence;

(b) where section 104(3) (but not section 104(2)) applied to him, as if he had been convicted of the offence and the order were a sentence passed on him for that offence;

(c) where the order was made on an application under section 104(5), to the Crown Court.

(2) A defendant may appeal to the Crown Court against the making of an interim sexual offences prevention order.

(3) A defendant may appeal against the making of an order under section 108, or the refusal to make such an order—

(a) where the application for such an order was made to the Crown Court, to the Court of Appeal;

(b) in any other case, to the Crown Court.

(4) On an appeal under subsection (1)(c), (2) or (3)(b), the Crown Court may make such orders as may be necessary to give effect to its determination of the appeal, and may also make such incidental or consequential orders as appear to it to be just.

(5) Any order made by the Crown Court on an appeal under subsection (1)(c) or (2) (other than an order directing that an application be re-heard by a magistrates' court) is for the purpose of section 108(7) or 109(7) (respectively) to be treated as if it were an order of the court from which the appeal was brought (and not an order of the Crown Court).

111. Appeals in relation to SOPOs and interim SOPOs: Scotland

In Scotland—

(a) an interlocutor granting, refusing, varying, renewing or discharging a sexual offences prevention order or interim sexual offences prevention order is an appealable interlocutor; and

(b) where an appeal is taken against an interlocutor so granting, varying or renewing such an order the order shall, without prejudice to any power of the court to vary or recall it, continue to have effect pending the disposal of the appeal.

112. Sections 104 and 106 to 109: Scotland

(1) Sections 104 and 106 to 109 apply to Scotland with the following modifications—

(a) subsections (1)(b), (2) and (3) of section 104 shall be disregarded;

(b) an application under subsection (5) of section 104 shall not be competent in respect of a person who is a qualifying offender by virtue only of a conviction or finding which relates to any offence listed at paragraphs 64 to 111 of Schedule 5;

(c) references to a chief officer of police and to his police area are to be read, respectively, as references to a chief constable and to the area of his police force;

(d) references to the defendant are to be read as references to the person in respect of whom the order is sought or has effect;

(e) an application for a sexual offences prevention order or interim sexual offences prevention order is made by summary application to any sheriff within whose sheriffdom lies—

(i)   any part of the area of the applicant's police force; or

(ii)   any place where it is alleged that the person in respect of whom the order is sought or has effect acted in a way mentioned in subsection (5)(b) of section 104, (references to 'the court' being construed accordingly);

(f)   an application for the variation, renewal or discharge of either such order is made by summary application to the sheriff who made the order or to a sheriff—

(i)   within whose sheriffdom the person subject to the order resides; or

(ii)   where the application is made by a chief constable, within whose sheriffdom lies any part of the area of the applicant's police force, (references to 'the court' being construed accordingly).

(2)   A record of evidence shall be kept on any summary application made by virtue of subsection (1)(e) or (f) above.

(3)   The clerk of the court by which, by virtue of that subsection, a sexual offences prevention order or interim sexual offences prevention order is made, varied, renewed or discharged shall cause a copy of, as the case may be—

(a)   the order as so made, varied or renewed; or

(b)   the interlocutor by which discharge is effected,

to be given to the person named in the order or sent to him by registered post or by the recorded delivery service (an acknowledgement or certificate of delivery of a copy so sent, issued by the Post Office, being sufficient evidence of the delivery of the copy on the day specified in the acknowledgement or certificate).

113. Offence: breach of SOPO or interim SOPO

(1)   A person commits an offence if, without reasonable excuse, he does anything which he is prohibited from doing by—

(a)   a sexual offences prevention order;

(b)   an interim sexual offences prevention order;

(c)   an order under section 5A of the Sex Offenders Act 1997 (c. 51) (restraining orders);

(d)   an order under section 2, 2A or 20 of the Crime and Disorder Act 1998 (c. 37) (sex offender orders and interim orders made in England and Wales and in Scotland);

(e)   an order under Article 6 or 6A of the Criminal Justice (Northern Ireland) Order 1998 (S.I. 1998/2839 (N.I. 20)) (sex offender orders and interim orders made in Northern Ireland).

(2)   A person guilty of an offence under this section is liable—

(a)   on summary conviction, to imprisonment for a term not exceeding 6 months or a fine not exceeding the statutory maximum or both;

(b)   on conviction on indictment, to imprisonment for a term not exceeding 5 years.

(3)   Where a person is convicted of an offence under this section, it is not open to the court by or before which he is convicted to make, in respect of the offence, an order for conditional discharge or, in Scotland, a probation order.

Foreign travel orders

114. Foreign travel orders: applications and grounds

(1)   A chief officer of police may by complaint to a magistrates' court apply for an order under this section (a 'foreign travel order') in respect of a person ('the defendant') who

resides in his police area or who the chief officer believes is in or is intending to come to his police area if it appears to the chief officer that—

(a) the defendant is a qualifying offender, and

(b) the defendant has since the appropriate date acted in such a way as to give reasonable cause to believe that it is necessary for such an order to be made.

(2) An application under subsection (1) may be made to any magistrates' court whose commission area includes any part of the applicant's police area.

(3) On the application, the court may make a foreign travel order if it is satisfied that—

(a) the defendant is a qualifying offender, and

(b) the defendant's behaviour since the appropriate date makes it necessary to make such an order, for the purpose of protecting children generally or any child from serious sexual harm from the defendant outside the United Kingdom.

115. Section 114: interpretation

(1) Subsections (2) to (5) apply for the purposes of section 114.

(2) 'Protecting children generally or any child from serious sexual harm from the defendant outside the United Kingdom' means protecting persons under 16 generally or any particular person under 16 from serious physical or psychological harm caused by the defendant doing, outside the United Kingdom, anything which would constitute an offence listed in Schedule 3 if done in any part of the United Kingdom.

(3) Acts and behaviour include those occurring before the commencement of this Part.

(4) 'Qualifying offender' has the meaning given by section 116.

(5) 'Appropriate date', in relation to a qualifying offender, means the date or (as the case may be) the first date on which he was convicted, found or cautioned as mentioned in subsection (1) or (3) of section 116.

(6) In this section and section 116 as they apply to Northern Ireland, references to persons, or to a person, under 16 are to be read as references to persons, or to a person, under 17.

116. Section 114: qualifying offenders

(1) A person is a qualifying offender for the purposes of section 114 if, whether before or after the commencement of this Part, he—

(a) has been convicted of an offence within subsection (2),

(b) has been found not guilty of such an offence by reason of insanity,

(c) has been found to be under a disability and to have done the act charged against him in respect of such an offence, or

(d) in England and Wales or Northern Ireland, has been cautioned in respect of such an offence.

(2) The offences are—

(a) an offence within any of paragraphs 13 to 15, 44 to 46, 77, 78 and 82 of Schedule 3;

(b) an offence within paragraph 31 of that Schedule, if the intended offence was an offence against a person under 16;

(c) an offence within paragraph 93 of that Schedule, if—

(i) the corresponding civil offence is an offence within any of paragraphs 13 to 15 of that Schedule;

(ii) the corresponding civil offence is an offence within paragraph 31 of that Schedule, and the intended offence was an offence against a person under 16; or

253

(iii) the corresponding civil offence is an offence within any of paragraphs 1 to 12, 16 to 30 and 32 to 35 of that Schedule, and the victim of the offence was under 16 at the time of the offence.

(d) an offence within any other paragraph of that Schedule, if the victim of the offence was under 16 at the time of the offence.

(3) A person is also a qualifying offender for the purposes of section 114 if, under the law in force in a country outside the United Kingdom and whether before or after the commencement of this Part—

(a) he has been convicted of a relevant offence (whether or not he has been punished for it),

(b) a court exercising jurisdiction under that law has made in respect of a relevant offence a finding equivalent to a finding that he is not guilty by reason of insanity,

(c) such a court has made in respect of a relevant offence a finding equivalent to a finding that he is under a disability and did the act charged against him in respect of the offence, or

(d) he has been cautioned in respect of a relevant offence.

(4) In subsection (3), 'relevant offence' means an act which—

(a) constituted an offence under the law in force in the country concerned, and

(b) would have constituted an offence within subsection (2) if it had been done in any part of the United Kingdom.

(5) An act punishable under the law in force in a country outside the United Kingdom constitutes an offence under that law for the purposes of subsection (4), however it is described in that law.

(6) Subject to subsection (7), on an application under section 114 the condition in subsection (4)(b) above (where relevant) is to be taken as met unless, not later than rules of court may provide, the defendant serves on the applicant a notice—

(a) stating that, on the facts as alleged with respect to the act concerned, the condition is not in his opinion met,

(b) showing his grounds for that opinion, and

(c) requiring the applicant to prove that the condition is met.

(7) The court, if it thinks fit, may permit the defendant to require the applicant to prove that the condition is met without service of a notice under subsection (6).

117. Foreign travel orders: effect

(1) A foreign travel order has effect for a fixed period of not more than 6 months, specified in the order.

(2) The order prohibits the defendant from doing whichever of the following is specified in the order—

(a) travelling to any country outside the United Kingdom named or described in the order,

(b) travelling to any country outside the United Kingdom other than a country named or described in the order, or

(c) travelling to any country outside the United Kingdom.

(3) The only prohibitions that may be included in the order are those necessary for the purpose of protecting children generally or any child from serious sexual harm from the defendant outside the United Kingdom.

(4) If at any time while an order (as renewed from time to time) has effect a defendant is not a relevant offender, the order causes him to be subject to the requirements imposed by

regulations made under section 86(1) (and for these purposes the defendant is to be treated as if he were a relevant offender).

(5) Where a court makes a foreign travel order in relation to a person already subject to such an order (whether made by that court or another), the earlier order ceases to have effect.

(6) Section 115(2) applies for the purposes of this section and section 118.

118. Foreign travel orders: variations, renewals and discharges

(1) A person within subsection (2) may by complaint to the appropriate court apply for an order varying, renewing or discharging a foreign travel order.

(2) The persons are—
    (a) the defendant;
    (b) the chief officer of police on whose application the foreign travel order was made;
    (c) the chief officer of police for the area in which the defendant resides;
    (d) a chief officer of police who believes that the defendant is in, or is intending to come to, his police area.

(3) Subject to subsection (4), on the application the court, after hearing the person making the application and (if they wish to be heard) the other persons mentioned in subsection (2), may make any order, varying, renewing or discharging the foreign travel order, that the court considers appropriate.

(4) An order may be renewed, or varied so as to impose additional prohibitions on the defendant, only if it is necessary to do so for the purpose of protecting children generally or any child from serious sexual harm from the defendant outside the United Kingdom (and any renewed or varied order may contain only such prohibitions as are necessary for this purpose).

(5) In this section 'the appropriate court' means—
    (a) the court which made the foreign travel order;
    (b) a magistrates' court for the area in which the defendant resides; or
    (c) where the application is made by a chief officer of police, any magistrates' court whose commission area includes any part of his police area.

119. Foreign travel orders: appeals

(1) A defendant may appeal to the Crown Court—
    (a) against the making of a foreign travel order;
    (b) against the making of an order under section 118, or the refusal to make such an order.

(2) On any such appeal, the Crown Court may make such orders as may be necessary to give effect to its determination of the appeal, and may also make such incidental or consequential orders as appear to it to be just.

(3) Any order made by the Crown Court on an appeal under subsection (1)(a) (other than an order directing that an application be re-heard by a magistrates' court) is for the purposes of section 118(5) to be treated as if it were an order of the court from which the appeal was brought (and not an order of the Crown Court).

120. Appeals in relation to foreign travel orders: Scotland

In Scotland—
    (a) an interlocutor granting, refusing, varying, renewing or discharging a foreign travel order is an appealable interlocutor; and

(b) where an appeal is taken against an interlocutor so granting, varying or renewing such an order the order shall, without prejudice to any power of the court to vary or recall it, continue to have effect pending the disposal of the appeal.

121. Sections 114 to 118: Scotland

(1) Sections 114 to 118 apply to Scotland with the following modifications—

(a) references to a chief officer of police and to his police area are to be read, respectively, as references to a chief constable and to the area of his police force;

(b) references to the defendant are to be read as references to the person in respect of whom the order is sought or has effect;

(c) an application for a foreign travel order is made by summary application to any sheriff within whose sheriffdom lies any part of the area of the applicant's police force (references to 'the court' being construed accordingly);

(d) for paragraphs (a) to (c) of section 118(5) there is substituted—

'(a) the sheriff who made the foreign travel order; or

(b) where the application is made by a chief constable, a sheriff whose sheriffdom includes any part of the area of the applicant's police force.'

(2) A record of evidence shall be kept on any summary application made by virtue of subsection (1)(c) above.

(3) The clerk of the court by which, by virtue of that subsection, a foreign travel order is made, varied, renewed or discharged shall cause a copy of, as the case may be—

(a) the order as so made, varied or renewed; or

(b) the interlocutor by which discharge is effected,

to be given to the person named in the order or sent to him by registered post or by the recorded delivery service (an acknowledgement or certificate of delivery of a copy so sent, issued by the Post Office, being sufficient evidence of the delivery of the copy on the day specified in the acknowledgement or certificate).

122. Offence: breach of foreign travel order

(1) A person commits an offence if, without reasonable excuse, he does anything which he is prohibited from doing by a foreign travel order.

(2) A person guilty of an offence under this section is liable—

(a) on summary conviction, to imprisonment for a term not exceeding 6 months or a fine not exceeding the statutory maximum or both;

(b) on conviction on indictment, to imprisonment for a term not exceeding 5 years.

(3) Where a person is convicted of an offence under this section, it is not open to the court by or before which he is convicted to make, in respect of the offence, an order for conditional discharge (or, in Scotland, a probation order).

Risk of sexual harm orders

123. Risk of sexual harm orders: applications, grounds and effect

(1) A chief officer of police may by complaint to a magistrates' court apply for an order under this section (a 'risk of sexual harm order') in respect of a person aged 18 or over ('the defendant') who resides in his police area or who the chief officer believes is in, or is intending to come to, his police area if it appears to the chief officer that—

(a) the defendant has on at least two occasions, whether before or after the commencement of this Part, done an act within subsection (3), and

(b) as a result of those acts, there is reasonable cause to believe that it is necessary for such an order to be made.

(2) An application under subsection (1) may be made to any magistrates' court whose commission area includes—

(a) any part of the applicant's police area, or

(b) any place where it is alleged that the defendant acted in a way mentioned in subsection (1)(a).

(3) The acts are—

(a) engaging in sexual activity involving a child or in the presence of a child;

(b) causing or inciting a child to watch a person engaging in sexual activity or to look at a moving or still image that is sexual;

(c) giving a child anything that relates to sexual activity or contains a reference to such activity;

(d) communicating with a child, where any part of the communication is sexual.

(4) On the application, the court may make a risk of sexual harm order if it is satisfied that

(a) the defendant has on at least two occasions, whether before or after the commencement of this section, done an act within subsection (3); and

(b) it is necessary to make such an order, for the purpose of protecting children generally or any child from harm from the defendant.

(5) Such an order—

(a) prohibits the defendant from doing anything described in the order;

(b) has effect for a fixed period (not less than 2 years) specified in the order or until further order.

(6) The only prohibitions that may be imposed are those necessary for the purpose of protecting children generally or any child from harm from the defendant.

(7) Where a court makes a risk of sexual harm order in relation to a person already subject to such an order (whether made by that court or another), the earlier order ceases to have effect.

124. Section 123: interpretation

(1) Subsections (2) to (7) apply for the purposes of section 123.

(2) 'Protecting children generally or any child from harm from the defendant' means protecting children generally or any child from physical or psychological harm, caused by the defendant doing acts within section 123(3).

(3) 'Child' means a person under 16.

(4) 'Image' means an image produced by any means, whether of a real or imaginary subject.

(5) 'Sexual activity' means an activity that a reasonable person would, in all the circumstances but regardless of any person's purpose, consider to be sexual.

(6) A communication is sexual if—

(a) any part of it relates to sexual activity, or

(b) a reasonable person would, in all the circumstances but regardless of any person's purpose, consider that any part of the communication is sexual.

(7) An image is sexual if—

(a) any part of it relates to sexual activity, or

(b) a reasonable person would, in all the circumstances but regardless of any person's purpose, consider that any part of the image is sexual.

(8) In this section, as it applies to Northern Ireland, subsection (3) has effect with the substitution of '17' for '16'.

125. RSHOs: variations, renewals and discharges

(1) A person within subsection (2) may by complaint to the appropriate court apply for an order varying, renewing or discharging a risk of sexual harm order.

(2) The persons are—

(a) the defendant;

(b) the chief officer of police on whose application the risk of sexual harm order was made;

(c) the chief officer of police for the area in which the defendant resides;

(d) a chief officer of police who believes that the defendant is in, or is intending to come to, his police area.

(3) Subject to subsections (4) and (5), on the application the court, after hearing the person making the application and (if they wish to be heard) the other persons mentioned in subsection (2), may make any order, varying, renewing or discharging the risk of sexual harm order, that the court considers appropriate.

(4) An order may be renewed, or varied so as to impose additional prohibitions on the defendant, only if it is necessary to do so for the purpose of protecting children generally or any child from harm from the defendant (and any renewed or varied order may contain only such prohibitions as are necessary for this purpose).

(5) The court must not discharge an order before the end of 2 years beginning with the day on which the order was made, without the consent of the defendant and—

(a) where the application is made by a chief officer of police, that chief officer, or

(b) in any other case, the chief officer of police for the area in which the defendant resides.

(6) Section 124(2) applies for the purposes of this section.

(7) In this section 'the appropriate court' means—

(a) the court which made the risk of sexual harm order;

(b) a magistrates' court for the area in which the defendant resides; or

(c) where the application is made by a chief officer of police, any magistrates' court whose commission area includes any part of his police area.

126. Interim RSHOs

(1) This section applies where an application for a risk of sexual harm order ('the main application') has not been determined.

(2) An application for an order under this section ('an interim risk of sexual harm order')—

(a) may be made by the complaint by which the main application is made, or

(b) if the main application has been made, may be made by the person who has made that application, by complaint to the court to which that application has been made.

(3) The court may, if it considers it just to do so, make an interim risk of sexual harm order, prohibiting the defendant from doing anything described in the order.

(4) Such an order—

(a) has effect only for a fixed period, specified in the order;

(b) ceases to have effect, if it has not already done so, on the determination of the main application.

(5) The applicant or the defendant may by complaint apply to the court that made the interim risk of sexual harm order for the order to be varied, renewed or discharged.

127. RSHOs and interim RSHOs: appeals

(1) A defendant may appeal to the Crown Court—

    (a) against the making of a risk of sexual harm order;

    (b) against the making of an interim risk of sexual harm order; or

    (c) against the making of an order under section 125, or the refusal to make such an order.

(2) On any such appeal, the Crown Court may make such orders as may be necessary to give effect to its determination of the appeal, and may also make such incidental or consequential orders as appear to it to be just.

(3) Any order made by the Crown Court on an appeal under subsection (1)(a) or (b) (other than an order directing that an application be re-heard by a magistrates' court) is for the purpose of section 125(7) or 126(5) (respectively) to be treated as if it were an order of the court from which the appeal was brought (and not an order of the Crown Court).

128. Offence: breach of RSHO or interim RSHO

(1) A person commits an offence if, without reasonable excuse, he does anything which he is prohibited from doing by—

    (a) a risk of sexual harm order; or

    (b) an interim risk of sexual harm order.

(2) A person guilty of an offence under this section is liable—

    (a) on summary conviction, to imprisonment for a term not exceeding 6 months or a fine not exceeding the statutory maximum or both;

    (b) on conviction on indictment, to imprisonment for a term not exceeding 5 years.

(3) Where a person is convicted of an offence under this section, it is not open to the court by or before which he is convicted to make, in respect of the offence, an order for conditional discharge.

129. Effect of conviction etc. of an offence under section 128

(1) This section applies to a person ('the defendant') who—

    (a) is convicted of an offence under section 128;

    (b) is found not guilty of such an offence by reason of insanity;

    (c) is found to be under a disability and to have done the act charged against him in respect of such an offence; or

    (d) is cautioned in respect of such an offence.

(2) Where—

    (a) a defendant was a relevant offender immediately before this section applied to him, and

    (b) the defendant would (apart from this subsection) cease to be subject to the notification requirements of this Part while the relevant order (as renewed from time to time) has effect,

the defendant remains subject to the notification requirements.

(3) Where the defendant was not a relevant offender immediately before this section applied to him—

(a) this section causes the defendant to become subject to the notification require-ments of this Part from the time the section first applies to him until the relevant order (as renewed from time to time) ceases to have effect, and

(b) this Part applies to the defendant, subject to the modification set out in subsection (4).

(4) The 'relevant date' is the date on which this section first applies to the defendant.

(5) In this section 'relevant order' means—

(a) where the conviction, finding or caution within subsection (1) is in respect of a breach of a risk of sexual harm order, that order;

(b) where the conviction, finding or caution within subsection (1) is in respect of a breach of an interim risk of sexual harm order, any risk of sexual harm order made on the hearing of the application to which the interim risk of sexual harm order relates or, if no such order is made, the interim risk of sexual harm order.

Power to amend Schedules 3 and 5

130. Power to amend Schedules 3 and 5

(1) The Secretary of State may by order amend Schedule 3 or 5.

(2) Subject to subsection (3), an amendment within subsection (4) does not apply to convictions, findings and cautions before the amendment takes effect.

(3) For the purposes of sections 106 and 116, an amendment within subsection (4) applies to convictions, findings and cautions before as well as after the amendment takes effect.

(4) An amendment is within this subsection if it—

(a) adds an offence,

(b) removes a threshold relating to an offence, or

(c) changes a threshold in such a way as to cause an offence committed by or against a person of a particular age or in certain circumstances, or resulting in a particular disposal, to be within a Schedule when it would not otherwise be.

General

131. Young offenders: application

This Part applies to—

(a) a period of detention which a person is liable to serve under a detention and train-ing order, or a secure training order,

(b) a period for which a person is ordered to be detained in residential accommodation under section 44(1) of the Criminal Procedure (Scotland) Act 1995 (c. 46),

(c) a period of training in a training school, or of custody in a remand centre, which a person is liable to undergo or serve by virtue of an order under section 74(1)(a) or (e) of the Children and Young Persons Act (Northern Ireland) 1968 (c. 34 (N.I.)),

(d) a period for which a person is ordered to be detained in a juvenile justice centre under Article 39 of the Criminal Justice (Children) (Northern Ireland) Order 1998 (S.I. 1998/1504 (N.I. 9)),

(e) a period for which a person is ordered to be kept in secure accommodation under Article 44A of the Order referred to in paragraph (d),

(f) a sentence of detention in a young offender institution, a young offenders institu-tion or a young offenders centre,

(g) a sentence under a custodial order within the meaning of section 71AA of, or paragraph 10(1) of Schedule 5A to, the Army Act 1955 (3 & 4 Eliz. 2 c. 18) or the Air Force Act 1955 (3 & 4 Eliz. 2 c. 19) or section 43AA of, or paragraph 10(1) of Schedule 4A to, the Naval Discipline Act 1957 (c. 53),

(h) a sentence of detention under section 90 or 91 of the Powers of Criminal Courts (Sentencing) Act 2000 (c. 6), section 208 of the Criminal Procedure (Scotland) Act 1995 or Article 45 of the Criminal Justice (Children) (Northern Ireland) Order 1998,

(i) a sentence of custody for life under section 93 or 94 of the Powers of Criminal Courts (Sentencing) Act 2000 (c. 6),

(j) a sentence of detention, or custody for life, under section 71A of the Army Act 1955 (3 & 4 Eliz. 2 c. 18) or the Air Force Act 1955 (3 & 4 Eliz. 2 c. 19) or section 43A of the Naval Discipline Act 1957 (c. 53),

as it applies to an equivalent sentence of imprisonment; and references in this Part to prison or imprisonment are to be interpreted accordingly.

132. Offences with thresholds

(1) This section applies to an offence which in Schedule 3 is listed subject to a condition relating to the way in which the defendant is dealt with in respect of the offence or (where a relevant finding has been made in respect of him) in respect of the finding (a 'sentencing condition').

(2) Where an offence is listed if either a sentencing condition or a condition of another description is met, this section applies only to the offence as listed subject to the sentencing condition.

(3) For the purposes of this Part (including in particular section 82(6))—

(a) a person is to be regarded as convicted of an offence to which this section applies, or

(b) (as the case may be) a relevant finding in relation to such an offence is to be regarded as made,

at the time when the sentencing condition is met.

(4) In the following subsections, references to a foreign offence are references to an act which—

(a) constituted an offence under the law in force in a country outside the United Kingdom ('the relevant foreign law'), and

(b) would have constituted an offence to which this section applies (but not an offence, listed in Schedule 3, to which this section does not apply) if it had been done in any part of the United Kingdom.

(5) In relation to a foreign offence, references to the corresponding UK offence are references to the offence (or any offence) to which subsection (4)(b)[a] applies in the case of that foreign offence.

(6) For the purposes of this Part, a person is to be regarded as convicted under the relevant foreign law of a foreign offence at the time when he is, in respect of the offence, dealt with under that law in a way equivalent to that mentioned in Schedule 3 as it applies to the corresponding UK offence.

(7) Where in the case of any person a court exercising jurisdiction under the relevant foreign law makes in respect of a foreign offence a finding equivalent to a relevant finding, the court's finding is, for the purposes of this Part, to be regarded as made at the time when the person is, in respect of the finding, dealt with under that law in a way equivalent to that mentioned in Schedule 3 as it applies to the corresponding UK offence.

(8) Where (by virtue of an order under section 130 or otherwise) an offence is listed in Schedule 5 subject to a sentencing condition, this section applies to that offence as if references to Schedule 3 were references to Schedule 5.

(9) In this section, 'relevant finding', in relation to an offence, means—

(a) a finding that a person is not guilty of the offence by reason of insanity, or

(b) a finding that a person is under a disability and did the act charged against him in respect of the offence.

133. Part 2: general interpretation

(1) In this Part—

'admitted to a hospital' means admitted to a hospital under—

(a) section 37 of the Mental Health Act 1983 (c. 20), section 57(2)(a) or 58 of the Criminal Procedure (Scotland) Act 1995 (c. 46) or Article 44 or 50A(2) of the Mental Health (Northern Ireland) Order 1986 (S.I. 1986/595 (N.I. 4));

(b) Schedule 1 to the Criminal Procedure (Insanity and Unfitness to Plead) Act 1991 (c. 25); or

(c) regulations under subsection (3) of section 116B of the Army Act 1955 (3 & 4 Eliz. 2 c. 18) or the Air Force Act 1955 (3 & 4 Eliz. 2 c. 19) or section 63B of the Naval Discipline Act 1957 (c. 53);

'cautioned' means—

(a) cautioned by a police officer after the person concerned has admitted the offence, or

(b) reprimanded or warned within the meaning given by section 65 of the Crime and Disorder Act 1998 (c. 37),

and 'caution' is to be interpreted accordingly;

'community order' means—

(a) a community order within the meaning of the Powers of Criminal Courts (Sentencing) Act 2000 (c. 6);

(b) a probation order or community service order under the Criminal Procedure (Scotland) Act 1995 or a supervised attendance order made in pursuance of section 235 of that Act;

(c) a community order within the meaning of the Criminal Justice (Northern Ireland) Order 1996 (S.I. 1996/3160 (N.I. 24)), a probation order under section 1 of the Probation Act (Northern Ireland) 1950 (c. 7 (N.I.)) or a community service order under Article 7 of the Treatment of Offenders (Northern Ireland) Order 1976 (S.I. 1976/226 (N.I. 40)); or

(d) a community supervision order;

'community supervision order' means an order under paragraph 4 of Schedule 5A to the Army Act 1955 or the Air Force Act 1955 or Schedule 4A to the Naval Discipline Act 1957;

'country' includes territory;

'detained in a hospital' means detained in a hospital under—

(a) Part 3 of the Mental Health Act 1983, section 71 of the Mental Health (Scotland) Act 1984 (c. 36), Part 6 of the Criminal Procedure (Scotland) Act 1995 or Part III of the Mental Health (Northern Ireland) Order 1986;

(b) Schedule 1 to the Criminal Procedure (Insanity and Unfitness to Plead) Act 1991; or

(c) regulations under subsection (3) of section 116B of the Army Act 1955 or the Air Force Act 1955 or section 63B of the Naval Discipline Act 1957;

'guardianship order' means a guardianship order under section 37 of the Mental Health Act 1983 (c. 20), section 58 of the Criminal Procedure (Scotland) Act 1995 (c. 46) or Article 44 of the Mental Health (Northern Ireland) Order 1986 (S.I. 1986/595 (N.I. 4));

'home address' has the meaning given by section 83(7);

'interim notification order' has the meaning given by section 100(2);

'interim risk of sexual harm order' has the meaning given by section 126(2);

'interim sexual offences prevention order' has the meaning given by section 109(2);

'local police area' has the meaning given by section 88(3);

'local probation board' has the same meaning as in the Criminal Justice and Court Services Act 2000 (c. 43);

'notification order' has the meaning given by section 97(1);

'notification period' has the meaning given by section 80(1);

'order for conditional discharge' has the meaning given by each of the following—

    (a) section 12(3) of the Powers of Criminal Courts (Sentencing) Act 2000 (c. 6);

    (b) Article 2(2) of the Criminal Justice (Northern Ireland) Order 1996 (S.I. 1996/3160 (N.I. 24));

    (c) paragraph 2(1) of Schedule 5A to the Army Act 1955 (3 & 4 Eliz. 2 c. 18);

    (d) paragraph 2(1) of Schedule 5A to the Air Force Act 1955 (3 & 4 Eliz. 2 c. 19);

    (e) paragraph 2(1) of Schedule 4A to the Naval Discipline Act 1957 (c. 53);

'parental responsibility' has the same meaning as in the Children Act 1989 (c. 41) or the Children (Northern Ireland) Order 1995 (S.I. 1995/755 (N.I. 2)), and 'parental responsibilities' has the same meaning as in Part 1 of the Children (Scotland) Act 1995 (c. 36);

'the period of conditional discharge' has the meaning given by each of the following—

    (a) section 12(3) of the Powers of Criminal Courts (Sentencing) Act 2000;

    (b) Article 2(2) of the Criminal Justice (Northern Ireland) Order 1996;

    (c) paragraph 2(1) of Schedule 5A to the Army Act 1955;

    (d) paragraph 2(1) of Schedule 5A to the Air Force Act 1955;

    (e) paragraph 2(1) of Schedule 4A to the Naval Discipline Act 1957;

'probation order' has the meaning given by section 228(1) of the Criminal Procedure (Scotland) Act 1995;

'probation period' has the meaning given by section 307(1) of the Criminal Procedure (Scotland) Act 1995;

'relevant date' has the meaning given by section 82(6) (save in the circumstances mentioned in sections 98, 100, 107, 109 and 129);

'relevant offender' has the meaning given by section 80(2);

'restriction order' means—

    (a) an order under section 41 of the Mental Health Act 1983, section 57(2)(b) or 59 of the Criminal Procedure (Scotland) Act 1995 or Article 47(1) of the Mental Health (Northern Ireland) Order 1986;

    (b) a direction under paragraph 2(1)(b) of Schedule 1 to the Criminal Procedure (Insanity and Unfitness to Plead) Act 1991 (c. 25) or Article 50A(3)(b) of the Mental Health (Northern Ireland) Order 1986 (S.I. 1986/595 (N.I. 4)); or

    (c) a direction under subsection (2) of section 116B of the Army Act 1955 (3 & 4 Eliz. 2 c. 18) or the Air Force Act 1955 (3 & 4 Eliz. 2 c. 19) or section 63B of the Naval Discipline Act 1957 (c. 53);

'risk of sexual harm order' has the meaning given by section 123(1);

'sexual offences prevention order' has the meaning given by section 106(1);

'supervision' means supervision in pursuance of an order made for the purpose or, in the case of a person released from prison on licence, in pursuance of a condition contained in his licence;

'term of service detention' means a term of detention awarded under section 71(1)(e) of the Army Act 1955 or the Air Force Act 1955 or section 43(1)(e) of the Naval Discipline Act 1957.

(2) Where under section 141 different days are appointed for the commencement of different provisions of this Part, a reference in any such provision to the commencement of this Part is to be read (subject to section 98(4)) as a reference to the commencement of that provision.

134. Conditional discharges and probation orders

(1) The following provisions do not apply for the purposes of this Part to a conviction for an offence in respect of which an order for conditional discharge or, in Scotland, a probation order is made—

(a) section 14(1) of the Powers of Criminal Courts (Sentencing) Act 2000 (c. 6) (conviction with absolute or conditional discharge deemed not to be a conviction);

(b) Article 6(1) of the Criminal Justice (Northern Ireland) Order 1996 (S.I. 1996/3160 (N.I. 24)) (conviction with absolute or conditional discharge deemed not to be a conviction);

(c) section 247(1) of the Criminal Procedure (Scotland) Act 1995 (c. 46) (conviction with probation order or absolute discharge deemed not to be a conviction);

(d) paragraph 5(1) of Schedule 5A to the Army Act 1955 (3 & 4 Eliz. 2 c. 18) or the Air Force Act 1955 (3 & 4 Eliz. 2 c. 19) or Schedule 4A to the Naval Discipline Act 1957 (c. 53) (conviction with absolute or conditional discharge or community supervision order deemed not to be a conviction).

(2) Subsection (1) applies only to convictions after the commencement of this Part.

(3) The provisions listed in subsection (1)(d) do not apply for the purposes of this Part to a conviction for an offence in respect of which a community supervision order is or has (before or after the commencement of this Part) been made.

135. Interpretation: mentally disordered offenders

(1) In this Part, a reference to a conviction includes a reference to a finding of a court in summary proceedings, where the court makes an order under an enactment within subsection (2), that the accused did the act charged; and similar references are to be interpreted accordingly.

(2) The enactments are—

(a) section 37(3) of the Mental Health Act 1983 (c. 20);

(b) section 58(3) of the Criminal Procedure (Scotland) Act 1995 (c. 46);

(c) Article 44(4) of the Mental Health (Northern Ireland) Order 1986 (S.I. 1986/595 (N.I. 4)).

(3) In this Part, a reference to a person being or having been found to be under a disability and to have done the act charged against him in respect of an offence includes a reference to his being or having been found—

(a) unfit to be tried for the offence;

(b) to be insane so that his trial for the offence cannot or could not proceed; or

(c) unfit to be tried and to have done the act charged against him in respect of the offence.

(4) In section 133—

(a) a reference to admission or detention under Schedule 1 to the Criminal Procedure (Insanity and Unfitness to Plead) Act 1991 (c. 25), and the reference to a direction under paragraph 2(1)(b) of that Schedule, include respectively—

(i) a reference to admission or detention under Schedule 1 to the Criminal Procedure (Insanity) Act 1964 (c. 84); and

(ii) a reference to a restriction order treated as made by paragraph 2(1) of that Schedule;

(b) a reference to admission or detention under any provision of Part 6 of the Criminal Procedure (Scotland) Act 1995, and the reference to an order under section 57(2)(b) or 59 of that Act, include respectively—

(i) a reference to admission or detention under section 174(3) or 376(2) of the Criminal Procedure (Scotland) Act 1975 (c. 21); and

(ii) a reference to a restriction order made under section 178(1) or 379(1) of that Act;

(c) a reference to admission or detention under regulations made under subsection (3), and the reference to a direction under subsection (2), of section 116B of the Army Act 1955 (3 & 4 Eliz. 2 c. 18) or the Air Force Act 1955 (3 & 4 Eliz. 2 c. 19) or section 63B of the Naval Discipline Act 1957 (c. 53) include respectively—

(i) a reference to admission or detention, and

(ii) a reference to a direction,

under section 46 of the Mental Health Act 1983, section 69 of the Mental Health (Scotland) Act 1984 (c. 36) or Article 52 of the Mental Health (Northern Ireland) Order 1986.

136. Part 2: Northern Ireland

(1) This Part applies to Northern Ireland with the following modifications.

(2) References to a chief officer of police are to be read as references to the Chief Constable of the Police Service of Northern Ireland.

(3) References to police areas are to be read as references to Northern Ireland.

(4) References to a complaint are to be read as references to a complaint under Part VIII of the Magistrates' Courts (Northern Ireland) Order 1981 (S.I. 1981/1675 (N.I. 26)) to a court of summary jurisdiction.

(5) Subject to subsection (6), references to a magistrates' court are to be read as references to a court of summary jurisdiction.

(6) References to a magistrates' court for the area in which the defendant resides are to be read as references to a court of summary jurisdiction for the petty sessions district which includes the area where the defendant resides.

(7) References to a youth court for the area in which the defendant resides are to be read as references to a youth court for the petty sessions district which includes the area where the defendant resides.

(8) References in sections 101, 110(1), (2), (3)(b), (4) and (5), 119 and 127 to the Crown Court are to be read as references to a county court.

(9) Any direction of the county court made under section 89(1) on an appeal under Article 143 of the Magistrates' Courts (Northern Ireland) Order 1981 (appeals in other cases) (other than one directing that an application be re-heard by a court of summary jurisdiction) is, for the purposes of section 90, to be treated as if it were made by the court from which the appeal was brought and not by the county court.

(10) Any order of the county court made on an appeal under Article 143 of the Magistrates' Courts (Northern Ireland) Order 1981 (other than one directing that an application be re-heard by a court of summary jurisdiction) is, for the purposes of section 108, to be treated as if it were an order of the court from which the appeal was brought and not an order of the county court.

PART 3
GENERAL

137. Service courts

(1) In this Act—

(a) a reference to a court order or a conviction or finding includes a reference to an order of or a conviction or finding by a service court,

(b) a reference to an offence includes a reference to an offence triable by a service court,

(c) 'proceedings' includes proceedings before a service court, and

(d) a reference to proceedings for an offence under this Act includes a reference to proceedings for the offence under section 70 of the Army Act 1955 (3 & 4 Eliz. 2 c. 18) or the Air Force Act 1955 (3 & 4 Eliz. 2 c. 19) or section 42 of the Naval Discipline Act 1957 (c. 53) for which the offence under this Act is the corresponding civil offence.

(2) In sections 92 and 104(1), 'court' includes a service court.

(3) Where the court making a sexual offences prevention order is a service court—

(a) sections 104(1)(a) and (4) to (6), 105, 109, 111 and 112 do not apply,

(b) in section 108, 'the appropriate court' means the Crown Court in England and Wales, and

(c) in section 110(3)(a), the references to the Crown Court and Court of Appeal are references to the Crown Court and Court of Appeal in England and Wales.

(4) In this section 'service court' means a court-martial or Standing Civilian Court.

138. Orders and regulations

(1) Any power to make orders or regulations conferred by this Act on the Secretary of State is exercisable by statutory instrument.

(2) A statutory instrument containing an order or regulations under section 21, 86 or 130 may not be made unless a draft of the instrument has been laid before, and approved by resolution of, each House of Parliament.

(3) Any other statutory instrument, except one containing an order under section 141, is to be subject to annulment in pursuance of a resolution of either House of Parliament.

139. Minor and consequential amendments

Schedule 6 contains minor and consequential amendments.

140. Repeals and revocations

The provisions listed in Schedule 7 are repealed or revoked to the extent specified.

141. Commencement

(1) This Act, except this section and sections 138, 142 and 143, comes into force in accordance with provision made by the Secretary of State by order.

(2) An order under subsection (1) may—

    (a) make different provision for different purposes;

    (b) include supplementary, incidental, saving or transitional provisions.

142. Extent, saving etc.

(1) Subject to section 137 and to subsections (2) to (4), this Act extends to England and Wales only.

(2) The following provisions also extend to Northern Ireland—

    (a) sections 15 to 24, 46 to 54, 57 to 60, 66 to 72, 78 and 79,

    (b) Schedule 2,

    (c) Part 2, and

    (d) sections 138, 141, 143 and this section.

(3) The following provisions also extend to Scotland—

    (a) Part 2 except sections 93 and 123 to 129 and Schedule 4, and

    (b) sections 138, 141, 143 and this section.

(4) Unless otherwise provided, any amendment, repeal or revocation made by this Act has the same extent as the provision to which it relates.

(5) Section 16B of the Criminal Law (Consolidation) (Scotland) Act 1995 (c. 39) continues to have effect despite the repeal by this Act of section 8 of the Sex Offenders Act 1997 (c. 51).

(6) For the purposes of the Scotland Act 1998 (c. 46), this Act is to be taken to be a pre-commencement enactment.

143. Short title

This Act may be cited as the Sexual Offences Act 2003.

SCHEDULES

SCHEDULE 1

Section 56

EXTENSION OF GENDER-SPECIFIC PROSTITUTION OFFENCES

Sexual Offences Act 1956 (c. 69)

1. In section 36 of the Sexual Offences Act 1956 (permitting premises to be used for prostitution), at the end insert '(whether any prostitute involved is male or female)'.

Street Offences Act 1959 (c. 57)

2. In section 1(1) of the Street Offences Act 1959 (loitering or soliciting for purposes of prostitution), after 'prostitute' insert '(whether male or female)'.

3.—(1) Section 2 of that Act (application to court by woman cautioned for loitering or soliciting) is amended as follows.

(2) In the heading of the section, for 'woman' substitute 'person'.

(3) In subsection (1)—

    (a) for 'woman' substitute 'person',

    (b) for 'her' in each place substitute 'his', and

    (c) for 'she' in each place substitute 'he'.

(4) In subsection (2)—

    (a) for 'woman' in the first place substitute 'person',

    (b) for 'he' substitute 'the chief officer', and

    (c) for 'woman' in the second place substitute 'person cautioned'.

(5) In subsection (3), for 'woman' substitute 'person cautioned'.

Sexual Offences Act 1985 (c. 44)

4.—(1) The Sexual Offences Act 1985 is amended as follows.

(2) For the heading 'Soliciting of women by men' substitute 'Soliciting for the purpose of prostitution'.

(3) In section 1 (kerb-crawling)—

    (a) for 'man' substitute 'person',

    (b) for 'a woman' substitute 'another person',

    (c) for 'women' in each place substitute 'persons', and

    (d) for 'the woman' substitute 'the person'.

(4) In section 2 (persistent soliciting of women for the purpose of prostitution)—

    (a) for the heading of the section substitute 'Persistent soliciting',

    (b) for 'man' substitute 'person',

    (c) for 'a woman' substitute 'another person', and

    (d) for 'women' substitute 'persons'.

(5) In section 4 (interpretation)—

    (a) omit subsections (2) and (3),

    (b) for 'man' substitute 'person',

    (c) for 'a woman' substitute 'another person',

    (d) for 'her' in the first place substitute 'that person', and

    (e) for 'her' in the second place substitute 'that person's'.

SCHEDULE 2

Section 72(7)

SEXUAL OFFENCES TO WHICH SECTION 72 APPLIES

England and Wales

1. In relation to England and Wales, the following are sexual offences to which section 72 applies—

    (a) an offence under any of sections 5 to 15 (offences against children under 13 or under 16);

(b) an offence under any of sections 1 to 4, 16 to 41, 47 to 50 and 61 where the victim of the offence was under 16 at the time of the offence;

(c) an offence under section 62 or 63 where the intended offence was an offence against a person under 16;

(d) an offence under—

(i) section 1 of the Protection of Children Act 1978 (c. 37) (indecent photographs of children), or

(ii) section 160 of the Criminal Justice Act 1988 (c. 33) (possession of indecent photograph of child),

in relation to a photograph or pseudo-photograph showing a child under 16.

Northern Ireland

2.—(1) In relation to Northern Ireland, the following are sexual offences to which section 72 applies—

(a) rape;

(b) an offence under—

(i) section 52 of the Offences against the Person Act 1861 (c. 100) (indecent assault upon a female person), or

(ii) section 53 or 54 of that Act (abduction of woman);

(c) an offence under—

(i) section 2 of the Criminal Law Amendment Act 1885 (c. 69) (procuration of girl under 21),

(ii) section 3 of that Act (procuring defilement of woman using threats, etc.),

(iii) section 4 of that Act of unlawful carnal knowledge of a girl under 14,

(iv) section 5 of that Act of unlawful carnal knowledge of a girl under 17, or

(v) section 7 of that Act (abduction of girl under 18);

(d) an offence under—

(i) section 1 of the Punishment of Incest Act 1908 (c. 45) (incest by males), or

(ii) section 2 of that Act (incest by females);

(e) an offence under—

(i) section 21 of the Children and Young Persons Act (Northern Ireland) 1968 (c. 34 (N.I.)) (causing or encouraging seduction, etc. of girl under 17), or

(ii) section 22 of that Act (indecent conduct towards a child);

(f) an offence under Article 3 of the Protection of Children (Northern Ireland) Order 1978 (S.I. 1978/1047 (N.I. 17)) (indecent photographs of children);

(g) an offence under Article 9 of the Criminal Justice (Northern Ireland) Order 1980 (S.I. 1980/704 (N.I. 6)) (inciting girl under 16 to have incestuous sexual intercourse);

(h) an offence under Article 15 of the Criminal Justice (Evidence, Etc.) (Northern Ireland) Order 1988 (S.I. 1988/1847 (N.I. 17)) (indecent photographs of children);

(i) an offence under—

(i) Article 19 of the Criminal Justice (Northern Ireland) Order 2003 (S.I. 2003/1247 (N.I. 13)) (buggery),

(ii) Article 20 of that Order (assault with intent to commit buggery), or

(iii) Article 21 of that Order (indecent assault on a male);

(j) an offence under—

(i) section 15 of this Act (meeting a child following sexual grooming etc.), or

(ii) any of sections 16 to 19 or 47 to 50 of this Act (abuse of trust, prostitution, child pornography).

(2) Sub-paragraph (1), apart from paragraphs (f) and (h), does not apply where the victim of the offence was 17 or over at the time of the offence.

General

3. A reference in paragraph 1 or 2(1) to an offence includes—

(a) a reference to an attempt, conspiracy or incitement to commit that offence; and

(b) a reference to aiding and abetting, counselling or procuring the commission of that offence.

SCHEDULE 3

Section 80

SEXUAL OFFENCES FOR PURPOSES OF PART 2

England and Wales

1. An offence under section 1 of the Sexual Offences Act 1956 (c. 69) (rape).

2. An offence under section 5 of that Act (intercourse with girl under 13).

3. An offence under section 6 of that Act (intercourse with girl under 16), if the offender was 20 or over.

4. An offence under section 10 of that Act (incest by a man), if the victim or (as the case may be) other party was under 18.

5. An offence under section 12 of that Act (buggery) if—

(a) the offender was 20 or over, and

(b) the victim or (as the case may be) other party was under 18.

6. An offence under section 13 of that Act (indecency between men) if—

(a) the offender was 20 or over, and

(b) the victim or (as the case may be) other party was under 18.

7. An offence under section 14 of that Act (indecent assault on a woman) if—

(a) the victim or (as the case may be) other party was under 18, or

(b) the offender, in respect of the offence or finding, is or has been—

(i) sentenced to imprisonment for a term of at least 30 months; or

(ii) admitted to a hospital subject to a restriction order.

8. An offence under section 15 of that Act (indecent assault on a man) if—

(a) the victim or (as the case may be) other party was under 18, or

(b) the offender, in respect of the offence or finding, is or has been—

(i) sentenced to imprisonment for a term of at least 30 months; or

(ii) admitted to a hospital subject to a restriction order.

9. An offence under section 16 of that Act (assault with intent to commit buggery), if the victim or (as the case may be) other party was under 18.

10. An offence under section 28 of that Act (causing or encouraging the prostitution of, intercourse with or indecent assault on girl under 16).

11. An offence under section 1 of the Indecency with Children Act 1960 (c. 33) (indecent conduct towards young child).

12. An offence under section 54 of the Criminal Law Act 1977 (c. 45) (inciting girl under 16 to have incestuous sexual intercourse).

13. An offence under section 1 of the Protection of Children Act 1978 (c. 37) (indecent photographs of children), if the indecent photographs or pseudo-photographs showed persons under 16 and—

    (a) the conviction, finding or caution was before the commencement of this Part, or

    (b) the offender—

        (i)   was 18 or over, or

        (ii) is sentenced in respect of the offence to imprisonment for a term of at least 12 months.

14. An offence under section 170 of the Customs and Excise Management Act 1979 (c. 2) (penalty for fraudulent evasion of duty etc.) in relation to goods prohibited to be imported under section 42 of the Customs Consolidation Act 1876 (c. 36) (indecent or obscene articles), if the prohibited goods included indecent photographs of persons under 16 and—

    (a) the conviction, finding or caution was before the commencement of this Part, or

    (b) the offender—

        (i)   was 18 or over, or

        (ii) is sentenced in respect of the offence to imprisonment for a term of at least 12 months.

15. An offence under section 160 of the Criminal Justice Act 1988 (c. 33) (possession of indecent photograph of a child), if the indecent photographs or pseudo-photographs showed persons under 16 and—

    (a) the conviction, finding or caution was before the commencement of this Part, or

    (b) the offender—

        (i)   was 18 or over, or

        (ii) is sentenced in respect of the offence to imprisonment for a term of at least 12 months.

16. An offence under section 3 of the Sexual Offences (Amendment) Act 2000 (c. 44) (abuse of position of trust), if the offender was 20 or over.

17. An offence under section 1 or 2 of this Act (rape, assault by penetration).

18. An offence under section 3 of this Act (sexual assault) if—

    (a) where the offender was under 18, he is or has been sentenced, in respect of the offence, to imprisonment for a term of at least 12 months;

    (b) in any other case—

        (i)   the victim was under 18, or

        (ii) the offender, in respect of the offence or finding, is or has been—

            (a) sentenced to a term of imprisonment,

            (b) detained in a hospital, or

            (c) made the subject of a community sentence of at least 12 months.

19. An offence under any of sections 4 to 6 of this Act (causing sexual activity without consent, rape of a child under 13, assault of a child under 13 by penetration).

20. An offence under section 7 of this Act (sexual assault of a child under 13) if the offender—

    (a) was 18 or over, or

    (b) is or has been sentenced in respect of the offence to imprisonment for a term of at least 12 months.

21. An offence under any of sections 8 to 12 of this Act (causing or inciting a child under 13 to engage in sexual activity, child sex offences committed by adults).
22. An offence under section 13 of this Act (child sex offences committed by children or young persons), if the offender is or has been sentenced, in respect of the offence, to imprisonment for a term of at least 12 months.
23. An offence under section 14 of this Act (arranging or facilitating the commission of a child sex offence) if the offender—
    (a) was 18 or over, or
    (b) is or has been sentenced, in respect of the offence, to imprisonment for a term of at least 12 months.
24. An offence under section 15 of this Act (meeting a child following sexual grooming etc).
25. An offence under any of sections 16 to 19 of this Act (abuse of a position of trust) if the offender, in respect of the offence, is or has been—
    (a) sentenced to a term of imprisonment,
    (b) detained in a hospital, or
    (c) made the subject of a community sentence of at least 12 months.
26. An offence under section 25 or 26 of this Act (familial child sex offences) if the offender—
    (a) was 18 or over, or
    (b) is or has been sentenced in respect of the offence to imprisonment for a term of at least 12 months.
27. An offence under any of sections 30 to 37 of this Act (offences against persons with a mental disorder impeding choice, inducements etc. to persons with mental disorder).
28. An offence under any of sections 38 to 41 of this Act (care workers for persons with mental disorder) if—
    (a) where the offender was under 18, he is or has been sentenced in respect of the offence to imprisonment for a term of at least 12 months;
    (b) in any other case, the offender, in respect of the offence or finding, is or has been—
        (i) sentenced to a term of imprisonment,
        (ii) detained in a hospital, or
        (iii) made the subject of a community sentence of at least 12 months.
29. An offence under section 47 of this Act (paying for sexual services of a child) if the victim or (as the case may be) other party was under 16, and the offender—
    (a) was 18 or over, or
    (b) is or has been sentenced in respect of the offence to imprisonment for a term of at least 12 months.
30. An offence under section 61 of this Act (administering a substance with intent).
31. An offence under section 62 or 63 of this Act (committing an offence or trespassing, with intent to commit a sexual offence) if—
    (a) where the offender was under 18, he is or has been sentenced in respect of the offence to imprisonment for a term of at least 12 months;
    (b) in any other case—
        (i) the intended offence was an offence against a person under 18, or
        (ii) the offender, in respect of the offence or finding, is or has been—
            (a) sentenced to a term of imprisonment,
            (b) detained in a hospital, or
            (c) made the subject of a community sentence of at least 12 months.

32. An offence under section 64 or 65 of this Act (sex with an adult relative) if—
    (a) where the offender was under 18, he is or has been sentenced in respect of the offence to imprisonment for a term of at least 12 months;
    (b) in any other case, the offender, in respect of the offence or finding, is or has been—
        (i) sentenced to a term of imprisonment, or
        (ii) detained in a hospital.
33. An offence under section 66 of this Act (exposure) if—
    (a) where the offender was under 18, he is or has been sentenced in respect of the offence to imprisonment for a term of at least 12 months;
    (b) in any other case—
        (i) the victim was under 18, or
        (ii) the offender, in respect of the offence or finding, is or has been—
           (a) sentenced to a term of imprisonment,
           (b) detained in a hospital, or
           (c) made the subject of a community sentence of at least 12 months.
34. An offence under section 67 of this Act (voyeurism) if—
    (a) where the offender was under 18, he is or has been sentenced in respect of the offence to imprisonment for a term of at least 12 months;
    (b) in any other case—
        (i) the victim was under 18, or
        (ii) the offender, in respect of the offence or finding, is or has been—
           (a) sentenced to a term of imprisonment,
           (b) detained in a hospital, or
           (c) made the subject of a community sentence of at least 12 months.
35. An offence under section 69 or 70 of this Act (intercourse with an animal, sexual penetration of a corpse) if—
    (a) where the offender was under 18, he is or has been sentenced in respect of the offence to imprisonment for a term of at least 12 months;
    (b) in any other case, the offender, in respect of the offence or finding, is or has been—
        (i) sentenced to a term of imprisonment, or
        (ii) detained in a hospital.

Scotland

36. Rape.
37. Clandestine injury to women.
38. Abduction of woman or girl with intent to rape.
39. Assault with intent to rape or ravish.
40. Indecent assault.
41. Lewd, indecent or libidinous behaviour or practices.
42. Shameless indecency, if a person (other than the offender) involved in the offence was under 18.
43. Sodomy, unless every person involved in the offence was 16 or over and was a willing participant.
44. An offence under section 170 of the Customs and Excise Management Act 1979 (c. 2) (penalty for fraudulent evasion of duty etc.) in relation to goods prohibited to be imported

under section 42 of the Customs Consolidation Act 1876 (c. 36) (indecent or obscene articles), if the prohibited goods included indecent photographs of persons under 16.

45. An offence under section 52 of the Civic Government (Scotland) Act 1982 (c. 45) (taking and distribution of indecent images of children).

46. An offence under section 52A of that Act (possession of indecent images of children).

47. An offence under section 106 of the Mental Health (Scotland) Act 1984 (c. 36) (protection of mentally handicapped females).

48. An offence under section 107 of that Act (protection of patients).

49. An offence under section 1 of the Criminal Law (Consolidation) (Scotland) Act 1995 (c. 39) (incest), if a person (other than the offender) involved in the offence was under 18.

50. An offence under section 2 of that Act (intercourse with a stepchild), if a person (other than the offender) involved in the offence was under 18.

51. An offence under section 3 of that Act (intercourse with child under 16 by person in position of trust).

52. An offence under section 5 of that Act (unlawful intercourse with girl under 16), save in the case of an offence in contravention of subsection (3) of that section where the offender was under 20.

53. An offence under section 6 of that Act (indecent behaviour towards girl between 12 and 16).

54. An offence under section 8 of that Act (abduction of girl under 18 for purposes of unlawful intercourse).

55. An offence under section 10 of that Act (person having parental responsibilities causing or encouraging sexual activity in relation to a girl under 16).

56. An offence under section 13(5) of that Act (homosexual offences) unless every person involved (whether in the offence or in the homosexual act) was 16 or over and was a willing participant.

57. An offence under section 3 of the Sexual Offences (Amendment) Act 2000 (c. 44) (abuse of position of trust), where the offender was 20 or over.

58. An offence under section 311(1) of the Mental Health (Care and Treatment) (Scotland) Act 2003 (asp 13) (non-consensual sexual acts).

59. An offence under section 313(1) of that Act (persons providing care services: sexual offences).

60. An offence in Scotland other than is mentioned in paragraphs 36 to 59 if the court, in imposing sentence or otherwise disposing of the case, determines for the purposes of this paragraph that there was a significant sexual aspect to the offender's behaviour in committing the offence.

Northern Ireland

61. Rape.

62. An offence under section 52 of the Offences against the Person Act 1861 (c. 100) (indecent assault upon a female) if—

(a) where the offender was under 18, he is or has been sentenced, in respect of the offence, to imprisonment for a term of at least 12 months;

(b) in any other case—

(i) the victim was under 18, or

(ii) the offender, in respect of the offence or finding, is or has been—

(a) sentenced to a term of imprisonment,

(b) detained in a hospital, or

(c) made the subject of a community sentence of at least 12 months.

63. An offence under section 53 or 54 of that Act (abduction of woman by force for unlawful sexual intercourse) if the offender—

(a) was 18 or over, or

(b) is or has been sentenced in respect of the offence to imprisonment for a term of at least 12 months.

64. An offence under section 61 of that Act (buggery) if—

(a) the offender was 20 or over, and

(b) the victim or (as the case may be) other party was under 18.

65. An offence under section 62 of that Act of assault with intent to commit buggery if the victim or (as the case may be) other party was under 18, and the offender—

(a) was 18 or over, or

(b) is or has been sentenced in respect of the offence to imprisonment for a term of at least 12 months.

66. An offence under section 62 of that Act of indecent assault upon a male person if—

(a) where the offender was under 18, he is or has been sentenced, in respect of the offence, to imprisonment for a term of at least 12 months;

(b) in any other case—

(i) the victim was under 18, or

(ii) the offender, in respect of the offence or finding, is or has been—

(a) sentenced to a term of imprisonment,

(b) detained in a hospital, or

(c) made the subject of a community sentence of at least 12 months.

67. An offence under section 2 of the Criminal Law Amendment Act 1885 (c. 69) (procuration) if the offender—

(a) was 18 or over, or

(b) is or has been sentenced in respect of the offence to imprisonment for a term of at least 12 months.

68. An offence under section 3 of that Act (procuring defilement of woman by threats or fraud, etc.) if the offender—

(a) was 18 or over, or

(b) is or has been sentenced in respect of the offence to imprisonment for a term of at least 12 months.

69. An offence under section 4 of that Act of unlawful carnal knowledge of a girl under 14 if the offender—

(a) was 18 or over, or

(b) is or has been sentenced in respect of the offence to imprisonment for a term of at least 12 months.

70. An offence under section 5 of that Act of unlawful carnal knowledge of a girl under 17, if the offender was 20 or over.

71. An offence under section 7 of that Act (abduction of girl under 18) if the offender—

(a) was 18 or over, or

(b) is or has been sentenced in respect of the offence to imprisonment for a term of at least 12 months.

72. An offence under section 11 of that Act (homosexual offences) if—

(a) the offender was 20 or over, and

(b) the victim or (as the case may be) other party was under 18.

73. An offence under section 1 of the Punishment of Incest Act 1908 (c. 45) (incest by males), if—

(a) where the offender was under 18, he is or has been sentenced in respect of the offence to imprisonment for a term of at least 12 months;

(b) in any other case—

    (i) the victim or (as the case may be) other party was under 18, or

    (ii) the offender, in respect of the offence or finding, is or has been—

        (a) sentenced to a term of imprisonment, or

        (b) detained in a hospital.

74. An offence under section 2 of that Act (incest by females), if—

(a) where the offender was under 18, he is or has been sentenced in respect of the offence to imprisonment for a term of at least 12 months;

(b) in any other case—

    (i) the victim or (as the case may be) other party was under 18, or

    (ii) the offender, in respect of the offence or finding, is or has been—

        (a) sentenced to a term of imprisonment, or

        (b) detained in a hospital.

75. An offence under section 21 of the Children and Young Persons Act (Northern Ireland) 1968 (c. 34) (causing or encouraging seduction or prostitution of a girl under 17) if the offender—

(a) was 18 or over, or

(b) is or has been sentenced in respect of the offence to imprisonment for a term of at least 12 months.

76. An offence under section 22 of that Act (indecent conduct towards a child) if the offender—

(a) was 18 or over, or

(b) is or has been sentenced in respect of the offence to imprisonment for a term of at least 12 months.

77. An offence under Article 3 of the Protection of Children (Northern Ireland) Order 1978 (S.I. 1978/1047 (N.I. 17)) (indecent photographs of children) if the offender—

(a) was 18 or over, or

(b) is or has been sentenced in respect of the offence to imprisonment for a term of at least 12 months.

78. An offence under section 170 of the Customs and Excise Management Act 1979 (c. 2) (penalty for fraudulent evasion of duty etc.) in relation to goods prohibited to be imported under section 42 of the Customs Consolidation Act 1876 (c. 36) (indecent or obscene articles), if the prohibited goods included indecent photographs of persons under 16, and the offender—

(a) was 18 or over, or

(b) is or has been sentenced in respect of the offence to imprisonment for a term of at least 12 months.

79. An offence under Article 9 of the Criminal Justice (Northern Ireland) Order 1980 (S.I. 1980/704 (N.I. 6)) (inciting girl under 16 to have incestuous sexual intercourse) if the offender—

(a) was 18 or over, or

(b) is or has been sentenced in respect of the offence to imprisonment for a term of at least 12 months.

80. An offence under Article 122 of the Mental Health (Northern Ireland) Order 1986 (S.I. 1986/595 (N.I. 4)) (offences against women suffering from severe mental handicap).

81. An offence under Article 123 of that Order (offences against patients) if—

    (a) where the offender was under 18, he is or has been sentenced in respect of the offence to imprisonment for a term of at least 12 months;

    (b) in any other case, the offender, in respect of the offence or finding, is or has been—

        (i) sentenced to a term of imprisonment,

        (ii) detained in a hospital, or

        (iii) made the subject of a community sentence of at least 12 months.

82. An offence under Article 15 of the Criminal Justice (Evidence, etc.) (Northern Ireland) Order 1988 (S.I. 1988/1847 (N.I. 17) (possession of indecent photographs of children) if the offender—

    (a) was 18 or over, or

    (b) is or has been sentenced in respect of the offence to imprisonment for a term of at least 12 months.

83. An offence under section 3 of the Sexual Offences (Amendment) Act 2000 (c. 44) (abuse of position of trust), if the offender, in respect of the offence or finding, is or has been—

    (a) sentenced to a term of imprisonment,

    (b) detained in a hospital, or

    (c) made the subject of a community sentence of at least 12 months.

84. An offence under Article 19 of the Criminal Justice (Northern Ireland) Order 2003 (S.I. 2003/1247 (N.I. 13)) (buggery) if—

    (a) the offender was 20 or over, and

    (b) the victim or (as the case may be) other party was under 17.

85. An offence under Article 20 of that Order (assault with intent to commit buggery) if the victim was under 18 and the offender—

    (a) was 18 or over, or

    (b) is or has been sentenced in respect of the offence to imprisonment for a term of at least 12 months.

86. An offence under Article 21 of that Order (indecent assault upon a male) if—

    (a) where the offender was under 18, he is or has been sentenced, in respect of the offence, to imprisonment for a term of at least 12 months;

    (b) in any other case—

        (i) the victim was under 18, or

        (ii) the offender, in respect of the offence or finding, is or has been—

            (a) sentenced to a term of imprisonment,

            (b) detained in a hospital, or

            (c) made the subject of a community sentence of at least 12 months.

87. An offence under section 15 of this Act (meeting a child following sexual grooming etc.).

88. An offence under any of sections 16 to 19 of this Act (abuse of trust) if the offender, in respect of the offence or finding, is or has been—

    (a) sentenced to a term of imprisonment,

    (b) detained in a hospital, or

    (c) made the subject of a community sentence of at least 12 months.

89. An offence under section 47 of this Act (paying for sexual services of a child) if the victim or (as the case may be) other party was under 17 and the offender—

(a) was 18 or over, or

(b) is or has been sentenced in respect of the offence to a term of imprisonment of at least 12 months.

90. An offence under section 66 of this Act (exposure) if—

    (a) where the offender was under 18, he is or has been sentenced in respect of the offence to imprisonment for a term of at least 12 months;

    (b) in any other case—

        (i) the victim was under 18, or

        (ii) the offender, in respect of the offence or finding, is or has been—

            (a) sentenced to a term of imprisonment,

            (b) detained in a hospital, or

            (c) made the subject of a community sentence of at least 12 months.

91. An offence under section 67 of this Act (voyeurism) if—

    (a) where the offender was under 18, he is or has been sentenced in respect of the offence to imprisonment for a term of at least 12 months;

    (b) in any other case—

        (i) the victim was under 18, or

        (ii) the offender, in respect of the offence or finding, is or has been—

            (a) sentenced to a term of imprisonment,

            (b) detained in a hospital, or

            (c) made the subject of a community sentence of at least 12 months.

92. An offence under section 69 or 70 of this Act (intercourse with an animal, sexual penetration of a corpse) if—

    (a) where the offender was under 18, he is or has been sentenced in respect of the offence to imprisonment for a term of at least 12 months;

    (b) in any other case, the offender, in respect of the offence or finding, is or has been—

        (i) sentenced to a term of imprisonment, or

        (ii) detained in a hospital.

Service offences

93.—(1) An offence under—

    (a) section 70 of the Army Act 1955 (3 & 4 Eliz. 2 c. 18),

    (b) section 70 of the Air Force Act 1955 (3 & 4 Eliz. 2 c. 19), or

    (c) section 42 of the Naval Discipline Act 1957 (c. 53),

of which the corresponding civil offence (within the meaning of that Act) is an offence listed in any of paragraphs 1 to 35.

(2) A reference in any of those paragraphs to being made the subject of a community sentence of at least 12 months is to be read, in relation to an offence under an enactment referred to in sub-paragraph (1), as a reference to being sentenced to a term of service detention of at least 112 days.

General

94. A reference in a preceding paragraph to an offence includes—

    (a) a reference to an attempt, conspiracy or incitement to commit that offence, and

    (b) except in paragraphs 36 to 43, a reference to aiding, abetting, counselling or procuring the commission of that offence.

95. A reference in a preceding paragraph to a person's age is—

(a) in the case of an indecent photograph, a reference to the person's age when the photograph was taken;

(b) in any other case, a reference to his age at the time of the offence.

96. In this Schedule 'community sentence' has—

(a) in relation to England and Wales, the same meaning as in the Powers of Criminal Courts (Sentencing) Act 2000 (c. 6), and

(b) in relation to Northern Ireland, the same meaning as in the Criminal Justice (Northern Ireland) Order 1996 (S.I. 1996/3160 (N.I. 24)).

97. For the purposes of paragraphs 14, 44 and 78—

(a) a person is to be taken to have been under 16 at any time if it appears from the evidence as a whole that he was under that age at that time;

(b) section 7 of the Protection of Children Act 1978 (c. 37) (interpretation), subsections (2) to (2C) and (8) of section 52 of the Civic Government (Scotland) Act 1982 (c. 45), and Article 2(2) and (3) of the Protection of Children (Northern Ireland) Order 1978 (S.I. 1978/1047 (N.I. 17)) (interpretation) (respectively) apply as each provision applies for the purposes of the Act or Order of which it forms part.

98. A determination under paragraph 60 constitutes part of a person's sentence, within the meaning of the Criminal Procedure (Scotland) Act 1995 (c. 46), for the purposes of any appeal or review.

SCHEDULE 4

Section 93

PROCEDURE FOR ENDING NOTIFICATION REQUIREMENTS FOR ABOLISHED HOMOSEXUAL OFFENCES

Scope of Schedule

1. This Schedule applies where a relevant offender is subject to the notification requirements of this Part as a result of a conviction, finding or caution in respect of an offence under—

(a) section 12 or 13 of the Sexual Offences Act 1956 (c. 69) (buggery or indecency between men), or

(b) section 61 of the Offences against the Person Act 1861 (c. 100) or section 11 of the Criminal Law Amendment Act 1885 (c. 69) (corresponding Northern Ireland offences).

Application for decision

2.—(1) The relevant offender may apply to the Secretary of State for a decision as to whether it appears that, at the time of the offence, the other party to the act of buggery or gross indecency—

(a) where paragraph 1(a) applies, was aged 16 or over,

(b) where paragraph 1(b) applies, was aged 17 or over,

and consented to the act.

(2) An application must be in writing and state—

    (a) the name, address and date of birth of the relevant offender,

    (b) his name and address at the time of the conviction, finding or caution,

    (c) so far as known to him, the time when and the place where the conviction or finding was made or the caution given and, for a conviction or finding, the case number,

    (d) such other information as the Secretary of State may require.

(3) An application may include representations by the relevant offender about the matters mentioned in sub-paragraph (1).

Decision by Secretary of State

3.—(1) In making the decision applied for, the Secretary of State must consider—

    (a) any representations included in the application, and

    (b) any available record of the investigation of the offence and of any proceedings relating to it that appears to him to be relevant,

but is not to seek evidence from any witness.

(2) On making the decision the Secretary of State must—

    (a) record it in writing, and

    (b) give notice in writing to the relevant offender.

Effect of decision

4.—(1) If the Secretary of State decides that it appears as mentioned in paragraph 2(1), the relevant offender ceases, from the beginning of the day on which the decision is recorded under paragraph 3(2)(a), to be subject to the notification requirements of this Part as a result of the conviction, finding or caution in respect of the offence.

(2) Sub-paragraph (1) does not affect the operation of this Part as a result of any other conviction, finding or caution or any court order.

Right of appeal

5.—(1) If the Secretary of State decides that it does not appear as mentioned in paragraph 2(1), and if the High Court gives permission, the relevant offender may appeal to that court.

(2) On an appeal the court may not receive oral evidence.

(3) The court—

    (a) if it decides that it appears as mentioned in paragraph 2(1), must make an order to that effect,

    (b) otherwise, must dismiss the appeal.

(4) An order under sub-paragraph (3)(a) has the same effect as a decision of the Secretary of State recorded under paragraph 3(2)(a) has under paragraph 4.

(5) There is no appeal from the decision of the High Court.

Interpretation

6.—(1) In this Schedule a reference to an offence includes—

    (a) a reference to an attempt, conspiracy or incitement to commit that offence, and

    (b) a reference to aiding, abetting, counselling or procuring the commission of that offence.

(2) In the case of an attempt, conspiracy or incitement, references in paragraph 2 to the act of buggery or gross indecency are references to the act of buggery or gross indecency to which the attempt, conspiracy or incitement related (whether or not that act occurred).

Transitional provision

7. Until the coming into force of the repeal by this Act of Part 1 of the Sex Offenders Act 1997 (c. 51), this Schedule has effect as if references to this Part of this Act were references to Part 1 of that Act.

SCHEDULE 5

Section 104

OTHER OFFENCES FOR PURPOSES OF PART 2

England and Wales

1. Murder.
2. Manslaughter.
3. Kidnapping.
4. False imprisonment.
5. An offence under section 4 of the Offences against the Person Act 1861 (c. 100) (soliciting murder).
6. An offence under section 16 of that Act (threats to kill).
7. An offence under section 18 of that Act (wounding with intent to cause grievous bodily harm).
8. An offence under section 20 of that Act (malicious wounding).
9. An offence under section 21 of that Act (attempting to choke, suffocate or strangle in order to commit or assist in committing an indictable offence).
10. An offence under section 22 of that Act (using chloroform etc. to commit or assist in the committing of any indictable offence).
11. An offence under section 23 of that Act (maliciously administering poison etc. so as to endanger life or inflict grievous bodily harm).
12. An offence under section 27 of that Act (abandoning children).
13. An offence under section 28 of that Act (causing bodily injury by explosives).
14. An offence under section 29 of that Act (using explosives etc. with intent to do grievous bodily harm).
15. An offence under section 30 of that Act (placing explosives with intent to do bodily injury).
16. An offence under section 31 of that Act (setting spring guns etc. with intent to do grievous bodily harm).
17. An offence under section 32 of that Act (endangering the safety of railway passengers).
18. An offence under section 35 of that Act (injuring persons by furious driving).
19. An offence under section 37 of that Act (assaulting officer preserving wreck).
20. An offence under section 38 of that Act (assault with intent to resist arrest).
21. An offence under section 47 of that Act (assault occasioning actual bodily harm).
22. An offence under section 2 of the Explosive Substances Act 1883 (c. 3) (causing explosion likely to endanger life or property).

23. An offence under section 3 of that Act (attempt to cause explosion, or making or keeping explosive with intent to endanger life or property).

24. An offence under section 1 of the Infant Life (Preservation) Act 1929 (c. 34) (child destruction).

25. An offence under section 1 of the Children and Young Persons Act 1933 (c. 12) (cruelty to children).

26. An offence under section 1 of the Infanticide Act 1938 (c. 36) (infanticide).

27. An offence under section 16 of the Firearms Act 1968 (c. 27) (possession of firearm with intent to endanger life).

28. An offence under section 16A of that Act (possession of firearm with intent to cause fear of violence).

29. An offence under section 17(1) of that Act (use of firearm to resist arrest).

30. An offence under section 17(2) of that Act (possession of firearm at time of committing or being arrested for offence specified in Schedule 1 to that Act).

31. An offence under section 18 of that Act (carrying a firearm with criminal intent).

32. An offence under section 8 of the Theft Act 1968 (c. 60) (robbery or assault with intent to rob).

33. An offence under section 9 of that Act of burglary with intent to—
    (a) inflict grievous bodily harm on a person, or
    (b) do unlawful damage to a building or anything in it.

34. An offence under section 10 of that Act (aggravated burglary).

35. An offence under section 12A of that Act (aggravated vehicle-taking) involving an accident which caused the death of any person.

36. An offence of arson under section 1 of the Criminal Damage Act 1971 (c. 48).

37. An offence under section 1(2) of that Act (destroying or damaging property) other than an offence of arson.

38. An offence under section 1 of the Taking of Hostages Act 1982 (c. 28) (hostage-taking).

39. An offence under section 1 of the Aviation Security Act 1982 (c. 36) (hijacking).

40. An offence under section 2 of that Act (destroying, damaging or endangering safety of aircraft).

41. An offence under section 3 of that Act (other acts endangering or likely to endanger safety of aircraft).

42. An offence under section 4 of that Act (offences in relation to certain dangerous articles).

43. An offence under section 127 of the Mental Health Act 1983 (c. 20) (ill-treatment of patients).

44. An offence under section 1 of the Prohibition of Female Circumcision Act 1985 (c. 38) (prohibition of female circumcision).

45. An offence under section 1 of the Public Order Act 1986 (c. 64) (riot).

46. An offence under section 2 of that Act (violent disorder).

47. An offence under section 3 of that Act (affray).

48. An offence under section 134 of the Criminal Justice Act 1988 (c. 33) (torture).

49. An offence under section 1 of the Road Traffic Act 1988 (c. 52) (causing death by dangerous driving).

50. An offence under section 3A of that Act (causing death by careless driving when under influence of drink or drugs).

51. An offence under section 1 of the Aviation and Maritime Security Act 1990 (c. 31) (endangering safety at aerodromes).

52. An offence under section 9 of that Act (hijacking of ships).

53. An offence under section 10 of that Act (seizing or exercising control of fixed platforms).

54. An offence under section 11 of that Act (destroying fixed platforms or endangering their safety).

55. An offence under section 12 of that Act (other acts endangering or likely to endanger safe navigation).

56. An offence under section 13 of that Act (offences involving threats).

57. An offence under section 4 of the Protection from Harassment Act 1997 (c. 40) (putting people in fear of violence).

58. An offence under section 29 of the Crime and Disorder Act 1998 (c. 37) (racially or religiously aggravated assaults).

59. An offence falling within section 31(1)(a) or (b) of that Act (racially or religiously aggravated offences under section 4 or 4A of the Public Order Act 1986 (c. 64)).

60. An offence under Part II of the Channel Tunnel (Security) Order 1994 (S.I. 1994/570) (offences relating to Channel Tunnel trains and the tunnel system).

61. An offence under section 51 or 52 of the International Criminal Court Act 2001 (c. 17) (genocide, crimes against humanity, war crimes and related offences), other than one involving murder.

62. An offence under section 47 of this Act, where the victim or (as the case may be) other party was 16 or over.

63. An offence under any of sections 48 to 53 or 57 to 59 of this Act.

Scotland

64. Murder.

65. Culpable homicide.

66. Assault.

67. Assault and robbery.

68. Abduction.

69. Plagium.

70. Wrongful imprisonment.

71. Threatening personal violence.

72. Breach of the peace inferring personal violence.

73. Wilful fireraising.

74. Culpable and reckless fireraising.

75. Mobbing and rioting.

76. An offence under section 2 of the Explosive Substances Act 1883 (c. 3) (causing explosion likely to endanger life or property).

77. An offence under section 3 of that Act (attempt to cause explosion, or making or keeping explosives with intent to endanger life or property).

78. An offence under section 12 of the Children and Young Persons (Scotland) Act 1937 (c. 37) (cruelty to persons under 16).

79. An offence under section 16 of the Firearms Act 1968 (c. 27) (possession of firearm with intent to endanger life).

80. An offence under section 16A of that Act (possession of firearm with intent to cause fear of violence).

81. An offence under section 17(1) of that Act (use of firearm to resist arrest).

82. An offence under section 17(2) of that Act (possession of firearm at time of committing or being arrested for offence specified in Schedule 1 to that Act).

83. An offence under section 18 of that Act (carrying a firearm with criminal intent).

84. An offence under section 1 of the Taking of Hostages Act 1982 (c. 28) (hostage-taking).

85. An offence under section 1 of the Aviation Security Act 1982 (c. 36) (hijacking).

86. An offence under section 2 of that Act (destroying, damaging or endangering safety of aircraft).

87. An offence under section 3 of that Act (other acts endangering or likely to endanger safety of aircraft).

88. An offence under section 4 of that Act (offences in relation to certain dangerous articles).

89. An offence under section 105 of the Mental Health (Scotland) Act 1984 (c. 36) (ill-treatment of patients).

90. An offence under section 1 of the Prohibition of Female Circumcision Act 1985 (c. 38) (prohibition of female circumcision).

91. An offence under section 134 of the Criminal Justice Act 1988 (c. 33) (torture).

92. An offence under section 1 of the Road Traffic Act 1988 (c. 52) (causing death by dangerous driving).

93. An offence under section 3A of that Act (causing death by careless driving when under influence of drink or drugs).

94. An offence under section 1 of the Aviation and Maritime Security Act 1990 (c. 31) (endangering safety at aerodromes).

95. An offence under section 9 of that Act (hijacking of ships).

96. An offence under section 10 of that Act (seizing or exercising control of fixed platforms).

97. An offence under section 11 of that Act (destroying fixed platforms or endangering their safety).

98. An offence under section 12 of that Act (other acts endangering or likely to endanger safe navigation).

99. An offence under section 13 of that Act (offences involving threats).

100. An offence under Part II of the Channel Tunnel (Security) Order 1994 (S.I. 1994/570) (offences relating to Channel Tunnel trains and the tunnel system).

101. An offence under section 7 of the Criminal Law (Consolidation) (Scotland) Act 1995 (c. 39) (procuring).

102. An offence under section 9 of that Act (permitting girl to use premises for intercourse).

103. An offence under section 11 of that Act (trading in prostitution and brothel-keeping).

104. An offence under section 12 of that Act (allowing child to be in brothel).

105. An offence under section 13(9) of that Act (living on earnings of male prostitution etc.).

106. An offence under section 50A of that Act (racially-aggravated harassment).

107. An offence under section 51 or 52 of the International Criminal Court Act 2001 (c. 17) (genocide, crimes against humanity, war crimes and related offences), other than one involving murder.

108. An offence under section 1 of the International Criminal Court (Scotland) Act 2001 (asp 13) (genocide, crimes against humanity, war crimes and related offences as specified in Schedule 1 to that Act).

109. An offence under section 22 of the Criminal Justice (Scotland) Act 2003 (asp 7) (traffic in prostitution etc.).

110. An offence to which section 74 of that Act applies (offences aggravated by religious prejudice).

111. An offence under section 315 of the Mental Health (Care and Treatment) (Scotland) Act 2003 (asp 13) (ill-treatment and wilful neglect of mentally disordered person).

Northern Ireland

112. Murder.

113. Manslaughter.

114. Kidnapping.

115. Riot.

116. Affray.

117. False imprisonment.

118. An offence under section 4 of the Offences against the Person Act 1861 (c. 100) (soliciting murder).

119. An offence under section 16 of that Act (threats to kill).

120. An offence under section 18 of that Act (wounding with intent to cause grievous bodily harm).

121. An offence under section 20 of that Act (malicious wounding).

122. An offence under section 21 of that Act (attempting to choke, suffocate or strangle in order to commit or assist in committing an indictable offence).

123. An offence under section 22 of that Act (using chloroform etc. to commit or assist in the committing of any indictable offence).

124. An offence under section 23 of that Act (maliciously administering poison etc. so as to endanger life or inflict grievous bodily harm).

125. An offence under section 27 of that Act (abandoning children).

126. An offence under section 28 of that Act (causing bodily injury by explosives).

127. An offence under section 29 of that Act (using explosives etc. with intent to do grievous bodily harm).

128. An offence under section 30 of that Act (placing explosives with intent to do bodily injury).

129. An offence under section 31 of that Act (setting spring guns etc. with intent to do grievous bodily harm).

130. An offence under section 32 of that Act (endangering the safety of railway passengers).

131. An offence under section 35 of that Act (injuring persons by furious driving).

132. An offence under section 37 of that Act (assaulting officer preserving wreck).

133. An offence under section 47 of that Act of assault occasioning actual bodily harm.

134. An offence under section 2 of the Explosive Substances Act 1883 (c. 3) (causing explosion likely to endanger life or property).

135. An offence under section 3 of that Act (attempt to cause explosion, or making or keeping explosive with intent to endanger life or property).

136. An offence under section 25 of the Criminal Justice (Northern Ireland) Act 1945 (c. 15) (child destruction).

137. An offence under section 1 of the Infanticide Act (Northern Ireland) 1939 (c. 5) (infanticide).

138. An offence under section 7(1)(b) of the Criminal Justice (Miscellaneous Provisions) Act (Northern Ireland) 1968 (c. 28) (assault with intent to resist arrest).

139. An offence under section 20 of the Children and Young Persons Act (Northern Ireland) 1968 (c. 34) (cruelty to children).

140. An offence under section 8 of the Theft Act (Northern Ireland) 1969 (c. 16) (robbery or assault with intent to rob).

141. An offence under section 9 of that Act of burglary with intent to—
    (a) inflict grievous bodily harm on a person, or
    (b) do unlawful damage to a building or anything in it.

142. An offence under section 10 of that Act (aggravated burglary).

143. An offence of arson under Article 3 of the Criminal Damage (Northern Ireland) Order 1977 (S.I. 1977/426 (N.I. 4)).

144. An offence under Article 3(2) of that Order (destroying or damaging property) other than an offence of arson.

145. An offence under Article 17 of the Firearms (Northern Ireland) Order 1981 (S.I. 1981/155 (N.I. 2)) (possession of firearm with intent to endanger life).

146. An offence under Article 17A of that Order (possession of firearm with intent to cause fear of violence).

147. An offence under Article 18(1) of that Order (use of firearm to resist arrest).

148. An offence under Article 18(2) of that Order (possession of firearm at time of committing or being arrested for an offence specified in Schedule 1 to that Order).

149. An offence under Article 19 of that Order (carrying a firearm with criminal intent).

150. An offence under section 1 of the Taking of Hostages Act 1982 (c. 28) (hostage-taking).

151. An offence under section 1 of the Aviation Security Act 1982 (c. 36) (hijacking).

152. An offence under section 2 of that Act (destroying, damaging or endangering safety of aircraft).

153. An offence under section 3 of that Act (other acts endangering or likely to endanger safety of aircraft).

154. An offence under section 4 of that Act (offences in relation to certain dangerous articles).

155. An offence under section 1 of the Prohibition of Female Circumcision Act 1985 (c. 38) (prohibition of female circumcision).

156. An offence under Article 121 of the Mental Health (Northern Ireland) Order 1986 (S.I. 1986/595 (N.I. 4) (ill-treatment of patients).

157. An offence under section 134 of the Criminal Justice Act 1988 (c. 33) (torture).

158. An offence under section 1 of the Aviation and Maritime Security Act 1990 (c. 31) (endangering safety at aerodromes).

159. An offence under section 9 of that Act (hijacking of ships).

160. An offence under section 10 of that Act (seizing or exercising control of fixed platforms).

161. An offence under section 11 of that Act (destroying fixed platforms or endangering their safety).

162. An offence under section 12 of that Act (other acts endangering or likely to endanger safe navigation).

163. An offence under section 13 of that Act (offences involving threats).

164. An offence under Article 9 of the Road Traffic (Northern Ireland) Order 1995 (S.I. 1995/2994 (N.I. 18)) (causing death or grievous bodily injury by dangerous driving).

165. An offence under Article 14 of that Order (causing death or grievous bodily injury by careless driving when under the influence of drink or drugs).

166. An offence under Article 6 of the Protection from Harassment (Northern Ireland) Order 1997 (S.I. 1997/1180 (N.I. 9) (putting people in fear of violence).

167. An offence under section 66 of the Police (Northern Ireland) Act 1998 (c. 32) (assaulting or obstructing a constable etc.).

168. An offence under Part II of the Channel Tunnel (Security) Order 1994 (S.I. 1994/570) (offences relating to Channel Tunnel trains and the tunnel system).

169. An offence under section 51 or 52 of the International Criminal Court Act 2001 (c. 17) (genocide, crimes against humanity, war crimes and related offences), other than one involving murder.

170. An offence under section 47 of this Act, where the victim or (as the case may be) other party was 17 or over.

171. An offence under any of sections 48 to 53 or 57 to 59 of this Act.

Service offences

172. An offence under—
    (a) section 70 of the Army Act 1955 (3 & 4 Eliz. 2 c. 18),
    (b) section 70 of the Air Force Act 1955 (3 & 4 Eliz. 2 c. 19), or
    (c) section 42 of the Naval Discipline Act 1957 (c. 53),
of which the corresponding civil offence (within the meaning of that Act) is an offence under a provision listed in any of paragraphs 1 to 63.

General

173. A reference in a preceding paragraph to an offence includes—
    (a) a reference to an attempt, conspiracy or incitement to commit that offence, and
    (b) a reference to aiding, abetting, counselling or procuring the commission of that offence.

174. A reference in a preceding paragraph to a person's age is a reference to his age at the time of the offence.

SCHEDULE 6

Section 139

MINOR AND CONSEQUENTIAL AMENDMENTS

Vagrancy Act 1824 (c. 83)

1. In section 4 of the Vagrancy Act 1824 (rogues and vagabonds) except so far as extending to Northern Ireland, omit the words from 'every person wilfully' to 'female'.

2. In section 4 of the Vagrancy Act 1824 as it extends to Northern Ireland, omit the words from 'wilfully, openly, lewdly' to 'any female; or'.

Town Police Clauses Act 1847 (c. 89)

3. In section 28 of the Town Police Clauses Act 1847 (penalty for committing certain acts), omit 'Every person who wilfully and indecently exposes his person:'.

Offences against the Persons Act 1861 (c. 100)

4. In the Offences against the Person Act 1861, omit sections 61 and 62.

Criminal Law Amendment Act 1885 (c. 69)

5. In the Criminal Law Amendment Act 1885, omit—
    (a) in section 2, subsections (2) to (4), and
    (b) section 11.

Vagrancy Act 1898 (c. 39)

6. The Vagrancy Act 1898 ceases to have effect.

Children and Young Persons Act 1933 (c. 12)

7. In Schedule 1 to the Children and Young Persons Act 1933 (offences to which special provisions of that Act apply), for the entry relating to offences under the Sexual Offences Act 1956 (c. 69) substitute—

'Any offence against a child or young person under any of sections 1 to 41, 47 to 53, 57 to 61, 66 and 67 of the Sexual Offences Act 2003, or any attempt to commit such an offence.

Any offence under section 62 or 63 of the Sexual Offences Act 2003 where the intended offence was an offence against a child or young person, or any attempt to commit such an offence.'

Visiting Forces Act 1952 (c. 67)

8.—(1) Paragraph 1 of the Schedule to the Visiting Forces Act 1952 (offences referred to in section 3 of that Act) is amended as follows.
    (2) Before sub-paragraph (a) insert—

'(za) rape and buggery (offences under the law of Northern Ireland);'.

    (3) In sub-paragraph (a), omit 'rape' and 'buggery'.

    (4) In sub-paragraph (b), after paragraph (xii) insert—

'(xiii) Part 1 of the Sexual Offences Act 2003.'

Army Act 1955 (3 & 4 Eliz. 2 c. 18)

9. In section 70(4) of the Army Act 1955 (person not to be charged with an offence committed in the United Kingdom where corresponding civil offence is within the subsection)—
    (a) omit 'or rape', and
    (b) after 'International Criminal Court Act 2001' insert 'or an offence under section 1 of the Sexual Offences Act 2003 (rape)'.

Air Force Act 1955 (3 & 4 Eliz. 2.c. 19)

10. In section 70(4) of the Air Force Act 1955 (person not to be charged with an offence committed in the United Kingdom where corresponding civil offence is within the subsection)—
    (a) omit 'or rape', and
    (b) after 'International Criminal Court Act 2001' insert 'or an offence under section 1 of the Sexual Offences Act 2003 (rape)'.

Sexual Offences Act 1956 (c. 37)

11. In the Sexual Offences Act 1956, omit—
    (a) sections 1 to 7, 9 to 17, 19 to 32 and 41 to 47 (offences), and
    (b) in Schedule 2 (prosecution, punishment etc.), paragraphs 1 to 32.

Naval Discipline Act 1957 (c. 53)

12. In section 48(2) of the Naval Discipline Act 1957 (courts-martial not to have jurisdiction as regards certain offences committed in the United Kingdom)—
    (a) omit 'or rape', and
    (b) before 'committed on shore' insert 'or an offence under section 1 of the Sexual Offences Act 2003 (rape)'.

Mental Health Act 1959 (c. 72)

13. In the Mental Health Act 1959, omit sections 127 (amendment of Sexual Offences Act 1956) and 128 (sexual intercourse with patients).

Indecency with Children Act 1960 (c. 33)

14. The Indecency with Children Act 1960 ceases to have effect.

Sexual Offences Act 1967 (c. 60)

15. In the Sexual Offences Act 1967, omit the following—
    (a) section 1 (amendment of law relating to homosexual acts in private),
    (b) section 4 (procuring others to commit homosexual acts),
    (c) section 5 (living on earnings of male prostitution),
    (d) section 7 (time limit on prosecutions),
    (e) section 8 (restriction on prosecutions), and
    (f) section 10 (past offences).

Firearms Act 1968 (c. 27)

16. In Schedule 1 to the Firearms Act 1968 (offences to which section 17(2) of that Act applies), for paragraph 6 substitute—

'6. Offences under any of the following provisions of the Sexual Offences Act 2003—
    (a) section 1 (rape);

(b) section 2 (assault by penetration);

(c) section 4 (causing a person to engage in sexual activity without consent), where the activity caused involved penetration within subsection (4)(a) to (d) of that section;

(d) section 5 (rape of a child under 13);

(e) section 6 (assault of a child under 13 by penetration);

(f) section 8 (causing or inciting a child under 13 to engage in sexual activity), where an activity involving penetration within subsection (3)(a) to (d) of that section was caused;

(g) section 30 (sexual activity with a person with a mental disorder impeding choice), where the touching involved penetration within subsection (3)(a) to (d) of that section;

(h) section 31 (causing or inciting a person, with a mental disorder impeding choice, to engage in sexual activity), where an activity involving penetration within subsection (3)(a) to (d) of that section was caused.'

Theft Act 1968 (c. 60)

17. In section 9 of the Theft Act 1968 (burglary), in subsection (2) omit 'or raping any person'.

Children and Young Persons Act (Northern Ireland) 1968 (c. 34 (N.I.))

18.—(1) The Children and Young Persons Act (Northern Ireland) 1968 is amended as follows.

(2) In section 21 (causing or encouraging seduction or prostitution of girl under 17), omit—

(a) in subsection (1), 'or the prostitution of,', and

(b) in subsection (2), 'or the prostitution of,' and 'or who has become a prostitute,'.

(3) In Schedule 1 (offences against children and young persons to which special provisions of that Act apply), at the end insert—

'Any offence against a child or young person under any of sections 15 to 19, 47 to 59, 66 and 67 of the Sexual Offences Act 2003 or any attempt to commit such an offence.'

Rehabilitation of Offenders Act 1974 (c. 53)

19. In section 7 of the Rehabilitation of Offenders Act 1974 (limitations on rehabilitation under that Act), in subsection (2), for paragraph (bb) substitute—

'(bb) in any proceedings under Part 2 of the Sexual Offences Act 2003, or on appeal from any such proceedings;'.

Sexual Offences (Amendment) Act 1976 (c. 82)

20.—(1) The Sexual Offences (Amendment) Act 1976 is amended as follows.

(2) In section 1 (meaning of 'rape'), omit subsection (2).

(3) In section 7 (citation, interpretation etc.)—

(a) for subsection (2) substitute—

'(2) In this Act—

(a) "a rape offence" means any of the following—

(i) an offence under section 1 of the Sexual Offences Act 2003 (rape);

(ii) an offence under section 2 of that Act (assault by penetration);

(iii)   an offence under section 4 of that Act (causing a person to engage in sexual activity without consent), where the activity caused involved penetration within subsection (4)(a) to (d) of that section;

(iv)   an offence under section 5 of that Act (rape of a child under 13);

(v)   an offence under section 6 of that Act (assault of a child under 13 by penetration);

(vi)   an offence under section 8 of that Act (causing or inciting a child under 13 to engage in sexual activity), where an activity involving penetration within subsection (3)(a) to (d) of that section was caused;

(vii)   an offence under section 30 of that Act (sexual activity with a person with a mental disorder impeding choice), where the touching involved penetration within subsection (3)(a) to (d) of that section;

(viii)   an offence under section 31 of that Act (causing or inciting a person, with a mental disorder impeding choice, to engage in sexual activity), where an activity involving penetration within subsection (3)(a) to (d) of that section was caused;

(ix)   an attempt, conspiracy or incitement to commit an offence within any of paragraphs (i) to (vii);

(x)   aiding, abetting, counselling or procuring the commission of such an offence or an attempt to commit such an offence.

(b)   the use in any provision of the word "man" without the addition of the word "boy" does not prevent the provision applying to any person to whom it would have applied if both words had been used, and similarly with the words "woman" and "girl".';

(b)   omit subsection (3).

Criminal Law Act 1977 (c. 45)

21. In the Criminal Law Act 1977, omit section 54 (inciting girl under 16 to have incestuous sexual intercourse).

Internationally Protected Persons Act 1978 (c. 17)

22. In section 1 of the Internationally Protected Persons Act 1978 (attacks and threats of attacks on protected persons)—

(a)   in subsection (1)(a)—

(i)   omit 'rape,';

(ii)   after 'Explosive Substances Act 1883' insert 'or an offence listed in subsection (1A)';

(b)   after subsection (1) insert—

'(1A)   The offences mentioned in subsection (1)(a) are—

(a)   in Scotland or Northern Ireland, rape;

(b)   an offence under section 1 or 2 of the Sexual Offences Act 2003;

(c)   an offence under section 4 of that Act, where the activity caused involved penetration within subsection (4)(a) to (d) of that section;

(d)   an offence under section 5 or 6 of that Act;

(e)   an offence under section 8 of that Act, where an activity involving penetration within subsection (3)(a) to (d) of that section was caused;

(f)   an offence under section 30 of that Act, where the touching involved penetration within subsection (3)(a) to (d) of that section;

(g)   an offence under section 31 of that Act, where an activity involving penetration within subsection (3)(a) to (d) of that section was caused.'

Suppression of Terrorism Act 1978 (c. 26)

23.—(1) Schedule 1 to the Suppression of Terrorism Act 1978 (offences for the purposes of that Act) is amended as follows.

(2) In paragraph 3, after 'Rape' insert 'under the law of Scotland or Northern Ireland'.

(3) For paragraph 9 substitute—

'9. An offence under any of the following provisions of the Sexual Offences Act 2003—

(a) sections 1 or 2 (rape, assault by penetration);

(b) section 4 (causing a person to engage in sexual activity without consent), where the activity caused involved penetration within subsection (4)(a) to (d) of that section;

(c) section 5 or 6 (rape of a child under 13, assault of a child under 13 by penetration);

(d) section 8 (causing or inciting a child under 13 to engage in sexual activity), where an activity involving penetration within subsection (3)(a) to (d) of that section was caused;

(e) section 30 (sexual activity with a person with a mental disorder impeding choice), where the touching involved penetration within subsection (3)(a) to (d) of that section;

(f) section 31 (causing or inciting a person, with a mental disorder impeding choice, to engage in sexual activity), where an activity involving penetration within subsection (3)(a) to (d) of that section was caused.'.

Protection of Children Act 1978 (c. 37)

24. In section 1(1) of the Protection of Children Act 1978 (indecent photographs of children), at the beginning insert 'Subject to sections 1A and 1B,'.

Rehabilitation of Offenders (Northern Ireland) Order 1978 (S.I. 1978/1908 (N.I. 27))

25. In Article 8 of the Rehabilitation of Offenders (Northern Ireland) Order 1978 (limitations on rehabilitation under that Order), in paragraph (2), for sub-paragraph (bb) substitute—

'(bb) in any proceedings under Part 2 of the Sexual Offences Act 2003, or on appeal from any such proceedings;'.

Magistrates' Courts Act 1980 (c. 43)

26.—(1) The Magistrates' Courts Act 1980 is amended as follows.

(2) In section 103 (evidence of persons under 14 in committal proceedings), in subsection (2)(c), after 'the Protection of Children Act 1978' insert 'or Part 1 of the Sexual Offences Act 2003'.

(3) In Schedule 7 (consequential amendments), omit paragraph 18.

Criminal Justice Act 1982 (c. 48)

27. In the Criminal Justice Act 1982, in Part 2 of Schedule 1 (offences excluded from early release provisions), after the entry relating to the Proceeds of Crime Act 2002 (c. 29) insert—

'Sexual Offences Act 2003

Sections 1 and 2 (rape, assault by penetration).

Section 4 (causing a person to engage in sexual activity without consent), where the activity caused involved penetration within subsection (4)(a) to (d) of that section.

Sections 5 and 6 (rape of a child under 13, assault of a child under 13 by penetration).

Section 8 (causing or inciting a child under 13 to engage in sexual activity), where an activity involving penetration within subsection (3)(a) to (d) of that section was caused.

Section 30 (sexual activity with a person with a mental disorder impeding choice), where the touching involved penetration within subsection (3)(a) to (d) of that section.

Section 31 (causing or inciting a person, with a mental disorder impeding choice, to engage in sexual activity), where an activity involving penetration within subsection (3)(a) to (d) of that section was caused.'

Police and Criminal Evidence Act 1984 (c. 60)

28.—(1) The Police and Criminal Evidence Act 1984 is amended as follows.

(2) In section 80(7) (sexual offences for purposes of compellability of spouse), after 'the Protection of Children Act 1978' insert 'or Part 1 of the Sexual Offences Act 2003'.

(3) In Schedule 1A (specific arrestable offences), after paragraph 25 insert—

'Sexual Offences Act 2003

26. An offence under—
    (a) section 66 of the Sexual Offences Act 2003 (exposure);
    (b) section 67 of that Act (voyeurism);
    (c) section 69 of that Act (intercourse with an animal);
    (d) section 70 of that Act (sexual penetration of a corpse); or
    (e) section 71 of that Act (sexual activity in public lavatory).'

(4) In Part 2 of Schedule 5 (serious arrestable offences), after the entry relating to the Obscene Publications Act 1959 (c. 66) insert—

'Sexual Offences Act 2003

16. Section 1 (rape).
17. Section 2 (assault by penetration).
18. Section 4 (causing a person to engage in sexual activity without consent), where the activity caused involved penetration within subsection (4)(a) to (d) of that section.
19. Section 5 (rape of a child under 13).
20. Section 6 (assault of a child under 13 by penetration).
21. Section 8 (causing or inciting a child under 13 to engage in sexual activity), where an activity involving penetration within subsection (3)(a) to (d) of that section was caused.
22. Section 30 (sexual activity with a person with a mental disorder impeding choice), where the touching involved penetration within subsection (3)(a) to (d) of that section.
23. Section 31 (causing or inciting a person, with a mental disorder impeding choice, to engage in sexual activity), where an activity involving penetration within subsection (3)(a) to (d) of that section was caused.'

Criminal Justice Act 1988 (c. 33)

29.—(1) The Criminal Justice Act 1988 is amended as follows.

(2) In section 32 (evidence through television links), in subsection (2)(c), after 'the Protection of Children Act 1978' insert 'or Part 1 of the Sexual Offences Act 2003'.

(3) In section 160(1) (possession of indecent photograph of child), at the beginning insert 'Subject to subsection (1A),'.

Criminal Justice Act 1991 (c. 53)

30. In section 34A of the Criminal Justice Act 1991 (power to release short-term prisoners on licence), in subsection (2)(da), for 'Part I of the Sex Offenders Act 1997' substitute 'Part 2 of the Sexual Offences Act 2003'.

Sexual Offences (Amendment) Act 1992 (c.34)

31.—(1) Section 2 of the Sexual Offences (Amendment) Act 1992 (offences to which that Act applies) is amended as follows.

(2) In subsection (1) (England and Wales)—

    (a) after paragraph (d) insert—

        '(da) any offence under any of the provisions of Part 1 of the Sexual Offences Act 2003 except section 64, 65, 69 or 71;';

    (b) in paragraph (e) for '(d)' substitute '(da)'.

(3) In subsection (3) (Northern Ireland)—

    (a) after paragraph (hh) insert—

        '(ha) any offence under any of sections 15 to 21, 47 to 53, 57 to 59, 66, 67, 70 and 72 of the Sexual Offences Act 2003.';

    (b) in paragraph (i) for '(hh)' substitute '(ha)'.

Criminal Justice and Public Order Act 1994 (c. 33)

32.—(1) The Criminal Justice and Public Order Act 1994 is amended as follows.

(2) In section 25 (no bail if previous conviction for certain offences), for subsection (2)(d) and (e) substitute—

    '(d)   rape under the law of Scotland or Northern Ireland;

    (e)   an offence under section 1 of the Sexual Offences Act 1956 (rape);

    (f)   an offence under section 1 of the Sexual Offences Act 2003 (rape);

    (g)   an offence under section 2 of that Act (assault by penetration);

    (h)   an offence under section 4 of that Act (causing a person to engage in sexual activity without consent), where the activity caused involved penetration within subsection (4)(a) to (d) of that section;

    (i)   an offence under section 5 of that Act (rape of a child under 13);

    (j)   an offence under section 6 of that Act (assault of a child under 13 by penetration);

    (k)   an offence under section 8 of that Act (causing or inciting a child under 13 to engage in sexual activity), where an activity involving penetration within subsection (3)(a) to (d) of that section was caused;

    (l)   an offence under section 30 of that Act (sexual activity with a person with a mental disorder impeding choice), where the touching involved penetration within subsection (3)(a) to (d) of that section;

    (m)   an offence under section 31 of that Act (causing or inciting a person, with a mental disorder impeding choice, to engage in sexual activity), where an activity involving penetration within subsection (3)(a) to (d) of that section was caused;

    (n)   an attempt to commit an offence within any of paragraphs (d) to (m).'

(3) Omit sections 142 to 144.

(4) In Schedule 10 (consequential amendments) omit paragraphs 26 and 35(2) and (4).

Criminal Law (Consolidation) (Scotland) Act 1995 (c. 39)

33. In section 5(6) of the Criminal Law (Consolidation) (Scotland) Act 1995 (which relates to construing the expression 'a like offence'), after paragraph (c) insert

'or (cc) any of sections 9 to 14 of the Sexual Offences Act 2003;'.

Criminal Injuries Compensation Act 1995 (c. 53)

34. In section 11 of the Criminal Injuries Compensation Act 1995 (approval by parliament of certain alterations to the Tariff or provisions of the Scheme)—
    (a) in subsection (3)(d), after "rape" insert 'or an offence under section 30 of the Sexual Offences Act 2003';
    (b) after subsection (8) insert—

'(9) In subsection (3) "rape", in relation to anything done in England and Wales, means an offence under section 1 or 5 of the Sexual Offences Act 2003.'

Sexual Offences (Conspiracy and Incitement) Act 1996 (c.29)

35. In the Schedule to the Sexual Offences (Conspiracy and Incitement) Act 1996 (sexual offences for the purposes of that Act), in paragraph 1—
    (a) for sub-paragraph (1)(b) substitute—

'(b) an offence under any of sections 1 to 12, 14 and 15 to 26 of the Sexual Offences Act 2003.';

    (b) in sub-paragraph (2), for 'In sub-paragraph (1)(a), sub-paragraphs (i), (iv), (v) and (vi) do' substitute 'Sub-paragraph (1)(b) does'.

Sexual Offences (Protected Material) Act 1997 (c. 39)

36. In the Schedule to the Sexual Offences (Protected Material) Act 1997 (sexual offences for the purposes of that Act)—
    (a) after paragraph 5 insert—

'5A. Any offence under any provision of Part 1 of the Sexual Offences Act 2003 except section 64, 65, 69 or 71.';

    (b) in paragraph 6, for '1 to 5' substitute '5 and 5A'.

Sex Offenders Act 1997 (c. 51)

37. The Sex Offenders Act 1997 ceases to have effect.

Crime and Disorder Act 1998 (c. 37)

38.—(1) The Crime and Disorder Act 1998 is amended as follows.
    (2) Omit sections 2, 2A, 2B and 3 (sex offender orders and interim orders).
    (3) In section 4 (appeals against orders)—
        (a) in subsection (1), omit 'a sex offender order or an order under section 2A above', and
        (b) in subsection (3), omit 'or 2(6) above'.

(4) Omit section 20.

(5) In section 21 (procedural provisions with respect to orders)—
    (a) omit subsection (2);
    (b) in subsection (4)—
        (i) omit 'or (2)'; and
        (ii) for 'either of those subsections' substitute 'that subsection';
    (c) in subsection (5), omit 'or 20';
    (d) in subsection (6), omit 'and sex offender orders' and 'or 20(4)(a)';
    (e) in subsection (7)(b)(i), omit 'or, as the case may be, chief constable';
    (f) omit subsections (7A) and (7B); and
    (g) in subsection (10), omit 'or 20'.

(6) Omit section 21A.

(7) In section 22 (offences in connection with breach of orders), omit subsections (6) and (7).

(8) In Schedule 8 (minor and consequential amendments), omit paragraph 144.

Criminal Justice (Children) (Northern Ireland) Order 1998 (S.I. 1998/1504 (N.I. 9))

39. In paragraph 1 of Schedule 1 to the Criminal Justice (Children) (Northern Ireland) Order 1998—
    (a) omit sub-paragraphs (c), (e) and (j);
    (b) after sub-paragraph (l) insert—

        '(m) Section 69 of the Sexual Offences Act 2003.'

Criminal Justice (Northern Ireland) Order 1998 (S.I. 1998/2839 (N.I. 20))

40. In the Criminal Justice (Northern Ireland) Order 1998, omit Articles 6, 6A, 6B and 7.

Youth Justice and Criminal Evidence Act 1999 (c. 23)

41.—(1) The Youth Justice and Criminal Evidence Act 1999 is amended as follows.

(2) In section 35 (cross examination of child witnesses), in subsection (3)(a), after sub-paragraph (v) insert

    'or (vi) Part 1 of the Sexual Offences Act 2003;'.

(3) In section 62 (meaning of 'sexual offence' etc.), for subsection (1) substitute—

    '(1) In this Part "sexual offence" means any offence under Part 1 of the Sexual Offences Act 2003.'

Criminal Evidence (Northern Ireland) Order 1999 (S.I. 1999/2789 (N.I. 8))

42.—(1) The Criminal Evidence (Northern Ireland) Order 1999 is amended as follows.

(2) In Article 3(1) (meaning of 'sexual offence'), after sub-paragraph (gg) insert—

    '(ga) any offence under any of sections 15 to 21, 47 to 53, 57 to 59, 66, 67, and 70 to 72 of the Sexual Offences Act 2003.'

(3) In Article 23 (protection of child complainants and other child witnesses)—
    (a) in paragraph (3), after sub-paragraph (c) insert—

'(cc) any offence under any of sections 15 to 21, 47 to 53, 57 to 59, 66 to 72 of the Sexual Offences Act 2003;';

  (b) in paragraph (4)(a), after '(3)(a)' insert 'or (cc)'.

Powers of Criminal Courts (Sentencing) Act 2000 (c. 6)

43.—(1) The Powers of Criminal Courts (Sentencing) Act 2000 is amended as follows.

(2) In section 91 (power to detain offenders under 18 convicted of certain offences), for subsection (1)(b) and (c) substitute—

'(b) an offence under section 3 of the Sexual Offences Act 2003 (in this section, 'the 2003 Act') (sexual assault); or

(c) an offence under section 13 of the 2003 Act (child sex offences committed by children or young persons); or

(d) an offence under section 25 of the 2003 Act (sexual activity with a child family member); or

(e) an offence under section 26 of the 2003 Act (inciting a child family member to engage in sexual activity).'

(3) In section 109 (life sentence for second serious offence), in subsection (5), after paragraph (f) insert—

'(fa) an offence under section 1 or 2 of the Sexual Offences Act 2003 (in this section, "the 2003 Act") (rape, assault by penetration);

(fb) an offence under section 4 of the 2003 Act (causing a person to engage in sexual activity without consent), where the activity caused involved penetration within subsection (4)(a) to (d) of that section;

(fc) an offence under section 5 or 6 of the 2003 Act (rape of a child under 13, assault of a child under 13 by penetration);

(fd) an offence under section 8 of the 2003 Act (causing or inciting a child under 13 to engage in sexual activity), where an activity involving penetration within subsection (3)(a) to (d) of that section was caused;

(fe) an offence under section 30 of the 2003 Act (sexual activity with a person with a mental disorder impeding choice), where the touching involved penetration within subsection (3)(a) to (d) of that section;

(ff) an offence under section 31 of the 2003 Act (causing or inciting a person, with a mental disorder impeding choice, to engage in sexual activity), where an activity involving penetration within subsection (3)(a) to (d) of that section was caused;

(fg) an attempt to commit an offence within any of paragraphs (fa) to (ff);'.

(4) In section 161 (definition of 'sexual offence' etc.), in subsection (2)—

  (a) after paragraph (f) insert—

'(fa) an offence under any provision of Part 1 of the Sexual Offences Act 2003 except section 52, 53 or 71;';

  (b) in paragraph (g), for '(a) to (f)' substitute '(f) and (fa)'.

(5) In Schedule 9 (consequential amendments), omit paragraphs 189, 190 and 193.

Criminal Justice and Courts Services Act 2000 (c. 43)

44.—(1) The Criminal Justice and Courts Services Act 2000 is amended as follows.

(2) Omit sections 39 and 66.

(3) In section 68 (sexual and violent offenders for the purposes of risk assessment etc.), in subsection (2), for 'Part I of the Sex Offenders Act 1997' substitute 'Part 2 of the Sexual Offences Act 2003'.

(4) In section 69 (duties of local probation boards in connection with victims of certain offences), in subsection (8)(b), for 'Part I of the Sex Offenders Act 1997' substitute 'Part 2 of the Sexual Offences Act 2003'.

(5) In Schedule 4 (offences against children for the purposes of disqualification orders)—

    (a) in paragraph 1, for sub-paragraph (m) substitute—

> '(m) an offence under any of sections 5 to 26 and 47 to 50 of the Sexual Offences Act 2003 (offences against children).';

    (b) in paragraph 2, for sub-paragraph (n) substitute—

> '(n) an offence under any of sections 1 to 4, 30 to 41, 52, 53, 57 to 61, 66 and 67 of the Sexual Offences Act 2003.';

    (c) in paragraph 3, after sub-paragraph (s) insert—

> '(sa) he commits an offence under section 62 or 63 of the Sexual Offences Act 2003 (committing an offence or trespassing with intent to commit a sexual offence) in a case where the intended offence was an offence against a child.'

(6) Omit Schedule 5.

Sexual Offences (Amendment) Act 2000 (c. 44)

45.—(1) The Sexual Offences (Amendment) Act 2000 is amended as follows.

(2) In section 1 (reduction in age at which certain sexual acts are lawful), omit subsections (1) and (2).

(3) In section 2 (defences available to persons under age), omit subsections (1) to (3).

(4) Omit sections 3 and 4 (abuse of position of trust) except so far as extending to Scotland.

(5) Omit section 5 (notification requirements for offenders under section 3).

(6) In section 6 (meaning of 'sexual offence' for the purposes of certain enactments), omit subsection (1).

Proceeds of Crime Act 2002 (c. 29)

46.—(1) The Proceeds of Crime Act 2002 is amended as follows.

(2) In paragraph 4 of Schedule 2 (lifestyle offences: England and Wales), for sub-paragraph (2) substitute—

> '(2) An offence under any of sections 57 to 59 of the Sexual Offences Act 2003 (trafficking for sexual exploitation).'

(3) For paragraph 8 of that Schedule substitute—

> *'Prostitution and child sex*
>
> 8 (1) An offence under section 33 or 34 of the Sexual Offences Act 1956 (keeping or letting premises for use as a brothel).

(2) An offence under any of the following provisions of the Sexual Offences Act 2003—

    (a) section 14 (arranging or facilitating commission of a child sex offence);

    (b) section 48 (causing or inciting child prostitution or pornography);

    (c) section 49 (controlling a child prostitute or a child involved in pornography);

    (d) section 50 (arranging or facilitating child prostitution or pornography);

    (e) section 52 (causing or inciting prostitution for gain);

    (f) section 53 (controlling prostitution for gain).'

(4) In paragraph 4 of Schedule 5 (lifestyle offences: Northern Ireland), for sub-paragraph (2) substitute—

    '(2) An offence under any of sections 57 to 59 of the Sexual Offences Act 2003 (trafficking for sexual exploitation).'

(5) In paragraph 8 of that Schedule—

    (a) after sub-paragraph (1) insert—

    '(1A) An offence under any of the following provisions of the Sexual Offences Act 2003—

        (a) section 48 (causing or inciting child prostitution or pornography);

        (b) section 49 (controlling a child prostitute or a child involved in pornography);

        (c) section 50 (arranging or facilitating child prostitution or pornography);

        (d) section 52 (causing or inciting prostitution for gain);

        (e) section 53 (controlling prostitution for gain).';

    (b) omit sub-paragraphs (2) to (5).

Adoption and Children Act 2002 (c. 38)

47. In section 74 of the Adoption and Children Act 2002 (status conferred by adoption not to apply for the purposes of certain enactments), in subsection (1) for paragraphs (b) and (c) substitute

    'or (b) sections 64 and 65 of the Sexual Offences Act 2003 (sex with an adult relative).'

Nationality, Asylum and Immigration Act 2002 (c. 41)

48. In the Nationality, Asylum and Immigration Act 2002, omit sections 145 and 146 (traffic in prostitution).

Criminal Justice (Scotland) Act 2003 (asp 7)

49. In section 21(9) of the Criminal Justice (Scotland) Act 2003 (power of adjournment where person convicted of sexual offence or offence disclosing significant sexual aspects to behaviour in committing it), for the words from '—(a) "three weeks" ' to 'each case' substitute ' "four weeks" there were'.

Protection of Children and Vulnerable Adults (Northern Ireland) Order 2003 (S.I. 2003/417 (N.I. 4))

50. In paragraph 1 of Schedule 1 to the Protection of Children and Vulnerable Adults (Northern Ireland) Order 2003, after sub-paragraph (n) insert—

    '(o) any offence under any of sections 15 to 21 and 47 to 50 of the Sexual Offences Act 2003.'.

Access to Justice (Northern Ireland) Order 2003 (S.I. 2003/435 (N.I. 10))

51. In Schedule 2 to the Access to Justice (Northern Ireland) Order 2003, in paragraph 2(d)—
    (a) omit sub-paragraph (x),
    (b) omit 'or' at the end of sub-paragraph (xi),
    (c) at the end of sub-paragraph (xii) insert

    'or (xiii) under section 89, 90, 97, 100, 104, 108, 109, 114, 118, 123, 125 or 126 of the Sexual Offences Act 2003,'.

Criminal Justice (Northern Ireland) Order 2003 (S.I. 2003/1247 (N.I. 13))

52. In the Criminal Justice (Northern Ireland) Order 2003, omit—
    (a) in Article 19(4), sub-paragraph (a) and
    (b) in Schedule 1, paragraphs 1, 2, 20 and 21.

SCHEDULE 7

Section 140

REPEALS AND REVOCATIONS

Reference	*Extent of repeal or revocation*
Vagrancy Act 1824 (c. 83)	In section 4 except so far as extending to Northern Ireland, the words from 'every person wilfully' to 'female'. In section 4 as it extends to Northern Ireland, the words from 'wilfully, openly, lewdly' to 'any female; or'.
Town Police Clauses Act 1847 (c. 89)	In section 28 the words 'every person who wilfully and indecently exposes his person:'.
Offences Against the Person Act 1861 (c. 100)	Sections 61 and 62.
Criminal Law Amendment Act 1885 (c. 69)	Section 2(2) to (4). Section 11.
Vagrancy Act 1898 (c. 39)	The whole Act.
Criminal Law Amendment Act 1912 (c. 20)	Section 7.
Visiting Forces Act 1952 (c. 67)	In the Schedule, in paragraph 1(a) the words 'rape, buggery'; paragraph 1(b)(viii).
Army Act 1955 (3 & 4 Eliz. 2 c. 18)	In section 70(4), the words 'or rape'.

Reference	Extent of repeal or revocation
Air Force Act 1955 (3 & 4 Eliz. 2 c. 19)	In section 70(4), the words 'or rape'.
Sexual Offences Act 1956 (c. 69)	Sections 1 to 7. Sections 9 to 17. Sections 19 to 32. Sections 41 to 47. In Schedule 2, paragraphs 1 to 32.
Naval Discipline Act 1957 (c. 53)	In section 48(2), the words 'or rape'.
Mental Health Act 1959 (c. 72)	Sections 127 and 128.
Indecency with Children Act 1960 (c. 33)	The whole Act.
Sexual Offences Act 1967 (c. 60)	Section 1. Section 4. Section 5. Sections 7 and 8. Section 10.
Theft Act 1968 (c. 60)	In section 9(2), the words 'or raping any person'.
Children and Young Persons Act (Northern Ireland) 1968 (c. 34 (N.I.))	In section 21, in subsection (1) the words 'or the prostitution of,' and in subsection (2) the words 'or the prostitution of,' and 'or who has become a prostitute,'.
Criminal Justice Act 1972 (c. 71)	Section 48.
National Health Service Reorganisation Act 1973 (c. 32)	In Schedule 4, paragraph 92.
Sexual Offences (Amendment) Act 1976 (c. 82)	Section 1(2). Section 7(3).
Criminal Law Act 1977 (c. 45)	Section 54.
National Health Service Act 1977 (c. 49)	In Schedule 15, paragraph 29.
Internationally Protected Persons Act 1978 (c. 17)	In section 1(1)(a), the word 'rape,'.
Suppression of Terrorism Act 1978 (c. 26)	In section 4(1)(a), the word '11,'. In Schedule 1, paragraph 11.

Reference	Extent of repeal or revocation
Magistrates' Courts Act 1980 (c. 43)	In section 103(2)(c), the words from 'the Indecency with Children Act 1960' to '1977 or'. In Schedule 1, paragraphs 23, 27 and 32. In Schedule 7, paragraph 18.
Criminal Attempts Act 1981 (c. 47)	In section 4(5), paragraph (a) and the word 'and' immediately after it.
Magistrates' Courts (Northern Ireland) Order 1981 (S.I. 1981/1675 (N.I. 26))	In Article 29(1), the words from 'or with an offence under section 1(1)(b) of the Vagrancy Act 1898' to 'homosexual act'. In Schedule 2, paragraphs 5(c), 10(c) and 22.
Criminal Justice Act 1982 (c. 48)	In Schedule 1, in Part 1, paragraph 2, and in Part 2, the cross-heading immediately before paragraph 12, and paragraphs 12 to 14.
Mental Health (Amendment) Act 1982 (c. 51)	In Schedule 3, paragraphs 29 and 34.
Homosexual Offences (Northern Ireland) Order 1982 (S.I. 1982/1536 (N.I. 19))	In Article 2(2), in the definition of 'homosexual act', the words from ', an act of gross indecency' to the end. Article 3. Article 7. Article 8. Article 10(2)(a) and (b). In Article 11(1), the words ', or gross indecency with,'. Article 12(1). Article 13. In the Schedule, paragraphs 3, 4 and 7.
Mental Health Act 1983 (c. 20)	In Schedule 4, paragraph 15.
Police and Criminal Evidence Act 1984 (c. 60)	In section 80(7), the words from 'the Sexual Offences Act 1956' to '1977 or'. In Schedule 1A, paragraph 4 and the cross-heading immediately before it. In Part 1 of Schedule 5, paragraphs 4 and 6 to 8. In Part 2 of Schedule 5, paragraph 2 and the cross-heading immediately before it. In Part 1 of Schedule 6, paragraph 9.
Sexual Offences Act 1985 (c. 44)	Section 3. Section 4(2) and (3). Section 5(2).
Mental Health (Northern Ireland) Order 1986 (S.I. 1986/595 (N.I. 4))	In Schedule 5, in Part II, the entry relating to the Homosexual Offences (Northern Ireland) Order 1982.

Reference	Extent of repeal or revocation
Criminal Justice Act 1988 (c. 33)	In section 32(2)(c), the words from 'the Sexual Offences Act 1956' to '1977 or'.
Children Act 1989 (c. 49)	In Schedule 12, paragraphs 11 to 14 and 16.
Criminal Justice and Public Order Act 1994 (c. 33)	Sections 142 to 144. In Schedule 10, paragraphs 26 and 35(2) and (4).
Criminal Procedure and Investigations Act 1996 (c. 25)	Section 56(2)(a).
Sexual Offences (Conspiracy and Incitement) Act 1996 (c. 29)	In the Schedule, paragraph 1(1)(a).
Sexual Offences (Protected Material) Act 1997 (c. 39)	In the Schedule, paragraphs 1 to 4.
Crime (Sentences) Act 1997 (c. 43)	Section 52.
Sex Offenders Act 1997 (c. 51)	The whole Act.
Crime and Disorder Act 1998 (c. 37)	Sections 2, 2A, 2B and 3. In section 4, in subsection (1) the words ', a sex offender order or an order under section 2A above' and in subsection (3) the words 'or 2(6) above'. Section 20. In Section 21, subsection (2); in subsection (4), the words 'or (2)'; in subsection (5), the words 'or 20'; in subsection (6), the words 'and sex offender orders' and 'or 20(4)(a)'; in subsection (7)(b)(i), the words 'or, as the case may be, chief constable'; subsections (7A) and (7B); and in subsection (10), the words 'or 20'. Section 21A. Section 22(6) and (7). In Schedule 8, paragraphs 36 and 144.
Criminal Justice (Children) (Northern Ireland) Order 1998 (S.I. 1998/1504 (N.I. 9))	In Schedule 1, paragraph 1(c), (e) and (j).
Criminal Justice (Northern Ireland) Order 1998 (S.I. 1998/2839 (N.I. 20)).	Articles 6, 6A, 6B and 7.
Youth Justice and Criminal Evidence Act 1999 (c. 23)	In section 35(3)(a), sub-paragraphs (i) to (iv).

Reference	Extent of repeal or revocation
Powers of Criminal Courts (Sentencing) Act 2000 (c. 6)	Section 161(2)(a) to (e). In Schedule 9, paragraphs 189, 190 and 193.
Care Standards Act 2000 (c. 14)	In Schedule 4, paragraph 2.
Criminal Justice and Courts Services Act 2000 (c. 43)	Section 39. Section 66. In Schedule 4, paragraphs 1(c) to (i), 2(g) to (m) and 3(b) to (r). Schedule 5.
Sexual Offences (Amendment) Act 2000 (c. 44)	Section 1(1), (2) and (4). Section 2(1) to (3) and (5). Sections 3 and 4 except so far as extending to Scotland. Section 5. Section 6(1).
Armed Forces Act 2001 (c. 19)	In Schedule 6, paragraphs 2 and 59.
Proceeds of Crime Act 2002 (c. 29)	In Schedule 5, paragraph 8(2) to (5).
Police Reform Act 2002 (c. 30)	Sections 67 to 74.
Nationality, Immigration and Asylum Act 2002 (c. 41)	Sections 145 and 146.
Access to Justice (Northern Ireland) Order 2003 (S.I. 2003/435 (N.I. 10))	In Schedule 2, in paragraph 2(d), sub-paragraph (x) and the word 'or' at the end of sub-paragraph (xi).
Criminal Justice (Northern Ireland) Order 2003 (S.I. 2003/1247 (N.I. 13))	In Article 19(4), sub-paragraph (a). In Schedule 1, paragraphs 1, 2, 20 and 21.

Appendix 2
Table of Changes

Old offence (SOA 1956 unless otherwise stated)	Penalty	Replacement section SOA 2003	Maximum penalty on indictment
Rape and associated offences		*Non-consensual sexual offences*	
s 1 rape on male/female vagina/anus	life	s 1 penile rape on male/ female vagina/anus/mouth male only commits	life
		s 5 rape of child under 13	life
Assault with intent to commit rape (common law offence fallen into disuse)	life	s 62 committing an offence with intent to commit a sexual offence	10 years
s 9 Theft Act 1968 burglary with intent to commit rape	14 years (dwelling) 10 years other cases	s 63 trespass with intent to commit a sexual offence	10 years
s 2 procuration of sexual intercourse of a woman by threat or intimidation	2 years	s 4 causing a person to engage in sexual activity without consent	life if penetration 10 years all other cases
s 3 procuration of sexual intercourse of a woman by false pretences/false representations	2 years	s 4 causing a person to engage in sexual activity without consent	life if penetration 10 years all other cases
s 4 administering drugs to a woman to obtain sexual intercourse	2 years	s 61 administering a substance with intent	10 years
Defilement		*Sexual activity*	
s 5 USI girl under 13	life	s 5 rape of child under 13	life
s 6 USI girl under 16	2 years	s 9 sexual activity with a child	14 years

Old offence (SOA 1956 unless otherwise stated)	Penalty	Replacement section SOA 2003	Maximum penalty on indictment
s 7 intercourse with a defective	2 years	ss 30–33 offences against persons with a mental disorder impeding choice ss 34–37 inducements, etc., to persons with a mental disorder	life if penetration 14 years where direct sexual touching 10 years where engages in presence or causes to watch
s 128 Mental Health Act 1956 Sexual intercourse with patients	2 years	ss 38–44 care workers for persons with a mental disorder	14 years if penetration 10 years where direct sexual touching 7 years where engages in presence or causes to watch
Incest s 10 incest by a man where girl under 13	life	*Familial sexual abuse* s 5 rape of child under 13	life
where girl over 13	7 years	s 25 sexual activity with a child family member under 18	14 years if penetration
with a woman	2 years	s 64 sex with an adult relative (penetration)	2 years
s 54 Criminal Law Act 1977 incitement of girls under 16 to commit incest	2 years	s 8 causing/inciting child under 13 to engage in sexual activity	14 years
		s 10 causing/inciting child under 16 to engage in sexual activity	14 years if penetration 5 years otherwise

Appendix 2. Table of Changes

Old offence (SOA 1956 unless otherwise stated)	Penalty	Replacement section SOA 2003	Maximum penalty on indictment
		s 26 inciting a child family member to engage in sexual activity	14 years/5 years
s 11 incest by a woman (consensual) with a man	7 years	s 8 sexual activity with child under 13	life
		s 25 sexual activity with a child family member	14 years (where aged 18 or over) otherwise 5 years
		s 65 sex with an adult relative (consenting to penetration)	2 years
Buggery and associated offences			
s 12 buggery consenting adults	2 years	no offence	n/a
bestiality	life	s 69 intercourse with an animal	2 years
s 13 gross indecency adult males not in private	5 years	no specific offence possibly s 71 sexual activity in a public lavatory	summary only, fine or 6 months
s 16 assault with intent to commit buggery	10 years	no specific offence	n/a
s 4 SOA 1967 procuring others to commit homosexual acts	2 years	no specific offence s 4 causing a person to engage in sexual activity	n/a 10 years
Indecent assault		*Sexual assault*	
s 14 indecent assault on female	10 years	s 2 assault by penetration s 3 sexual assault	life 10 years
where girl under 13		s 6 assault of child under 13 by penetration s 7 sexual assault of child under 13	life 14 years

Old offence (SOA 1956 unless otherwise stated)	Penalty	Replacement section SOA 2003	Maximum penalty on indictment
s 15 indecent assault on male	10 years	s 2 assault by penetration	life
		s 3 sexual assault	10 years
where boy under 13		s 6 assault of child under 13 by penetration	life
		s 7 sexual assault of child under 13	14 years
Gross indecency with a child under 16		*Child sexual offences*	
s 1 Indecency with Children Act 1960—act of gross indecency with child under 16 incites child under 16 to commit act of gross indecency	10 years	s 7 sexual assault of child under 13	14 years
		s 9 sexual activity with a child	14 years
Abuse of position of trust		*Abuse of position of trust*	
s 3 SO(A)A 2000 abuse of position of trust	5 years	s 16 abuse of position of trust	5 years
		s 17 causing/inciting	5 years
		s 18 sexual activity in presence of child	5 years
		s 19 causing child to watch a sexual act	5 years
Abduction			
s 17 abduction of a woman by force or for property	14 years	s 62 committing an offence with intent to commit a sexual offence	life if kidnapping or false imprisonment 10 years otherwise
s 19 abduction of unmarried girl under 18 from parent or guardian	2 years	no specific offence	n/a
s 21 abduction of defective from parent or guardian	2 years	s 62 committing an offence with intent to commit a sexual offence	life if kidnapping or false imprisonment 10 years otherwise

Old offence (SOA 1956 unless otherwise stated)	Penalty	Replacement section SOA 2003	Maximum penalty on indictment
Prostitution		*Sexual exploitation and trafficking*	
s 22 causing prostitution of women	2 years	s 52 causing or inciting prostitution for gain	7 years
s 23 procuration of girl under 21 for USI anywhere in world	2 years	s 50 arranging or facilitating child prostitution	14 years
s 28 causing or encouraging prostitution of girl under 16	2 years	s 48 causing or inciting child prostitution	14 years
s 29 causing or encouraging prostitution of a defective	2 years	s 52 causing or inciting prostitution for gain	7 years
s 30 man living on the earnings of prostitution	7 years	s 53 controlling prostitution for gain	7 years
		s 49 controlling a child prostitute	14 years
s 31 woman exercising control over prostitute	7 years	s 53 controlling prostitution for gain	7 years
		s 49 controlling a child prostitute	14 years
s 32 solicitation by men for immoral purposes	2 years	s 1 Street Offences Act 1959 amended to include male prostitutes	summary only—fine or 6 months
ss 1–2 SOA 1985 kerb-crawling	fine	amended to be gender-neutral	same
No equivalent		s 47 paying for sexual services of a child	if child under 13 life 13–16, 14 years 16–18, 7 years
Pornography			
s 1 Protection of Children Act 1978	10 years	amended to raise age of child to someone under 18 years	same
s 160 Criminal Justice Act 1988	5 years	amended to raise age of child to someone under 18 years	same

Old offence (SOA 1956 unless otherwise stated)	Penalty	Replacement section SOA 2003	Maximum penalty on indictment
No equivalent		s 48 causing or inciting child pornography	14 years
		s 49 controlling a child involved in pornography	14 years
		s 50 arranging or facilitating child pornography	14 years
No equivalent		ss 57–59 trafficking into, within, or out of the UK	14 years
Public decency		*Exposure*	
Indecent exposure s 4 Vagrancy Act 1824	3 months 1 year on second conviction	s 66 exposure	2 years
s 28 Town Police Clauses Act 1847	14 days		
s 5 Public Order Act 1986	Fine	s 71 sexual activity in a public lavatory	summary only—6 months or fine
No equivalent		s 67 voyeurism	2 years
Outraging public decency (common law offence) *R v Gibson and Sylveire* [1990] Crim LR 738	life	no change	
Miscellaneous			
Charged as accessories aiding and abetting		s 4 causing person to engage in sexual activity	10 years
No equivalent		s 70 sexual penetration of a corpse	2 years

Appendix 3
Official Publications and Responses

Achieving Best Evidence in Criminal Proceedings, Guidance for Vulnerable and Intimidated Witnesses, including Children, (Home Office Communication Directorate, January 2002)

Association Chief Police Officers, Media Group Advisory Guidelines No. 5 Sex Offenders **http://www.acpo.police.uk/policies/index.html**.

British Crime Survey 2000, (Home Office Statistical Bulletin 18/00 October 2000)

Code for Crown Prosecutors, (Director of Public Prosecutions, Crown Prosecution Service) **http://www.cps.gov.uk/Home/CodeForCrownProsecutors/**

Complex Child Abuse Investigations: Inter-Agency Issues Guidance, (Home Office/Department of Health May 2002)

Consultation Paper on the Review of Part I of the Sex Offenders Act 1997, (Home Office Communication Directorate, July 2001)

COPINE Project, Combating Paedophile Information Networks in Europe, (NSPCC 2003)

Criminal Justice and Court Services Act 2000: Protection of Children Guidance, (Home Office, December 2002)

An Evaluation of the Live Link for Child Witnesses, (Home Office, Davies and Noon 1991)

Home Office Circular 39/1997 Sex Offenders Act 1997, Sentencing and Offences Unit, (Home Office August 1997)

Home Office Circular 20/2000 Children Involved in Prostitution, Sentencing and Offences Unit, (Home Office May 2000)

Joint Committee on Human Rights Twelfth Report, House of Lords, House of Commons, (Parliamentary Publications, 9 June 2003)

Liberty's response to the Home Office consultation paper on reform of rape laws, (Liberty March 2001)

Liberty's Second Reading Briefing on the Sex Offences (Amendment) Bill in the House of Commons, (Liberty July 2003)

Memorandum of Good Practice on Video Recorded Interviews with Child Witnesses for Criminal Proceedings, (Department of Health/Home Office 1992)

Metropolitan Police Service Response to the Sex Offences Bill, (Metropolitan Police Service June 2000)

The Police Perspective on Sex Offender Orders, (Police Research Series report, HO May 2003)

Protecting the Public: Strengthening Protection Against Sex Offenders and Reforming the Law on Sexual Offences, (Home Office Consultation Paper Cmnd 5668 Home Office, November 2002)

Rape and Sexual Assault of Women: the extent and nature of the problem: Findings from the British Crime Survey, (Myhill and Allen, Home Office Research Study 237, Home Office Development and Statistics Directorate, March 2002)

Report of the Interdepartmental Working Group on Preventing Unsuitable People from Working with Children and Abuse of Trust, Sentencing and Offences Unit, (Home Office December 1998; *Update* July 2000)

Report on the Joint Investigation into the Investigation and Prosecution of Cases Involving Allegations of Rape, (HMCPSI Inspectorate, April 2002)

Risk Assessment and Management of Known Sexual and Violent Offenders: A Review of Current Issues, (Policing and Reducing Crime Unit Home Office 2001)

Risk Management of Sexual and Violent Offenders: The Work of Public Protection Panels, (Home Office 2001)

Setting the Boundaries: Reforming the Law on Sex Offences vol.1
Supporting Evidence vol.2,
Report and Recommendations, (Home Office Communication Directorate, July 2000)

Sex Offences Review: Response by The Christian Institute, (The Christian Institute January 2001)

Sex Offending Against Children, (Grubin, Home Office, Police Research Series Paper 99, 1998)

Sexual Freedom Coalition Response to Home Office Consultation Paper, (Sexual Freedom Coalition, January 2003)

The Sexual Offences (Amendment) Bill: Age of Consent and Abuse of Position of Trust, (House of Commons Research Paper 94/4 21 January 1999)

Spanner Trust Submission to the Home Office Review Board on Sexual Offences (March 2001)

Stopping Traffic: Exploring the extent of, and responses to, trafficking in women for sexual exploitation in the UK, (Kelly and Regan, Home Office, Police Research Series Paper 125, 2000)

Witness in Court, (Home Office Communications Directorate 2002)

Working Together to Safeguard Children, (Department of Health, Home Office Department of Education and Employment, 1999)

Index

References to the text of the Sexual Offences Act 2003 have the page references in italics

Index

disqualification orders—*continued*
  misunderstandings in relation to 28
  provisions of new law in relation to 26–7

evidential presumptions as to consent *230–1*
  administration of substance or drug 20
  burden to adduce 17
  circumstances when apply 17–18
  inability to communicate 19
  relevant act 17
  unconsciousness or asleep 19
  unlawful detention 19
  violence or threats of 13, 18–19, 27
evidential provisions
  competency 149
  corroboration 156
  inferences and presumptions 156–8
  see also **cross-examination; previous sexual
    history; Special Measures**
exposure *228*
  offence of 137–8
  previous law relating to 137
External Reference Group *3*

familial child sex offences *210–13*
  adoptive relationships 105
  consent 103–4
  defences 107–8
  eugenics issue 101–2
  foster parents 104–5
  inciting a child family member 106
  penalties 108
  reasonable belief aged over 18 years 106–7
  relevant family relationships 104–6
  sexual activity with a child family member 56,
    103–4
  see also **familial sexual offences; incest**
familial sexual offences 6
  acts of penetration 111
  age requirements 111
  consenting adults 109
  knowledge of relationship 112
  need for 109
  offences involving adult relatives 109–10
  penalties 112
  prohibited degrees of relationship 110–11
  sexual activity 109–10, 111
  see also **familial child sex offences; incest**
foreign travel orders *252–6*

gender reassignment therapy 33–4, 40
gender-neutral 3, 39, 49, 103, 106, 109, 126, 145
gender-specific prostitution offences, extension
  of (Schedule 1) *267–8*
general interpretation
  Part 1 *232*
  Part 2 *262–4*

genitalia 137
  surgically reconstructed 33–4, 40
grooming *see* **meeting a child following sexual
  grooming**
gross indecency with a child 61

homosexual offences
  abolition of 160
  discriminatory aspect of 125, 127, 144–5, 160

images
  definition of 114–15, 122
  indecent 115–16, 122
  see also **indecent photographs of children**
incest 6
  previous law relating to 101, 102–3
  reasons for repeal 102
  see also **familial child sex offences; familial
    sexual offences**
indecent assault 32, 42, 71
indecent photographs of children *220–1*
  age of child 115, 116
  changes to existing law 115–16
  criminal investigations and proceedings 117–18
  defences to 116–18
  definitions of 115
  offences relating to 114–15
  possession of 115
  relevant relationship 116–17
  sentencing guidelines 118–19
information about release or transfer *243*
information for verification *242–3*
intercourse with an animal 141–3, *228–9*
  need for offence 141–2
intimate samples
  refusal to provide 157

learning disability, persons with a 87–8, 89, 91,
  92
Liberty 54, 68, 73, 134, 139, 163, 176

marriage
  defence of 32, 100, 107, 116–17
meeting a child following sexual grooming
  criticisms of 73
  examples of 71–3, 75
mental disorder, persons with a 5–6
  agreement secured by inducement, threats or
    deceit 94–5
  capacity to consent 14, 17
  care workers, interpretations of 96–8
  care workers, offences committed by 95–100
  defences to 91–2, 93
  marriage and 100
  meaning of 92
  offences involving sexual activity with 90–4
  pre-existing relationships and 100